Humana Festival 2000
The Complete Plays

Humana Inc. is one of the nation's largest
managed health care companies
with approximately 6 million members in its health care plans.

The Humana Foundation was established in 1981
to support the educational, social, medical and cultural development
of communities in ways that reflect
Humana's commitment to social responsibility
and an improved quality of life.

SMITH AND KRAUS PUBLISHERS
Contemporary Playwrights / Collections

Act One Festival '95
Act One Festival '95

EST Marathon '94: The One-Act Plays
EST Marathon '95: The One-Act Plays
EST Marathon '96: The One-Act Plays
EST Marathon '97: The One-Act Plays
EST Marathon '98: The One-Act Plays

Humana Festival: 20 One-Acts Plays 1976–1996
Humana Festival '93: The Complete Plays
Humana Festival '94: The Complete Plays
Humana Festival '95: The Complete Plays
Humana Festival '96: The Complete Plays
Humana Festival '97: The Complete Plays
Humana Festival '98: The Complete Plays
Humana Festival '99: The Complete Plays

Women Playwrights: The Best Plays of 1992
Women Playwrights: The Best Plays of 1993
Women Playwrights: The Best Plays of 1994
Women Playwrights: The Best Plays of 1995
Women Playwrights: The Best Plays of 1996
Women Playwrights: The Best Plays of 1997
Women Playwrights: The Best Plays of 1998
Women Playwrights: The Best Plays of 1999

If you require pre-publication information about upcoming Smith and Kraus books, you may receive our semi-annual catalogue, free of charge, by sending your name and address to *Smith and Kraus Catalogue, 4 Lower Mill Road, North Stratford, NH 03590. Or call us at (800) 895-4331, fax (603) 643-1831. www.SmithKraus.com.*

Humana Festival 2000
The Complete Plays

Edited by Michael Bigelow Dixon
and Amy Wegener

Contemporary Playwrights Series

SK
A Smith and Kraus Book

A Smith and Kraus Book
Published by Smith and Kraus, Inc.
177 Lyme Road, Hanover, New Hampshire 03755
www.SmithKraus.com

Manufactured in the United States of America

Cover and Text Design by Julia Hill Gignoux
Layout by Jennifer McMaster
Cover artwork © Brian Cronin

First Edition: October 2000
10 9 8 7 6 5 4 3 2 1

Library of Congress Cataloguing-in-Publication Data
Contemporary Playwrights Series
ISSN1067-9510

Contents

Acknowledgments

The editors wish to thank the following persons for their invaluable assistance in compiling this volume:

Andrew Crocker
Lindsay Cummings
Tsue French
Adrien-Alice Hansel
Ginna Hoben
Dottie LaBry
Jennifer McMaster
Kelly Lea Miller
Kerry Mulvaney
Liz Nofziger
Emily Roderer
Jeff Rodgers
Jimmy Seacat
Kyle Shepherd
Alexander Speer

John Buzzetti
William Craver
Peter Franklin
Mary Harden
Morgan Jenness
Carl Mulert
Howard Rosenstone
Susan Schulman
Carolyn Smith
Wendy Streeter

Foreword

One is reminded that it's all about stories. Sometimes the various skirmishes between adherents of various styles obscure the fact that there is still a story being told. The 24th Humana Festival is all over the map stylistically, but a single storyteller in a single light could hold us rapt with the recognizable human dramas at the heart of these fascinating texts.

The 31 writers who illuminated this year's festival seem, in many ways, to be focused on responsibility. In *Tape* it's an examination of our responsibility for our past actions. In *Touch* it's our responsibility to ourselves to find a way to go on. In *Back Story* it's family and our sacrifices on behalf of it. In *Big Love* it's, in part, our responsibility to defend ourselves when no one else will. I could go on, but the point is made.

In fact, in 31 fascinating ways these writers address not only what we do but how we feel about what we do, and this explosive melding of doing and feeling has magnified the actors' contributions to the Humana Festival. More than ever, I thought these plays were revealed in performance. These are *theatre* pieces that need and count on acting, directing, and design.

I suppose this is what distinguishes writing for the stage from other forms of literature. How does the playwright know how to leave room for acting? What kind of three-dimensional sense is necessary to make texts that can exist in space? What does a playwright need to know about rhythm and tone?

This playwriting is a mysterious business. The playwright has much in common with the decathlon athlete who must have many skills to survive and prosper. As the plays in this collection demonstrate, these are writers who have those interlocking understandings. Here's to the plays that make possible that thing we call "theatricality" in all its guises while remaining stone-simple stories at the same time. Now, there's a good trick.

Jon Jory
Producing Director
Actors Theatre of Louisville

Editors' Note

It didn't start out this way and certainly no one ever imagined it would come to this, but the 2000 Humana Festival of New American Plays turned out to be a great finale for Jon Jory. As Producing Director of Actors Theatre of Louisville for 31 years, Jon invented and steered the Humana Festival through its first 24 seasons. His artistic talent, his dramaturgical insight, and his producing prowess are evident in the critical success of the festival and the numerous awards that have been bestowed upon festival plays.

From our perspective, what seems most noteworthy about this year's festival is that it embodied so many of Jon's passions. Each year Jon looked for plays that might generally fit the following categories, and this year he landed them all: emotionally charged American drama; irreverent character comedy brimming with social satire; explorations of new forms in bold theatrical terms; ensemble works created with non-traditional methodologies; ten-minute plays in all their political, spiritual and whimsical glories; off-beat experiments in venue and media; the celebration of young writers; premieres of work by distinguished and established American dramatists; and a reunion with previous Humana Festival playwrights who devote their time, ideas and talents to the American stage.

That such variety could be embraced by a single festival is a tribute to the brilliance of American playwrights who continue to question traditions of the world and of the theatre they've inherited. The success of the festival is theirs, of course, but Jon had the good sense to invite them to his party. And what a farewell gala his last festival turned out to be. Attendance records were set, awards were presented (including one for career achievement to Jon from the American Theatre Critics Association), panels explored issues in criticism and new plays around the world, and an exhibit documented the various ways in which scenic designers approach new plays.

This book captures only a piece of all that action, but without a doubt the most important piece of the Humana Festival puzzle. Scripts are where it all begins at Actors Theatre of Louisville; they provide the meanings and inspiration for a hundred theatre artists, whose work in turn engages and amazes thousands of audience members—as the scripts engaged and amazed us to begin with. We hope they'll do the same for you now.

Michael Bigelow Dixon & Amy Wegener

Actors Theatre of Louisville Staff Credits

Producing Director. . . . . Jon Jory
Executive Director . . . . Alexander Speer

ADMINISTRATION

BUDGET AND MANAGEMENT

General Manager. . . . . James Roemer
Assistant General Manager. . . . . Jeffrey S. Rodgers
Systems Manager . . . . Dottie LaBry
Bookkeeper. . . . . Mary Ann Thompson
Assistant Bookkeeper . . . . Shirley Bruce

BUSINESS OFFICE

Executive Secretary. . . . . Wanda Snyder

DEVELOPMENT

Director of Development & External Affairs . . . . Jennifer Lennon
Director of Annual Giving . . . . Brian Smith
Corporate & Foundation Officer. . . . . Kate Carpenter
Director of Community Relations. . . . . Debra Farmer
Associate . . . . Janna Burch

FESTIVAL

Coordinator . . . . Andrew C. Crocker

MARKETING AND PUBLIC RELATIONS

Director. . . . . James Seacat
Senior Marketing Associate. . . . . Randy Blevins
Media & Publicity Coordinator . . . . Kyle Shepherd
Graphics Coordinator . . . . Liz Nofziger
Associate . . . . Danielle Minnis
Telemarketing Manager . . . . Allison Hammons
Marketing/Mail Services . . . . Tsue French

LITERARY

Manager. . . . . Michael Bigelow Dixon
Assistant Manager. . . . . Amy Wegener
Associate . . . . Val Smith

SPECIAL PROJECTS
Director. . . . . Debra Farmer

TICKET SALES
Director. . . . . Emma E. Oberdieck
Managers . . . . Saundra Blakeney, Steve Clark,
Julie Gallegos
Customer Service. . . . . Brenda Blazer, Eric Federspiel,
Kristy Kannapell, Todd McMichael,
Barbara Maggard, Jay Menchan,
Lynn T. Smith, Kae Thompson
Corporate Subscriptions Manager . . . . Kim McKercher
Group Sales Manager. . . . . Judy Osborne
Group/Corporate Sales Assistant . . . . Holli Lewis

HOUSE STAFF
Director of Operations . . . . Daniel T. Wetzel
Maintenance Staff. . . . . Jim Wantland
Custodian. . . . . Walter Miller, Jr.
Receptionist . . . . Dorothy King
Housekeeping Supervisor. . . . . Charlene Brown
Housekeeping Asst. Supervisor. . . . . Hank Hunter
Housekeeping Staff . . . . LaTonya Yarbor, Gwen Small,
Zidkijah Zabad, Palva Surrell

VOLUNTEER AND AUDIENCE RELATIONS
Director . . . . Carol Baker
House Managers . . . . Diane Kane, Bill Nusz, Candy Pierce,
Nancy Stephen, Whit Stokes
Coat Check Attendants . . . . Scott Stauble, Michael Fraytak

PRODUCTION
Production Manager . . . . Frazier W. Marsh
Artistic Manager . . . . Zan Sawyer-Dailey
Production Stage Manager . . . . Deb Acquavella
Stage Managers. . . . . Paul Mills Holmes, Juliet Penna,
Kathy Preher

Company Manager. . . . . Paul Bauer
Richin Casting Associate . . . . Judy Bowman

DESIGN AND TECHNOLOGY
Scenic Designer . . . . Paul Owen
Assistant to Scenic Designer . . . . Tom Burch
Technical Director. . . . . Michael Reynolds
Asst. TD/Shop Foreman. . . . . Robert Waltz
Draftsman/Rigger . . . . Ted Thomas
Carpenters . . . . Kevin Anderson, Kelley O'Donnoghue,
Jerry J. Prasser, Sam Sgroi
Journeyman Carpenter . . . . Scott Sprehn
Bingham Deck Carpenter . . . . Karen L. Griffin
Pamela Brown Deck Carpenter. R. Kevin Gose
Scenic Artist . . . . Katrina Johansen
Props Masters . . . . Ben Hohman, Mark Walston
Pamela Brown Deck Supervisor . . . . Jennifer Parker
Props Carpenter . . . . Doc Manning
Props Artisans . . . . Tracey Rainey, Dan Tracy,
Amahl Lovato, Nathan Michael
Props Journeyman . . . . Ann Marie Morehouse
Costume Shop Manager . . . . Margret Fenske
Assistant to Costume Designer . . . . Kevin R. McLeod
Drapers. . . . . Kris Brady, Susan P. Williams
First Hands. . . . . Julianne Johnson, Bronwyn Klaphaak
Stitchers. . . . . Michelle Bazeley, Rose Maluda,
Margaret St. John, Terry Gullickson
Crafts Master . . . . Shari Cochran
Wig Master . . . . Bobb Terrell
Costume Journeyman. . . . . Jessica Watters
Pamela Brown Wardrobe Master . . . . Kimberly J. Donze
Bingham Wardrobe Journeyman . . . . Karen Hall
Sound Designer . . . . Martin R. Desjardins
Sound Engineer. . . . . David Preston
Assistant Sound Engineer. . . . . Richard Dionne
Sound Technicians . . . . Kelly Kress, Jason Tratta
Lighting Supervisor . . . . Paul Werner
Assistant Lighting Supervisor . . . . Cindy Bowman

Pamela Brown Master Electrician. . . . . Brian Scott
Electrician . . . . Jon Mulvaney
First Electrician. . . . . Matt Shuirr
Swing Electrician/Board Operator . . . . Andrew Vance
Pamela Brown Light Board Operator. . . . . Zak Al-Alami

APPRENTICE/INTERN COMPANY
Director. . . . . Sullivan Canaday White
Associate Director . . . . Meredith McDonough

APPRENTICES
Shawna Joy Anderson, Molly M. Binder, Philip Bolin, Rachel Burttram,
Cary Calebs, Christy Collier, Patrick J. Dall'Occhio, Samantha Desz,
Melody G. Fenster, J. Matthew Jenkins, Tom Johnson, Aimeé Kleisner,
Cabe McCarty, Kimberly Megna, Tom Moglia, Holly W. Sims, Stephen
Sislen, Heather Springsteen, Mark Watson, Zach Welsheimer, Jessica
Wortham, Travis York

INTERNS
Apprentice/Intern. . . . . Melissa Lee Denton
Arts Administration. . . . . Cara Miller
Costumes. . . . . Marcy Rector
Directing. . . . . Pascaline Bellegarde, Aimée Hayes, Dano Madden
Festival . . . . Erin M. Everson
Literary . . . . Ginna Hoben, Kelly Lea Miller, Kerry Mulvaney
Marketing/Public Relations . . . . Sara Kellogg, Cheryl Winkelman
Stage Management . . . . Nichole A. Shuman, Juliane Taylor

Humana Festival 2000
The Complete Plays

Tape
by Stephen Belber

1

BIOGRAPHY

Plays by Stephen Belber include *The Death of Frank* (Synchronicity Space), *Through Fred* (Soho Repertory), *The Wake* (Via Theater), *Broken Fall* (Juilliard), *Steve* (Expanded Arts), *Wind* (Lincoln Center Living Room at HERE), *Stone Cold Lyricism* (Harold Clurman Theater), and *Tape* at the Humana Festival of New American Plays. *Tape* was made into a movie by Indigent Films starring Ethan Hawke, Uma Thurman and Robert Sean Leonard, and directed by Richard Linklater. Mr. Belber has also performed several of his shows in New York and elsewhere, and they include *Finally, One Million Butterflies, Eclectic Mulatto Moondance,* and *Psychotic Busboy Blues*. He is an associate writer and actor on *The Laramie Project* by Moisés Kaufman and the members of Tectonic Theater Project, which had its world premiere at the Denver Center Theater in 2000 and opened off-Broadway the same year. His work has been workshopped by New York Stage & Film, The Sundance Theater Lab, New York Theater Workshop, Second Stage, and the Chatauqua Institute. Another new play, *The Transparency of Val,* also played in 2000 at the Trustus Theater in Columbia, South Carolina. Mr. Belber is a graduate of the playwrights program at the Juilliard School.

HUMANA FESTIVAL PRODUCTION

Tape premiered at the Humana Festival of New American Plays in February 2000. It was directed by Brian Jucha with the following cast:

Vince	Dominic Fumusa
Jon	Stephen Kunken
Amy	Erica Yoder

and the following production staff:

Scenic Designer	Paul Owen
Costume Designer	Suttirat Larlarb
Lighting Designer	Greg Sullivan
Sound Designer	Martin R. Desjardins
Properties Designer	Mark Walston
Stage Manager	Charles M. Turner III
Assistant Stage Manager	Juliet Penna
Dramaturg	Michael Bigelow Dixon
Casting	Laura Richin Casting

CHARACTERS

VINCE: Beat-up jeans, no shoes, perhaps a tank top tee shirt; lovable, self-destructive type.

JON: Dressed casually but well, with a degree of "hip" thrown in—V-neck sweater, no tee shirt, retro, perfectly fitting jeans, worn leather jacket, brown leather shoes.

AMY: Dressed smartly—the way a young attorney might be on a Friday night. She's not overweight.

TIME & PLACE

A Motel 6 motel room in Lansing, Michigan.

The play is performed without an intermission.

Stephen Kunken, Dominic Fumusa and Erica Yoder
in *Tape*

24th Annual Humana Festival of New American Plays
Actors Theatre of Louisville, 2000
photo by Richard Trigg

Tape

Vince, 28, stands alone at the sink outside the bathroom pouring the contents of a can of Schlitz into the sink with one hand while holding and drinking from a second can of Schlitz in the other. When the first can is empty, he chucks it casually onto the floor. He opens another can from a six-pack which rests on the sink and repeats the action. When it is empty, he tosses it across the room. At about this time, he finishes the beer he is drinking and throws it towards the TV. He opens another beer to drink and another one to empty. But first, he takes off his blue jeans and throws them on the bed. He returns to his task of emptying beers. A moment later there is a knock on the door. Vince finishes emptying the beer and chucks it onto one of the beds as he goes to the door. He opens it and Jon, 28, enters. They hug. Several seconds.

[NOTE: Vince is listening to a song by Eddie Cochrane during the opening actions of the play.]

VINCE: Hey, man.

JON: Hey, Vince. *(The hug continues—warm, genuine, obviously an old friendship.)* This is great, man.

VINCE: Yeah.

JON: This is great.

VINCE: How are you?

JON: Can't complain.

VINCE: Cool.

JON: Totally. It is, I'm very psyched.

VINCE: You should be, Jonny, it's a great thing.

JON: Thanks, man. Thanks.

VINCE: It's great to be alive!

JON: Totally. *(Beat.)* What's up?

VINCE: Not much.

JON: You're not dressed.

VINCE: Lay off.

JON: It's not that I don't like it—

VINCE: But?—

JON: But nothing.

VINCE: So?—

JON: So nothing—

VINCE: OK.

JON: OK.

VINCE: Excellent.

JON: Fine. *(Beat.)* I swear to God you get stranger each year.

VINCE: You look good, Jon.

(Jon enters the room more fully now, looking around.)

JON: Where's Leah?

VINCE: Didn't make the trip.

JON: Why not?

VINCE: We broke up.

JON: Shut up.

VINCE: I'm serious—

JON: Shut up—

VINCE: I'm serious—

JON: You broke up?!

VINCE: We broke up.

JON: Why?

VINCE: Complicated.

JON: Why?

VINCE: She didn't like the way I dress.

JON: Don't joke—

VINCE: I'm not.

JON: What happened?

VINCE: I get stranger each year.

JON: Vince!!—

VINCE: She thinks I'm a dick. *(Pause.)* She sends apologies for not coming. She says she's sure it'll go well.

JON: I don't believe it.

VINCE: I'm serious, man, she does—

JON: Why did you break up?

VINCE: I don't know.

(Silence.)

JON: I'm sorry, man.

VINCE: Me too.

JON: *(Beat.)* Is it permanent?

VINCE: Permanent as a dead horse, amigo.

JON: *(Beat.)* Did you do something?

VINCE: Why do you say that?

JON: Because I know you.

VINCE: You think I'm a dick—

JON: No, it's just that I know that you occasionally have a tendency to act in a phallic fashion.

VINCE: I'm not like that anymore.

JON: What—you're not a dick?

VINCE: See what I mean?

JON: I'm just asking what happened.

VINCE: Lots of things.

JON: Like?—

VINCE: Like she thinks I'm reckless.

JON: In general?

VINCE: Yes.

JON: *(Pause.)* Were you at all specifically reckless recently?

VINCE: Not particularly specifically.

JON: Be honest, Vince.

VINCE: I am.

JON: Did you fuck around?

VINCE: No!

JON: Vince?—

VINCE: I didn't!

JON: So what happened?

VINCE: She says I have violent tendencies.

JON: …Oh boy….

VINCE: I never touched her, Jon.

JON: I didn't say you did.

VINCE: It's just that she thinks I have "unresolved issues which occasionally manifest themselves in potentially violent ways." *(Beat.)* What?

JON: I think it's fair to say she has a point.

VINCE: No one's saying she doesn't have a point.

JON: So—?

VINCE: So she has to break up with me?

JON: She's probably scared.

VINCE: Of what? I never threatened her.

JON: You present a threatening appearance.

VINCE: Dude, we've been together three years!

JON: So?

VINCE: So you think she'd be used to it by now!

JON: It's a tricky one, Vin.

VINCE: What're you talking about?

JON: I'm just saying, it's tricky. Women these days have no reason to hang around potentially violent guys. It's not an attractive quality to them anymore. Too many other guys out there with resolved violent tendencies.

VINCE: So I'm just out of fashion?

JON: Don't be a fool—

VINCE: Don't be a politically correct fuck!

JON: I'm not, I'm telling you that you're an idiot if you think chicks are gonna put up with your bullshit.

VINCE: What bullshit?

JON: Like playing rough.

VINCE: I didn't play rough with her.

JON: Vince.

VINCE: What?

JON: I love you—

VINCE: Good—

JON: —but c'mon.

VINCE: What?

JON: You don't not play rough.

VINCE: I totally do not play rough.

JON: You're swarthy.

VINCE: That's a stereotype.

JON: True.

VINCE: Bigot.

JON: I can't be a bigot—I'm a Jew.

VINCE: I know plenty of Jewish bigots.

JON: Who?

VINCE: Irving Berlin.

JON: *(Beat.)* OK, let's move onto the next subject—

VINCE: Fine.

JON: I'm sorry you guys broke up. Really. I'm sorry for you both.

VINCE: Don't be sorry for that bitch.

JON: Fine, I'm just sorry for you. Next subject.

(Beat.)

VINCE: She says if I get my act together, stick with the meetings and stop being a dick, she might consider talking to me again.

(Jon gives a slight kick to one of the empty beer cans on the floor.)

JON: Good. *(Beat.)* Should we get some dinner?

VINCE: I gotta wait for a call.

JON: From who?

VINCE: None of your business.

JON: Leah?

VINCE: *(Indignant.)* No.

JON: ...O-K.

(Silence.)

VINCE: *(Sulky.)* So are you ready for tomorrow?

JON: You're mad.

VINCE: I'm not mad—

JON: You're allowed to be—

VINCE: I'm not mad. I'll find someone else.

JON: It's true—

VINCE: Who appreciates my dark side.

JON: Exactly. *(Pause.)* But the thing is, if you could maybe find a way to learn something from this, then you won't have as large of a dark side.

VINCE: *(Beat.)* Learn what?

JON: Learn to deal with some of your violent desires.

VINCE: *(Skeptical.)* How?

JON: By acknowledging them, by making some type of truce with yourself where you're not always in constant battle to prove your integrity, or your self worth or whatever it is that you think nobody gets about you.

VINCE: I don't think there's anything to get about me. I'm a simple man.

JON: Yeah, but your idea of manhood is putting on Eddie Cochrane and screwing your girl. It's not like that anymore. Women want other things.

VINCE: Like what?

JON: I don't know. *(Beat.)* ...Enya.

VINCE: *(Beat. Unconvinced.)* Yeah.

(Silence.)

JON: Vince—

VINCE: So where're you staying?

JON: *(Pause.)* They got me over at the Radisson in town.

VINCE: Nice!

JON: Yeah, it is.

VINCE: Lansing Film Festival!

JON: Yeah, that and Cannes.

VINCE: Still, it's a good gig.

JON: It's a good cheap thrill.

VINCE: Why do you have to dump on it? It's a good gig.

JON: Because I have big expectations. I spent two years on this film, I want it to be in a theater near you.

VINCE: It is.

JON: Yeah, but you had to come out to the middle of fucking Michigan to be there. For one screening. For which I'm getting paid a whopping five hundred bucks.

VINCE: Yeah, but all you need is for one guy from—whatever—from Disney to be there tomorrow—he likes it—boom, next thing you know, you're directing *Free Willy Four.*

JON: Starring David Hasselhoff.

VINCE: Hey.

JON: Hey.

VINCE: Hey.

JON: Hey. *(Beat.)* Dude, I'm starving.

VINCE: What time is it?

JON: *(Looks at watch.)* Quarter of.

VINCE: You wanna have a beer?

JON: Aren't you supposed to be getting your act together?

VINCE: I'll do it when I get back.

JON: See, this is what she's talking about—

VINCE: Jon—if I wanted to hang out with my mother...right?

JON: Well put, Vince.

VINCE: What Leah doesn't know won't hurt her.
(Vince carefully reaches into his bag and gets a beer, tosses it to Jon. He then carefully takes one for himself.)

JON: Whattayou got goin' in that bag, Vince?

VINCE: Beer.

JON: How much?

VINCE: Lot.

JON: I don't know why I said you had violent tendencies.

VINCE: Why?—

JON: Warm beer, boxers, Motel 6. Who needs Betty Ford?

VINCE: We can't all be at the Radisson.

JON: Hey—you know, if you wanna stay with me—

VINCE: No—

JON: Seriously, I thought you'd be with Leah, that's why I didn't offer earlier—

VINCE: It's not a problem—

JON: It's not a problem—they gave me a double; 11th floor overlooking a park—

VINCE: No, man, you probably wanna get laid.

JON: *(Pause.)* That's true.

VINCE: It's your big weekend, chicks are gonna flock to you.

JON: You're right.

VINCE: I'll be fine here.

JON: Cool.

VINCE: Should I twist your arm?

JON: Yeah. More.

VINCE: Schmuck.

JON: Prick.

VINCE: Putz.

JON: Suck-ass. *(Beat.)* I appreciate you coming out here. Seriously. We've come a long way.

VINCE: Since—?

JON: I dunno. High school.

VINCE: You think?

JON: Some of us. *(Pause.)* Dude, I'm totally giving you shit.

VINCE: No but you're right—

JON: No I'm not—

VINCE: You are, face it—

JON: I'm right only in that I think you can do better than you are, Vince.

VINCE: Why?—

JON: Because I believe in you. If I didn't, we wouldn't still be friends and I wouldn't be able to say that to you.

VINCE: Why not?

JON: Because it sounds totally pretentious.

VINCE: You're right—

JON: But the thing is—I mean it. I'm sorry but it's true. It's like this thing with Leah—if it is permanent, then you should view it as an opportunity to change—

VINCE: Change what?

JON: I don't know—find a new job, new way of doing things—

VINCE: I like my job.

JON: What is your job?

VINCE: Volunteer firefighter.

JON: I know, but how do you make your money?

VINCE: Lay off.

JON: I'm just saying—

VINCE: What?

JON: —it's immature.

VINCE: You try doing it—

JON: That's not the point—

VINCE: Besides, the majority of my clients happen to be over fifty. If that's not mature, I'm baffled as to what is.

JON: Private dope delivery to ex-hippies does not a mature man make, Vince. It's not that different than standing on the corner selling to teenagers—

VINCE: Why're you lecturing me?

JON: I'm not, I'm just pointing things out—

VINCE: Such as?

JON: Such as I think you can do better.

VINCE: Than what?

JON: Than pissing your life away. You're a smart guy, why're you still dealing drugs?

VINCE: Because I'm smart. If I was dumb, I would've gotten caught by now. Besides—I'm a firefighter.

JON: You deal to the fire chief, Vince!

VINCE: He needs me.

JON: That's not the point—

VINCE: Why is what you do better?!

JON: Why is what I do better?

VINCE: Yeah.

JON: *(Pause.)* What I'm trying to do is better because it's an attempt at figuring things out. I would like to, eventually, become good enough at it to the point where I can contribute to a larger debate about why this country is so fucked up. I would like to try and examine why it is that a fifty-whatever-year-old fire chief feels the need to get stoned every night. What is it about life in America that's driving that urge in him?

VINCE: He likes it.

JON: Fine, but then there's something slightly wrong with the fact that someone with that type of responsibility is constantly high. There's maybe
some sort of symbolism there worth examining.

VINCE: His firehouse happens to have the best record in the city.

JON: Vince—if my house was on fire, I wouldn't want him anywhere near it—

VINCE: You're such a fucking bigot!—

JON: The guy has a good record because he's lucky!—

VINCE: Says who?

JON: It's obvious! He's living a big, luck-driven lie.

VINCE: What're you—high?

JON: I'm serious—

VINCE: You're making movies about people who rob Popeye's Fried Chicken!—

JON: I'm telling a story which aims to resonate the notion of where our society's
headed if we're not careful. The only reason it sounds pompous is because
I haven't fully honed my skills yet—

VINCE: It doesn't sound pompous, it sounds like you're talking out your ass—

JON: Why?

VINCE: Because you have no idea where society is headed. You're just like everybody else—you're following the latest trend which you hope will get you
laid until the trend switches to something else, at which point you'll drop
the old one and make a movie about—whatever—like turtles that get
caught in fishing nets. Starring, like…Cindy Hasselhoff. *(Beat.)* His niece.

JON: You don't like my work?

VINCE: I like it like I like a shot of whiskey first thing in the morning—it's
good for about ten minutes, then I want my coffee.

JON: Wow.

VINCE: What?

JON: Did I say something to piss you off? Or is it that you're just a dick?

VINCE: Both.

JON: Good to see that you're finally admitting it.

VINCE: Unlike some of us.

JON: What—that I'm a dick?

VINCE: Yeah.

JON: When?

VINCE: I'm speaking figuratively.

JON: When was I figuratively a dick?

VINCE: High school.

JON: I was too shy to be a dick in high school.

VINCE: Oh I think you held you own.

JON: That's because everyone's a dick in high school, Vince. It's the white-male-football-playing prerogative. The trick is to evolve into something else once you're out.

VINCE: Jon, you're wearing two-hundred-dollar shoes.

JON: First of all, that's not true—

VINCE: One-fifty.

JON: I'm less shy than in high school.

VINCE: So you're an overt dick.

JON: No, actually, I'm a thoughtful person who wears nice shoes.

VINCE: And is, occasionally, full of shit.

JON: Is there something I'm not doing that you want me to do, Vince?

VINCE: I don't want you to do anything.

JON: No?—because seems like I'm being asked to do something by a twenty-eight-year-old pot dealer who refuses to progress with the rest of the world—which would be OK if it was a legitimate rebellion instead of just some lonely guy hanging out in his boxer shorts acting like a potentially violent dick.

VINCE: *(Beat.)* You wanna get high?

JON: No.

VINCE: C'mon, Jon, get high—

JON: I'm not getting high—

VINCE: Why—only violent dicks get high?

JON: No—

VINCE: So let's get high.

JON: I'm not getting high.

VINCE: I am.

> *(Vince goes into his duffel bag and carefully pulls out a very well-rolled joint. Jon watches as he lights it up.)*

JON: Whattayou got goin' on in that bag, Vince?

VINCE: Pot.

JON: How much?

VINCE: Lot.

> *(He takes a large hit from the joint, then offers it to Jon, who—after a moment—accepts. They smoke in silence…)*

VINCE: You know who's out here?

JON: Where?

VINCE: Here. Lansing.

JON: Who?

VINCE: Amy Randall.

JON: Really?

VINCE: Yep. I heard that from Tracy about two years ago, then when you got this thing, I looked her up on the Net, and she's out here. She's like an assistant county prosecutor or something.

JON: Did you call her?

VINCE: I thought about it.

JON: You should, especially now that Leah's…

VINCE: Out of the picture?

JON: Yeah.

VINCE: Yeah.

JON: *(Pause.)* I wonder if she's still…

VINCE: Hot?

JON: Yeah.

VINCE: That's not a very politically appropriate way to think about women, Jon.

JON: OK—here's the thing with being appropriate: It's better to *try* and do that than to be a complete asshole. The choice to respect people is actually a good one, despite people like you who insist on calling fat people "fat" to their face.

VINCE: What if they're fat?

JON: If they're fat they already realize it without your having to remind them. It basically has to do with having a couple manners.

VINCE: Is that what it is?

JON: That's it.

VINCE: So why'd you ask if she was hot?

JON: Because she is. Was. It's not a bad word. If the word is essentially a compliment, then saying it isn't bad manners. Human beings like to be called attractive. I'm not labeling Amy Randall anything she doesn't already know. And I'm sure she's smart, too.

VINCE: Well if we call her and she weighs 320 pounds, then I think we should go up to her and say, "Gee, we're really glad we dated you in high school instead of now because in high school you were really hot and now…well, I'm sure you already realize about now."

JON: You know what, Vince?—why don't you shut up for awhile.

VINCE: Oh I see—I made a point so now I have to shut up?

JON: No, it's that you like being rude for the sake of it; either that or you do it to prove that nobody can make you be nice. Either way, it gets tiresome.

And the thing is, you and I don't see each other often enough to make worthwhile this little competition for "who's more authentic." It's not about that anymore. OK? We should just accept the fact that we're a little different from each other, and let the friendship go from there.

VINCE: "Accept the fact that we're a little different from each other"?

JON: Yeah.

VINCE: Would you like to make me?

JON: Make you what?

VINCE: Make me "accept that fact."

JON: No.

VINCE: Why not?

JON: 'Cause it's stupid.

VINCE: No it's not—

JON: Yes it is—

VINCE: No it's not because how else will I know that you're different?

JON: You'll just have to trust me.

VINCE: No. Prove it.

JON: Or else what?

VINCE: I kick your ass.

JON: *(Pause.)* I guess this means you're potentially violent.

VINCE: Only when it comes to you.

JON: Funny how you get this way every time we talk about Amy Randall.

VINCE: No I don't.

JON: I don't even think you realize it, Vince.

VINCE: Fuck off.

JON: OK, you know what?—I'm outta here—

VINCE: Fuck off—

JON: Thanks for coming—

VINCE: Fuck off—

JON: Vincent—

VINCE: Fuck you, Jon—

JON: I'm sorry you still feel bad about Amy Randall, and that every time you get stoned and drunk around me this comes up. But it was ten years ago; I've explained to you a million times that I felt that it was OK for me to be with her because you guys had broken up, and that I now have a better understanding as to the fragility of human emotions—especially those belonging to swarthy Italian-Americans like yourself—and thus if the situation arose again today, I wouldn't let what happened happen. But these things do happen, especially in high school, and I'm sorry that I hurt your feelings.

VINCE: That's not what I'm talking about.

JON: What're you talking about?

VINCE: I'm talking about what happened.

JON: So am I.

VINCE: So what happened?

JON: We slept together.

VINCE: How?

JON: What do you mean?

VINCE: How did you sleep together?

JON: OK—so now this is about that?

VINCE: Isn't it?

JON: Is it?

VINCE: You tell me.

JON: We slept together.

VINCE: How?

JON: You know how.

VINCE: No, actually, I don't. I have an idea, but I don't know because we've never actually talked about it. We've laughed about it; we thought it was kinda funny, but you've never actually told me what happened.

JON: So what do you wanna know?

VINCE: I wanna know what happened.

JON: We slept together.

VINCE: How?

JON: What do you mean "how"?

VINCE: *How.*

JON: You have to be more specific, Vince.

VINCE: In what fashion did you sleep with her?

JON: We had sex.

VINCE: And—?

JON: And that was it.

VINCE: Was it good sex?

JON: I've had better since.

VINCE: Was it fun?

JON: It was all right.

VINCE: Was it on the rough side?

JON: Hard to say. We were both drunk.

VINCE: Did you rape her?

JON: No.

VINCE: Kind of?

JON: No!

VINCE: Was it like date rape?

JON: "Like date rape"?

VINCE: Did you "kind of" force her to have sex with you?

JON: No.

(Silence.)

VINCE: Jon?

JON: I'm not sure what you want me to say, Vince.

VINCE: I want you to tell me what happened. You're a filmmaker—lay out the scene for me; show me the dailies.

JON: Can we talk about this sometime when you're not high?

VINCE: Maybe the only reason I'm high is so that you get high so that for once you can tell me the truth instead of changing the subject.

JON: Yes, it was a little rough. Which is obviously something that doesn't make me proud.

VINCE: (Beats.) And did you ever talk to her after that?

JON: No.

VINCE: Why not?

JON: Because I wouldn't know what to say to her. I'm a completely different person than I was then.

VINCE: Maybe she is too.

JON: Maybe.

VINCE: Maybe she's fat.

JON: That's really not funny.

VINCE: I didn't say it was. (Beat.) Does anyone else know what happened?

JON: I didn't tell anyone.

VINCE: Maybe you should.

JON: I don't actually consider it a crime, Vince. It was not a good thing; it was morally somewhat questionable and I wish it hadn't happened, but I don't think it's the type of thing where I need to turn myself into the police ten years later.

VINCE: I'm not talking about the police.

JON: So what're you talking about?

VINCE: I dunno. Her.

JON: I think she already knows.

VINCE: Maybe you should apologize.

JON: Oh Jesus—

VINCE: What?

JON: You want me to apologize to her?

VINCE: Why not?

JON: It wasn't even date rape, Vince!—It was just something that got a little out of hand—

VINCE: I thought you weren't sure what date rape was.

JON: Look—I'm sorry.

VINCE: Don't apologize to me.

JON: *(Recomposing.)* I'm not. What I'm trying to say is that ten years ago I did something wrong, and when I think about it now, it seems like the person who did that is a complete stranger to me. A dumb, drunk, high school senior who thought she was just being a little prudish and needed some coercion. It was bad and I regret it but it was a far cry from rape. And I don't think she would look back on it and call it that either.

VINCE: What would she call it?

JON: I don't know what she'd call it.

VINCE: What if she called it rape?

JON: Listen to me, I highly, highly doubt that she even remembers it—

VINCE: You remember it—

JON: I remember it because it was a pivotal thing for me—

VINCE: Your first rape?

JON: Stop being an asshole—

VINCE: Tell me why it was pivotal—

JON: Because it was one of the first times I looked at myself objectively and decided that I would try to avoid becoming a certain type of person. OK? For her it might have been nothing particularly important one way or another; for me, it constituted something more significant.

VINCE: So you'd like to think.

JON: Why are you suddenly high and mighty?—

VINCE: I'm not high and mighty—I'm too high to be high and mighty! I'm just a lowly, drug-dealing, boxer-wearing scum of the earth.

JON: You said it—

VINCE: No, actually, you did.

JON: I didn't mean it like that.

VINCE: How'd you mean it?

JON: That you should change your life a bit.

VINCE: This coming from a rapist.

JON: You're an idiot—

VINCE: Sorry—this coming from a big low-budget moviemaker who makes movies about "where society is possibly headed if we can just manage to forget about the date rape we didn't kind of really commit in high school."

JON: You're seriously disturbed.

VINCE: No, actually, I *am* high and mighty. I was wrong before.

JON: What do you want me to say, Vince?—I'm sorry.

VINCE: Stop apologizing to me, Jon—

JON: I'm not! I'm apologizing in general. I wish it had never happened. I don't think I'm an evil person.

VINCE: No one's saying you're evil—

JON: It sure as hell feels like it—

VINCE: Do *you* think you're evil?

JON: No—

VINCE: So then you're not evil. *I'm* the evil one here. You're the morally conscious movie-maker.

JON: Whatever.

VINCE: Whatever.

JON: Can we stop now?

VINCE: Totally.

JON: Thank you.

VINCE: *(Beat.)* I just think you should call her.

JON: I'm not gonna call her.

VINCE: I think you should—

JON: Stop! OK? To call her would be to trivialize the entire matter. It would be like saying, "How's life—oh by the way, I'm sorry I date-raped you ten years ago."

VINCE: So you *did* date-rape her?

JON: No, I didn't—

VINCE: What did you do?

JON: I coerced her to have sex with me.

VINCE: How?

JON: Verbally.

VINCE: You verbally coerced her?

JON: Yes. By applying excessive linguistic pressure, I persuaded her to have sex with me.

VINCE: And then things got rough?

JON: Things got rough in that after awhile they became aggressively playful.

VINCE: *They* did?

JON: We did.

VINCE: Meaning what?

JON: Meaning I probably still thought I was being playful but others might interpret my actions as being rough.

VINCE: —i.e., rape.

JON: No—rough.

VINCE: Look—Jon, only you two know what happened, so only you two can "interpret" your actions. So why don't you just tell me the facts and interpret them later.

JON: I'm telling you—I argued her into it—

VINCE: You're fucking lying, Jon!

(Silence.)

JON: What is your problem?

VINCE: How can you sit here with your oldest friend in the world and continuously tell lies?

JON: What makes you think I'm lying?

VINCE: Because only you would come up with the term "excessive linguistic pressure." That's not a normal expression, Jon, it's a clear sign of excessive bullshit. If you had really done only that, you'd be more specific. You'd say that you told her that if she didn't put out you'd start telling people she had VD, or smelled bad, or had a penis, or any of the normal things guys say. But you come up with your typical crap which sounds mature but contains nothing. But it's bullshit, because the reason you are where you are today is because you always insist on getting things your way. It's what you're good at, so why don't you just own up and admit what you did?

JON: *(Beat.)* Fuck off, Vince.

(Jon heads for the door.)

VINCE: Fine. I'll call her.

(Vince reaches for the phone.)

JON: Don't do that.

VINCE: Why not?

JON: Because I would like you not to.

VINCE: Why not?

JON: Because you've already made your point.

VINCE: What's my point?

JON: Your point is that nobody's perfect, including me, so it offends you when I tell you how I think you should live your life.

VINCE: That's not my point, Jon.

JON: It should be.

VINCE: It's not.

JON: Why?

VINCE: Because I haven't gotten to my point yet.

JON: So then get to it.

VINCE: Maybe I don't have one.

JON: Then I'm gonna go.

VINCE: Wrong.

JON: No—right.

(Jon starts for the door but Vince beats him to it. Vince locks the door and stands firmly in front of it.)

VINCE: Admit it.

JON: Admit what?

VINCE: What you did to Amy.

JON: What even makes you think I did something?

VINCE: Because I know—

JON: How?

VINCE: Because she told me.

JON: Told you what?

VINCE: What you did.

JON: What did she say?

VINCE: What?

JON: What did she say?

VINCE: Nothing.

JON: Get outta my way, Vincent.

VINCE: It was obvious—

(Jon reaches for the door handle only to have Vince shove him forcefully in the chest. The confrontation has reached a whole new level.)

VINCE: Tell me what you did and I'll let you go.

JON: Stop being a dick, Vince—

VINCE: Tell me what you did—

JON: Why do you care?

VINCE: Cause I wanna hear it—

JON: What would that change?

VINCE: I don't know!—

JON: So then what does it matter?—

VINCE: I don't know—

JON: —We both know I did something wrong—

VINCE: So then tell me—

JON: I pinned her arms back and stuck my dick in! OK?! For Christ fucking sakes! Shit happens! I already said I'm sorry!

(Beat.)

VINCE: Thank you.

(Vince now unlocks the door and opens it, as though an invitation for Jon to exit. Jon remains still. Vince then goes to his duffel bag, reaches inside and carefully rummages around for a second. Jon wearily looks on. After a moment, Vince takes out a small tape recorder from the bag. He looks at it briefly to make sure it is still running, then presses the "stop" button. He then places the tape recorder on the floor in front of him. Beat. Jon, having registered the import of this, stares at the recorder, and then at Vince. More silence.)

JON: What the hell did you just do?

VINCE: Taped our conversation.

JON: *(Pause.)* Why?

VINCE: I wanted to make sure I heard you right.

(Beat; Vince picks up the recorder, presses "rewind" briefly, then presses "play.")

TAPE: "I pinned her arms back and stuck my dick in! OK?! For Christ fucking sakes! Shit happens!"

(Vince presses "stop," then places the recorder back onto the floor.)

VINCE: I guess you're right—you are a completely different person.

JON: I can't believe you just did that.

VINCE: Beer?

(Vince now takes a sticker label for the tape and writes on it, then methodically places the label onto the tape. He then puts the tape in the pocket of his pants, which lie strewn on the bed. He puts his pants on. He then goes to his bag once more and takes out two beers. He offers one to Jon, who does not respond, still staring in disbelief at the recorder. Vince tosses the beer anyway. Without even looking up, Jon "swacks" the beer out of mid-air, back in the direction of Vince. Beat. Vince picks up the fallen beer from the floor.)

VINCE: You're mad?

JON: How could you do something like that?

VINCE: Like what?

JON: I'm not messing around, Vince—

VINCE: It offends you?

JON: It offends me fucking immensely.

VINCE: Why?

JON: I'm not even…

VINCE: All I'm suggesting is that you call her up and apologize for the actions of a drunk high school senior.

JON: *(Pause.)* You know you just ended our friendship.

VINCE: It's just a cheap little tape recorder. It's Kmart, man.

JON: Why did you do that?

VINCE: I'm trying to make a point.

JON: Which is what?

VINCE: That there's something wrong here.

JON: Where?—With you and I?

VINCE: Yeah. And everyone else.

JON: You think that everyone else in the world should call up and apologize for what they've done wrong in their life?

VINCE: I don't know.

JON: You honestly think that would help? You don't think it'd just end up being a bunch of hypocrites walking around raping people and apologizing?

VINCE: You have a better idea?

JON: Yeah—not do it next time.

VINCE: That's it?

JON: Yeah.

VINCE: You don't even think she'd want it for herself?

JON: Want what?

VINCE: The tape.

JON: Why would she want it?

VINCE: To know that you admitted it.

JON: I doubt she even remembers it happening, Vince.

VINCE: So then she might wanna be reminded.

JON: Why?

VINCE: Because *I'd* wanna be reminded if you pinned down my arms and fucked *me* without permission.

JON: Don't talk like that—

VINCE: That's what you did, Jon, it's on the tape.

JON: This is ridiculous.

VINCE: Why?

JON: Because my apologizing now won't make a difference to her. She's probably dealt with the whole issue and moved on.

VINCE: Maybe she has, but if you're such a different guy than you were ten years ago, then you technically shouldn't have a problem apologizing for something that, in effect, the real you didn't even do. Now, on the other hand, if you're still the kind of guy who could do something like that, then I can understand your feeling hesitant to apologize. Wouldn't want to come across as a hypocrite.

JON: *(Beat.)* Give me the tape, Vince.

VINCE: No way.

JON: Why not?

VINCE: Because—as you imply to me on a daily basis whenever we spend the day together—I wouldn't have the guts to tell her all the interesting tidbits that this tape herewith contains. It'll be much easier to simply hand it to her. If I even have the guts to do that.

(Vince goes into his duffel bag again and takes out a tiny plastic bag. He goes to the table and lays out three lines of coke, arranging them carefully with the edge of a credit card taken from his pocket.)

[NOTE: Vince turns on Eddie Cochrane music as part of the action of taking out the coke.]

VINCE: I think I'm gonna skip dinner. I'm not really hungry.

(He snorts a line of coke.)

JON: You're not gonna give her that tape, Vince.

VINCE: Hard to say, Jon.

JON: Tell me what you're gonna do with it.

VINCE: Hard to say.

(He snorts another line of coke.)

JON: Stop being a dick.

VINCE: I'm sorry—did you want to do a line?

JON: What are you gonna do with the tape?

VINCE: I was gonna make it into a movie and apply to next year's Lansing Film Festival. *(Sits at table calmly.)* Seriously, you should go. *(Beat.)* I'll tell her you said hello.

JON: What're you talking about.

VINCE: She should be calling at any minute.

JON: Why?

VINCE: 'Cause she said she'd call me at eight.

JON: I thought you said you didn't call her.

VINCE: No, I said I *thought* about calling her. And I actually did. It's cool. We're hooking up for dinner.

(Vince sits at the table, placing the tape in front of him. He snorts the last line of coke.)

VINCE: Really, Jon, you should go. I mean, I probably won't even follow through with the whole thing. *(Beat.)* Unless, of course, she sees·it sitting there and keeps pestering me about what it is.

(Beat. Vince sips his beer. Jon does not know whether to stay or go. Beat. The phone rings. Vince answers.)

VINCE: Hello?…Hey, Amy! How are you?…Yeah? Well, are you still up for some chow?…Cool. So did I tell you why I was out here?…That's true, the film festival, but the reason for that is because—well you remember Jon Saltzman, right?…Yeah? Well he's actually made a movie that's being shown as part of the festival, so I came out for that…huh?…Yeah, he is out here, staying at the Radisson…hmm hmm, 11th floor, overlooking a park. Anyway, so, I don't know how you wanna work this, I'm over at the Motel 6 on West Saginaw…exactly…cool, well only thing is that I don't have wheels, so maybe—…well that'd be great, if you wanna just pick me up and we can take it from there…Great, so you know where it is?…Cool, I'm in room 32…OK, I'll see you in a few.

(He hangs up the phone and begins to get dressed.)

VINCE: Dude, can I borrow a couple bucks?

JON: Why are you doing this?

VINCE: Well, at first it was a moral crusade, but now I'm not really sure except for the fact that you don't want me to.

JON: And that's worth more than our entire friendship?

VINCE: Jon, if you weren't my oldest friend, I don't think I would have ever assumed that I possess the power to make you think twice about something like this. Assuming you are thinking twice.

JON: There are better ways to go about making someone do that.

VINCE: How? Convince you with a really good argument? *(No answer.)* I'm not a very moral guy, Jon, much less a highly articulate poet-moviemaker. I can barely pay my rent much less persuade someone like you to stop being an asshole.

JON: No one's asking you to be articulate, Vince, it's just that you pick potentially the most important weekend of my life to bring up something I haven't even thought about in ten years!

VINCE: *(Beat.)* Yeah. I guess so.

(Vince is now fully dressed and ready to go.)

VINCE: You gonna stay here?

JON: Give me the tape.

VINCE: No.

JON: Give me the tape, Vince.

VINCE: Why?

JON: Because it doesn't belong to you.

VINCE: I bought it at Kmart!

JON: What's on it doesn't belong—

VINCE: Bullshit! I had to be like Aldrich Ames to make this tape. It's the most planned-out thing I've done my whole life.

JON: It's mine, Vince.

VINCE: I'm gonna give it to you and you're gonna destroy it—

JON: No I'm not.

VINCE: What're you gonna do with it? Put it in your closet and not think about it for another ten years?

JON: Where did you get this whole self-righteous thing? It's really not like you to have a spine.

VINCE: What can I say? I'm a fireman.

JON: *(Sitting on bed.)* I'm not leaving until you give it up.

VINCE: I don't care if you're not leaving, just don't finish my coke.

JON: Tell me something—have you ever done something that you regretted?

VINCE: Yes.

JON: That you never apologized for?

VINCE: Yes.

JON: So then why're you doing this now?

VINCE: I don't know, it must be because I have guilt about all that stuff that I never apologized for and I'm taking it out on you.

JON: OK, so then it's irrational.

VINCE: I agree.

JON: So give me the tape.

VINCE: No fucking way. *(Beat.)* You know, I wasn't even gonna give it to her at all, but the way you're acting, it's like I have no choice.
(Silence.)

VINCE: She was on her cell, man. Said she was five minutes away.

JON: Give me the tape, Vince.

VINCE: No.

JON: Vincent—

VINCE: What?

JON: Give me the tape.

VINCE: Feel free to leave anytime, Jon—

JON: Stop being a dick—

VINCE: —I won't get in your way this time—

JON: VINCENT!

VINCE: *(Mimic.)* "VINCENT!"

> *(Suddenly Jon charges Vince and tackles him onto the bed. Entwined in each other's arms, they now wrestle ferociously, rolling together off the bed and onto the floor. The fight is not so much about the tape as about their anger with each other, which is intense, deep-rooted and filled with violent tendencies... although there is also something oddly comic about this wrestling match, seeing as it is the exact type of "roughhousing" they might have done in 6th grade—and yet they are both 28. It continues, with both gaining an upper edge...until Jon gains an advantage on Vince by pinning him partially up against the base of the wall in a position that looks comfortable for neither man. They remain somewhat stuck here...until there is a knock on the door. They stop struggling. Beat. Vincent disengages himself from Jon, stands, and goes to the door; opens it. Amy Randall, 28, enters.)*

> [SUGGESTION: Amy catches Vince and Jon in the act of fighting, perhaps in a physical position of aggression that is reminiscent of the actual rape event. Either the door to the room is left slightly ajar and/or Amy knocks once and then opens the door motivated by the commotion she is hearing inside.]

VINCE: Hello, Amy—

AMY: Hi, Vincent.

> *(They give a brief, tentative but genuine hug.)*

VINCE: Wow. You look good.

AMY: You, too—

VINCE: Naw, it's nothing.

> *(Amy enters; she spots Jon as Vincent says his next line.)*

VINCE: You're not gonna believe who just showed up—

AMY: Jon?

JON: Hi, Amy—

AMY: Wow—

JON: Yeah—

AMY: Quite the reunion—

VINCE: He just swung by to say hello—

AMY: *(To Jon.)* I haven't seen you in…

JON: Since high school, probably.

VINCE: I saw you at Tracy's, right?—

AMY: That's right, about five years ago.

JON: I couldn't make it that time—

AMY: That's right. You were in grad school?

JON: USC.

AMY: For film?—

JON: Yeah—

AMY: Obviously—"Lansing Film Festival"—

JON: Right, that's why I'm here—

AMY: Vince told me.

JON: Right—

AMY: Right. *(Beat.)* I think I'm gonna wait outside, Vincent—

VINCE: No, don't.

AMY: It's just that I didn't lock my car.

VINCE: That's OK. Really. I can watch it from here.

    (Vince looks out the window.)

VINCE: *(Continues.)* It's fine.

    (Vince stands next to Amy, facing Jon.)

VINCE: *(Continues.)* I'll just stand here.

AMY: OK.

    (Silence.)

VINCE: So.

AMY: Yeah.

VINCE: It's good to see you, Amy.

AMY: You too, Vincent.

VINCE: Why do you live in Lansing?

AMY: I guess I like it. It's sort of mellow.

VINCE: Totally.

AMY: I went to school in Ann Arbor.

VINCE: That's right.

AMY: So I just decided to stay.

VINCE: I admire that.

JON: *(Beat.)* Vince told me but…what kind of law is it—?

AMY: I'm an assistant district attorney.

JON: Right. That's cool.

AMY: Yeah, I like it a lot.

JON: Yeah?

AMY: Definitely. It's good, it's a pretty good job.

JON: So you, like, what—you basically prosecute criminals?

AMY: Yeah.

JON: *(Pause.)* Cool.

AMY: Yeah. *(Beat.)* So what are *you* up to, Vincent?

VINCE: Me?

AMY: Yeah.

VINCE: Not much.

AMY: I can't believe you just called me out of the blue like that this morning.

VINCE: Yeah?

AMY: I actually love it when people do that.

VINCE: Why?

AMY: I don't know. I never have the courage to do that kind of thing.

VINCE: I just figured what the hell.

AMY: Yeah, but you could've easily not done it.

VINCE: Not what?

AMY: Not called. Most people don't.

JON: That's true.

AMY: It is true.

VINCE: Like Jon.

JON: *(In explanation.)* I didn't know you lived out here.

AMY: And if you had?

JON: I'm probably one of those people who don't have the courage.

AMY: You think?

JON: It's hard to say.

AMY: It is. Half the time it's not even worth it. People change, they end up having nothing to say to each other, even if they were best friends a year earlier.

VINCE: *(Beat.)* I'm glad you're not fat.

AMY: Is that right?

VINCE: Yeah.

AMY: You should of seen me in college.

VINCE: Fat?

AMY: Quite.

VINCE: Me too.

AMY: Probably for different reasons. *(Beat.)* So, you didn't answer my question.

VINCE: Which one?

AMY: What are you doing these days?

VINCE: Oh. I live in California.

AMY: Where?

VINCE: Oakland.

AMY: Nice.

VINCE: I'm a firefighter.

AMY: Are you serious?

VINCE: I'm totally serious.

AMY: That's pretty cool, Vincent.

VINCE: It keeps me busy.

AMY: I'm sure.

VINCE: Yeah.

AMY: Lotta fires in Oakland?

VINCE: Average.

JON: I should get going.

VINCE: I thought you were coming to dinner with us.

JON: No, I never said that.

VINCE: Well why don't you?

JON: I can't, I gotta get some sleep for tomorrow.

VINCE: No you don't—

JON: Yeah, actually, I do—

VINCE: Dude, they're showing your movie, you're not running a marathon—

JON: I know, but—

VINCE: Plus they're showing it at 2 o'clock in the afternoon.

JON: I know, but I have some meetings in the morning.

AMY: You haven't changed, have you Vincent?

VINCE: Whattayou mean?

AMY: I can remember you doing the exact same thing when we were dating.

VINCE: Doing what?

AMY: Putting pressure on people to follow whatever schedule you've already worked out in your head.

VINCE: That's not true.

AMY: It is, but it's nice. It's like you stayed up the night before thinking for hours how the next day was going to work and now you just want people to partake in your vision.

VINCE: That's not true—

AMY: OK.

VINCE: Jon can do anything he wants—

AMY: I know—

VINCE: I'm just suggesting he joins us for dinner.

JON: Why?

VINCE: Because I'm sentimental. Is that so wrong? I like it when old friends get together. It makes me feel warm.

AMY: Maybe Jon doesn't feel like it—

VINCE: I know he doesn't because he doesn't have the courage. It's like you said, he lets these things go.

AMY: I didn't mean him specifically.

VINCE: Well you should have. He always does it.

JON: Does what?

VINCE: Let things go. If you saw your mother on the street, you'd cross to the other side.

JON: What are you—high?

VINCE: Yes.

AMY: Are you high, Vincent?

VINCE: A bit.

AMY: You've been smoking pot since high school?

VINCE: It's no different than drinking—

AMY: I know, but do you also still drink?—

VINCE: So?

AMY: I'm just saying you should be careful—

VINCE: What is this, "Lecture Vince Night"?

AMY: Who's lecturing you?

VINCE: You are. He did, I'm waiting for the Motel 6 desk guy to come in here next.

AMY: It's only because I care about you.

VINCE: You haven't seen me for five years.

AMY: But you were my first boyfriend, Vincent. It's inevitable. You could turn into a dirty old man and I'd still care.

VINCE: Really?

AMY: Of course. It's one of those things.

VINCE: *(Beat.)* Do you wanna get married?

AMY: I can't right now.

VINCE: Why?

AMY: I have a boyfriend.

VINCE: Who is he?

AMY: He's the district attorney.

VINCE: That is so typical…

AMY: Why?

VINCE: I don't know, it just is.

AMY: If it doesn't work out, I'll give you a call in Oakland.

VINCE: Yeah, right—

JON: So I should get going.

VINCE: *(To Amy.)* Why don't you give *him* a lecture?

AMY: On what?

VINCE: Taking better care of himself.

AMY: He looks like he's doing OK.

JON: *(Standing.)* It was good to see you again, Amy.

VINCE: Whoa, whoa, whoa—

AMY: Vince—

VINCE: No, he's not getting out of here just like that.

JON: Maybe I'll see you tomorrow.

VINCE: No, bullshit—

JON: Vince—

VINCE: What?!

JON: I have to go.

> *(Beat; Jon reaches out to shake Amy's hand.)*

VINCE: You see, it's actually really nice of you to say that, Amy, because I always thought Jon was your first love. *(Beat.)* I mean, I know you guys didn't really date that much, but I guess I always assumed—even though I didn't know about it till later—I always assumed that when you guys got together there at the end of senior year, it was sort of like some long-awaited love affair that was bound to happen. *(Beat.)* Am I characterizing that correctly?

JON: *(Beat.)* I don't think anyone would call it a long-awaited love affair, Vince.

VINCE: What would you call it?

JON: I'd call it us getting together at the end of senior year.

VINCE: *(Pause; to Amy.)* Oh. Maybe I'm just jealous because...you know, *I* wanted to be your first boyfriend.

AMY: You were.

VINCE: I know, but...you know what I mean.

AMY: Oh.

VINCE: I shouldn't care about that kind of stuff, but like I say, I'm sentimental.

AMY: That's not sentimental, Vincent.

VINCE: What is it?

AMY: It's stupid.

VINCE: …I agree, but see, I didn't know that in high school. Back then, you not wanting to have sex with me was sort of like being disinvited to Christmas dinner at my grandparents'. *(Pause.)* Which is something I'm very sentimental about.

AMY: You shouldn't have taken it personally.

VINCE: I know, but I did. *(Pause.)* Especially when you guys ended up getting together. Literally. *(Quiet. To Amy.)* But I guess I blew it out of proportion.

AMY: What're you talking about, Vincent?

VINCE: I'm talking about you guys getting together at the end of senior year. It hurt my feelings at the time. But according to Jon, it was less of a long-awaited love affair and more like just two kids getting giddy before graduation. In which case, I suppose I really shouldn't hold a grudge. *(Beat.)* Is that what it was?

AMY: *(Beat.)* I would say that it was a crush that never amounted to much.

VINCE: For you or for him?

AMY: For me.

JON: Vince, it doesn't seem like Amy really wants to talk about this.

VINCE: Why not, we're all mature adults. We can talk about a high school crush that happened ten years ago.

JON: Fine, then I'm gonna let you two have this discussion without me.

VINCE: OK, but before you leave, I'm just curious as to why nothing ever came of Amy's crush for you. Amy?

AMY: Why nothing ever came of it?

VINCE: Yeah. Why didn't it develop into something more serious. I mean, it wasn't like you and I got back together afterwards. I don't think you even dated anyone after that. At least not anybody from our school.

AMY: *(Beat.)* I guess it just didn't work out.

VINCE: Oh. *(Pause.)* And there's no specific *reason* for that?

AMY: I'm sure there was.

VINCE: But?

AMY: No but. I'm sure there was.

VINCE: Oh. *(Beat.)* Why're you so anxious to leave, Jon?

JON: Because this is awkward for me.

VINCE: And so you'd rather leave?

JON: Fine, Vince. *(He stretches his arms out, palms up.)* Here I am. Would anyone like to say anything to me? *(Silence.)* Amy?

AMY: *(Beat.)* No thanks.

JON: Vince?

VINCE: Yeah.

(Vince takes the tape from his pocket and tosses it to Jon.)

VINCE: It's your call, Jon. I can't speak for you.

(Jon holds the tape; silence.)

JON: *(Beat.)* It was good to see you again, Amy.

AMY: *(Pause.)* You too.

VINCE: That is so fucking typical…

JON: I gotta go.

(Jon prepares to leave, with a small, unsuccessful attempt to make eye contact with Amy before doing so…. He opens the door.)

VINCE: Jon?

JON: What?

VINCE: Can I have that back?

(Beat. Jon tosses Vince the tape. Beat.)

JON: Goodbye, Amy.

(She does not answer. Beat; Jon exits. Silence.)

AMY: Oakland must be a pretty safe place.

VINCE: Why?

AMY: There don't seem to be enough fires to keep you busy.

VINCE: What do you mean?

AMY: Can you tell me what that was about?

VINCE: I wanted to know what happened between you two.

AMY: When?

VINCE: That night. *(Beat.)* I wanted him to apologize to you.

AMY: Why?

VINCE: So you could hear it. *(Beat.)* He admitted it to me.

AMY: What did you do?

VINCE: I got him to admit it. It's on the tape.

AMY: Admit what?

VINCE: What he did to you. *(No answer.)* He did do it, didn't he? Amy?

AMY: What?

VINCE: That night. Am I wrong? He raped you. Didn't he?

AMY: *(Pause.)* Why would that be any of your business?

VINCE: You're missing my point—

AMY: And even if he had, the last thing I would want is a taped confession.

VINCE: Why not?

AMY: Because I'm not the one who needs it.

VINCE: What're you talking about?

(She starts to leave.)

AMY: I'm not the one who needs it.

VINCE: So then who needs it?

AMY: I'll see you later—

VINCE: Where are you going?

AMY: Home.

VINCE: I don't think you understand, I was trying to do the right thing.

AMY: *(Turning back to him.)* For whom?

VINCE: For you.

AMY: Is that really what you mean, Vincent?

VINCE: Of course it's what I mean!—

AMY: Because I don't think it is.

VINCE: I thought you'd appreciate it.

AMY: Well I don't.

VINCE: Why not?

AMY: Because he didn't rape me.

> *(Beat.)*

VINCE: What?

AMY: He didn't. *(Pause.)* So the only person you're trying to make feel better is yourself.

> *(Silence. Beat. Then a knock on the door. Beat. Vince puts the tape back in his pants pocket. Vincent goes and opens the door. Jon is there. He looks at them both; beat.)*

JON: Hey.

VINCE: *(Pause.)* Hey.

> *(Jon closes the door behind him and enters the room more fully; more silence.)*

VINCE: What are you doing?

JON: I came back.

VINCE: Why?

JON: Because I felt like it.

> *(Silence.)*

JON: Vince, can you give us a couple minutes in private?

VINCE: *(Beat.)* Are you kidding me?

JON: I'm serious.

VINCE: You want me to leave you alone with her?

JON: Yeah—

VINCE: No—

JON: You can wait outside the door.

VINCE: No fucking way!

JON: Why not?

VINCE: Because of the whole—no. No.

JON: I just need two minutes—

VINCE: Why?

JON: I want to tell her something.

VINCE: What?

JON: It's none of your business.

VINCE: Yes it is—

JON: Why?

VINCE: Because I'm the one who brought it up!

AMY: It's all right, Vincent.

VINCE: No it's not.

AMY: Yes it is.

VINCE: Well I don't care, I'm not leaving.

(Vince folds his arms and sits down. Silence. Beat.)

JON: *(To Amy.)* I wanted to apologize.

VINCE: For what?

JON: Vince—

VINCE: What?!

JON: Shut up. *(Beat. To Amy.)* I wanted to apologize. *(Beat.)* For what it's worth. *(Pause.)* I'm sorry. I really, honestly, truly am.
    (Silence.)

AMY: For what?

JON: For what happened between us in high school.

AMY: What happened between us?

JON: I'm talking about what happened at the end of senior year, which Vince was trying to get me to talk about before.

AMY: Before when?

JON: Like five minutes ago.

AMY: About when you and I got together in high school?

JON: Right.

AMY: Right. So tell me again what happened?

JON: *(Beat.)* Do you know which day I'm talking about?

AMY: At the end of senior year? At Rebecca's party?

JON: Yeah.

AMY: Yeah.

VINCE: *(Beat.)* What are you guys doing?

AMY: I'm just curious. I don't want there to be a communication gap here.

JON: I'm not sure what I'm supposed to say.

AMY: I think you think you did something to me.

JON: Yes.

AMY: What do you think you did?

JON: Why?

AMY: Because this is very interesting to me.

JON: Do you not think that something happened?

AMY: Well of course something happened.

JON: But are you saying you don't remember what it was?

AMY: C'mon, Jon—there are certain things one doesn't forget.

JON: I agree.

AMY: I'm just wondering how you would describe it.

JON: Probably the same way as you.

AMY: You think?

JON: *(Beat.)* The whole reason this thing started is because Vince taped this conversation he and I had earlier.

VINCE: Dude, I'm sorry—

JON: It's fine—

VINCE: I didn't realize—

JON: I'm just saying, that that's why I'm here.

AMY: You're here because Vince taped you?

JON: Yes.

AMY: Why?

JON: Why?

AMY: Why?

JON: …Because it made me think.

AMY: Oh.

JON: Which is why I came back.

AMY: Good—so tell me what happened.

JON: *(Beat.)* I think I raped you.

AMY: *(Beat.)* No. You didn't rape me.

JON: *(Beat.)* Yes, I did.

AMY: No. You didn't.

JON: *(Beat.)* Are you trying to make fun of this?

AMY: No.

JON: Amy. I know what happened.

AMY: Apparently not.

JON: I do.

AMY: Says who?

JON: Me.

AMY: Why?

JON: Because I just admitted it.

AMY: On what—the tape?

JON: Yeah.

AMY: What's on it?

JON: It's me confessing what I did.

AMY: What did you do?

JON: I just told you.

AMY: But that doesn't prove you did it—

JON: Why not?—

AMY: Because if no one's accusing you of anything, then there's no reason to confess.

JON: ...I'm having trouble realizing what you're doing.

AMY: I'm not doing anything—

JON: This is not an easy thing for me.

AMY: You sure about that?

VINCE: Jon?

JON: What?

VINCE: Do you know what you're saying?

JON: I'm saying what you wanted me to say.

VINCE: But are you sure you have the right girl?

JON: Yes!

VINCE: She says nothing happened.

JON: She's lying—

AMY: No I'm not.

JON: Amy?!

AMY: What?

JON: You're mocking this!

AMY: Why would I do that?

JON: I don't know, but if you are, I have better things to do.

AMY: I just think we just have differing perceptions of what happened.

JON: I really don't see how that could be.

AMY: Why, because you decided you did something?

JON: I did do something.

AMY: Well I say you didn't.

JON: So then what happened?

AMY: When?

JON: Then.

AMY: We had sex.

JON: Amy—

AMY: What?

JON: I'm trying to be honest.

AMY: Why now?

JON: Because I haven't seen you in ten years.

AMY: But why *now*?

JON: Because when Vince played me back that tape, it hit me what I had done.

AMY: And if he *hadn't* played back the tape?

JON: Yeah—?

AMY: Would you be saying this?

JON: Probably not.

AMY: Or is it just that I'm here?

JON: What do you mean?

AMY: If I lived in Alaska, would you have sought me out?

JON: I don't really know.

AMY: You should look into that.

JON: Fine.

AMY: *(Pause.)* Or is it just that you're jealous. *(Beat.)* Does that make me sound conceited?

JON: A bit.

AMY: Why? *I* loved *you*. *(Beat.)* I did. I was totally in love with you that night. *(Beat…)* Did you love *me*?

JON: *(Beat.)* No.

AMY: So why were you with me?

JON: I'm not sure.

AMY: Maybe it's the same reason you came back to apologize just now.

JON: Which is what?

AMY: You like pissing off Vincent.

JON: Why would it piss him off if that's what he wanted in the first place!?

AMY: Because he's confused.

VINCE: Exactly.

AMY: It's never too late to one-up your best friend by telling him once and for all that you raped the love of his life in high school. *(Pause.)* Especially if you get to do it in front of her.

JON: You really think I'm like that?

AMY: I don't know, I have a very poor record of judging you accurately. *(Beat.)* Maybe you just came back to get the last word. You didn't like what was on the tape, so you came back to hear yourself phrase it more eloquently.

JON: *(Beat.)* The reason I came back is to apologize, which I can assure you is not at all disingenuous. I honestly am sorry.

AMY: Why, because you had your hand over my mouth?

JON: Yes.

AMY: Well hey, Jon...I let everybody do that.

JON: Can you please just tell me the truth?

AMY: I am. *(Beat...Jon starts for the door.)*

VINCE: Where are you going?

JON: I think I should leave.

VINCE: Why?—

JON: Because no matter what I say, there's nowhere for this to go.

AMY: You want the last word, Jon, but it's not yours to have.

VINCE: Why don't you guys just figure out what the fuck you're talking about?—

JON: Vince!

VINCE: What?

JON: She's in denial.

VINCE: Amy?

AMY: *(To Vince.)* What was it that even made you think something happened?

VINCE: At Rebecca's?

AMY: Yeah.

VINCE: Because I thought it did. I thought later that that's what you were trying to tell me.

AMY: Why?

VINCE: Because why else would you have slept with Jon when you were supposed to be dating me?

AMY: You and I had already broken up.

VINCE: I know, but *we* hadn't even slept together, so what the hell were you doing sleeping with him?

AMY: It's none of your business.

VINCE: Well that's partly why I figured something happened.

AMY: Why, because if I wasn't sleeping with you, why would I sleep with somebody else?

VINCE: Yeah...I guess...I guess...I thought something like that.

(*Beat.*)

JON: I'm gonna go. (*To Vince.*) Maybe I'll see you tomorrow. Amy, I'm sorry. And I'm sorry you're not in a place where you can hear that right now. (*Pause.*) I hope you have a good life.

(*Jon heads for the door.*)

AMY: Why did you say that?

JON: What?

AMY: That I'm not in a place to hear that.

JON: Because you don't seem to realize that I'm serious. I don't know how else to put it to you other than to say what I've said. Even if you really do think it wasn't a big deal, it was for me, and I want you to know that I'm sorry it happened.

(*Jon finishes, his words lingering in the air a moment. He has made Amy think. It seems as though she will not answer him. Beat.*)

AMY: (*Beat; calm on the surface.*) Well you should be. And I hope you die for it and go to hell; and if there is no hell, I hope that you suffer on your way *to* death, and that your last living sensation is that of a steel rod being shoved repeatedly up your insides so that it batters your heart and punctures your stomach; and when you die and your sphincter finally collapses, my hope is that your last bowel movement be saturated with blood from the draining backwash of your rotted, fucking, pathetic guts. (*Silence.*) Is that along the lines of what you wanted? (*No answer; beat…to Jon.*) I really don't know what you want me to say to you.

JON: (*Pause.*) Nothing.

VINCE: (*Beat…lost.*) So was I right?

(*Amy has pulled a cell phone from her purse and now calmly dials three numbers.*)

AMY: (*Into her phone.*) Yes, could you please dispatch a squad car over to the Motel 6 on Saginaw, room 32. There seems to be a significant amount of illegal substance in the room…it appears to be cocaine…yes, and by the way, you might want to run a check on one of the two gentlemen here, Jon Saltzman S-a-l-t-z-m-a-n—possible history of sexual misconduct including a verified first degree CSC ten years ago…thank you.

(*Amy folds the phone and returns it to her purse. Silence. Jon and Vince are both staring at her.*)

AMY: (*Beat.*) You guys can make a run for it if you like.

VINCE: Did you really just do that?

AMY: The average response time in Lansing is four minutes. It's one of the top departments in the country.

JON: Why does it have to be like this?

AMY: Because if you're truly repentant, then you should be willing to pay the price.

JON: Why can't you just accept the fact that I'm sorry?

AMY: It does me no good.

JON: Is that my fault?

AMY: No, that's the way it is.

JON: But I'm the one who has to run out of here like a criminal?

AMY: It's up to you.

JON: Because I'm not going to.

AMY: Is that because you think the statute of limitations ran out?

JON: I have no idea.

AMY: There is none for a sexual misconduct felony. *(Pause.)* Just to let you know.

VINCE: *(Beat.)* I really don't feel like getting busted for a couple lines of coke.

AMY: Then I guess I'll see you later, Vincent.

(Vincent is unsure what to do for a moment, then he quickly wipes the rest of the cocaine back into the bag and sticks in his pocket.)

AMY: Just do me a favor and leave that tape behind. *(Pause.)* So I can give it to Officer Friendly. *(Beat; Vince is quite unsure what to do.)*

VINCE: You want me to give you the tape?

AMY: Yeah.

(Vince looks at Jon.)

AMY: You don't need his permission.

VINCE: I feel like I do.

AMY: You didn't need his permission to make it; why would you need it now?

VINCE: *(Pause.)* Protocol?

AMY: Fine, then I'll just stay here and tell them myself.

(Beat; Vince starts for the door; he stops, turns to Jon.)

VINCE: Dude, it might be in your best interest to come with me.

JON: I'm staying.

VINCE: Why?

JON: Because if this is the only way she knows how to deal with this, then this is what should happen.

VINCE: Fine but what about me?

JON: What about you?

VINCE: I didn't really do anything wrong!

AMY: You're in possession of an illegal substance—

VINCE: I know but I was just trying to blow off some steam.

AMY: You should've blown it off with beer.

VINCE: I did, I just needed to blow off a little extra.

JON: You better go, Vince, they're on their way.

VINCE: Come with me.

JON: No.

VINCE: Don't be an idiot, they'll arrest you.

(Beat…Jon remains still.)

VINCE: *(To Amy.)* Is this really what you want?

AMY: Jon's a big boy, he can make his own decisions.

VINCE: Fine, then I'm outta here.

JON: Thanks, Vince.

VINCE: What?

JON: Thanks.

VINCE: For what?

JON: For all your honesty.

VINCE: *(At a loss.)* What do you mean?

JON: Nothing. I'll see you later.

(Vince starts again for the door, but then stops. He knows he wouldn't be able to live with himself if he left—for it is he who got Jon into this.)

VINCE: FUCK!

(In a change of plans, he now hurriedly takes the bag of coke from his pocket, then reaches into his duffel bag and produces an enormous bag of marijuana; he then takes both bags and goes into the bathroom. We hear the flush of a toilet. A moment later, Vincent comes back out empty-handed; he goes to the table and attempts to wipe clean any potential remnants of the cocaine. All of this is done with a large amount of frustration and bitter dejection. He then goes to the window and looks out. Seeing that he still has at least a minute or two, he takes the cassette from his pocket, looks momentarily at Jon, then methodically breaks the cassette in half, pulling out the tape so as to ensure the cassette's total destruction. Finally, he sits on the bed. Silence. There is silence for perhaps an entire minute as the three of them regard one another intently and curiously. Then, a notion slowly begins to enter Vince's mind. Beat.)

[SUGGESTION: The author notes that Vince might NOT break the tape before Amy leaves, and that Vince takes it out after Amy exits and that it is

included as part of a final ambiguous blackout image of Jon and Vince at the end of the play.]

VINCE: Did you really call the police?

AMY: No.

VINCE: Jesus Christ.

AMY: Sorry.

VINCE: Why'd you do that?

AMY: I felt like it.

VINCE: You're fucked up.

AMY: What did you expect?

VINCE: *(Beat.)* ...Fine, but do you know how much those drugs cost?

AMY: There'll be other drugs, Vincent.

VINCE: I know, but I really liked *those* ones!

    (Silence. Amy now stands; she regards Jon for a very long moment.)

AMY: *(Beat. To Jon.)* Good luck tomorrow.

JON: Thank you.

AMY: Goodbye, Vincent.

VINCE: Bye, Amy.

    (Amy opens the door to go.)

VINCE: It was good to see...

    (Amy exits, closing the door behind her.

    Beat. Jon and Vince sit in silence. Vince starts to say something, then decides not to. Beat. Lights fade to black.)

END OF PLAY

No. 11 (Blue and White)
by Alexandra Cunningham

BIOGRAPHY

Alexandra Cunningham grew up in Darien, Connecticut. A graduate of Johns Hopkins University, she studied at the Samuel Beckett School for Theatre and Drama at Trinity College, Dublin and received her M.F.A. in playwriting from Columbia University, where she was awarded the Oscar Hammerstein II Center Award for Playwriting and the John Golden Award for Best Play. Her plays have been workshopped and produced at Juilliard, Columbia University, Trinity College, New Dramatists, the Irish Arts Center and New York Stage and Film, and she has been a playwriting instructor at the Sewanee Young Writers Conference. Ms. Cunningham is currently a playwright-in-residence at the Juilliard School, where she has taught playwriting in the Juilliard Intersession twice and received two Lincoln Center LeComte du Nuoy grants.

HUMANA FESTIVAL PRODUCTION

No. 11 (Blue and White) premiered at the Humana Festival of New American Plays in March 2000. It was directed by Brian Mertes with the following cast:

Alex	Savannah Haske
Suzanne Callahan	Lauren Klein
Reid Callahan	Blair Singer
Danny	Patrick J. Dall'Occhio
Brian	Patrick Darragh
Paige	Jessica Wortham
Tammy	Christy Collier
Coach Coyle/Dad/Lieutenant Cleary	William McNulty
Jenny/Voice of Kristin	Shawna Joy Anderson
Lindsay	Woodwyn Koons

and the following production staff:

Scenic Designer	Paul Owen
Costume Designer	Suttirat Larlarb
Lighting Designer	Greg Sullivan
Sound Designer	Martin R. Desjardins
Properties Designer	Ben Hohman
Stage Manager	Janette L. Hubert
Production Assistant	Trudy L. Paxton
Fight Director	Drew Fracher
Dramaturg	Amy Wegener
Assistant Dramaturg	Kelly Lea Miller
Casting	Laura Richin Casting

CHARACTERS

REID CALLAHAN, 18
SUZANNE CALLAHAN, his mother
ALEXANDRA, 17
BRIAN, 18
DANNY, 17
COACH COYLE/DAD/LIEUTENANT CLEARY, to be played by the same actor
TAMMY, 18
LINDSAY, 16
PAIGE, 17
JENNY, 17/KRISTIN'S VOICE, 19—to be played by the same actress

TIME & PLACE

In Connecticut, right now.

I showed him some of my poems, one of which
began "Mirrored images of bitches' murderous
beauty," and another, "The girl who came with
doves to sell will die."
He said, "Lots of libido."
That made me smile.

—Paul Theroux

Shawna Joy Anderson, Patrick Darragh, Patrick J. Dall'Occhio,
Savannah Haske, Blair Singer and Jessica Wortham
in *No. 11 (Blue and White)*

24th Annual Humana Festival of New American Plays
Actors Theatre of Louisville, 2000
photo by Richard Trigg

No. 11
(Blue and White)

Lights.

ALEX: When they hear the name, they always ask me, and they always expect me to say: Well I knew *of* him, yeah, but I didn't *know* him. And then they always want to hear the story. They never expect the one I have to tell.

Reid at the table. Suzanne enters with a bouquet.

SUZANNE: Look at these, aren't they just gorgeous. I *love* them. He always remembers what I like. Look at them. *Look* at them.
(*She waves the flowers in front of Reid.*)
Hyacinths, tulips and freesia. Look.

REID: Thcrumptious.

SUZANNE: Oh, you, you don't know anything.

REID: I know Mr. McGraw's a fucking loser.

SUZANNE: You don't *know* that, you *think* it, and watch your language.

REID: Yeah, I definitely think it.

SUZANNE: Well, that might end up making things a little difficult...but I guess we'll just have to see.
(*She starts arranging the flowers.*)

REID: Why would it make things difficult?...*Mom? Why* would it—

SUZANNE: Oh, you know. You never know.

REID: You would marry him?...You would marry him?

SUZANNE: Oh, hold your horses. Nobody's marrying anybody.

REID: I *hate* him.

SUZANNE: You've said. Are you wearing that shirt?

REID: Yeah, I *thought* so, I *thought* this was me.

SUZANNE: No, I mean, to school. Look, the neck is all pulled out of shape, it's just awful.

(Beat.)

Go put something else on, okay? Just humor me, do it for me.

REID: Why? You're not going to be there.

SUZANNE: When people see you, they see me, honey, all right? Just put on something that has a collar that doesn't...*do* that.

REID: I'm wearing this.

SUZANNE: *Fine.*

REID: I'm outta here, I'm gonna be late.

SUZANNE: Did you eat anything? You should have something to eat before school.

REID: *Is* there anything?

SUZANNE: Oh, I don't know. Why don't you look?

REID: If there's no food, do you want me to buy the stuff for the team dinner or are you going to get it when you go?

SUZANNE: When I go where? What?

REID: The dinner, the pasta dinner for the team!

(She stares blankly at him.)

We have one every Friday night before the Saturday afternoon game, a different player hosts it every time, this week it's our turn, Earth to Mom, hello.

SUZANNE: Well, not this week, I can't do it. Some other time maybe.

REID: What? Fuck *maybe*, Mom—

SUZANNE: Listen to the way you talk to me! If your father was alive he would never let you get aw—

REID: You've been on the list for this Friday for months, they made up the schedule in January, I wrote it on your stupid calendar—

SUZANNE: Well, I can't *do* it, Reid, so that's *it*, all right? Switch me with one of the other mothers or something. Throwing a tantrum isn't going to make me magically able to do it, haven't you learned that by now?

(She places the arranged flowers decisively in the middle of the table.)

I thought you said you were going to be late. Didn't you say that?

(She exits. Reid crosses to a drawer, takes out a pair of scissors and advances on the blooms. He delicately snips the head off one, then another. He braces himself against the table and moans with pleasure.)

REID: Ohhh.

Scene. The school day dawns over the parking lot. Brian and Danny huddle in their lacrosse team jackets.

DANNY: Is he still sitting in the car? Why is he still sitting in the car?

BRIAN: Hey, check this shit out.

(He takes a drag off his cigarette and french-inhales.)

DANNY: …that's fucking fantastic, I feel totally complete.

BRIAN: It's a french-inhale.

DANNY: I don't believe this. I can see him from here and he's just sitting behind the wheel like some kind of moron.

BRIAN: He's got fifteen minutes, lay off.

DANNY: My ass he's got fifteen minutes, he's got like four minutes.

BRIAN: It's only—*(Looks at his watch.)*—Heeeyyy, shit.

DANNY: What the hell is he doing? Hey, Callahan! Shitsmear! What's up!…All right, wait, he's getting out of the car, we will sneak by with a couple of minutes to spare, give me a drag.

BRIAN: *(Doesn't really care.)* You've got asthma.

(He passes Danny the cigarette.)

DANNY: Okay, look at me, am I doing it? Here, wait—look.

BRIAN: Uh, well, you're pretty close. I can see what you might look like if you actually *were* doing it. It's a shitty habit anyway, dude, you don't want to get into smoking. I mean, besides making me look totally dropdead cool and fuckable I can't think of too much else it does for me, really.

DANNY: So tell me how to do it.

BRIAN: You inhale the smoke, right? But you don't take it into your lungs, you just hold it in your mouth. Then you exhale all the air out of your lungs through your nose, still holding the smoke in your mouth, and then when you inhale again, you suck the air in only through your nose, and you open your mouth as you inhale and let the smoke drift out and you'll take it straight up your nose. Take it from me, they fall right over and spread.

DANNY: Okay, here I go.

(He inhales. Reid enters and slaps him on the back. The smoke goes the wrong way.)

DANNY: *(Coughing.)* Glad you finally decided to get out of the car and join us. What the hell were you doing? Beating off?

(Reid smiles.)

Oh, sure, I should have known, right?

(Brian smiles now.)

Oh, my God, you were! You were beating off in the car? In the car?

REID: *(Matter-of-fact.)* Helps me concentrate.

DANNY: You're like some giant mutant jackrabbit.

REID: I get horny in the mornings. I'm not the only one.

DANNY: Right in the parking lot. Eight forty fucking five in the morning. Not to mention it's about two degrees out. I'm surprised you didn't get stuck to the steering wheel.

BRIAN: Think of it this way, Dan, if old Reid gets his rocks off and over with now, he won't feel the need to do it in the library stacks during third period study hall.

REID: *(Agreeing.)* Hey, yeah.

BRIAN: 'Cause, me, I like the old flaky crusty shit on the edges of the books to be the *binding.*

REID: *(Chuckling.)* I like it in the stacks. Kinda dark and spooky.

BRIAN: Knowing he got it out of the way early always makes me feel better. Comforts me in my hour of needing to use the encyclopedia.

REID: I don't *do* it in the reference section. I do it in the Virginia Woolf section. There were a lot of long lonely nights last year that I wanted to spend beating off that I *couldn't*, because I had to read that *To The Lighthouse* piece of shit for Clements's class? What a nightmare. So now I make up for all those lost opportunities and punish the bitch at the same time.

DANNY: You're a freak, Reid.

REID: I don't like to see you in fetters, Danny, pal. Set yourself free.

DANNY: Well, I abuse myself as much as the next guy but this just strikes me as excessive, I'm sorry.

BRIAN: Yeah, well, when Reid drove us all home from practice Monday I saw you use one of the wads of Kleenex on the floor of the passenger well to actually *blow your nose.*
(Reid snorts scornfully.)
I mean, you're a guy, aren't you? Don't you recognize one of those when you see it? Even my *mom* knows what those are. She empties my garbage, she learned from experience.
(Beat.)

DANNY *(Chastened.)* Well, we're gonna be late now.

BRIAN: For assembly, boo hoo hoooo.

REID: Aaah, it was worth it. It's always worth it.
(He throws his arm around Danny's shoulders.)
Isn't it? Huh?

DANNY: Oh, yeah, this is great. Please, paw me some more, since I know you haven't gotten a chance to wash your hands yet and everything.

REID: I hate to break it to you, Dan, but it's going on around you all the time. Girls? Doing it all day long. 'Cause they don't even need to use their hands. They just squeeze their thighs together and massage the goldmine. God, how great is that.

BRIAN: Or they can contract their vagina muscles—

REID: *(Likes the turn this conversation is taking.)* Sweet!

BRIAN: —they kind of pulse them. It's called Kegeling, or something. Women learn to do it so after they have a baby they can get tight again.

REID: Wow, is the Discovery Channel finally living up to its name or what.

BRIAN: Missy can do it.

REID: Missy *Bel*mont? Don't shit the Pope.

BRIAN: In third grade she was scared of the girls' bathroom so she trained herself to hold it till she got home and then later she discovered...it could be...put to other uses.

(A bell rings.)

DANNY: Shit, I can't remember if I have thirteen demerits or fourteen. I think thirteen, I think I'm cool for one more.

REID: So ol' Missy can pulse her cunt muscles. That is fascinating, I mean it. She hides her light under a bushel. What's it look like?

BRIAN: Don't know. I know what it feels like, though.

DANNY: *Knew* what it *felt* like, since she dumped you.

REID: ...oh ho, you guys, this is all just too interesting, I think I might have to pay a visit to the *library*.

DANNY: Oh, man, come on, I have to finish my *Brideshead Revisited* thing for Schwartz, third period is the only time I have free before class, you can't go in there then.

BRIAN: Ha, ha, Evelyn *Waugh*, starts with *W*, you'll find it in the Woolf stack, have a good time, Dan.

(Alex passes in front of them. Reid grabs her; Danny and Brian keep going.)

REID: Alex, baby, hold up, gotta ask you—

ALEX: I already said, no way.

REID: Please. Come on please please.

ALEX: No. You have to show your work, you know, you have to show how you *got* the answers, what're you gonna do? Copy my scratch paper too? Forget it. Be a man, take the F. You've seen one before, it holds no surprises for you.

REID: Let me worry about showing how I got the answers, okay? Anyway, he'll figure if you were letting me copy off you, you would have warned me about needing to show my work too, so if I can't, you'll look like the sweet little innocent morsel that you are. Looking so hot in that uniform skirt.

ALEX: Do you know, some lady came up to me Wednesday at Carvel and offered me a hundred dollars for this skirt? She said Dress Campbell was her family tartan. Whatever she was smoking, I want some. But I had nothing I could change into, so I missed the boat.

REID: Well, that's a crying shame but I'd miss that skirt. It's so short and sweet. It's taken you three years to get tall enough to make that skirt the length it should be and now it's perfect.

(Beat.)

ALEX: Oh, no, no. You're not fooling anyone, you know.

REID: *(Fake surprise.)* I'm not? I'm not fooling anyone?

ALEX: It's still no dice, Reid, I'm not doing it. And who still thinks a teacher is going to let them wear a baseball cap during an exam anyway? That's like Cheating 101.

REID: I'm not *fooling* anyone?

ALEX: Shit, we're so late now, and I'm wearing ankle socks, I'm dead.

REID: I'm not fooling *anyone?*

ALEX: Shut up!

Scene. Suzanne speaks to the audience.

SUZANNE: On behalf of the Community Against Drugs and Alcohol, I'd like to welcome you all here this evening. For those of you who don't know us, I'm the co-chairman of CADA, Suzanne Callahan, and this is my fellow co-chairman and president of the PTA, Charlotte Sanders, and I think I can say for both of us, it's good to see such a big turnout at a meeting. There's nothing more important than that we as parents try to take an active role in our children's lives. I mean, we just don't have a choice. So let's get started!

(Paige speaks to the audience.)

PAIGE: I was fourteen, I just didn't want it to be this big issue anymore, I wanted to get it over with. I was going out with this guy, Jeb McNeil, he was a freshman at Boston College, and he was pretty experienced, and he just kept saying I would love it, I would love it, love it —*(Disgust.)*—uhhhh!

SUZANNE: Tonight we're going to discuss something that was prepared for us by Police Chief Larson, for when you go on vacation and leave your children to housesit—this is a list of things to look out for on your return that will tell you if they had a party while you were gone.

PAIGE: Well, wait, actually he didn't say, "Paige, you *would* love it," he said, "Paige, you *will* love it."

SUZANNE: Because unless you come home unexpectedly, you'll never know anything went on. Unless you know where to look.

PAIGE: I just thought my first time should be with someone who knew what he was doing.

SUZANNE: Number one. If you own a pet—dog, cat, hamster—check for signs that the animal has recently been sick.

PAIGE: When I think about it now, I wish I'd told him beforehand, made like an announcement, you know? Then at least I would have the memory of it having been my *plan*. Instead of something that sort of just *happened*.

SUZANNE: That's always been a favorite at my house. I'll add to that: see if the dog or cat's water bowl smells like beer.

PAIGE: It was funny, since I'd already decided beforehand that I was gonna go through with it, once we got really into the heat of the whole thing I practically didn't even notice we'd kept going into actually doing it except after... *(Distastefully.)*—sticky.

(Beat.)

SUZANNE: Everybody got that? Okay, number two.

PAIGE: It wasn't anything real out of the ordinary for him either, he just said something like *(Panting.)* "Are you sure?" but we were almost finished pretty much before he even said that anyway, so.

SUZANNE: Heavy drape-like or pile fabrics especially retain odors for long periods of time, so check to see if the curtains or carpets smell like smoke.

PAIGE: *(Sighs.)* Every time I think about it, I'm totally humiliated.

SUZANNE: Seriously, let's talk about that. No one wants to feel like a Nazi to their own children. I used to think, what does it hurt? A little fun, no big deal. But the point isn't, can they clean up after themselves. The point is they are flying in the face of the rules you have set down, and also, incidentally, they're also breaking the law.

PAIGE: I mean, say the guy who got Jeb's room in the dorm the next year had a girlfriend who was a virgin like I was? And say they had sex on the same bed that Jeb and I did it on, and *she* bled all over the mattress, and then the poor guy figures, okay, I'll just flip the mattress over to the other side to hide the stain?

SUZANNE: And for *letting* them break the law, whether you're even *in* the house at the time, you're the one who's going to be fined and given a court date. So it's even more in *your* interest to put a stop to this kind of behavior. We can do this, or we can just give up.

PAIGE: Unless they put new mattresses in the dorms every year. But I bet they don't. I bet they just leave the same mattresses there year after year after year. Disgusting.

SUZANNE: Yes, of *course* it is. And of course it would be nice if our children behaved responsibly and maturely and never gave us any trouble. But the fact is, they're out to get away with whatever there is to get away with, any way they can.

PAIGE: Look—I know my mom paid for the full session and everything, but I didn't want to come anyway, and I don't really have anything to talk about, and it's stupid that I'm even here, I mean—I'm not *crazy*, so couldn't I just leave early? You already have the money. I won't tell if you won't.

SUZANNE: They're teenagers, after all, that's the way they are. And we have to make the decision before it's too late; we're either going to let them get away with murder or we're not.

Scene. Lacrosse tri-captains party. Reid in a bright ski jacket stands in the driveway drinking from a glass bottle of Grovestand and Tanqueray. Alex stalks back into the vicinity, wearing a scarf.

ALEX: I'd like to smash him in the side of the head with an oar. That'd wipe that smile off his face pretty damn quick.

REID: Stop whirling around like that, you're making me feel like I'm drinking shroom juice and gin instead of orange. Brrr.
    (He shivers. Danny walks up in a t-shirt, nicely toasted. He points in the direction Alex is already glaring.)

DANNY: Hey, Allie-Al, Price is here, he's over there, see him?

REID: *Leave* it, okay, she knows. Look at you in a t-shirt, nad, you lost your mind?

DANNY: *(Sweetly.)* It's spring.

REID: In name only.

DANNY: Look at the lawn, there's little purple and yellow and…purple crocuses popping out all over it. Spring.

REID: You know when you get pneumonia sometimes they have to carve a hole in your throat just so you can breathe.

DANNY: They're like little mini-pinwheels, they're like little colored—fan blades, imagine if you could float in the air on your stomach looking

down at them all what would you see, it would be like a white and green and yellow and purple…uh, *quilt*—
(*He notices a look on Reid's face.*)
—what? What is it?

REID: Nothing. I just thought I heard sirens.
(*Danny takes off running. Reid looks after him. He tips up the bottle and wipes his mouth on his sleeve.*)
Moron.

ALEX: (*Enraged.*) Look at him. Look at him grinning, having a check-me-out moment. Check him out! Oh, he's so cool, how can we stand it? How are we physically able to *stand* here and *stand* it!

REID: I told you not to fuck him.

ALEX: Yeah, lot of help that was—You should have told me not to *date* him!

REID: So he's a lush, so you're out of it now, so just never look back.

ALEX: Okay, this is how *not*-out-of-it I am, all right? He's over there being sweated down by Vida—

REID: That bitch has no chance, you're letting her upset you?

ALEX: I know she has no chance, Reid, and I don't want him *back*, all right, this is the point, they're ragging on each other and he says to her, "Suck my cock," and she says, "You wish," and he says, "Not that I'd ever let you near it, but if you *did* ever suck my cock you wouldn't be able to *wish* for anything *else* for the rest of your *life*," and I happen to be lucky enough to be nearby during this shit and he grabs me and shoves me at her and says, "Alex, you've sucked my cock *lots* of times—tell Vida what she's *missing*."
(*Beat.*)

REID: Okay, that is definitely not on. That has to be paid for.

ALEX: Is what I'm saying.

REID: Okay, here's one thing we could do—You go over there now while he has his back to us and tap him on the shoulder, with your left hand because you're a righty and you gotta keep that hand free, and when he turns around you clock him, and if he recovers and comes after you I'll step in and finish him off. That way, you would not only get him taken care of but you could get a good one in first yourself.

ALEX: Or.

REID: Or I'll just do it all, but I want to go on the record as saying I'm really disappointed in you, Woman Warrior of the Apocalypse.

ALEX: …I just want to be avenged, okay, I don't want to do any *work*.

REID: Fine, but I don't expect any adverse comments on my form or style. And if Vida gets in the way I'm taking her down too, stupid vadge.

(He watches Alex looking at her ex and getting misty.)

Don't cry, toughie. Hey. Don't cry, you little toughie. Come on.

ALEX: Try not to let him lose consciousness. I don't want him to miss anything.

REID: That's my girl.

(He hugs her, smothering her face into his coat. She starts making muffled noises and flailing her arms around trying to get free, which he finds funny. Brian strolls up. Reid releases Alex.)

BRIAN: What's happening, y'all.

REID: We're mauling Price Wetherall for casting aspersions on Alex. Get your chuckle hat on and let's go.

BRIAN: I thought you were *with* Price.

ALEX: We broke up!

BRIAN: *(Comprehending.)* Okay, I caught the bus, let's go.

(Brian tosses his beer away and follows Reid, who calls out over his shoulder as they leave.)

REID: If you get tired of watching you could go inside and bring us out some chips.

(Tammy walks up and stands next to Alex.)

TAMMY: Hi, Alex.

ALEX: *(Indifferent to Tammy.)* Hey, Tammy, how you doing.

TAMMY: What's going on.

ALEX: Not much. You know.

(They watch the fight. Beat.)

TAMMY: …Are you still going out with that guy?

ALEX: No, not really.

TAMMY: Oh. That's probably good, right.

(Reid comes over and hands Alex his jacket.)

REID: Hold this for me a second. S'restricting my wingspan.

TAMMY: Hi, Reid.

(Reid leaves. He barely acknowledges Tammy.)

REID: Hey.

Scene. Spenser School campus. Coach stands watching an impromptu touch football game. After a moment, Reid approaches him, breathless.

REID: Hey, Coach. Buddy. Don't be mad.

COACH: You know how they determine whether or not a criminal's legally insane? They establish that the guy may have been nuts enough to think doing something sounded like a good idea, but at the same time the guy knew society was going to condemn him for doing whatever it was.

So you're not insane, Callahan. You're a moron, but you're not insane. Otherwise you would think I walked over here for my health. Instead, I can see you already know what I'm gonna say. Go ahead, though, I think you were about to give me a really stupid explanation for something.

REID: It's just a little football. Bishop and Charlie Hall, they came down from Ithaca for the weekend—

COACH: It's 10 a.m. on Tuesday. Today is *Tuesday*.

REID: *(Laughing.)* Well, so I guess they're skipping some classes. Anyway, we're just playing a little football, here. Alumni versus seniors, you know.

COACH: Hey, it's your funeral, Callahan, okay? Not mine. You want to fuck up the chance for the whole team, that's fine. You don't want to play middie for Hopkins or Princeton, that's fine too. You blow out your knee or your shoulder or your ankle playing some crappy pickup game with your buddies and shoot your whole lacrosse career straight to hell, don't come crying to me. I shouldn't have to even tell you this shit. You should know it. I'm sick of following you around making sure you don't act like an asshole.

REID: Other people are sick of it too, don't worry. Jenny went away yesterday, she went to Atlanta with her mother for the week to look at colleges or some shit. She had a few choice things to say about my general demeanor before she left.

COACH: Well…while the cat's away, huh?

REID: *(Shrugging.)* Who knows.

COACH: And who cares, as long as you're not out fucking *yourself,* playing touch football with a bunch of jerks, risking your whole season, your whole shot. You don't even like Bill Bishop.

REID: Aw he's all right. He's actually mellowed out a lot since he went to—

COACH: Hello? Am I talking to myself?

REID: No, I'm listening. I'll get out of the game.

COACH: You sound like you think you're doing me a favor. Hey, I coach the best lacrosse team in the state of Connecticut—

REID: The second best.

COACH: All right, snotnose. And whose fault is that? Who was dancing around celebrating their hat trick when they should have been paying attention?

REID: Willy Schaeffer.

COACH: All right, did I *say* it was you? *Did* I? All I'm saying is, that's not gonna happen again. Because—

Willy fucking Schaeffer is not the point. Goddamnit, I hate it when you make me think about that game.

The point is, just take it from me, there's nothing more pathetic than listening to somebody talk about what a superhero they were when they were seventeen. Before they fucked up their *knee*, blah blah *blah*. Okay? Okay?

REID: Yeah.

COACH: When's your cootchie coming back?

REID: Next Thursday.

COACH: You gonna last till then?

REID: *(Pretending to think.)* Um, *probably*, yeah.

COACH: She'll be missing the game. That's pretty rough. No little poon bouncing up and down in the stands waving her varsity jacket for you, Callahan.

How're you gonna make it a whole week and a half without a *girl*.
(The football is thrown very hard and purposefully at Coach, who catches it. Reid looks over his shoulder and laughs at his friends.)

REID: *(Unfazed.)* See you at practice, Coach.

(He exits. Coach searches in his pocket, pulls out a Swiss Army Knife, unsheathes the largest blade and plunges it in and out of the football. The ball deflates between his squeezing hands. He glares off, and brandishes the flabby pigskin at someone.)

COACH: I don't know what you're bitching about, Bishop. I'm the head of Spenser Athletics, so that makes this *my* football. I can do whatever the hell I want to it. I can eat it if I want. I can make you eat it. I thought you graduated anyway, Why are you still here? We gave you that diploma so you would go away.

Scene. Paige and Alex sit in the cafeteria the same morning.

PAIGE: Yeah, well, I can't help it.

ALEX: It really is a good book; you don't know what you're missing.

PAIGE: Maybe someday when we have to be in the car for a long time or we have to go on the bus to play an away game you can tell me what happens in it and then if it sounds good to me, then I'll read it.

ALEX: *(Dry.)* …I'll live for that moment.

(Brian enters. Paige likes Brian. I mean she likes-him likes him.)

BRIAN: Ladies, it's that time again.

PAIGE: Huh. Get a life.

BRIAN: Are you refusing to participate? I know what that usually means.

ALEX: She's not refusing, she's up to it, come on, let's go.

(Each girl extends her bare leg toward Brian. He takes each one in turn by the ankle and slowly runs his palm all over the leg, up to the knee, then in a more deliberate sweep back down.)

PAIGE: Are we done for today, or what?

BRIAN: Hm—Well, Alex passes, but Paigey, you're a little stubbly. Tsk tsk.

PAIGE: *(Incredulous.)* What are you, shitting me?

BRIAN: Not at all.

PAIGE: I did it. I did it this morning!

BRIAN: Hey, I'm as disappointed as you are.

(Alex is smiling.)

PAIGE: Alex passes and I don't?

ALEX: What's that supposed to mean?

BRIAN: Yeah, what does that mean? I only even bother to check Alex out of a respect for form and appearances. She under*stands* that she has her job and I have mine.

PAIGE: Let me feel what it takes to pass around here, all right. Let me feel what *you* all say is close.

ALEX: Go ahead, it's your funeral.

(Alex extends her leg to Paige, who runs her hand up and down it and then violently pushes it away.)

ALEX: Home sugaring kit, you should try it. A total breeze. *Semper fidelis.*

BRIAN: *(Smiling at her.)* That's my girl.

(Paige sticks out her leg angrily.)

PAIGE: Fuck you, feel me again.

BRIAN: *(Mock huffy.)* Okay, but I think I know what I'm doing.

(He rubs her leg again.)

Ah, ah, ah. It's especially scruffy back here, where the calf muscle starts. That's a beginner's mistake, I expect more from you. Maybe you need to change the blade, or try a different brand. I hear those Gillette Daisy ones are hot.

(Brian lets go of her leg and starts to leave. He calls over his shoulder.)

You have sixth period free, don't you? That's enough time for you to get home and take care of this and come back, if you skip lunch.

(Paige turns to Alex who is getting up to leave.)

PAIGE: Alex! Come here, feel this, tell me he's kidding.

ALEX: Hey, you knew your mission and you failed; accept it before it destroys you.

Scene. A bell rings. Reid stands at his locker, unloading his backpack. Alex hurries by him, tapping him on the left shoulder as she goes. Reid looks to his left but she has already passed. She laughs and so does he.

ALEX: *(Leaving.)* You're so sly—but so am I.
    (Tammy sidles up and stands behind Reid. She stands on his left and taps him on the shoulder. He turns.)

REID: *(Unreadable.)* Hey, Tammy, how they hanging.

TAMMY: Good. How's it going with you.

REID: It's going. You got a class?

TAMMY: No, I was going out to have a cigarette really fast before I go to the library. You want to come?

REID: Where you going?

TAMMY: Behind the Lower School building. If you sit sort of kitty corner to the back entrance you can see if someone's coming before they see you.

REID: I hate to break this to you, but there is no place you can smoke at this school that Brian hasn't already been nailed in by the Dean, and he spoiled *that* one for you Tuesday morning.

TAMMY: Oh, shit. Shit.

REID: You could always try quitting.

TAMMY: I did. But I didn't last very long.

REID: Well, Tam, I gotta mosey.

TAMMY: Wait—there was something I wanted to ask you.

REID: Yeah? What was that?

TAMMY: Well, I wanted to know if—Oh, God, now you put me on the spot. I hate this.

REID: Wow, this sounds pretty good. This sounds big. Come on, spill it.

TAMMY: *(Laughing nervously.)* I—mmmm. Oh fuck. Just forget it. I'm sorry. Forget it.

REID: *(Quietly.)* Now you've got me wondering, Tammy. You're not getting off the hook now. Now I really have to know.
    (She looks up at him. He smiles.)

TAMMY: I was wondering if you would want to go to this thing with me on

Friday, it's like a house party these people I know who go to Kent are having, it's gonna be an all-nighter, this guy's parents went to Antigua.

REID: A house party. Like a big sleepover. You want me to go to a sleepover with you.

TAMMY: Well, it wouldn't be just us. There'll be lots of Spenser people, and people from Staples, and—

REID: *(Interested in this concept.)* You never ask me to go to things, Tam.

TAMMY: Well, I just thought this sounded like something you—

REID: I mean, this is a little weird to me. I can't really figure this out. Because, you know, you're a friend of Jenny's and everything—

TAMMY: I know! Why, what do you think I—

REID: Is it because Jenny's not here? You wait for her to leave town to make your move? Because you knew I'd be all alone and lonely…. Is that it?

TAMMY: What? No.

REID: I always thought you guys were really close. What a shame.

TAMMY: Oh, just—Forget I said anything.

REID: *(Smoothly.)* I can't do that, Tammy. Come on. I mean, this is serious. I never knew this was the deal with you. I'm sorry, but I can't just forget it.

TAMMY: There's no deal. I just thought you might like to go to this thing. I remember you were pissed off when you missed the one Pete Scofield had. *I'm* sorry you think I'm asking you on a *date* or something. *I'm* sorry you're probably going to go act like a jerk and get Jenny mad at me for no reason. I was just trying to be nice. *Sorry.*

(She leaves angrily. Reid watches her go. He looks down at himself and smiles. He reaches inside his jeans to adjust himself. Brian enters and rushes him.)

BRIAN: You gonna stand there all day playing pocket pool or you gonna come lift with me?

REID: Duh.

BRIAN: What'd old Tammy have to say for herself.

REID: She wants you.

BRIAN: Yeah? Well, bring her on.

REID: She asked me out.

BRIAN: You're shitting me.

REID: I shined her on.

BRIAN: Yeah…Wait, you're serious.

REID: But of course.

BRIAN: No offense, okay, but what the hell is the matter with you?

REID: I got too much on my plate at the moment, okay, pardon me.

BRIAN: Well, eat faster.

(Reid laughs. They are leaving.)

I can't live vicariously through you if you don't do anything, pal. Okay?…

Scene. Jenny speaks to the audience.

JENNY: My mom wants me to look at Emory University in Georgia because she says Atlanta's such a great city, full of art and culture, Jenny, don't you want to expand your horizons, blah blah blah. But I know that's all bullshit.

(Danny speaks to the audience.)

DANNY: I heard a good one today.

JENNY: It's because they don't play lacrosse in the South. Anyone who wants to play Division I lacrosse in college would have to stay in the Northeast, so of course Reid's going to go to school somewhere up here.

I know she wants me to go to Emory because she thinks the distance will make me forget about him.

DANNY: Wait, I have to remember it, I always fuck these up.

JENNY: She's wrong.

DANNY: Okay, I got it, here goes. You ready?

JENNY: I said, I'll go look at it, but you're not fooling anybody. You should just wear a sign.

DANNY: How many feminists does it take to change a light bulb?

JENNY: President of the I Hate Reid Callahan Club.

(Brian speaks to the audience.)

BRIAN: *(Laconically.)* I don't know, Dan, how many.

JENNY: I said, you hate him but I guess he's good enough to drive us to the airport, huh.

DANNY: Two.

JENNY: Hypocrite.

DANNY: One to change the light bulb and the other to suck my dick.

BRIAN: *(Not impressed.)* I've heard that one.

JENNY: It's funny, Reid's not good enough for me, right, but whenever he's in our house Mom always seems to drop at least one thing on the floor in front of him and then has to bend *way* over to pick it up.

BRIAN: Here, I've got a good joke.

JENNY: Everybody wants him, and he wants me.

BRIAN: Reid told me this one.

DANNY: *(Laughing already.)* Oh, man.

JENNY: Kristin Baker, she's at Wesleyan now, surrounded by hot college guys, but she still wants Reid. I saw her trying to talk to him at Missy Belmont's Christmas party, it was pathetic.

Reid says he feels bad for Kristin; she still loves him the same way she always did, except now he loves *me* like that, so he knows how she feels, he can understand her in a way that maybe I can't.

He's right about *that.*

BRIAN: What do you call the useless piece of flesh around the vagina?

JENNY: I understand one thing though.

DANNY: I don't know. What do you call that useless piece of flesh around the vagina.

JENNY: No way am I going to college in Georgia and leaving him up here.

BRIAN: The woman.

Scene. Reid is trying to call Kristin. Alex is lying on the bed reading the Lacrosse Universe Spring Hot Sheet Blowout Sale catalog.

REID: God, who has this bitch been *talk*ing to for twenty minutes?

ALEX: Who bitch?

REID: Kristin.

ALEX: Maybe her roommate's using the phone. College, you know. Look at this price. $22.99. I could stock up for that kind of price. I could have a different one for every day of the week. *Then* I'd be cool.

REID: You need to get out of that whole wooden stick mindset you've been riding since fifth grade, Al. You're not an Onondoga Indian. You need to go aluminum. Or the way you play, titanium.

ALEX: I like linseed oil, and the old sticks that have the *cat*gut pockets. And the smell of the hickory and the leather ties when they get wet down playing in the rain...You don't get any of that with a metal shaft. Wooden handle is old school. I'm part of the chain of history.

REID: You're not part of anything, honey. The Iroquois Nation didn't let women play lacrosse and they don't even today, the elders think it brings the bad mojo. You only have history if *I* make it *for* you.

(He tosses her another catalog.)

Look in that one, every stick is like thirty dollars off retail, at least. Even the fucking hickory dickory sticks.

(She opens it and starts flipping through the pages.)

Find me some rib pads and some arm guards, and I'll order them up, they're open till 9 on weekdays. And I tell you what, you pick out an aluminum stick for yourself and I'll buy it, my treat. Just 'cause I like your face.

ALEX: Sugar *daddy.*

REID: You *can*not lose.

ALEX: You know what's nice about the metal sticks? They have cool names. The wooden ones don't get names, but the metal ones you can choose from the Edge, the Shotgun, the Wave, the Shutout, the Wall, the Viper, the Raptor, the Excalibur, the Sam II—The Sam II?

REID: That would be—the Son of Sam.

ALEX: I see. And the Dominator.

REID: I have three of those.

(He has been repeatedly dialing the same number and hanging up at the busy signal throughout the above; at last he gets through.)

KRISTIN'S VOICE: Hello?

REID: Damn, Kristin, you call me and tell me to call you but then you tie up your damn phone all fucking night.

KRISTIN'S VOICE: *(Gooey.)* Hi, Reidy.

REID: …Call me *sir.*

(Alex starts laughing, then tries to stifle herself. Reid smiles at her.)

KRISTIN'S VOICE: Is somebody there with you?

(Alex rolls off the bed and grabs her bag.)

ALEX: *(Whispering.)* I'm gonna put some makeup on before we hit it.

REID: *(Whispering, covering the phone.)* Thank God.

KRISTIN'S VOICE: *(Over this.)* Whose voice is that? Who are you talking to?

REID: You.

KRISTIN'S VOICE: *(Trying something different.)* I miss you so much, I haven't seen you in so long—come up here.

REID: I can't come up, I got practice every day at 5 for the semis this weekend. This is the big show.

KRISTIN'S VOICE: Come on, it only takes an hour, you could come tonight and be back in time for class tomorrow…do you have me on speaker phone?

REID: *(Does.)* No.

KRISTIN'S VOICE: I hate it when you do that.

REID: I don't. I'm not. Anyway I thought you told me you had some kind of exam the end of this week.

KRISTIN'S VOICE: I do. But I'll blow it off if you'll come up here.

REID: Oh noooho. What kind of boyfriend would I be if I let you do something like that?

KRISTIN'S VOICE: *(Adoring; whispering.)* A shitty one.

REID: Shitty, that's right. You speak the truth. I'm looking out for you, I'm not gonna let you drop the ball. I am ordering you now—go study.
(Alex comes out of Reid's bathroom with her hair taken down and her face painted, jingling her car keys in one hand.)

KRISTIN'S VOICE: Ooh, I love it when you order me around. What're you gonna do while poor me goes to study?
(Alex finds the Jeep keys and jingles them at Reid with her other hand.)

REID: I don't know, I guess I could study too.

Scene. Instantly, loud music. Post-game party. Paige is dancing to techno, holding a bottle of beer in her hand. Lindsay approaches to continue an earlier argument.

PAIGE: Stop looking at me like that. If you think I'm so bombed then get someone from Safe Rides to take you home, that's what they're for.

LINDSAY: How come you didn't just tell me you were planning to kiss the sky tonight? Then I would have found another ride home, back when I still could.

PAIGE: *(Dignified.)* It was not a *plan.*

LINDSAY: If I don't leave in the next half hour I'm dead.

PAIGE: So call them.

LINDSAY: *(Disbelieving.) Call* them.

PAIGE: Whoooo, echo.

LINDSAY: Would *you* call *your* parents? If it was your ass and not mine, you're telling me you would call them?

PAIGE: Jesus Christ, who knows. Maybe. It's a moral dilemma. Quit harshing my mellow.

LINDSAY: They think I'm on a date. A date with Justin from yearbook.

PAIGE: Poor heartbwoken pizzaface.

LINDSAY: They would never have let me go to a lax party. The only reason I pulled off going to this one was because I figured you'd drop me off and Dad would never know the difference. As long as he hears a car and then I walk in, it all works out.

PAIGE: Do you know who does this song, I really like it but when they play it on the radio I never get to hear them say who it is—

LINDSAY: Don't try to get out of this, Paige! I'm fucking pissed at you, I mean it!

PAIGE: I'm not trying to get out of *any*thing. I don't even know what's going *on*.

LINDSAY: Last time this happened, Dad said next time I'd be in deep shit. Thanks to you, next time is now.

PAIGE: Oh, please. This town is so fucking small, you're telling me no one at this entire party lives anywhere near you? The chances of that are slim to none and slim's on *vacation*. And I am *not* driving like this.

LINDSAY: Oh, great, get all responsible on me now.

PAIGE: Sorry, Linds, I would love to stand around and debate this all night long if possible, but I really have to take a whazz so I just will see you when I see you.

(She wobbles away. Alex is crossing the dance floor; Lindsay turns, distraught, and accidentally bumps into her. Alex does not know Lindsay.)

ALEX: *(Freezing cold; leaving.)* Excuse *you*, jailbait.

LINDSAY: *(Calling out after her; contrite.)* I'm sorry—I'm sorry!

(Paige staggers back up. Lindsay looks hopeful.)

PAIGE: Hey—make sure you call me tomorrow sometime so I know you got home okay.

LINDSAY: *(Trying not to panic because panic is uncool.)* Okay.

(Paige staggers off again. Reid strolls up to Lindsay, holding a plastic cup of beer.)

REID: You look upset. Everything okay?

LINDSAY: I don't have a ride home, I'm going to miss my curfew, and then I'm going to get killed.

REID: That's not a good reason to be upset. We'll find you a ride home, or if we can't I'll drive you myself. Problem solved. See how easy that was.

LINDSAY: *(Relieved; laughing.)* Oh thank God. Thank you so much.

REID: *(Smiling at her.)* Just let me finish my beer.

LINDSAY: Thank you so much. I know I'm overreacting but I really get in trouble with my parents over this kind of stuff.

REID: Well, I've got a big game coming up this weekend and everyone's blowing it off, no one's coming to watch it. *That's* something to get all worked up about. *I've* got problems, *I'm* upset.

LINDSAY: *(Sympathetic.)* I'm sorry.

REID: You should be.

(Lindsay giggles.)

REID: I'm Reid, by the way.

LINDSAY: *(Staring at him.)* Oh, I know who you are.

Scene. Coach speaks to the audience.

COACH: He's an unbelievable player, a once-in-a-lifetime player. He's the kind of perfect prayer answering player that at first as a coach you try to take the credit for him, like "He had raw talent, sure, but it took me to discipline him into the player he is today." Except with Reid I can't do that, because it's been pretty obvious from the beginning that he's a force unto himself and he doesn't need anyone or anything. So I just hopped on the ol' bandwagon.

(Danny speaks to the audience.)

DANNY: Yeah. Yeah, she is. She totally is. I'd fuck her in a heartbeat. You know who else is? This is gonna sound weird maybe, but…her *mom* is really hot.

(Brian speaks to the audience.)

BRIAN: *Duh.* She's a MILF.

COACH: Sometimes during a game when I call Reid off the field to do a little Man-and-Superman-ing, I look at him while I'm talking and I can see his mind working, I can see his total concentration, and I find myself wanting to say to him, "You know what? Just go. You don't need my help or anyone else's. Whatever you do out there, I know it's gonna be right, it's gonna be exactly what needs to be done."

DANNY: A what?

BRIAN: A MILF.

DANNY: What the hell is that?

BRIAN: A "Mom I'd Like To Fuck."

COACH: All I can say is, you better get to Reid while you can. I know for a fact there's at least six other scouts coming to look at him this weekend. You're interested in him, you better talk to him while he still wants to listen, cause I'm telling you, with this kid the rules just don't apply.

DANNY: That's not right. It should be MILTF. *Mom I'd Like To F*uck, MILTF.

BRIAN: Leave it to you to worry about the fucking spelling.

DANNY: I just like things to be…right.

BRIAN: Iddn't that sweet.

Scene. One in the morning. Lindsay's jeans are torn and the button is missing. Her hair looks like it's been raked. Dad enters enrobed.

DAD: *(Jovial.)* Three minutes to one—this is a first. Congratulations.

LINDSAY: Thanks.

DAD: No, thank *you*. So how was it.

LINDSAY: What.

DAD: Your date. What'd you do?

LINDSAY: Oh, you know, nothing.

DAD: Nothing? You did *nothing*.

LINDSAY: Well, you know, we drove around, we went to…places, it was—whatever.

DAD: What's so great about that? You swan around in some kid's car, he doesn't even take you out to eat or anything—

LINDSAY: We *ate*.

DAD: Yeah? What. What'd you eat.

LINDSAY: …We went to Post Corner—

DAD: Oh, *yeah*, a couple greasy slices of shitty pizza—shitty *Greek* pizza, not even real Italian, why people go to Greek pizza joints is beyond me. You know, when I grew up in Syracuse we had the best Italian food, I'm telling you, the best, you couldn't *get* bad Italian food in upstate New York. We were spoiled. So you ate Greek pizza and drove around. That's it?

LINDSAY: …What?

DAD: When I was your age I was busy, All County Baseball, Regents Exams to study for, the *draft*, but when I made time to take a girl out, I did it right. Came to the door to pick her up, walked her *back* to the door to say good night. Made it an occasion. Otherwise, what's the point. I didn't hear a car in the driveway just now.

LINDSAY: He dropped me off at the circle, I walked from the circle.

DAD: He dropped you *off*—

LINDSAY: I walked. It was fine. It was fine.

DAD: He have somewhere else to go? He doesn't have the *time* to drive you all the way to your door, he drops you off halfway? Save a little time by making his date walk two blocks in the dark? You like guys who act like that? Seriously, I'm asking, 'cause I don't know.

LINDSAY: I wanted to walk. I wouldn't like it but I wanted to walk.

DAD: That's not how a gentleman behaves. I know there aren't any, any more, there aren't any more gentlemen, but if there were, they wouldn't be caught dead letting their girlfriend walk a quarter of a mile in the dark. I swear, I could kill these little pissy-ass snotnoses. Pulling up here in their Mommy's Wagoneer and honking, they expect you to come running.

Next time that little shit comes to pick you up I'm gonna spread nails in the driveway.

LINDSAY: Dad?

DAD: Nails and tacks. That'll be a big surprise for that little jerk.

LINDSAY: *(Tiny.)* …Dad?

DAD: *(Spideysense finally kicking in partially.)* What?…What's the matter? What's going on?

LINDSAY: …um, do we have any juice?

DAD: What is going on?

LINDSAY: Nothing. I'm going to bed.

DAD: …Good. Get some sleep…. You're a beautiful girl, Lindsay. You know that? Back when I was in school they would have been lining up around the block. They'd take you anywhere you wanted to go. *And*, walk you to the door when it was over. You know that? Don't accept anything less.

LINDSAY: I know, you've said.

DAD: Having to sit here and listen to you tell me what passes for a date these days. How this guy treated you tonight. What passes for politeness, what you girls let them get away with.

　　'Cause you know, if you all put your foot down, this crap would stop. If you told them how you wanted to be treated, they'd have to go along with it. They would. Because they wouldn't have a choice.

LINDSAY: Yeah. Good night.

DAD: Good night. Don't put up with it, sweetheart. You know what I'm saying?

LINDSAY: Yeah. Good night.

Scene. Suzanne waits in her bathrobe. Reid enters looking a little more than a little worse for wear and begins foraging for food.

REID: Hey, Mom, burning the midnight oil?

SUZANNE: What were you doing?

REID: Watching New Canaan whip our asses because we can't play hockey for shit.

SUZANNE: I don't mean what were you doing this evening, I mean what were you doing just now.

REID: What is this, Twenty Questions?

SUZANNE: No, not twenty questions, just one question.

REID: Gee, you promise?

SUZANNE: You pulled into the garage half an hour ago. Why did it take you so long to come into the house?

REID: Why, did you miss me? Hey, now that's two questions. Pick one, either what was I doing or why did it take me so long.

SUZANNE: Reid, I'm not in the mood for your lip.

REID: You got something stashed out there? Is that it? Afraid I'll accidentally stumble on your treasure trove?

SUZANNE: No.

REID: Well, don't worry. I wasn't out there rooting around looking for your hidden bottles of Stoli or your *Playgirls* or whatever you got. Your secrets are safe with me.

(Pause.)

SUZANNE: Jenny called.

REID: When?

SUZANNE: About an hour after you left. She said you could call their hotel room up until 2 but not after because her mother would be asleep after 2.

REID: Or I could blow the whole thing off completely and just not call at all. I'm gonna go with that.

SUZANNE: Did you do something to the Jeep?

REID: What? No. Like what would I *do* to it? I drove it. Is that what you mean?

SUZANNE: If you did something to it, why don't you just tell me so we can get it fixed. We only have four days till they get back, so if you did something to it tell me now.

REID: The fucking Jeep is fine, Mom, okay. Lay off.

SUZANNE: Well, maybe Jenny's going to think whatever you did is funny but her mother didn't want to leave it with you in the first place, she didn't trust you.

REID: Fuck her, she was perfectly cool giving it to me so I could fucking chauffeur them to the *airport*, right? Anyway, how do you know.

SUZANNE: I could tell from the look on her face.

REID: Oh, whatever. She's a bitch. That's not a secret. Who gives a shit. I'm hitting the hay.

SUZANNE: Did you spill something? Is that what you did?

REID: No, Mom, I did not spill anything.

SUZANNE: The last thing I need now is to listen to Debbie Fleming telling me how irresponsible you are. Again.

REID: Don't start on that, Mom, or I swear to God I'll pop you one, I don't care who you are!

SUZANNE: I'll take my chances! First she finds you and Jenny naked on her dining room table, now you wreck her car? She'll have a field day! It's like you don't care about me at all!

(Reid heaves a big sigh.)

REID: I didn't do anything. I didn't spill anything. I didn't *do* anything to the *Jeep*. Mom. Get it into your skull. Everything is copacetic. Good *night*.

SUZANNE: *(Building to rage.)* You were doing something climbing around inside that damn Wagoneer for half an hour. All I can say is it must be one hell of a stain. I wish I could get you to scrub your *bathtub* like that. If you don't tell me what you did I can't help you clean it up. I wouldn't mind so much if you just never asked for help at all. But you do—it's just always when it's too late, when you've already broken it or cheated on it or crashed it or stolen it!

REID: You were spying on me. You were hiding like some fucking ratfink and watching me?

SUZANNE: Not the whole time. And I didn't hide. I was just standing there by the door, you could have looked up and seen me. But you were too busy, and I couldn't figure out what you were doing and then I got cold so I came back in to wait. *What*—were you *doing*!

REID: None of your goddamn business!

SUZANNE: You're sure about that now.

REID: Yes! God, you drive me nuts!

SUZANNE: Fine. Just remember that I asked you. More than once. You had your chance.

REID: *(Vicious.)* Good for you. It must be shitty to always be right about everything, Mom, how do you stand it.

SUZANNE: *(On the verge of hysteria.)* Huh—If that's blood on your shirt you can wash it yourself. Not that it'll come out. Not that you would know that. *(She slams out. Reid looks down at his shirt, startled.)*

REID: Where?—
(He finds the smears of blood at the bottom of the front hem.)
Oh.

Scene. Paige is on the phone with Kristin.

KRISTIN'S VOICE: I thought they'd give me a much harder time here about Reid than they actually did. I mean, it was nothing at Spenser, senior girls went out with junior boys all the time. Right?

PAIGE: *(Bored.)* Oh, sure.
(Suzanne speaks to the audience.)

SUZANNE: Girls have been calling this house for years now. All hours of the day and night. I knew it would happen, everyone could see even when he was a baby what he would grow into, and of course *I* think he's beautiful, I'm his mother, but even I was surprised at how early it started.

KRISTIN'S VOICE: Remember when Reva took Chris Nichols to the prom? He was a sophomore. Which actually was a bit much but she got away with it because he's just unbelievably hot. People didn't say to her, "God, you're taking a sophomore?" They said, "You're going with Chris Nichols? God, you're so *lucky.*" And it's the same with Reid. Only about a million times *more* so. That's why the girls up here don't rag on me about Reid any more—because they've *seen* him.

PAIGE: *(Bored.)* Yeah, cool.

SUZANNE: Although girls start all that kind of thing sooner than boys, so I think Reid was actually as surprised as I was, he hadn't started to think that way yet. He didn't know what they wanted from him.

KRISTIN'S VOICE: You can't get away from it. It's always been that way with him. I don't think he even realizes it.

PAIGE: Oh, he doesn't, huh?

SUZANNE: Now he does.

KRISTIN'S VOICE: A couple of them still make the babysitting cracks and all that but whatever, like I give a shit.

PAIGE: *(Bored again.)* Shake it off, baby.

KRISTIN'S VOICE: Huh, yeah. I'm glad they don't get it. Anyway, next fall he'll be in college, hopefully here, and then it'll be no big deal again. It's just the college-girl high-school-guy thing that freaks some people out. It has nothing to do with Reid as a person. He doesn't even notice or care about anything. I wish I could be like that.

(Alex enters, taking off her coat. She sees Paige is on the phone and looks at her inquiringly. Paige rolls her eyes, then makes a crocodile jaw with the fingers of one hand and snaps it open and shut rapidly over and over. Alex laughs.)

KRISTIN'S VOICE: Who is that? Who's laughing?

SUZANNE: You can hear they're terrified when they ask to speak to him, you can hear the fear in their voices, they're just shaking with the excitement: is he there, what will he say. I think it's cute. He doesn't think it's cute; but I don't know what he thinks it *is.*

ALEX: *(Still laughing.)* Pathetic.

Scene. Chilly out. Tammy is bundled up and waiting outside the ice rink for her ride. She looks impatiently at her watch. Reid materializes.

REID: You going home?

TAMMY: Well, I will be.

REID: The game's not over.

TAMMY: I didn't really come to see the game. I just came to procrastinate. I don't like hockey that much anyway.

REID: That's a nice color.

TAMMY: What?

REID: *(Indicating her sweater.)* Your, ah—

TAMMY: *(Cutting him off.)* Thanks.

(Silence.)

REID: *(Gently.)* Are you mad at me or something, Tam?

TAMMY: What? No.

REID: Are you okay?

TAMMY: I'm fine.

REID: Okay.

TAMMY: I mean, you know, you acted like a real asshole to me the other—

REID: I know.

TAMMY: You *did.* You acted like an assho—

REID: I know. I know I did.

TAMMY: You *know?*

(He smiles at her. She starts to smile back.)

Is this supposed to be like your idea of an apology or something? Because if it is, it's really lame.

(Reid continues to stare at her, smiling. He reaches out and flips her hair off her shoulder into her face; she slaps him away. They both laugh.)

Scene. Paige enters Lindsay's dark bedroom like a missile.

PAIGE: Lindsay, baby, up and at 'em. I have finally discovered the key to defeating hangovers. If I just drink the same thing all night I don't get one. Not even a little one. It's when I mix that I get nailed. Every…single…time. Hey, I hooked up with Brian Sanders last night and I think I'm in love.
(Lindsay has been lying all along in a heap on the floor. Paige throws herself down beside her, suddenly terrified.)
…Lindsay! Lindsay! Are you okay?
(Silence.)

LINDSAY: *(Hoarse.)* …who the fuck is Brian Sanders?

PAIGE: *(Relieved.)* Oh, I always forget, you don't go to our school. You look…really bad. Why are you lying down there on the floor?

LINDSAY: …maybe I like it down here.

PAIGE: …What does that *mean*?

Scene. Tammy speaks to the audience.

TAMMY: *(Defiantly.)* Nothing. It means *nothing*.

No reason, okay. *What* look.

Well, what am I supposed to do about it, Mom. I don't know what my face looks like to you. And I don't have a *look* on my face, anyway, so I can't get it off.

Fine, *don't* talk to me then. Whatever.

(She stares out the car window.)

Hey, do you mind, I turned that on. I wanted to *lis*ten to that song, I like it. Well, fine then, *let* me drive.

Well, I guess you *didn't have* to come pick me up, Mom, you're right. I guess you could have just blown it off, I guess you could have let me stay at the rink all night.

(She is crying.)

Or I guess you could turn around and take me back there and just *leave* me…

Scene. Brian speaks to the audience.

BRIAN: No, you couldn't, you bone, who would do that? The point is to establish that it's *her* and *you* against everyone else, all right? It's called divide and conquer, heard of it? If you don't want to know then don't fucking *ask* me, okay? She'll say, I thought the lax players just partied all the time. You say, Well, I come to these things because my friends throw them and it is kind of a team spirit issue and also I do occasionally enjoy partaking of the Brotherhood of the Grape, but after a certain point the scene grows old and I'd really rather just be home. *Writing*. And she'll go, Wow, really, what do you write? And you go, oh, just some *poet*ry, it's really nothing. And she'll say it's not nothing, can I hear one, you're totally wowing her with the killer one-two of simultaneously being really sensitive to literature and also fucking built like a *warrior*, and so you lean in real close and probably take her hand and hold it to your heaving chest so she can see what it would have been like to have been in a clinch with an actual *Viking*, and you let her have it.

No! With a poem. What the hell is the matter with you? You let her have it with a *poem.*

Wanna hear the one I've been using lately? Listen up, scrote.

Oh terrible darling,
How have you sought me,
Enchanted and caught me
See now where you've brought me—
I sleep by the roadside and dress out in rags.
Think how you found me;
Dreams wash around me—
The dew of my childhood, and life's morning beam;
My heart that sang merrily while I was young
Swells up like a billow and bursts in despair.
And the wreck of my hopes on sweet memory flung
Are all that is left of the dream.
You'll burn in my heart till these thin pulses stop;
Your fragrance I'll drain
To the last brilliant drop.
The dream of my longing and wreck of my soul
Dancing, inspiring
My wild blood to firing
Oh terrible glory
Oh beautiful siren
Come tell the old story again.

...I'm telling you, they hear that and like my Dad says about his old Camaro, "She starts right up!"

Love and death. They're the keys, pal. They make it a whole new ballgame out there, and I do mean *ball*game.

No, I didn't write it. But who the fuck's gonna know that? Nobody knows anything anymore anyway, and even if they did, what are the odds that some dippy gash you meet at Eric Hanford's wake-and-bake is gonna be the one who does.

Scene. Danny speaks to the audience.

DANNY: I never get anywhere with Spenser girls...until they remember I'm on the lacrosse team.

I can't wait to get the hell out of this place. Life's gonna be totally different then…because it *has* to be.

Scene. Lindsay speaks to the audience.

LINDSAY: At the party my friend Paige told me the Jeep belonged to his girl-friend Jenny who only wasn't there because she was away visiting colleges; so when he offered me a ride home and I saw we were going in the Jeep it made me feel comfortable because it was sort of like her being there in a weird way, reminding him not to forget about her. He was a good guy, he was safe, he was in a relationship, he was just being nice.

What?

Oh, sorry.

I was just saying, what I was thinking when I—

(Tammy speaks to the audience.)

TAMMY: I was waiting outside the ice rink for a friend of mine to pick me up—

I don't know, nine thirty?

—and Reid came out and came up to me. After a couple of minutes he asked me if I wanted to go sit in his car with him while we talked because it was really chilly and wet out. We'd had kind of a fight a couple of days before and he was apologizing for what he'd said to me.

What?

Nothing. It was just a stupid fight.

Why does it matter what it was about?

(Reid appears. He stands watching them with his hands in his pockets.)

LINDSAY: We got to the four-way intersection where Brookfield meets Maple Ridge and he pulled the Jeep over by the stop sign and tried to kiss me.

I said I was sorry but I didn't want him to do that.

TAMMY: He said it looked like my friend wasn't coming and he could drive me home if I needed a ride. I said no thanks but he pulled out anyway and started driving—

LINDSAY: We got to my house and then we passed it. I said that's my house, please stop, but he just kept on driving.

TAMMY: Because he already *had* the engine running.

LINDSAY: He said he would turn around, so he drove down to the circle but halfway around he pulled over again and turned the Jeep and the lights off.

TAMMY: *(Defensive.)* He had it on so we could have the heater on.

No, why would I think it was strange? People do it all the time.

(Reid smiles dismissively. He shifts his weight, bored.)

LINDSAY: Then he came over to my side and started kissing me again, only this time he was on top of me.

TAMMY: He drove really fast to Maple Ridge Road and pulled into a parking lot and turned the Jeep off and started to kiss me. I said I didn't come with him for that and he should either take me home or back to the ice rink.

LINDSAY: I said please stop and he put his hands around my neck and started choking me, he said

REID: if you don't shut up and fuck, I'm going to kill you. Shut up.

LINDSAY: I didn't know him. I didn't know if he would, I didn't know if he was like that. He looked like he was like that then.

TAMMY: No, he *didn't* answer me. He *grabbed* me by the neck of my sweater and forced me over the hump between the two front seats into the back of the car and he followed me.

LINDSAY: I thought he would kill me. I didn't want him to hurt me.

TAMMY: He started kissing me again and putting his hands all over me, being really rough. Then he said

REID: take off your clothes.

LINDSAY: He lifted me by the lapels of my coat and shoved me into the back seat of the Jeep. He told me to

REID: *(Private-joke smile.)* take off your clothes!

LINDSAY: and he started taking off his jeans.

TAMMY: I told him to fuck off

REID: *(Laughing in disbelief.)* Fuck off, huh. Ooooooo.

TAMMY: I tried to get my leg up and knee him but he shoved it away

REID: Want to play that way? I can too.

TAMMY: and ripped my sweater up over my head. Then he grabbed my throat and started squeezing it hard and saying he would

LINDSAY: I didn't take my clothes off, I don't know what happened, I just couldn't make myself take them off even though he kept saying he was going to

REID: *(Vehemently.)* kill you, goddamnit.

LINDSAY: so he ripped my jeans down and off, they got stuck over my boots so he took those off too, and my underwear. Then he said

REID: take your fucking shirt off, don't make me have to do it.

(He bends at the waist and rests his hands on his thighs, his shoulders slumping, his head hanging down as if in exhaustion.)

TAMMY: He put his arm across my throat and pinned me to the seat and he took my pants off and my underwear. Then he took his own jeans off

(Reid lifts his head quickly as if catching someone in an act and points his finger at the audience.)

REID: don't you move. Don't even think about it.

(He starts to lower his head again, then lifts it fast.)

Don't you move, Tammy, I mean it.

TAMMY: and had sex with me.

LINDSAY: I said I'd never done it before. I was hoping if he knew I was a virgin maybe he wouldn't want to do it with me.

TAMMY: *(Horribly embarrassed.)* When he was done, he pulled me up and over and made me get on my knees. Then he, ah, went in from

REID: Oh, my God, that's it. That's it. There.

TAMMY: I had never done it, ahhh, *that* way and it hurt me a lot.

LINDSAY: I don't know if he heard me. He might have. I don't know.

TAMMY: I couldn't help it, it hurt so much when he started I tried to pull away from him, but he grabbed a handful of my hair and slammed my head down against the back of the seat.

REID: Shut up. Shut *up*. Just shut up.

LINDSAY: I did, I said it at least three times, I don't know if he could tell that I was one when he started, that it was my first time.

REID: See? See? Can you feel that? Can you feel it? Oh my God.

LINDSAY: It hurt me a lot and a couple of times I screamed and he got really

REID: *(Breathless.)* I'll kill you. I'll kill you.

TAMMY: I was woozy but the pain was still really bad, I screamed a few times

REID: Shut up! Shut up or I'll fucking kill you, I swear to God I will.

LINDSAY: I could feel that I was really bleeding but it didn't stop him.

REID: I will. I will. I will.

LINDSAY: When he finished he got off me and I saw that some of my blood was on the carpet but I didn't say anything and he didn't notice either.

TAMMY: When he finished he went back to the front seat. I was scared to move because I didn't know if he was done. But then the car started and

(Reid straightens up. He brushes himself off lovingly.)

REID: Come on, put them on. Hurry up. Christ.

LINDSAY: I got out of the Jeep and he drove away and I walked home from there. But he

TAMMY: He took me back to the ice rink and after he drove away I went inside and called my mom. But first he

REID: So, uh…

LINDSAY: *(Choking up.) Linds*ay.

REID: Lindsay, right.

TAMMY: Let me out. Let me *out*!

REID: *(Scornful.)* You're out.

LINDSAY: I was glad it was dark on my street.

TAMMY: Nobody at the rink saw me.

LINDSAY: He said that he

TAMMY: would kill me if

REID: you tell anyone.

You hear me?

LINDSAY: Don't let him.

TAMMY: Don't let him.

REID: Oh, *please*.

(Lindsay and Tammy sink to their knees. A phone is ringing. Alex rolls over in bed and knocks it violently off the cradle, then picks it up.)

ALEX: *(Clearing her cloggy throat.)* What.

REID: What are you doing.

ALEX: What are you, high? Look at the fucking time, what am I *doing*.

REID: Do you want to go for a drive?

ALEX: Not bloody likely.

REID: We'll go to the beeeeeach.

ALEX: Uh-uh, Midnight Rider, not tonight.

REID: Come on, Alex. Come *on*.

ALEX: —What is the matter?

REID: We'll—just—go to the beach, okay. We'll go to Cumberland Farms and get hot chocolate and go to the beach. And talk.

ALEX: …Cumbies isn't open this late anymore. No.

REID: I'll buy you waffles. We'll smoke a little hash and watch *The Last Boy Scout.*

ALEX: No. NO.

REID: Jesus Chr—Don't be a bitch!

ALEX: Excuse *me*, what?

REID: I'm, I'm coming over there—I'm gonna *come over there* and we are *going to*—

ALEX: *(Over this.)* Fuck you, okay. Fuck you!

REID: *(Collecting himself.)* …Sorry.

ALEX: You—Go to sleep, for fuck's sake. What is wrong with you. Why don't you sleep? Why can't you *ever sleep*!

REID: I can sleep.

ALEX: *Prove* it. Go *do* it. *God.*

(*She hangs up. Reid collapses into a chair and turns on the TV with the remote. After a moment he calls out.*)

REID: Mom. *Mom!*

(*Suzanne can be heard approaching. She stands in the doorway, wiping her hands.*)

SUZANNE: Yes? What is it?

(*Reid ignores her. She stands looking at him.*)

SUZANNE: It's late…Shouldn't you try to get some sleep?

(*Reid ignores her.*)

I think you should.

(*Silence. Reid stands up and finds his jacket.*)

It's late; where are you going?

(*Beat. Reid stares at her then abruptly turns away.*)

REID: Where *is* there.

Scene. *Jenny's room. Jenny leans over Reid in the bed and kisses him. He doesn't wake up. She kisses him again; he wakes up instantly and shies away from her.*

REID: *What.*

JENNY: Nothing. I just. Kiss you good night, you know, I was kissing you good night.

REID: You have to wake me up to do it?

JENNY: That was an accident. But now that you are awake…you could come out and play with me. If you want. No pressure—

REID: If it was an accident that you woke me up, it's no big deal if I go back to sleep.

JENNY: …Why'd you come here then? You have a bed at home.

REID: I'm proving a point.

(*Beat.*)

JENNY: …What?

REID: (*Over this.*) You asked me to come. Wasn't that you who left all those messages? I mean, if you want me to take off I'll cut out right now, no sweat if you want me to go—What.

JENNY: I don't want you to go, I only got back today, I haven't seen you for a week, why do you always *do* th—

REID: All right, stop, come here, come here.

(*Jenny comes to him.*)

I've got to get up really early, I've got to get my shit together for the game, no fighting, okay, sleeping now.

JENNY: I just—

REID: What.

JENNY: You act like you hate me.

REID: Oh, like you're on your best behavior when someone wakes you up out of a great dream.

JENNY: What was it about?

REID: Skiing.

JENNY: *(Cranky.)* You always dream about *skiing.*

REID: Double black diamond trails and nobody on them and the air is so clean and cold it hurts to breathe it and I don't know anyone and they don't know me. Somewhere I can concentrate, I need to concentrate. I can't...*think*, right now. *(Yawns.)* And I don't want to.

(Jenny is bored. She waits until she thinks he has finished talking, then goes for his t-shirt, pulls it up, reaches for him and then stops.)

JENNY: Mm—*(Hisses in surprise.)* Did you get in a fight? Did you get in a fight? How did you get these? Reid, wake *up*. How can you sleep? Why are you always sleeping?

Scene. Suzanne walks into Reid's room and flips on the light. His bed is empty and the window is open. She crosses to the window angrily, slams it down and locks it at the top, and starts to leave the room. Then she wheels around, rushes back, unlocks the window and pulls it up, adjusting it so it is exactly as it was. She leaves, switching the light off.

Scene. Alex is in bed, trying to get back to sleep. The phone rings. She moans and smacks it off the rest; then answers it.

ALEX: *(Groggy.)* For the love of *God.*

TAMMY: Um, who is this? Is this Alex?

ALEX: *(Taken aback.)* You called *me*, you say who *you* are, that's how it works.

TAMMY: ...I need to—I didn't want to call but I have to talk to you, I have to know, because I know that you and he are—

(Alex hangs up. An irate parental voice is heard.)

VOICE: Alex, tell your friends to stop calling so late! Some of us are trying to sleep! Have some respect!

ALEX: *(Calling out.)* I have respect! I don't *tell* anybody to do *anything*! God!

(She rolls over. After a moment her hand swings out from under the covers ready for violence, then freezes; instead her hand gently picks the phone receiver off the cradle and rests it on the floor.)

Scene. Paige and Lindsay at Rite-Aid. A cashier is calling for price check at Register 4.

PAIGE: You can't use that on it, that's antibiotic cream. If you use that on it you'll just make it worse.

LINDSAY: *(Wants to leave.)* It says you can use it.

PAIGE: Not for what you have. If you use that down there you'll get a yeast infection that'll make what you have now look like a birthday present. Even guys get yeast infections if they take antibiotics for too long, haven't you ever heard about that? Put it back. Just get the Monisefrin. If you're embarrassed to buy it, I'll buy it, all right.

LINDSAY: I'm not embarrassed, you're just talking *really* loudly.

PAIGE: I don't understand how you can have cystitis. You have to *do* it to get cystitis, you have to do it really really *hard*—

LINDSAY: I'm buying this one.

PAIGE: You should get the seven day one, not the three, three isn't enough for what you've got.

LINDSAY: Fine.

PAIGE: You know, these all say you should be seeing the doctor if you've never had this problem before.

LINDSAY: *(That's not going to happen.)* Yeah.
(Paige reads the box as they walk to the registers.)

PAIGE: "Do not use in girls less than 12 years of age." *(Laughs evilly.)* That sounds funny doesn't it? And who are they talking to, anyway?

Scene. The Callahan breakfast table, early morning. Reid sits in sweats, punching his stick pocket repeatedly with a lacrosse ball in his fisted hand.

SUZANNE: Would you like some, uh...toast?

REID: I already had six English muffins and two bowls of Chex.

SUZANNE: Is there anything *left* that I can offer you?

REID: I'm carbo-loading. Make me some spaghetti...I'm just kidding.

SUZANNE: Wouldn't matter if you weren't. Shouldn't you have left by now?

REID: Only takes twenty minutes to get to Northfield.

SUZANNE: Not at the speed limit.

REID: …I don't know—what that *is*.

SUZANNE: Coach Coyle called, he needs you there to work with the goalie before the—

REID: I need money.

SUZANNE: …My purse is in the hall closet.

REID: Purse, hall closet. Purse, hall closet.

(He exits. The doorbell starts ringing.)

REID: *(Yelling, off.)* Mom, the door.

SUZANNE: So answer it, you're out there! Reid? Oh—

(She pads out of the room and returns followed by Lieutenant Cleary.)

Well, Richard, this is a surprise. I mean, we all know policemen only come out at night.

(Lieutenant Cleary smiles.)

Thank you for coming by the meeting the other night, incidentally.

LT. CLEARY: Oh—it was my pleasure.

SUZANNE: I don't think any of us had realized just how many different household items can be used as bongs and bowls.

(She laughs.)

Well, what can I do for you? I know I shouldn't park in the fire lane, but I'm basically just a very lazy woman, I just can't be bothered to shlep my groceries that extra twenty feet to the actual parking *spaces*—

(Lieutenant Cleary places a piece of paper on the table.)

LT. CLEARY: I'm going to just leave this with you, all right?

SUZANNE: Well, of course—What is —

LT. CLEARY: It authorizes me and Detective Valentine, he's out in your driveway, it authorizes us to take possession of ah, that 1993 Jeep Grand Cherokee parked out there, registered to a Deborah Fleming of 18 Clearwater Lane.

SUZANNE: *(Thinks she has it figured out.)* Oh—that car's not stolen, Debbie left it for Reid to drive while she and Jenny, he's going out with her daughter Jenny, he took them to the *air*port in it, they're in Atlanta—

LT. CLEARY: *(Starting to enjoy himself.)* They're *not*, actually—they're back. I have to ask you—where is Reid?

SUZANNE: Reid? Why? I told you, it's not stolen.

LT. CLEARY: Is he here now?

SUZANNE: Well, yes but he has to go, he has a lacrosse game up at Northfield today, it's a big one, he's late, there'll be scouts there—

(Reid is in the doorway. Lieutenant Cleary turns and sees him and chit-chat time is over.)

LT. CLEARY: Reid Callahan?

SUZANNE: You know it is, Richard—What is this?

LT. CLEARY: Do you know why I'm here, Reid?

(Pause.)

SUZANNE: Reid?

REID: No.

LT. CLEARY: Are you sure?

REID: Yes.

LT. CLEARY: *(Mildly.)* Okay, well, if you're sure you don't know, then I'll tell you.

Scene. Jenny speaks to the audience.

JENNY: It's not true. No way is it true. No way would he do that. No way would he have to. If it wasn't so terrible, I would totally be laughing, because it's so completely ridiculous, the whole idea. I mean, look at him. Does he look that desperate? I'll tell you who looks desperate. Those two bitches, *that* is *who*.

(Coach speaks to the audience.)

COACH: So they're called, Concerned Parents Against Varsity Sports. What would that be? CPAVS. Wow, *that's* catchy, huh? Christ. And they want to abolish varsity sports because they encourage aggression in males, make them feel privileged, make them feel like they can behave with, ah, *(He looks at a printed manifesto he is holding.)* im*pu*nity. "The attitude of these athletes leads them to treat women with a casual kind of violence, as if sex instead of a mutual decision has become yet another of the spoils of the entitled victor." Uh-*huh*.

JENNY: That's right, I *would* know.

COACH: What *I* think is, if anyone would bother to ask me, it allows these guys to work out their aggression on the field, in play, blow off steam, learn to channel their energy in a healthy way and learn the value of teamwork, compe*ti*tion, I can't believe I have to *explain* this, let alone defend it.

JENNY: And anyway, even if he did, I don't care. I do *not care.*

COACH: Fifteen sixteen seventeen years old, barely the fucking age of reason, little cupcakes waiting outside the locker room to fawn all over these punks and bend over backwards to get their attention and why? Because they love *sports* so much? I don't think so.

JENNY: Yes, I *do*, I do *so* mean it, I *do so*.

COACH: All I know is, if a bunch of little cookies weren't there giving it away, these young guys wouldn't come to start thinking it was free.

JENNY: *I* just want to know when they're going to give me my *Jeep* back.

Scene. Paige and Lindsay.

PAIGE: Making a play for attention, is that it? Pretty fucked up way to try to get some spotlight on you, Lindsay.

I mean, I'm *with* Brian, okay. Remember? I'm like a…friend, of Reid's, I hang out with those guys. And—*and*, I was there that night, too, okay. I saw you. I saw you. "Oh *(Fake giggling.)* whose Jeep is that, I love it." I don't know who you think you're fooling.

LINDSAY: *(Starting to cry.)* I'm not fooling anyone. I'm not fooling *anyone!*

PAIGE: —that's right. You're *not*.

Scene. Tammy speaks to the audience.

TAMMY: I heard he has a trust fund that's worth like nine times as much as that. Obviously he wasn't going to have any trouble paying it. So why did they even bother to arrest him? He was back pretty much before he was even gone. And I come out of class and he's walking down the hallway and he *looks* at me, and his *friends*—and I'm *not* dropping out, I'm not dropping out of this school, but I stay awake at night and I remember their eyes on me and I try to imagine what's the worst thing they could do to me, what's the worst thing they could do to me *now*, and all I can think is that I'm not going to know until it happens.

Scene. Paige on the phone with Kristin.

KRISTIN'S VOICE: *(Hysterical.)* She was right there, I saw it on Channel 8! That girl who used to do her nails in chem lab!

PAIGE: *(Bored but sort of pleased too.)* Oh, yeah, Penny something.

KRISTIN'S VOICE: Jenny!

PAIGE: Jenny, right.

(Alex is nearby, listening to Paige's end of the conversation. Paige looks at her.)

ALEX: Well, we knew this was coming, we just didn't know when, right?

PAIGE: *(Evil.)* Huh.

KRISTIN'S VOICE: What was she doing there!

PAIGE: Who?

KRISTIN'S VOICE: *(Almost a shriek.) Jenny!*

(Alex can hear Kristin from where she is sitting. She laughs.)

ALEX: Attention all shoppers—We have a little shit here that says it's lost; has anyone lost their shit?

KRISTIN'S VOICE: They were leaving the courthouse and he had his mom on one side and then that *Jenny* girl was on the other side, holding his *hand!*

PAIGE: Well—maybe she just happened to be at the courthouse dealing with a totally unrelated matter and they ran into each other on the steps.

(Paige waves at Alex. Alex leans over to the mouthpiece.)

ALEX: *(Imitating call waiting.)* Beep.

PAIGE: I'm sorry, I've got another call.

KRISTIN'S VOICE: Call me back!

PAIGE: Of course.

(She hangs up and snorts.)

Jesus Christ.

ALEX: Screw her, tell me about the girl.

PAIGE: Well, she goes to St. Lucie's, I've known her since like second grade...I played travel soccer with her about a million years ago, on that team where Michael Lipton was the goalie.

ALEX: *(Confused.)* Michael *Lip*ton...

PAIGE: Yeah, you know, the kid who got hit in the neck with the ball and—

ALEX: *(With her now.)* —choked to death, oh yeah, God.

PAIGE: Yeah, and it's the exact same story. Gave her a ride, pulled over, threw her in the back, totally identical plotline—I mean, it's *her* lie, she's the star, you'd figure she'd at least give herself a few original twists, make her tale stand out.

ALEX: God, that was the *last* time they tried to abolish varsity sports, when Michael Lipton died, and it didn't work then, why would they try again? What's her name?

PAIGE: Lindsay Potter. Yeah, remember his mom watched the whole thing from the stands, she was cheering 'cause she thought he stopped the shot, she was too far away to see his face was turning black.

ALEX: What's her phone number?

PAIGE: It's written in on my phone, it's number 5.

(Alex picks up Paige's phone.)

Why, what are you going to do?

ALEX: Why do you ask?

PAIGE: *(Laughing.)* Well, okay—how far are you going to go? How *much* are you going to do?

ALEX: Far. Much.

Scene. Danny speaks to the audience.

DANNY: You got your smaller weaker country, suddenly free, thrilled to be exhibiting its rich and mineable natural resources, flaunting its open borders, showing the world how much it wants to form alliances and promote tourism. And maybe it goes overboard, just a little bit, being unskilled in the art of diplomacy, and brings itself to the attention of the big strong country, which notices maybe for the first time how attractive the small weak country is and starts thinking maybe the time is ripe for the expansion of empire. And the little country isn't prepared for invasion and is taken completely unawares, not that it could defend itself even if it *knew* what was coming...and the tanks roll in and the aerial assaults start dive-bombing the cathedral and laying waste to the cultural landmarks, and *then* your Lichtenstein or your Luxembourg or your Kuwait starts screaming for help. Which is terrible, and tragic, but, in the general geopolitical scheme of things, nobody is ever really that surprised.

Well, yeah, I thought it was kind of *iffy*, you know. I mean, although it didn't come out of nowhere, we're in this history class, "Age of Conflict," and we were supposed to be doing papers on the Domino Theory, so—But still, rape is like war? Rape as global microcosm? I still thought it was a weird thing to say. Except—if you know Reid it's not as weird a thing to say as maybe it would be if someone *else* said it. That's all I'm saying.

Scene. The school cafeteria. Tammy faces Alex.

ALEX: That's what I said.

TAMMY: Because you would know.

ALEX: Yeah, I would.

TAMMY: You're that close, you know him that well.

ALEX: Isn't that why you're trying to talk to me? *Yeah*, I *do*.

TAMMY: Maybe you do—but you weren't there.

ALEX: Well if you'll excuse me my Jell-O is getting cold.

TAMMY: Maybe you will be someday.

ALEX: Listen. He did not call me when he got home. He did not call me and tell me what he *did* to you because nothing was done and there was *nothing* to *tell.*

TAMMY: You know he did it, Alex. You know what he did to me. He tells you everything...he tells you *everything.*

(Alex looks around to make sure she has an audience.)

ALEX: I know you asked him out while Jenny was gone and he turned you down. He *told* me that, *that's* something I *know.*

(There is some gleeful clapping and cheering for this statement from other areas of the caf.)

TAMMY: *(Weakly.)* ...well, but that wasn't anything. That was nothing. That had nothing to do with anything.

(Tammy sits down with her lunch, alone. After a moment, Brian and Danny join her, sitting facing her. Long pause.)

BRIAN: ...So, Tam. Drinking a little chocolate milk? Having a little...salad? Good for you.

(He smiles at her. Danny just stares at her. She picks up her tray and flees. Brian turns and beckons Alex.)

BRIAN: Alex baby, come back and sit here, we cleaned it all up for you, just like you asked.

Scene. Reid speaks to the audience.

REID: Wherever I go, always, all day, all night. Can't get away from it, it's all I can think about, it's destroying my life. There's one of them parked in the lot when I leave practice every day, they bug my friends, one of them stopped me about a mile away from Brian's house the other night to check my license and *registration,* oh yeah, like they don't know it's my goddamned car, like they don't know who I *am.*

The school's gonna graduate me early. To get me out of there, because it's upsetting a lot of people, it's creating a "negative atmosphere." You know, like that has anything to do with anything, I have as much of a right to be there as anybody, I'm *awaiting* trial, right, it hasn't even *happened* yet. But it's fine with me—well, at first I was pretty burned up about it but then it started to seem okay, because the fucking cops are all over my back all the time and I can't take it anymore. So since I'm done with school whether I wanted to be or not, and I have to wait however many months for my trial date to come up, I'm gonna get the hell out of Dodge, I'm gonna go to Montana, I know somebody who's working in

Big Sky, I'm gonna go there and ski and hit the half-pipes, and whatever happens, happens. This is bullshit.

I made bail. I can go to Montana. They can't stop me.

I can do whatever I want.

(Alex appears.)

ALEX: This is a nice picture. This is probably the only nice passport picture I've ever seen.

REID: Thank you, Peaches.

ALEX: But news flash, Montana is in America.

REID: I'm not allowed to have a fucking passport? You've had one since you were in kindergarten—I remember.

ALEX: But if they just mailed this to you, that means you had to have applied for it after your bail hearing.

REID: The same day, funnily enough. The office was right down the street from the courthouse. It was so *handy*.

ALEX: ...Neat.

REID: It is "neat," isn't it, Kitten With A Whip.

ALEX: Don't *call* me that.

REID: I just wanted a passport, I just *wanted* one. It just struck me as something I *wanted*.

(Beat. Alex studies the passport.)

ALEX: Have any of them ever bothered to ask you if you had a passport?

REID: Not in so many words. Or in any words.

ALEX: So, you're out on bail even though you're a probable flight risk with a trust fund and no one is even interested in finding out whether the idea of leaving the country has ever crossed your mind or is crossing it now?

REID: You know, it's funny 'cause it's true.

ALEX: *(Smiling.)* ...you would think the cops would make it their business to know this kind of thing was going on, wouldn't you.

REID: You would, and I would, but since they apparently don't—keep it to yourself.

Scene. Tammy speaks to the audience. Alex appears as she does and stands behind her wearing a faint smile.

TAMMY: I had it, I checked before lunch that I had it and I did, but it's not there now and it's not in my locker and I called home but I know I didn't leave it at home, I know I had it, it was in my bag. I *know*, it's *very* important, it's like one third of my whole *grade*. I *did*. Well, I—mm. I just *(It comes out in a rush.)*—I think someone went in my bag and took it. That's what I think happened. Someone stole my paper…. No, I don't. I don't know who it was.

Scene. Brian speaks to the audience.

BRIAN: Hey, truth is always stranger than fiction, 'cause at least fiction has to make sense. I mean, I personally don't see why he doesn't just stay and face the music, since he didn't do anything wrong so there won't *be* any music. I would. I'd stay. Duke it out. Fuck 'em all. But if he thinks this way is better, then maybe it is. Maybe he knows something I don't. It wouldn't be the first time. All right, here it is, I found it, listen.

> Let not young souls be smothered out before
> They do quaint deeds and fully flaunt their pride.
> It is the world's one crime its babes grow dull
> Its poor are ox-like, limp and leaden-eyed.
> Not that they starve, but starve so dreamlessly,
> Not that they sow, but that they seldom reap,
> Not that they serve, but have no gods to serve,
> Not that they die, but that they die like sheep.

Well, because I don't know, you could be right, I just don't know. I mean, I know it's a good poem and all, but it doesn't make me hot.

Scene. Tammy lowers a heavy pile of textbooks to the floor and pulls open her locker door to put them inside. Brian walks up to her and slams it shut. He watches her as she spins the combination again and pulls open the door; he slams it again. She opens it; he slams it. She leans down and shoulders the load of books again and walks away.

Scene. Coach speaks to the audience.

COACH: Graduate him early because the sight of him makes that girl upset? I cut Chip Kennedy from varsity right before the semi against Fairchester last year because he developed this debilitating, heartbreaking syndrome, it was really tragic, it was called the Didn't-Listen-To-A-Damn-Thing-I-Said Syndrome, and since he was counting on lacrosse to coast him right into college, I guess the sight of *me* made Chip Kennedy pretty damned *upset*, but *I'm* still here. And judging by the four flat tires my car some-how developed while sitting in my driveway this past St. Patrick's Day, Chip Kennedy's still with us too, but *Reid* has to be graduated early? I mean, we may be undefeated, but that junior Wilton has on longstick this year is playing like he's the right hand of *God*, and if Reid isn't there to stop him, then we won all those battles only to lose the war…I've lived in this town all my life and I guarantee I won't be the only one who finds that unacceptable. So don't say I didn't warn you.

Scenes. Alex and Paige.

PAIGE: *(Distraught.)* I should have kept my mouth shut. Why is this happening?

ALEX: It's not. He's not.

PAIGE: *Yes*, he *said*, "I can't stand it when a woman gets jealous—Jealousy is probably the number one reason why I broke up with Missy."

ALEX: Brian broke up with Missy because she cheated on him…so actually, Missy broke up with Brian…. He's just being a jerk.

PAIGE: *(Momentarily thrilled.)* So he's *not* breaking up with me? Or—he's just lying about why.

ALEX: *(Not being sarcastic.)* …God, I'm tired.

Alex and Brian.

BRIAN: I'm trying to get *out* of this thing with her, Alex, okay, you're under-mining me. Why can't you just tell her you think she's better off without me or something, help me *out*.

ALEX: *(Irritated with him.)* You want to break up with her, be a man and just *do* it, Brian, just stand up and be *counted*, okay? Just say… "Paige…have you ever danced with the devil in the pale moonlight? I ask that question of all my friends; I just like the sound of it."

BRIAN: …You want me to quote Batman at her?

(Alex yawns.)

ALEX: I don't *want* you to do *anything*, but I think you'll find that you would actually be quoting the Joker.

Alex and Danny. Alex is starting to slouch with weariness. Danny is nicely, nicely toasted.

DANNY: Brian wants you.

ALEX: Yeah, great.

DANNY: You think it's great?

ALEX: No.

DANNY: No, you don't think it's great?

ALEX: No, I don't *think*.

DANNY: …Do you have any crackers?
(Alex has her head in her hands.)
Alex?

ALEX: *(Weary.)* No.

Alex and Jenny.

JENNY: But this memo says you have to.

ALEX: I'll wait until they actually tell me I'm off the team unless I go—then I'll go, but not until then.

JENNY: But you're the ones who should be going, anyway, not us.

ALEX: Why, because lacrosse is full body contact and tennis isn't? If they're going to get rid of varsity sports programs in this school they're going to do it whether you and I go and talk to their fucking freelance sports psychologist about how rape makes us feel, or not. So why bother? I mean, unless you want to.

JENNY: I don't.

ALEX: What you should be wondering about is why nobody on any of the *guys'* teams got this memo.

JENNY: *(Instantly uptight.)* Why, why should I?
(Alex drags her hands over her face and purrs with exhaustion.)

ALEX: Well…the school wants pseudoshrinks to talk to us about how we would feel after being raped, but they apparently *don't* want to ask anybody who is potentially capable of *doing* it to us, about *why*. I just hope somebody remembers to sign my diploma.

PAIGE: I just want this not to be happening—I don't even know what I said or how to fix it—help me, Alex, tell me what to do.

BRIAN: *(Flirtatious but serious.)* I think you know why I want to break up with her. Don't you…. Don't you?

JENNY: I just thought that when you said I should wonder why none of the *guys* got the memo, that you were talking about Re—

ALEX: No. *No.* Of course I wasn't.

(Reid appears.)

REID: You look tired.

ALEX: ...I am, I really, really am.

REID: You should sleep.

ALEX: Well, I would, except—

PAIGE: Can I ask you something?

BRIAN: Can I ask you something?

DANNY: Can I ask you something?

ALEX: *(Weary.)* Yeah.

JENNY: Can I just ask you something?

ALEX: Sure.

PAIGE: What would you have done if you were in my place?

BRIAN: Have you ever thought about me?

DANNY: What about Milk-Bones? I'd eat those.

JENNY: Tammy's one thing, it's easy to get to her, but what about the other girl, is there any way we can find out—

ALEX: I'm way ahead of you.

REID: Can I ask you something?

ALEX: *(Alert.)* ...Okay.

PAIGE: I just want to be with him. What should I do?

JENNY: You know who she is? How did you find out?

DANNY: Do you have anything crunchy at all?

(Alex is trying to focus on Reid. The cacophony is distracting her.)

ALEX: *(Tensing.)* Ssshhh, ssh.

JENNY: Can I help you do it?

PAIGE: *(Tearful.)* Why does this always happen? Why is this always always happening to me?

BRIAN: I just want you and me, I want us to—

ALEX: Brian, we can't talk about this right now, we're gonna be late.

BRIAN: Shit, you're right. Come on, let's go.

(Paige and Jenny and Danny leave. Brian follows them separate. Alex starts to go, then turns and looks inquiringly at Reid.)

ALEX: What did you want to ask me?

REID: Never mind; forget it.

ALEX: Oh—okay. Are you sure?

REID: *(Smiling at her.)* Yeah. Go take a nap.

ALEX: I can't now. Maybe later.

Scene. Tammy speaks to the audience. Alex appears as before and stands behind her.

TAMMY: No, I can't, can't you just look at it? I know you're the nurse, but you already said it wasn't broken, why do I need an x-ray? I didn't fall off a building, I just fell down some steps. Can you just...what?... The ones by the library. *(Upset.)* Well, I *was* holding onto the railing, okay? I didn't *expect* someone to *push* me.... Sorry. It's not your fault. Um, I need a couple of Band-Aids for my palms too. They broke my fall.

Scene. Brian and Alex in the parking lot of Lindsay's school.

BRIAN: Is that her?

ALEX: *(Looking where he's looking.)* Too tall. She's shorter than Paige.

BRIAN: Is that her?

ALEX: Too blonde.

BRIAN: ...Is that her?

ALEX: What are you, the blind guy and I'm the dog?

BRIAN: —Never, baby—

ALEX: *Shut* up—*Look* at the picture, okay? You can look at it just like I can, don't make me do all the work.

(Brian takes the picture from her and studies it.)

BRIAN: This picture makes them both look like trolls. Little preppie trolls.

ALEX: *(Spotting Lindsay.)* That's her.

BRIAN: She and Paige look like they're the same height here, Al. How do you get this Lindsay girl being shorter by looking at this?

ALEX: *Look at her.*

(She points.)

That's her.

BRIAN: That?

ALEX: *That,* in the yellow. Getting into the Infiniti.

BRIAN: *(Watching.)* ...sucks to have your dad pick you up.

ALEX: Yeah, but she doesn't have to wear a uniform. Ted Bundy could drive me to school and back every day until graduation if I could wear jeans.

(They watch Lindsay and her father drive away. Brian tosses his keys into the air and catches them.)

BRIAN: Well, so now we've seen her.

ALEX: Yeah, and contrary to popular belief that's just gonna make it *easier.*

(They begin to mosey toward Brian's car.)

BRIAN: …Can we go to Dairy Queen now?

ALEX: Do you think you could not ask me that for like two minutes? *Thanks.*

Scene. Phone ringing.

LINDSAY: Hello?

TAMMY: Is this Lindsay?

LINDSAY: *(Hopeful.)* Paige?

TAMMY: No, you don't know me, but I know something about you, I heard something happened to you that happened to me.

LINDSAY: …I don't know what that me—

TAMMY: I go to school with him, and no one believes me.

(Beat.)

I have a lawyer and I'm the reason he got arrested but it's not enough, I'm not enough and if you—

(Lindsay hangs up the phone, takes it off the hook and stares at it. Dad passes by in shirtsleeves.)

DAD: Honey, hang that up, I'm waiting for Somerset to call and give me some specifications, okay.

(Lindsay reluctantly replaces the receiver. It rings. She stares at it. Dad calls from off.)

DAD: Lindsay, it's for you.

(She picks it up.)

TAMMY: Was that your dad who answered?

LINDSAY: *(Moans.)* Ohh—

TAMMY: I know it's you now, you know, if you won't help me because you know you should then I'll *make* you—

(Lindsay hangs up again. After a moment the phone rings again. She stares at it. Her father enters. She stares at him.)

LINDSAY: I'm not home. I'm not home.

DAD: *(Puzzled.)* Okay…. Hello?

BRIAN: Hello, Mr. Potter, can I please speak to Lindsay?

DAD: She's not here at the moment; can I give her a message?

BRIAN: That would be great, sir, I'd really appreciate it. Tell her I saw her at school today but she left before she knew I was there.

DAD: *(Amused.)* Well, all right.

BRIAN: Tell her Reid said yellow is her color.

DAD: *(Chuckling; young love is so cute sometimes.)* That the message?

BRIAN: Yeah. Yeah, that's enough for right now.

DAD: Okay; you have a good night.

BRIAN: You too.

(Brian hangs up and turns to Alex. Dad hangs up and smiles at Lindsay.)

ALEX: Well, that went about as well as could be expected.

BRIAN: Yeah, it felt pretty good.

ALEX: Good.

(She evades Brian and picks up the phone.)

BRIAN: *(Not pleased.)* Now who are you calling?

ALEX: I'm trying him again.

BRIAN: He wasn't home.

ALEX: He might be, now. Ow—don't—*grab* me.

DAD: *(Smiling.)* Reid says you look nice in yellow.

(Lindsay looks down at herself and lets out a cry. The phone rings again. Tammy waits for an answer. Dad starts to reach for the phone but Lindsay won't let him pick it up. They stare at each other. Another phone rings. Reid hesitates, then.)

REID: Yeah?

ALEX: Where were you? I called like ten times.

(Brian is pissed. He walks out of the room.)

REID: Mom and I had some shit we had to take care of before I…

(He stops; beat.)

ALEX: Hello?

REID: …just—come over. You need to come over. You need to leave right now and come here. Okay?

(Alex appears. They stare at each other.)

ALEX: Okay.

REID: …You need to know something.

Scene. Reid and Suzanne at the airport. Suzanne is getting teary. She hugs him violently as he tries to pick his bag up off the floor.

REID: You're gonna make me miss final boarding.

SUZANNE: I don't like this idea anymore, I'm changing my mind, I don't want you to go.

REID: Well, it's a good thing I don't listen to you then, isn't it.

(Her face crumples.)

Come on, Mom, you know this is better. You know this is the wise move. Only idiots let themselves get railroaded. And?

SUZANNE: …you're not an idiot.

REID: Nope.

SUZANNE: But—

REID: And neither are you. Right?

SUZANNE: What is the account number? Do you have it?

REID: I told you, I wrote it down.

(Suzanne reaches out and starts fastening the front of Reid's jacket.)

Oh, man, don't, I'm gonna burn up inside this thing.

SUZANNE: It's still cold out West this time of year, you need to dress warm.

REID: Yeah, well, maybe it is, but it's not cold on the *plane* to out West. And I'm not going to be in Montana for very long anyway. Right?

SUZANNE: I know, but who knows when the next time I'll get to button up your coat will be. Maybe never.

(He is trying to undo the jacket; she brushes his hands away and finishes fastening it up.)

Let me at least do one thing for you, before you go. One little thing. There.

REID: 'Bye, Mom.

(She pats his chest and releases him. He starts walking away.)

SUZANNE: *(After him.)* I love you. Okay? Don't get lost. Well—don't get too lost.

Scene. Coach at the Varsity Lacrosse Spring Awards Ceremony Dinner.

COACH: …And the award for Best Sportsmanship goes to—Danny Whitton.

(Danny approaches the podium, smiling shyly. He trips on the steps to the stage.)

Yeah, Dan, just 'cause it's silly to be nervous doesn't mean everyone's not *watching* you, huh.

(Danny takes the award, shakes Coach's hand and exits, wishing one of the two of them could drop dead.)

And now for the most important and eagerly awaited award of the season. Or perhaps, I should say—and now is when I would normally announce the name of the winner of the most important and eagerly awaited award of the season, the MVP award, except this year we find ourselves in a bit of a situation. Up until recently we had a player on this varsity team whose abilities and natural gifts redefined the words "most valuable." He's the reason we went undefeated all season, and if we fell at the last hurdle, if we lost this year's New England Conference Championship to… *(Wants to say the word "fuck.")*…Wilton, it was only because he wasn't there to hold us together on the field and lead by example and remind us of who we *are*.

(Starting to feel the effects of the coaching staff open bar.)
And you know something? If I'm not allowed to give him the MVP award this year because of some pissant academic regulation, I'm not going to give it to anyone. I don't *have* to give one, you know, this isn't the Oscars. The MVP this year is gonna be conspicuous by his *absence*. In fact, I'll go that one better. I'm going to get my own award made up, with my own money, the *Coach's* Award. And I'll give it to him the next time I see him and I'll say, this is from someone who appreciates his achievements and knows what they mean, and recognizes his God-given skills for the rarity that they are. This MVP award belongs to him, he earned it, it's still his, regardless of whether he is still technically actually enrolled at this candyass school or not, and in a world where justice existed it would have been given to him in front of all of you, to honor what he did and what he still will do.

But because that's not going to happen any time soon and also they're not going to serve the desserts until I've given out all the goddamn prizes, I'll just take this opportunity to say that this year's Varsity MVP Most Valuable Player Award *would have* gone to Reid Callahan. But then you all already knew that, anyway.

Scene. Alex in the sports psychologist's office.

ALEX: Well so now let me ask you something, Dr. Patterson. They always want us to *talk* to someone, right? But they never want it to be *them*. And then we end up talking to *you*, because *why*? Because you can't be shocked? Sure, you can—I mean, look at you after what I just told you, and believe me, I could tell you some stuff that would burn off both your ears. Because it's better to get it all out in the open? Well, it all *happens* in the open—so what makes you think it's hiding now? Because you're objective? I never get that. I have never understood that, at all, ever. Objective just means you weren't there.

Scene. Brian, Alex and Danny. Danny is on the phone. The other two are watching him. Brian flicks ash and stares soulfully at Alex.

ALEX: Brian, use the damn ashtray, this isn't a barn.
BRIAN: …Sorry.
(Danny lights a cigarette; Alex takes it out of his hand and smokes it.)

ALEX: And you, don't smoke my last one, Asthma Poster Child.

BRIAN: Is it ringing, or what?

DANNY: Yeah.

BRIAN: How many rings?

DANNY: Six. Seven, eight.

ALEX: That's too many. That's weird.

BRIAN: Weird how?

ALEX: Weird like caller ID weird. Hang up. Hang up. We'll try something else.

TAMMY: Hello?

LINDSAY: Hello?

(Reid appears. He is not part of their scene.)

BRIAN: Dan, what's happening?

ALEX: Hang *up*, Danny! God!

TAMMY: Hello?

LINDSAY *(Whispering.)* Hello?

REID: Dear Alex,

Montana is great, and you know something funny? When you go to buy a snowboard there are almost as many different styles as there are for lacrosse sticks. You can get an Extreme, a Supermodel, a Carver, a Master, a Free, a Natural, a Mountain or a Levitation. And also, you can choose between a synthetic or a wooden core, which means there'd be one to make *you* happy, too.

I wonder if anyone will be screening this letter before you read it. Not if I mail it right after I finish it, right? They probably won't be able to get their act together that fast, will they? I mean, if they didn't even know I had a passport, no way will they be prepared for this. I'll have a few days lead time at least. They're going to ride my mom hard, but they'll have their work cut out for them there. And I know they won't get anything out of you. Hold the fort, okay? Fly the flag. I know you will.

TAMMY: *(Crying.)* You—Hello? Hello?

REID: …So can you guess which board I ended up buying? I'll say this much— it has a timber topsheet instead of plastic and its core is made from aspen and poplar wood and it snaps back like you would not believe. Now I know what you were talking about all this time. I'm enclosing the spare copy of the picture they took the day I got my passport, since you liked it so much; we can probably safely say the next time you see me I won't be looking like that any more. Don't forget me, okay? Don't forget me.

TAMMY: *(Crying.)* Who is this? God—You're not going to stop me, you know, so—Leave me alone. Please just leave me alone!

REID: Oh—and my snowboard is called the Free.

(Alex looks at Reid. She holds out the letter.)

ALEX: Dear Reid. I held the fort. I flew the flag. You knew I would. You know what else? If you fall, on the inside you'll never get all the way back up, no matter how good, or kind, or—vigilant you try to be from then on. You can't hide. I'm sure you're still trying, but don't kid yourself. The worst thing you've ever done—that's who you are. Now I know who you are. Who am I?

(Brian takes out a cell phone.)

ALEX: What are you doing?

BRIAN: It's my turn, right?

ALEX: Yeah, but give her a minute. Let her relax and think it's over. Then we call.

(Danny picks up Alex's cigarette from the ashtray.)

DANNY: Can I have this?

ALEX: *(Irritated.)* What?

DANNY: Are you finished with this? Can I have it?

(Alex snatches it from him.)

ALEX: Do I look like I'm finished?

DANNY: Yeah, sometimes.

(Blackout.)

END OF PLAY

The Divine Fallacy
by Tina Howe

BIOGRAPHY

Tina Howe is the author of *The Nest, Birth and After Birth, Museum, The Art of Dining, Painting Churches, Coastal Disturbances, Approaching Zanzibar, One Shoe Off, Pride's Crossing* and, most recently, *Women in Flames.* These works premiered at the Los Angeles Actors Theater, the New York Shakespeare Festival, the Kennedy Center, the Old Globe Theatre, Lincoln Center Theater and Second Stage. Her awards include an Obie for Distinguished Playwriting, an Outer Circle Critics Award, a Rockefeller Grant, two NEA Fellowships, a Guggenheim Fellowship, an American Academy of Arts and Letters Award in Literature, an American Theatre Wing Award, the Sidney Kingsley Award, the New York Drama Critics' Circle Award and two honorary degrees. In 1987, she received a Tony nomination for Best Play (*Coastal Disturbances*). Ms. Howe has been a Visiting Professor at Hunter College since 1990 and an Adjunct Professor at New York University since 1983. Her works can be read in numerous anthologies as well as in *Coastal Disturbances: Four Plays by Tina Howe, Approaching Zanzibar and Other Plays* and *Pride's Crossing* published by Theatre Communications Group. Ms. Howe has served on the council of the Dramatists Guild since 1990.

HUMANA FESTIVAL PRODUCTION

The Divine Fallacy was commissioned by Actors Theatre of Louisville and premiered at the Humana Festival of New American Plays in April 2000. It was directed by Jon Jory with the following cast:

Victor . . . . Tom Nelis
Dorothy . . . . Woodwyn Koons

and the following production staff:

Scenic Designer . . . . Paul Owen
Costume Designer . . . . Kevin R. McLeod
Lighting Designer. . . . . Paul Werner
Sound Designer. . . . . Martin R. Desjardins
Properties Designer. . . . . Ben Hohman
Stage Manager . . . . Janette L. Hubert
Assistant Stage Manager . . . . Juliet Penna
Dramaturgs . . . . Amy Wegener & Kelly Lea Miller
Casting . . . . Laura Richin Casting

CHARACTERS

VICTOR HUGO: A photographer, late 30's
DOROTHY KISS: A writer, mid 20's

SETTING

Victor's studio in downtown Manhattan. It's a freezing day in late February.

Woodwyn Koons and Tom Nelis
in *The Divine Fallacy*

24th Annual Humana Festival of New American Plays
Actors Theatre of Louisville, 2000
photo by Richard Trigg

The Divine Fallacy

Victor's studio in downtown Manhattan. It looks like a surreal garden blooming with white umbrellas and reflective silver screens. As the lights rise we hear the joyful bass-soprano duet, "Mit unser Macht ist nichts getan," from Bach's chorale, Ein feste Burg ist unser Gott, BWV 80. *It's a freezing day in late February. Victor, dressed in black, has been waiting for Dorothy for over an hour. There's a tentative knock at his door.*

VICTOR: Finally! *(Rushing to answer it.)* Dorothy Kiss?
  (Dorothy steps in, glasses fogged over and very out of breath. She's a mousy woman dressed in layers of mismatched clothes. An enormous coat covers a bulky sweater which covers a gauzy white dress. A tangle of woolen scarves is wrapped around her neck.)
DOROTHY: *(Rooted to the spot.)* Victor Hugo?
VICTOR: At last.
DOROTHY: I'm sorry, I'm sorry, I got lost.
VICTOR: Come in, come in.
DOROTHY: I reversed the numbers of your address.
VICTOR: We don't have much time.
DOROTHY: *(With a shrill laugh.)* I went to 22 West 17th instead of 17 West 22nd!
VICTOR: I have to leave for Paris in an hour.
DOROTHY: The minute I got there, I knew something was wrong.
VICTOR: *(Looking at his watch.)* No, make that forty-five minutes.
DOROTHY: There were all these naked people milling around. *(Pause.)* With pigeons.
VICTOR: The spring collections open tomorrow.
DOROTHY: They were so beautiful.
VICTOR: It's going to be a mad house… Come in, please…
  (He strides back into the studio and starts setting up his equipment.)
DOROTHY: I didn't realize they came in so many colors.

DOROTHY:	VICTOR:
Red, green, yellow, purple…	A tidal wave of photographers
I think they'd been dyed.	and fashion editors is descending
	from all over the world.

(Pause.)

VICTOR: I swore last year would be my last, but a man's got to make a living, right? *(Turning to look for her.)* Hey, where did you go?

(Dorothy waves at him from the door.)

VICTOR: Miss Kiss… we've got to hurry if you want me to do this.

(Dorothy makes a strangled sound.)

VICTOR: *(Guiding her into the room.)* Come in, come in… I won't bite.

DOROTHY: *(With a shrill laugh.)* My glasses are fogged over! I can't see a thing!

(She takes them off and wipes them with the end of one of her scarves.)

VICTOR: Here, let me help you off with your coat.

(They go through a lurching dance as he tries to unwrap all her scarves, making her spin like a top.)

VICTOR:	DOROTHY:
Hold still…easy does it…atta girl…	Whoops, I was just…sorry, sorry,
	sorry, sorry, sorry, sorry, sorry…

(He finally succeeds. They look at each other and smile, breathing heavily.)

VICTOR: So *you're* Daphne's sister?!

DOROTHY: Dorothy Kiss, the *writer*…

(Victor struggles to see the resemblance.)

DOROTHY: I know. It's a shocker.

VICTOR: No, no…

DOROTHY: She's the top fashion model in the country, and here I am… Miss Muskrat!

VICTOR: The more I look at you, the more I see the resemblance.

DOROTHY: You don't have to do that.

VICTOR: No really. There's something about your forehead…

DOROTHY: I take after my father. The rodent side of the family… Small, nondescript, close to the ground… *(She makes disturbing rodent faces and sounds.)*

VICTOR: You're funny.

DOROTHY: I try.

(Silence.)

VICTOR: So…

DOROTHY: *(Grabbing her coat and lurching towards the door.)* Goodbye, nice meeting you.

VICTOR: *(Barring her way.)* Hey, hey, just a minute…

DOROTHY: I can let myself out.

VICTOR: Daphne said you were coming out with a new novel and needed a photograph for the back cover.

DOROTHY: Another time…

VICTOR: It sounded wild.

DOROTHY: Oh God, oh God…

VICTOR: Something about a woman whose head keeps falling off.

DOROTHY: This was *her* idea, not mine! I hate having my picture taken! *(Struggling to get past him.)* I hate it, hate it, hate it, hate it, hate it, hate it, hate it, hate it…

VICTOR: *(Grabbing her arm.)* She told me you might react like this.

DOROTHY: *Hate it, hate it, hate it, hate it!*

VICTOR: Dorothy, Dorothy…

(Dorothy desperately tries to escape. Victor grabs her in his arms as she continues to fight him, kicking her legs. He finally plunks her down in a chair. They breathe heavily. A silence.)

DOROTHY: Why can't you set up your camera in my brain? Bore a hole in my skull and let 'er rip. *(She makes lurid sound effects.)* There's no plainness here, but heaving oceans ringed with pearls and ancient cities rising in the mist… Grab your tripod and activate your zoom, wonders are at hand… Holy men calling the faithful to prayer as women shed their clothes at the river's edge… *Click!* Jeweled elephants drink beside them, their trunks shattering the surface like breaking glass. *Click!* Their reflections shiver and merge, woman and elephant becoming one… Slender arms dissolving into rippling tusks, loosened hair spreading into shuddering flanks… *Click, click, click!* Now you see them, now you don't… A breast, a tail, a jeweled eye… *Click!* Macaws scream overhead *(Sound effect.)*, or is it the laughter of the women as they drift further and further from the shore, their shouts becoming hoarse and strange… *(Sound effect.) Click!* *(Tapping her temple.)* Aim your camera here, Mr. Hugo. *This* is where beauty lies… Mysterious, inchoate and out of sight!

(Silence as Victor stares at her.)

DOROTHY: *(Suddenly depressed.)* I don't know about you, but I could use a drink.

VICTOR: *(As if in a dream.)* Right, right…

DOROTHY: VICTOR?! *(Pause.)* I'd like a drink, if you don't mind!

VICTOR: Coming right up. What's your poison?

DOROTHY: Vodka, neat.

VICTOR: You got it! *(He lurches to a cabinet and fetches a bottle of vodka and a glass.)*

DOROTHY: That's alright, I don't need a glass. *(She grabs the bottle and drinks an enormous amount.)* Thanks, I needed that!

VICTOR: Holy shit!

DOROTHY: *(Wiping her mouth.)* Where are my manners? I forgot about you. *(Passing him the bottle.)* Sorry, sorry…

VICTOR: *(Pours a small amount in a glass and tips it towards her.)* Cheers!

(She raises an imaginary glass.)

DOROTHY: Could I ask you a personal question?

VICTOR: Shoot.

DOROTHY: Are you really related to Victor Hugo?

VICTOR: Strange but true.

DOROTHY: Really, really?

VICTOR: *Really!* He was my great great grandfather! *(Bowing.)* A votre service.

DOROTHY: He's my favorite writer! He's all I read… Over and over and over again! I can't believe I'm standing in the same room with you!

(She suddenly grabs one of his cameras and starts taking pictures of him.)

VICTOR: Hey, what are you doing? That's a two thousand dollar camera you're using!

(He lunges for it. She runs from him, snapping his picture.)

DOROTHY: A direct descendant of Victor Hugo…

VICTOR: *(Chasing her.)* Put that down!

DOROTHY: *(Snapping him at crazy angles.)* No one will believe me!

VICTOR: Give it here! *(Finally catching her.)* I SAID: GIVE ME THAT CAMERA!

(They struggle. A torrent of blood gushes from her hand.)

DOROTHY: Ow! Ow!

VICTOR: *(Frozen to the spot.)* Miss Kiss… Miss Kiss… Oh my God, my God…

(Dorothy gulps for air.)

VICTOR: What did I do?

(Her breathing slowly returns to normal.)

VICTOR: Are you alright?

DOROTHY: *(Weakly.)* A tourniquet… I need a tourniquet.

VICTOR: On the double! *(He races around looking for one.)*

DOROTHY: Wait, my sock… *(She kicks off one of her boots and removes a white sock.)*

VICTOR: *(Running to her side.)* Here, let me help.

DOROTHY: No, I can do it. *(She expertly ties it to stop the flow of blood.)*

VICTOR: How are you feeling?

DOROTHY: Better thanks.

VICTOR: I'm so sorry.

DOROTHY: It's not your fault.

VICTOR: I didn't mean to hurt you.

DOROTHY: I have a stigmata.

VICTOR: *What?*

DOROTHY: I said I have a stigmata. It bleeds when I get wrought up.

VICTOR: *You have a stigmata?*

DOROTHY: Several, actually.

VICTOR: Jesus Christ!

DOROTHY: Jesus Christ, indeed.

VICTOR: A *stigmata?* In *my* studio?

    (Silence.)

DOROTHY: I'm afraid you're going to miss your plane to Paris. I'm sorry. *(A silence. She hands him his camera.)* Well, I guess you may as well take my picture.

VICTOR: Right, right… your picture.

    (She removes her glasses and bulky sweater and looks eerily beautiful in her white gauzy dress.)

DOROTHY: I'm as ready as I'm ever going to be.

    (Victor is stunned, unable to move.)

DOROTHY: Yoo hoo… Mr. Hugo?

VICTOR: You're so beautiful!

DOROTHY: *(Lowering her eyes.)* Please!

VICTOR: You look so sad… Like an early Christian martyr.

    (A great light starts to emanate from her. Victor races to get his camera and begins taking her picture.)

VICTOR: *(Breaking down.)* I can't…I can't…I just…can't.

DOROTHY: Victor, Victor, it's alright… We all have something… You have your eye, Daphne has her beauty and I have this. It's OK. It makes me who I am.

    (Victor struggles to control himself.)

DOROTHY: Listen to me… Listen… When the Navahos weave a blanket, they leave in a hole to let the soul out—the flaw, the fallacy—call it what you will. It's part of the design, the most important part—faith, surrender, a mysterious tendency to bleed…

VICTOR: I'm so ashamed.

DOROTHY: You did your job. You took my picture.

VICTOR: But I didn't see you.

DOROTHY: Shh, shh…

VICTOR: I was blind.

DOROTHY: Shhhhhh…

VICTOR: *(Breaking down again.)* Blind, blind, blind…

> *(Dorothy rises and places her hands over his eyes, and then raises them in a gesture of benediction.)*

DOROTHY: There, there, it's alright. It's over.

> *(The lights blaze around them and then fade as the closing measures of Bach's duet swell.)*

END OF PLAY

War of the Worlds
Conceived by Anne Bogart
Written by Naomi Iizuka
Created by The SITI Company

BIOGRAPHY

Naomi Iizuka made her Actors Theatre of Louisville debut three years ago with *Polaroid Stories*, which won the 1998 PEN Center USA West Award for Drama. Her next play, *Aloha, Say the Pretty Girls*, premiered in the 1999 Humana Festival. Her other plays include *Scheherazade, Skin, Language of Angels* and *Tattoo Girl*. Her work has been produced in theatres across the country, and published by TCG, Sun and Moon, and Dramatic Publishing. Ms. Iizuka is the recipient of Princeton University's Hodder Fellowship, a McKnight Fellowship, a Jerome Playwriting Fellowship, and a Whiting Award. She received her B.A. from Yale University and her M.F.A. in playwriting from the University of California–San Diego.

HUMANA FESTIVAL PRODUCTION

War of the Worlds premiered at the Humana Festival of New American Plays in March 2000. It was directed by Anne Bogart with the following cast:

Beatrice Nelson . . . . Akiko Aizawa
Thompson . . . . J. Ed Araiza
Bernstein . . . . Will Bond
Stratten . . . . Tom Nelis
Leni Zadrov . . . . Ellen Lauren
Stephen Webber . . . . Barney O'Hanlon
Orson Welles . . . . Stephen Webber
Entourage . . . . Phil Bolin, Carey Calebs,
Cabe McCarty, Mark Watson

and the following production staff:

Scenic Designer . . . . Neil Patel
Costume Designer . . . . James Schuette
Lighting Designer . . . . Mimi Jordan Sherin
Sound Designer . . . . Darron L. West
Properties Designer . . . . Mark Walston
Stage Manager . . . . Megan Wanlass
Assistant Stage Manager . . . . Jason Szalla
Dramaturg . . . . Meghan Davis
Assistant Dramaturg . . . . Kelly Lea Miller

CHARACTERS

ORSON WELLES, also THIRD MAN

THOMPSON

BERNSTEIN, also FIRST MAN, CALLER #5, VOICE #2, STRANGER #2, REPORTER #1, PERSONALITY #4

STEPHEN WEBBER, also SECOND MAN, SILENT ASSISTANT, CALLER #1, VOICE #3, STRANGER #3, REPORTER #2, PERSONALITY #2

STRATTEN, also FILM SCHOLAR, CALLER #2, TAYLOR, SCHAEFER, VOICE #5, HOLLYWOOD REPORTER #1, PERSONALITY #3

LENI ZADROV, also CALLER #3, WARDROBE GIRL #1, VOICE #4, HOLLY-WOOD REPORTER #2, PERSONALITY #1

BEATRICE NELSON, also CALLER #4, WARDROBE GIRL #2, VOICE #6, ACTRESS, FOREIGN STARLET, PERSONALITY #5

J. Ed Araiza, Ellen Lauren, Barney O'Hanlon,
Stephen Webber and Will Bond
in *War of the Worlds*

24th Annual Humana Festival of New American Plays
Actors Theatre of Louisville, 2000
photo by Richard Trigg

War of the Worlds

1.

A soundstage. The set of an unfinished movie in Arizona, the mid-1980s. An empty swimming pool, a hole in the ground the color of bone. A brilliant, technicolor sunset plays out in the distance. Footsteps. Orson Welles enters the frame. He is larger than life. He smokes a cigar. He is droll and dapper and, almost imperceptibly, unwell. He speaks to an audience, seen and unseen.

WELLES: Good evening, ladies and gentlemen, my name is Orson Welles. I'd like to take a moment, before we begin, to tell you a little bit about what we're going to do here tonight. What you're about to see is a modern American story. It's the story of one man's life, his life's work. It's my story. On the face of it, it's a simple yarn. I was born in Kenosha, Wisconsin, a long time ago, a long way from here.
(The first magic trick. Welles pulls a tiny box out of thin air. Inside the box is a room. Inside the room is a woman from another place in time. Her name is Beatrice Nelson. She listens to piano music on a radio. In the background is a window. The month is May. Almost a century ago. Outside the window is a cherry blossom tree. White blossoms. As they fall, they look like snow.)

WELLES: When I was a much younger man, I was behind a bit of radio hokum called *War of the Worlds*. Perhaps you've heard of it. It caused quite a stir.
(The piano music fades. Static. An announcer's voice breaks through. A fragment from an ancient radio broadcast of The War of the Worlds. *Beatrice Nelson moves closer to the radio.)*

WELLES: After that, I went to Hollywood. I made a few movies. You may have seen one or two. No, now I'm being coy, and I don't want to do that. Not now. I'm here now before you to plead my case, to set the record straight. I have to, you see. It's very important to me. The truth is very important to me. What you're about to hear is the real story, behind the scenes, uncut. And this is another promise—listen carefully: During the next hour, everything you hear will be absolutely true and based on solid fact. Nothing more, nothing less. And now with your permission, a small act of magic. With the sympathetic support of yourselves, ladies and gentlemen, this just might work. Imagine this, if you will: It is night, but not a real night—a night of the mind and of a soundstage. We have no curtain, real or imaginary. There's only the illusion I'd like to create—

(Orson Welles disappears in the middle of speaking. The glass shatters. Music. News on the March. Highlights from the life of Orson Welles. Moments of a public life captured on film, video, TV interviews, home movies, outtakes, fragments of a documentary. Voiceover narration.)

ANNOUNCER: Time On The March. Hollywood. Entertainment Capital of the World. Legendary are the tales of the inhabitants of this sprawling mecca, this city of stars, but none of these are so loved and hated more than the potent figure laid to rest this week. Legendary actor-director-writer-orator-magician. Born May 6, 1915, in Kenosha, Wisconsin. Dubbed a genius virtually from the time he could talk. Reading at two, playing the violin at seven. Playing Shakespeare at ten. His first film. His first Broadway performance. His first wife. But not his last. The year 1937, he founded The Mercury Theatre with John Houseman. His resonant voice then took him to the world of radio and one night made broadcasting history. Halloween 1938. *War of the Worlds.* As millions of terrorized citizens swarmed the streets, he was packing his bags for Hollywood. The year 1941. Creates the motion picture masterpiece, *Citizen Kane.* How many movies did he create in his lifetime? No man can say. Then last week, as it must for all men, death came to George Orson Welles—

(The sequence ends with footage of Orson Welles at the end of his life. His back is to us. He is an enormous figure in a black cloak and hat—the magician from F For Fake. He's in the distance, striding away from the camera. We watch as he disappears from view. The picture cuts out. A blank screen. Sound of the projector.)

2.

A projection room. Present are the producers of a documentary on the late Orson Welles. Stratten is the executive producer. Thompson is the interviewer. A room full of anonymous men. Silhouettes. Their faces are invisible. The bright white light of the projection booth cuts through the dimness. The men are smoking. Dust motes swirl in the air.

THOMPSON: That's it.

FIRST MAN: Hello.

SECOND MAN: Hello.

FIRST MAN: Stand by. I'll tell you if we want to run it again.

THOMPSON: Well, how about it, Mr. Stratten?

STRATTEN: How do you like it, boys?

SECOND MAN: Well, seventy years of a man's life—

THIRD MAN: That's a lot to try and get into one film.

STRATTEN: It's a good start, Thompson. But it needs an angle. All we saw on that screen is Welles doing Welles. I already know all about that. Everybody knows all about that.

THIRD MAN: We need to get behind the image. It isn't enough to see the public persona. You've got to tell us who the man was, who he really was.

SECOND MAN: The part of him he didn't even know about.

STRATTEN: Or the part he knew about, and wanted to keep hidden from view. Remember, boys, this was a man who was putting on a show till the day he died. Wait a minute, wait a minute. What were his last words? Do you remember, boys? What were the last words Welles said on earth? Maybe he told us all about himself on his deathbed.

THIRD MAN: Yeah, and maybe he didn't.

SECOND MAN: All we saw on that screen was a big American.

FIRST MAN: One of the biggest.

STRATTEN: Yes, but how is he different from John Houston, or William Randolph Hearst, for that matter—Or John Doe? Yes, sure—

THIRD MAN: I tell you, Thompson, a man's dying words—

FIRST MAN: What were they?

THOMPSON: You don't watch the news.

SECOND MAN: When Welles died, he said just one word.

THIRD MAN: Thorne.

FIRST MAN: That's all he says, Thorne?

SECOND MAN: What the hell is "Thorne?"

THIRD MAN: Just one word.

SECOND MAN: What was it?

THIRD MAN: Or who was it?

FIRST MAN: Could be a woman.

SECOND MAN: Could be a lot of things.

STRATTEN: Here's a man who was a genius—or so they say—a man who was as loved and hated and talked about as any man in our time—a genius or a charlatan, the real thing or a very good fake, I don't know which—but when he comes to die, he's got one thing on his mind, something called Thorne. What does that mean?

FIRST MAN: Maybe it was a horse he bet on once.

SECOND MAN: Yeah, and didn't come in.

STRATTEN: All right, but where was the race?

FIRST MAN: Thorne.

STRATTEN: Thompson!

THOMPSON: Yes, sir.

STRATTEN: Hold the release date up a week, two weeks if you have to. Find out about Thorne.

THIRD MAN: Thorne.

STRATTEN: Get in touch with everybody that ever knew Welles, or knew him well—that manager of his, Bernstein, the best friend. He's still living.

THIRD MAN: Stephen Webber.

SECOND MAN: And that lady friend of his, too, the actress—

FIRST MAN: Leni Zadrov—

SECOND MAN: Right.

STRATTEN: See them all. Get in touch with everybody that ever worked for him—whoever loved him, whoever hated his guts. I don't mean going through the city directory, of course.

THOMPSON: I'll get on it right away, Mr. Stratten—

STRATTEN: Good! Thorne dead or alive! It'll probably turn out to be a very simple thing.

(Lightning. Leni Zadrov is suddenly illuminated by light. Rain. Music.)

3.

Music. An ancient movie already in progress. The living area of a hotel suite. A generic hotel on the outskirts of a city. Thousands of strangers have slept here. A soundless television. Leni Zadrov holds a tumbler of scotch. Her silent assistant and Thompson stand by.

LENI ZADROV: What does it matter what I say, what anyone says? A person is all things to all people. Get me another.

THOMPSON: Miss Zadrov—

LENI ZADROV: He died in the middle of the night, working on a script, he was always working, even at the end. What do you want?

THOMPSON: I thought maybe we could talk about Orson Welles.

LENI ZADROV: Talk about Orson. Talk about old times. Old times, for old
    times' sake. When times are gone they're not old, they're dead—Who
    told you you could sit down?

THOMPSON: I thought we could just talk.

LENI ZADROV: They called me right after he died, but I couldn't, I couldn't—
    he was a great man, the greatest—nobody understood how great he was.
    Why don't you people leave him alone, just leave him alone—

THOMPSON: Maybe later—

LENI ZADROV: Get out—

THOMPSON: Some other time—

LENI ZADROV: Get out. I said, get out.
    (Thunder. Lightning. Freeze frame.)

4.

*A film scholar interjects. A Film Archives. An air-conditioned mausoleum to
the art of cinema. Thompson is dwarfed by the machinery of filmmaking.*

FILM SCHOLAR: Then the camera pans up, and we see through the telephone
    booth, Thompson talking in the foreground, and in the background,
    through the glass, we see Susan Alexander at the table where he left her,
    and the waiter watching. It's this frame within a frame effect Welles was
    able to get, depth of field and sharpness of focus—*Citizen Kane*—Some
    people say it's the greatest movie ever made. It was the only Oscar Welles
    ever won. Won it for the screenplay. Shared it with Mankiewicz. Then,
    Pauline Kael comes along thirty years later, says he didn't really write it.
    Welles, that is.

THOMPSON: Can you tell me anything about his life?

FILM SCHOLAR: What's there to tell? Child prodigy. Apple of his mother's eye.
    His mother was an artist. Played the piano. She was a beauty, they say.
    Died when Welles was just a boy. He talked about her dying—Oh, don't
    tell me you're one of those people who thinks the artist's life has anything
    to do with anything? Well, have fun figuring it out. His life, I mean.
    Which part's real and which part's fancy—with Welles, it's sometimes
    hard to tell.

5.

Music. A frame within a frame. The image from the top of the play. A tiny box. Inside the box is a room. Inside the room is Beatrice Nelson. Behind her is a window. The music stops. She walks to the window. She looks out into a giant, unknown vastness. Night sky. Light on the old-fashioned radio. The sky is all of a sudden full of light. The light grows brighter. She watches from within, from another place in time.)

NEWSCASTER: Ladies and gentlemen, here is the latest bulletin from the Intercontinental Radio News. Toronto, Canada: Professor Morse of McGill University reports observing a total of three explosions on the planet Mars, between the hours of 7:45 p.m. and 9:20 p.m., Eastern Standard Time. This confirms earlier reports received from American observatories. Now, nearer home, comes a special bulletin from Trenton, New Jersey. It is reported that at 8:50 p.m. a huge, flaming object, believed to be a meteorite, fell on a farm in the neighborhood of Grovers Mill, New Jersey, twenty-two miles from Trenton. The flash in the sky was visible within a radius of several hundred miles and the noise of the impact was heard as far north as Elizabeth. We have dispatched a special mobile unit to the scene, and will have our commentator, Carl Phillips, give you a word picture as soon as he can reach there from Princeton.
(A giant hand passes over the window and the image disappears. The hand belongs to Orson Welles. A magic trick in process.)

6.

In the darkness, through an old radio, we hear fragments from The War of the Worlds *broadcast sped up, fast-forwarded, rewound. Orson Welles speaks into a microphone. New York City, 1938.*

WELLES: You're listening to a CBS presentation of Orson Welles and the Mercury Theater on the air. In an original adaptation of the *The War of the Worlds* by H.G. Wells. The performance will continue after a brief intermission. This is the Columbia Broadcasting System.
(The last notes of The War of the Worlds *broadcast. Phones are beginning to ring. The switchboard at CBS glitters with incoming calls. The callers speak through a field of static. Their voices seem scratchy, tinny, faraway.)*

CALLER #1: Don't you know New Jersey's been destroyed by Martians—it's on the radio.

CALLER #2: Right now, I don't know what to believe.

CALLER #3: And then I said to him, "O God, save us, please save us."

CALLER #2: Is it real? Is the world coming to an end? Hello—?

CALLER #3: I looked in the icebox and saw some chicken I was saving for Monday. I said to my nephew, "We may as well eat this chicken—we won't be here in the morning."

CALLER #4: I've been running all through my apartment building telling everybody the Martians are coming—

CALLER #1: Hello—?

CALLER #2: I want to know what's going on? What's really going on here—?

CALLER #4: It's crazy, it's just crazy. I've never seen anything like it. Everybody's just gone crazy—

CALLER #1: Hello—?

CALLER #3: I can't get through to my father in East Orange. He's older and not well, and I'm worried about him. He's all alone and he's not well—

CALLER #2: I want to know the truth. I mean, what's real and what's bunk. I just want to be clear—

CALLER #1: Hello—?

CALLER #3: Frankly, I'm scared. Right now I'm very scared—

CALLER #5: Is this your idea of a joke? Do you people have any idea what you've done? There are mobs in the streets. There are women and children huddled in churches. There's violence and looting—

CALLER #1: Hello—?

CALLER #5: It's a travesty and a disgrace, and before I'm through, I promise you, I'm going to sue you and Taylor and CBS and that Orson Welles fellah, and anybody else I can think of—

CALLER #1: Hello—?

CALLER #3: I'm calling from Trenton. I live in Trenton. I just turned on the radio. I was listening for the weather broadcast. I was with my little boy. My husband was at the movies. I thought it was all up for us. I grabbed my boy and sat and cried.

CALLER #2: I don't know what to think. I just don't know. I don't know what to think anymore—

CALLER #1: 2X 2L Calling CQ. 2X 2L Calling CQ. Isn't there anyone on the air? Isn't there anyone on the air? Isn't there anyone?

(A dial tone. It grows.)

7.

A fictive fragment from an ancient movie. Black and white, a scratchy print. Headlines from tomorrow's papers.

TAYLOR: Radio Listeners Take War Drama as Fact. Fake Radio 'War' Stirs Terror and Hysteria. End of the World—Real Thing or Radio 'Hoax'?
(Taylor throws the papers aside, revealing a young Orson Welles. An inner room in the CBS Studios. Elsewhere in the building, reporters, police officers, and CBS employees vie for control. Phones are ringing. Pandemonium just outside the closed door.)

TAYLOR: Is this your idea of entertainment?
(Enter Bernstein with a telegram.)

WELLES: I don't know how to entertain, Taylor. I just try everything I can think of.

TAYLOR: I don't think you realize the potential consequences—
(Enter Webber.)

WELLES: Hello, Bernstein.

TAYLOR: Lawsuits, potential liabilities—

BERNSTEIN: Excuse me. Mr. Welles, this just came in.

WELLES: Mr. Bernstein, I'd like you to meet Mr. Taylor.

WEBBER: I'll just borrow a cigar.

BERNSTEIN: How do you do, Mr. Taylor?

WELLES: Mr. Webber.

WEBBER: Hello.

WELLES: Mr. Taylor is vice-president for the Columbia Broadcasting System.

BERNSTEIN: We just got a cable from Mr. Woollcott.

WELLES: That's alright. We have no secrets from our listeners. Mr. Taylor is one of our most avid listeners, Mr. Bernstein. Read it to me.

BERNSTEIN: Dear Orson: This only goes to prove, my beamish boy, that all the intelligent people were listening to a dummy named Charlie, and all the dummies were listening to you.

TAYLOR: I assure you, gentlemen, this is no laughing matter. We have an obligation to our listeners, Orson. They rely on us to tell the truth. They believe us, don't you see—

WELLES: Look here, Taylor, it's my duty—and I'll let you in on a little secret, it's also my pleasure—to see to it that decent, hard-working Americans aren't taken in by what the powers-that-be have to say. I scared the

American public tonight—some of them, at least. And they should be scared. Not of Martians, but of people like yourself and the interests you represent. They should be very scared.

TAYLOR: You better hope the Crossley figures back you up, and that you keep your audience tuned in next week and the week after that.

WELLES: Tell your bosses not to worry Taylor. I have a lot of tricks up my sleeve. I can be a very entertaining fellow, you know.

(Taylor exits.)

WEBBER: Very entertaining and very idealistic.

WELLES: I thought so.

WEBBER: Do you believe any of it?

WELLES: I believe some of it. How do I look?

WEBBER: Like you need a shave and a good night's sleep.

WELLES: Good. That's exactly how I want to look.

VOICES: How about a photo Mr. Welles?

(The door opens. The roar of reporters. The blinding flash of cameras.)

8.

The film scholar interjects. Thompson takes notes. An interview already in progress.

FILM SCHOLAR: There but for the grace of God, goes God. Mankiewicz said that. You see—and this is what you have to understand—after *War of the Worlds*, Welles was a celebrity, a household name. He arrived in Hollywood with a two-picture deal, carte blanche, complete artistic control. It was unheard of. Welles operated outside of the system. He reported to no one but himself. Hollywood hated him for it. He hated them right back. He made *Kane* in 1940. After *Kane*, he made *The Magnificent Ambersons*. Botched it in the editing, well, let's just say left it to the studio. Went to Rio. The studio hacked it to pieces, reshot the ending. But that's another story. Remember this? The scene where Susan Alexander leaves Kane.

(The sound of a projector. In darkness, a clip from Citizen Kane *begins to play out. Actors play Kane and Susan Alexander. The volume is muted. The voice of the film scholar narrates. Thompson watches.)*

FILM SCHOLAR: *Kane* was all about pan, focus, dissolve. Welles and Toland were using a lot of low angle shots. They had to drill holes in the floor to get the camera low enough. And another thing, too: the ceiling. The ceiling is part of the shot. That was rare back then. Ceilings were a kind of fourth wall. They hid microphones up there, underneath the muslin. Remember this? The scene where Susan Alexander leaves Kane. The rest of it they shot in a single take. They had to. Welles destroyed the place. It's the heart, I think, of his character and his story, and in a way, it's a rather mysterious moment. It doesn't feel like acting. It feels real. Wow. I've never understood—

(*The projector sputters to a halt. Bright white light. The sound of a clock.*)

FILM SCHOLAR: Forgive me. I lost track of time.

THOMPSON: Who did location sound on *Kane?*

FILM SCHOLAR: Fesler. And another guy.

THOMPSON: Who was that?

WELLES: (*Off camera.*) Stewart.

FILM SCHOLAR: Stewart. I think his name was Stewart. Why do you ask?

THOMPSON: Never mind.

(*Footsteps. Susan Alexander makes her exit as the next scene begins. Lap dissolve.*)

9.

Bernstein and Thompson. In the middle of a conversation. Thompson has just asked a question. We enter midway into their conversation.

BERNSTEIN: Thorne—why do you ask? It's just a name after all, some random thing. You'd be surprised what one remembers at the end. I saw a woman once, this was years ago. I was on a street in Paris. Heard her footsteps before I saw her. She wore a black dress, I remember—tall, pale, she had strange grey eyes—It could've been out of a movie, but that's how it was. Sometimes, years later, I'd hear that sound, and I'd think it was her, but it wasn't.

(*The actress playing Susan Alexander exits.*)

BERNSTEIN: Who else have you seen?

(*Bernstein picks up a cigarette. Thompson lights it. The click of the lighter.*)

BERNSTEIN: Leni? Thank you. I called her right after he died, she couldn't even come to the phone. Who else? Let me guess—some film buff somewhere. I bet he had a lot to say. Orson had no patience. He loved to string them along. They never figured him out. I'm not sure anyone ever did. You ought to see Webber, if you haven't already. He was there from the beginning, from before the beginning, in the Mercury Theatre days, pre-*Kane*, pre-everything. When Orson went to Hollywood, he brought him along for the ride.

10.

The RKO lot at Culver City. Welles and Webber stand outside the doors to a soundstage. A memory from half a century ago.

WELLES: Take a look at it, Stephen. The biggest electric train set a boy ever had. Stephen.

WEBBER: After you, Mr. Welles.

WELLES: Stephen, welcome to Hollywood.

WEBBER: The Mercury Theater comes to Hollywood. Who would have believed.

WELLES: *(Shouting into the empty space.)* Hello?

WEBBER: *(Echoing Welles.)* Hello?

WELLES: We're going to try something new here, Stephen. They might not understand at first, but they will. Trust me. I might even make you a star.

WEBBER: Would you?

WELLES: You have my word. Let's get to work. We've got some movies to make. *(Music. Welles and Webber enter the gates of the RKO lot. A musical number. Extras in costume, Starlets, and studio personnel whiz by. An old-fashioned spectacle. Hollywood in the 1930s. The machinery of filmmaking in action.)*

WELLES: *(To a P.A.)* Excuse me. Excuse me.

BERNSTEIN: Excuse me, I'm looking for Mr. Orson Welles. Has anyone seen Mr. Orson Welles? He's come directly from New York, New York City. He's a director, a writer, an actor as well, theatre and radio. The voice behind Mercury Theatre, Mercury Playhouse, *War of the Worlds*. He's come to Hollywood to make a movie, a motion picture. He's a large man. Six two, six three. His weight—well, his weight, it's hard to say with his weight. It fluctuates. He's big, he's tall, he's very hard to miss. You'd recognize his face. He has a boyish face. You can see the boy in the man, a chubby little boy with strange almond eyes. Right now he's got a beard. Nobody cares much for the beard. Handsome, I would call him handsome. Excuse me, have you seen Mr. Welles? Orson Welles. His name is Orson Welles. I know he's here. He's just arrived in Hollywood. He's just arrived at RKO. From New York City. The Mercury Playhouse. *War of the Worlds.* He's very young. You wouldn't know to hear his voice. What a voice. Excuse me. Excuse me. I'm looking for Mr. Orson Welles? Has anyone seen Mr. Orson Welles.

(The P.A. recognizes Welles, and motions to Schaefer. The music stops. The lot instantly quiets down. Silence. The Extras and the studio personnel appraise the newcomers.)

SCHAEFER: *(To Webber.)* Mr. Welles. Welcome. Welcome to the RKO lot, Mr. Welles.

WEBBER: Oh, this—

SCHAEFER: I'm George Schaefer, vice-president of development and production.

WELLES: Thank you, Mr. Schaefer. This is Mr. Webber—

SCHAEFER: How do you do, Mr. Webber.

WELLES: —the leading man in my motion picture. I hope I haven't made a mistake, Stephen, have I? It is the leading man you want to be.

WEBBER: That's right.

WELLES: Are they waiting for me?

SCHAEFER: You—Oh, Mr. Welles.

WELLES: That's right. Yes, please go about your business, gentlemen, ladies. How do you do?

SCHAEFER: How do you do? Here you are in the flesh. Welcome, welcome. I didn't know your plans, nobody did—

WELLES: I don't know my plans myself.

SCHAEFER: —So I was unable to make any preparations, I'm afraid.

WELLES: But I have a few ideas.

(A loud crash. Bernstein enters with boxes, trunk, and suitcases.)

BERNSTEIN: Oops.

WELLES: Mr. Bern—Stein.

BERNSTEIN: Yes, Mr. Welles.

WELLES: Mr. Bernstein, would you come here a moment, please.

BERNSTEIN: Yes, Mr. Welles.

WELLES: Mr. Schaefer, this is Mr. Bernstein.

BERNSTEIN: How do you do?

WEBBER: Mr. Bernstein.

WELLES: Mr. Bernstein is an old family friend.

BERNSTEIN: How do you do, Mr. Schaefer.

WELLES: Mr. Schaefer—

SCHAEFER: Yes? How do you do?

WELLES: Mr. Schaefer—

SCHAEFER: Yes, Mr. Bernstine.

BERNSTEIN: Steen.

SCHAEFER: Welles.

WELLES: Mr. Schaefer—Do you know *The Heart of Darkness*, Mr. Schaefer?

SCHAEFER: The heart of darkness?

WARDROBE GIRL #1: Excuse me.

SCHAEFER: I don't think I understand.

BERNSTEIN: Excuse me.

WELLES: Conrad's *Heart of Darkness*, a trip downriver into the jungle, seen through Marlowe's eyes, the human eye, the subjective camera, the camera is an "I"—

WEBBER: Mr. Schaefer.

SCHAEFER: The camera is an "I"?

WEBBER: Mr. Schaefer.

SCHAEFER: Yes?

WEBBER: Excuse me.

SCHAEFER: But this is all somewhat unorthodox. A movie studio, Mr. Welles, after all—

WARDROBE GIRL #1: Excuse me.

SCHAEFER: Around here, we have ways we do things. We have a system, a formula, if you will—

WELLES: Mr. Schaefer, my movie will not adhere to any formula, I'm afraid. It'll be more like a séance, an extended dream.

SCHAEFER: A séance?

WARDROBE GIRL #2: Excuse me.

WELLES: That's right, Mr. Schaefer.

WEBBER: Excuse me.

BERNSTEIN: Excuse me.

SCHAEFER: But Mr. Welles, I'm afraid I don't understand. I don't understand. I don't understand.

(Freeze frame. Static snow. Welles steps out of the picture. An empty soundstage.)

WELLES: I don't understand—that's a direct quote, true to form, true to life. It's what was said to me time and time again—"I don't understand." I have spent a lifetime listening to "I don't understand." What is there not to understand? It's right there. It's as plain as day. It's as plain as the nose on your face. It's about the frame, you see, it's all about the frame—

(Orson Welles signals for music. He signals for lights. He signals the actors.)

11.

(Fast forward. 1939-1941. A chorus of Hollywood voices. Studio brass, Variety, The Hollywood Insider, *Hedda Hopper, Louella Parsons, Big Boy Williams, a disgruntled audience member from Pomona, et al.)*

WELLES: Who is he? Who the hell does he think he is?

VOICE #4: Who is he? Who does he think he is?

VOICE #2: Orson Welles? Why, he's an exhibitionist—

VOICE #6: A publicity seeker—

VOICE #2: A headline hunter—

VOICE #6: And a cheap sensationalist.

VOICE #3: Orson at twenty-six is still overshadowed by the glorious memory of Orson at six.

VOICE #2: He's a sort of Lord Byron meets Oscar Wilde. But he has a peculiarly American audacity. The man's an octopus of an ego.

VOICE #4: Too bad Orson Welles isn't an Englishman. If he had been, Hollywood wouldn't give him such a run-around. We reserve that for our own. But Mr. Welles doesn't scare easy. I'm thinking he'll make Hollywood sit up and beg for mercy.

VOICE #3: If Mr. Welles makes a great picture, I'll be the first to say so.

VOICE #5: Look Chappie, dear—one thing I want to warn you about. Orson is a very fascinating personality. He sings a siren song to anybody who listens. Just keep your feet on the ground, and whatever you do, don't let him hypnotize you.

VOICE #6: Genius.

VOICE #4: Welles is a genius.

VOICE #5: The man's a genius.

VOICE #3: Genius.

VOICE #4: He's a genius.

VOICE #2: An absolute genius.

VOICE #1: You don't know how sick to death I am of that word.

VOICE #3: From now on our motto at RKO is: Showmanship, not genius.

VOICE #4: People like to laugh. We do not need trouble-pictures, especially now. Make pictures to make us forget, not remember.

VOICE #5: It was, I would say it was a disappointment.

VOICE #3: *Kane* and then *Ambersons.*

VOICE #2: Box office disappointments.

VOICE #3: We were all, we were all disappointed.

VOICE #4: There were many disappointments, one after the next.

VOICE #5: Afterwards, he couldn't help but feel a certain disappointment.

VOICE #6: 2X 2L Calling CQ. 2X 2L Calling CQ.

(A Babel of gossips, naysayers, and critics. The sound grows loud.)

WELLES: Cut. Cut. Cut. Quiet please.

(Silence.)

WELLES: What were they all saying? So many voices chattering at once, each one laying claim to the truth. It's funny how you can make a person believe almost anything. The power of suggestion. Ladies and gentlemen, if you would indulge me for a moment, please close your eyes.

(Darkness. No sound, no light. The darkness is complete, electric.)

WELLES: What if I told you now that there was something lurking in the shadows, something alive but not quite human, something just beyond the edges of what you can see? It's very dark, isn't it?

(The sound of a match being struck. The lit end of a cigar glows in the darkness.)

12.

A clip from The Magnificent Ambersons *flickers in and out of view, fast forwards, rewinds, and then plays out. A black and white memory. A flawed print, incomplete. The volume is muted. Orson Welles smokes a cigar. A nimbus of smoke. He remembers out loud.*

WELLES: There it is. Magic. When we first got to Hollywood, we were trying to make a kind of magic, to do something new, something that was, in its own way, revolutionary. With *Ambersons*, I wanted the sense, I wanted it to flow from one scene to the next. A sense of rhythm—that's what it's all about. I know. It's difficult to dissect the creative process. In this scene, the camera never moves. Four minutes, and it doesn't move, not once. Look at them. They were wonderful, they really were—Tim and Ray and Aggie.

(The clip from Magnificent Ambersons *flickers in a kind of suspended animation. The actors are frozen in time. A frame within a frame. Welles seems all of a sudden old. He is watching the studio cut of* Ambersons *on a hotel room TV. Stratten interrupts from offstage.)*

STRATTEN: Hey, Mr. Welles!

THOMPSON: Ssh.

WELLES: Look at Aggie. God, she was something. I wish you could see how she wrapped up the whole story at the end. Joe Cotten goes to see her after all those years in a cheap boarding house and there's nothing left between them at all. Everything's over—her feelings and her world—his world, too—

STRATTEN: Hey, Mr. Welles!

(*A flash. The picture breaks up.*)

13.

Stratten leaps onstage. He's dressed like Uncle Sam. A skit from the Mercury Wonder Show. An interlude.

STRATTEN: Ever been to Rio? Rio de Janeiro? Beaches. Carnival. Girls. Lots of pretty girls. What if I told you, RKO will foot the bill? All expenses paid. How'd you like to take a trip down there? Shoot a little film. That's what you do, isn't it? In case you forgot, my friend, we're in a war. It's World War II, I'm talking about. Everybody's gotta do their part, pitch in. See it's like this: Some suit in DC, he got this idea, make a movie, show the people back home just how big our Americas truly are. Remind us what our boys are fighting for. Democracy and freedom, from Peoria all the way down to Rio. We forget our southern neighbors, my friend. We forget how vast and great America truly is. You could change all that. You could make a difference. Rio de Janeiro—What do you think, Welles? Feeling patriotic? Hit it, Harry!

WEBBER: Who's that?

WELLES: Nelson Rockefeller.

BERNSTEIN and WEBBER: Nelson Rockefeller?!

STRATTEN: *It's All True*, Mr. Welles. It's all true. Next stop, Rio de Janeiro!

(*Enter dancing girls with elaborate headdresses, feathers and glitter. A song and dance number.*)

STRATTEN and THE DANCING GIRLS:

Here is a man, *Here is a man*

American, *American*

And for the war you can be sure

He will do all he can

Who loves to smoke, *Who loves to smoke*

Enjoys a joke, ha, ha, ha, ha

And down in Rio de Janeiro

He will go for broke
Who buys the food? *Who buys the food?*
Who buys the drinks? *Who buys the drinks?*
Who knows that dough is meant to spend
And that's the way he thinks
Now should he go?
No, no, no, no *No, no, no, no*
Oh, what the hell,
He knows what sells
It's Mr. Welles!
(The dancing girls pull Orson Welles away. Orson Welles dances in the background.)
WELLES: *(Taking off his cape.)* Stephen, catch.
(Bernstein and Webber look on in the foreground. A close-up. They shout above the music.)
BERNSTEIN: What's wrong?
WEBBER: I don't understand what he's doing, I don't understand what he's thinking.
BERNSTEIN: It's just a diversion, Stephen, a little entertainment. The man knows what he's doing.
WEBBER: Does he? I'm not so sure.
(The music and the dancing drown out Webber's voice. Iris out.)

14.

THE VOICE OF ORSON WELLES: Tomorrow night the Mercury Theatre starts for South America. I've been asked to do a motion picture especially for Americans in all the Americas. I hope to see you again. Until then I remain, as always, obediently yours. This is Orson Welles. Good night.
(Samba music. Welles shoots scenes from carnival. Telegrams from RKO staff in Rio.)
BERNSTEIN: Rio is one expensive town. Stop. Spending through the roof. Stop.
WEBBER: Welles is over budget. Stop. No sign of progress on *It's All True.*
BERNSTEIN: Destroyed hotel room last night. Stop. Drinking and carousing with natives. Stop. Please reply.
WEBBER: Welles has disappeared. Stop. No word on when he'll return. Stop. Situation getting serious. Stop. Please reply.
BERNSTEIN: There is no script. Stop. No movie. Stop. Spending through the roof. Stop. Welles is out of control. Please reply.

WEBBER: Brazilian actor killed. Stop. What do we do now? What do we do?

(The dance begins to break down. The music becomes louder. Sweat and chaos.)

WELLES: Stop. Stop. Stop.

(Silence. The image disintegrates before our eyes.)

WELLES: *It's All True.* It was called *It's All True.* If you could see it, you'd know.

WEBBER: What are we doing here? Stop. When are we going home?

(The clip from The Magnificent Ambersons *reanimates. Stratten emerges from the darkness.)*

WELLES: God, the work that went into that. None of the ending survives, you know. I left, and they cut it up. They destroyed it all. There's nothing left of it.

STRATTEN: It's tragic what the studio did. You never made the movie you wanted to. And now, I guess, you never will. Would you have done things differently, in retrospect?

WELLES: Who can say.

STRATTEN: You can give me a better answer than that.

WELLES: When I was in Rio, I got a letter from Joe Cotten in which he said, "You don't realize you've made a sort of dark movie. It's more Chekhov than Tarkington." And of course that's what I intended all along. It just wasn't box office. So the studio destroyed *Ambersons* and then *Ambersons* destroyed me. I got over it. I had my whole life ahead of me still. You forget: If you want a happy ending it depends on where you stop your story. Next, I said next!

(The flash of a camera. Followed by many camera flashes one after the next. The roar of an unseen crowd. The actors from the clip break out of the frame. Stratten disappears into the future.)

HOLLYWOOD REPORTER #2: RKO pulls plug on *It's All True.*

HOLLYWOOD REPORTER #1: Back home, *Citizen Kane* shut out at Oscars.

HOLLYWOOD REPORTER #2: *Magnificent Ambersons:* Box Office Flop.

HOLLYWOOD REPORTER #1: Boy Wonder turned has-been almost overnight.

HOLLYWOOD REPORTER #2: Item: Saw Bad Boy Welles the other day at Harry Cohn's. He was sporting a moustache and twenty extra pounds. What're you going to do, Orson, now that you're out of a job?

HOLLYWOOD REPORTER #1: Item: Director, Actor, Radio Personality Mr. Orson Welles marries "It" Girl, Miss Rita Hayworth, in a small, private ceremony in Santa Monica, California. Our best wishes go out to the happy newlyweds. May you two love-birds live happily ever after.

(A Hollywood ending. Credits. The actors disperse. Welles exits. Lap dissolve.)

15.

Bernstein and Thompson in the middle of an interview. The sound of a clock ticking.

BERNSTEIN: The way things turned out, I don't need to tell you.

THOMPSON: It didn't end well.

BERNSTEIN: The marriage to Rita? Well, that was what it was. As for *It's All True*—well, I've seen bits and pieces. It might be a masterpiece—it's hard to tell—but what does that matter in the end? It's what people say about a thing, and what people say is that it was a disaster. The studio wrote it off. They didn't lose a dime. Orson was the only one who lost anything. He lost a great deal.

THOMPSON: Lost or squandered?

BERNSTEIN: It's easy to judge. Lesser men have made whole careers for themselves judging Orson. He made mistakes. I won't say he didn't. He was a complicated man. You ought to talk to Webber. Of course, he and Orson had a falling out. Then again, Orson had a falling out with just about everybody he knew. Artistic differences. Maybe more than that. I wouldn't know.

(Cut.)

16.

A blindingly bright light. Stephen Webber and Thompson.

WEBBER: It's funny how memory works. It's very unpredictable.

THOMPSON: What about Thorne?

WEBBER: Ah, yes. His dying words. All I can tell you is what I know first-hand, my own imperfect memories. Orson and I, we started out together in the theatre. I met him in '34. I saw him onstage. He was a strange, beautiful boy. And he had the most remarkable voice.

(Shakespeare. Young men rehearse a scene. A scene from a lifetime ago.)

WELLES: Now, Hal, what time of day is it, lad?

WEBBER: What a devil hast thou to do with the time of the day? Unless hours were cups of sack, and minutes capons.

WELLES: Why, Hal, 'tis my vocation, Hal; 'tis no sin for a man to labor in his vocation. Poins! Now shall we know if Gadshill have set a match.

WEBBER: Good Morrow, Ned.

BERNSTEIN: Good Morrow, sweet Hal. What says Monsieur Remorse? What says Sir John sack-and-sugar? Jack, how agrees the devil and thee about thy soul, that thou soldest him on Good-Friday last for a cup of Madeira and a cold capon's leg?

WELLES: Sir John stands to his word, the devil shall have his bargain.

BERNSTEIN: Then art thou dammed for keeping thy word with the devil.

WEBBER: Else he had been dammed for cozening the devil.

BERNSTEIN: But, my lads, my lads, to-morrow morning, by four o'clock, early at Gadshill! There are pilgrims going to Canterbury with rich offerings, and traders riding to London with fat Purses: I have bespoke supper to-morrow night in Eastcheap: we may do it as secure as sleep. If you will go, I will stuff your purses full of crowns; if you will not, tarry at home and be hanged.

WELLES: Hear ye, Yedward; if I tarry at home and go not, I'll hang you for going.

BERNSTEIN: You will, chops?

WELLES: Hal, wilt thou make one?

WEBBER: Who, I rob? I a thief? Not I, by my faith.

WELLES: There's neither honesty, manhood, nor good fellowship in thee, nor thou camest not of the blood royal, if thou darest not stand for ten shillings.

BERNSTEIN: Sir John, I pr'ythee, leave the prince and me alone: I will lay him down such reasons for this adventure that he shall go.

WELLES: Well, God give thee the spirit of persuasion. Farewell: you shall find me in Eastcheap.

WEBBER: Farewell, thou latter spring! Farewell, All-hallown summer!

(The memory begins to fade. Bits and pieces.)

THOMPSON: You and Welles were close.

WEBBER: We were friends. And then we weren't. We didn't speak for years. He'd felt I betrayed him. Maybe I never really knew him. I wonder what it means to know a man, to know his private self, the inner workings of his heart—I changed the subject, didn't I? You'd think with all the interviews Orson gave towards the end, you'd know all there was to know. But then again he never gave himself away, did he? He never gave anything away. He was a great man. But in the end, he destroyed himself. He'd like for you to think he didn't. He'd like for you to think he was some kind of maverick, that there was some kind of Hollywood conspiracy to keep him back.

WELLES: Marry, then, sweet wag, when thou art king.

WEBBER: It's an intriguing version of events.

WELLES: Let not us that are squires of the night's body be called thieves of the day's beauty

WEBBER: It's just not true.

WELLES: Let us be Diana's foresters—

WEBBER: Orson had trouble with the truth.

WELLES: Gentlemen of the shade

WEBBER: Which is to say he lied.

WELLES: Minions of the moon—

WEBBER: He lied about his past.

WELLES: And let men say we be men of good government—

WEBBER: He lied about himself.

WELLES: Being governed, as the sea is, by our noble and chaste mistress the moon—

WEBBER: I think after a while, he couldn't tell the difference between the lies and the truth.

WELLES: Under whose countenance we steal.

(Welles vanishes.)

17.

A blindingly bright light. Webber and Thompson. Crew people move back and forth in the background. A pause between questions.

THOMPSON: Was he ever in love?

WEBBER: Love? Why, I think what he did, everything he ever did, he did for love. I think that's why he made movies. And why he couldn't stop making them.

THOMPSON: How about that actress?

WEBBER: Which one? There were so many, I lost count. Orson—well, after a while, let's just say they all began to blend together.

(The sound of Leni Zadrov laughing.)

18.

Orson Welles is in the shadows. An evening in Hollywood, circa 1942. Post-Ambersons, post-It's All True. A dark, cavernous hall. The guests have gone home. Leni Zadrov is out of frame, laughing. Her laughter fills the space.

WELLES: What are you laughing at?

(*Leni Zadrov approaches in her* Mercury Wonder Show *costume. An echo of Susan Alexander and Charles Foster Kane in their first encounter.*)

ZADROV: You. You know, you don't gain weight if nobody sees you eat.

WELLES: Is that right?

ZADROV: It's a known, scientific fact.

WELLES: I'm absolutely starving.

ZADROV: Still?

WELLES: Always. And you?

ZADROV: Starving.

WELLES: Where is this going exactly?

ZADROV: It's a digression.

WELLES: Is that what it is?

ZADROV: I like digressions, don't you? One mad little digression can make all the difference in the world.

(*A door closes. Darkness. Zadrov and Welles laugh in the darkness. Light returns, like a door opening. The feel of the world is different. Welles and Zadrov are not where we last saw them. A different angle. A different point in time.*)

ZADROV: How did you do that?

WELLES: Like all good magic, the secret is ridiculously simple. You smile. I'm being serious. I'm a great fan of yours, you know. I saw you in *Bird of Paradise*. I was seventeen. You were naked. You were underwater. You were rescuing a wounded sailor. Do you always rescue wounded sailors?

ZADROV: Always. I can't help it. There's no logic. It's my character.

WELLES: Let's drink to character.

(*Lap dissolve. Welles snaps his fingers. Leni Zadrov awakes from a trance.*)

ZADROV: Did you really hypnotize me?

WELLES: You were in a deep, deep sleep.

ZADROV: Why did you wake me?

WELLES: I was getting a little lonely. I like people to talk to me, you see.

ZADROV: What do you like them to say?

WELLES: That depends.

ZADROV: I'm afraid I never saw your movie, Mr. Welles.

WELLES: (*Performing a magic trick.*) It was a fiction, Miss Zadrov, make-believe.

ZADROV: Leni. A fiction based on fact.

WELLES: (*Performing another magic trick.*) A fiction with a little fact thrown in. Am I holding your interest?

ZADROV: Yes, you are. You're very good. Are you a professional magician, Mr. Welles?

WELLES: Orson. George Orson.

ZADROV: Where did you learn all your tricks, George Orson?

WELLES: My father knew Houdini. He taught me a thing or two. The rest I picked up in the Orient. I travelled there when I was a boy. I learned from gurus and mystics. They showed me how to charm snakes, and how to make things disappear.

ZADROV: And your mother? What did she think of your magic?

WELLES: Oh, well, women, you know, most women, they hate magic. It irritates them. They don't like to be fooled. My mother was like most women. She died a long time ago. Are you watching? Watch closely.

(Welles performs another magic trick. And another one after that.)

ZADROV: God, you're crafty.

WELLES: Not really. How old are you anyway?

ZADROV: Ancient.

WELLES: Is Leni Zadrov, is that your real name?

ZADROV: No.

WELLES: What is?

ZADROV: I'll never say.

WELLES: Have you always acted?

ZADROV: Ever since I can remember.

WELLES: And are you acting now?

ZADROV: I am. And you?

WELLES: You don't think I'm Orson Welles?

ZADROV: I suppose you are, if you say you are, if you seem to be. I also sing and dance, you know. That's how I started.

WELLES: Would you sing for me now?

ZADROV: Oh, you wouldn't want to hear me sing.

WELLES: Yes. Yes, I would.

(Zadrov sings. And the world changes yet again. A party in progress. They are, for a little while, the happiest people in the world. Music.)

ZADROV: I've flown around the world in a plane

I've settled revolutions in Spain

The North Pole I have charted

Still I can't get started with you

Around the golf course I'm under par

And RKO has made me a star

I've got a house and a showplace
Still I can't get no place with you
You're so supreme
Lyrics I write of you
Scheme, just for the sight of you
Dream, both day and night of you
But, what good does it do
I've been consulted by Franklin D
And Greta Garbo has asked me to tea
You got me down-hearted
'Cause I can't get started with you
(Orson Welles applauds. Zadrov and Welles dance. The final magic trick. The world shifts once more. Dissolve to: one lone man applauding in a dark, cavernous space. The camera pans across time and space.)

19.

Camera pans down. The clip from The Stranger *plays out. The murder scene. Welles acts and directs. Webber stands apart.*

WEBBER: By the time he made *The Stranger*, we weren't speaking. What was there to say? Hollywood had brought out the worst in him—his selfishness, his arrogance, his fear. I could see it in his eyes. He was afraid. He was slipping, and he knew it. Everyone knew it. He'd started out a genius, and now he was doing voice-overs for two-bit westerns, any work that came his way he'd do it. He needed the money. He was spending it all. And he was drinking. He was a terrible drunk, abusive, cruel. The smallest thing would set him off. He'd get in fights. People were talking. I knew him better than anyone else. And a part of me loved him still, even then, despite everything. He hated me for that. When things went wrong, he blamed me. He said, I'd turned against him, that I turned others against him. He said I was trying to destroy him. All these years, you sonofabitch, you've been trying to destroy me. The look in his eye when he said that—you'd think he wanted to kill me.
(The scene ends with a gunshot. The character Welles is playing dies.)
WELLES: Cut!
(Welles moves on.)
WELLES: Sorry I've been jumping around like this, but that's the way it was. I can't explain it. I make the damnedest, the most elaborately detailed plans

you ever saw, and then I throw them all away. I just can't do it any other way. I may be dead wrong, but I'm so certain that nothing can shake it. It's the only thing I'm certain of.
(Dissolve to.)

20.

Music. And then voices, the clink of glass and china, laughter. A restaurant in Paris. Circa 1949. A dinner party in progress. Welles is presiding. He is a celebrity, the guest of honor. The people at the table are strangers. Their faces are unfamiliar. The sense of a great man in a foreign place, surrounded by strangers. Beatrice Nelson watches Welles from a distance. Her expression is unreadable. An echo of Kane's wife watching as her husband delivers his campaign speech. Thompson watches, too. He watches from a distant future.

STRANGER #3: What about *The Stranger?*

WELLES: Awful. There's nothing of me in that picture.

STRANGER #2: Why did you take it on?

WELLES: For money. What a silly question. I was deeply ashamed, but in need of money.

STRANGER #2: Are you up to trying *Kane?*

WELLES: Oh, Christ.

STRANGER #3: Why did you use the shrieking cockatoo?

WELLES: To wake them up.

STRANGER #3: Why does the light in his bedroom suddenly go off, and then come on again. Then you cut inside.

WELLES: Why not? Have another drink. I don't know. Who knows? Who cares?

STRANGER #2: Why did you begin and end with the "No Trespassing" sign?

WELLES: What do you think?

STRANGER #2: A man's life is private.

WELLES: Is it? That should theoretically be the answer, but it turns out that maybe it is and maybe it isn't.

STRANGER #3: You act as though it's painful to remember.
(Stratten and Zadrov are speaking out of earshot, laughing. Stratten begins a magic trick. Zadrov is his volunteer. Welles watches them. They continue their performance.)

STRANGER #3: Can we talk about Leland's betrayal of Kane?

WELLES: He didn't betray Kane. Kane betrayed him.

STRANGER #2: Why is that, do you suppose?

WELLES: Because he wasn't the man he pretended to be.

STRANGER #2: Yes, but in a sense, didn't Leland—

WELLES: I don't think so.

STRANGER #2: I was going to say something else, because if you were put in a position like that—

WELLES: I'm not his character. I'm not a friend of the hero. And he's a born friend of the hero. He's the loyal companion of a great man.

STRANGER #3: I certainly felt that Leland betrays him. I felt that emotionally.

WELLES: You're wrong, you're dead wrong. He's cruel to him, but he doesn't betray him. It's Kane who betrays the friendship. There is no betrayal of Kane. The betrayal is by Kane.

STRANGER #3: Then why do I dislike Leland so much?

WELLES: Because he doesn't have the size and person to love Kane for his faults. But that's not betrayal. He simply doesn't have the humanity, the generosity of spirit. He can't help it, you see. It's his nature. That's the story. How Leland discovers that this great man, his oldest friend in the world, that he's empty inside.

(Beatrice Nelson interrupts.)

BEATRICE NELSON: George. George Orson.

(Welles turns back. The world grows strange and unfamiliar. The faces are cold and indifferent. The laughter is mocking.)

STRATTEN: People say that after *Kane* you had trouble seeing things through. That you'd rather have a good meal, spend time with a pretty girl, that you'd rather talk about the one good movie you made, then try to make another one. And meanwhile, of course, time is passing, and you're not as young as you were, and people around you, they're beginning to wonder: What is Welles doing? What is he doing with all that genius? Sure, he's talented, but can you trust him?

(Stratten walks away. As Welles speaks, his voice grows louder. He overturns the table. Dishes and glasses crash to the ground.)

WELLES: I don't want to talk about *Kane.* I don't want to talk about *Kane.* I don't want to talk about *Kane.* I have no regrets, none. If I had it to do over, I wouldn't change a goddamn thing. I don't care if you believe me or not. Believe whatever the hell you want to believe.

(Stratten continues to walk. He walks towards the camera. His body fills the screen. Welles becomes a figure in the distant background. His image recedes. His voice grows faint. The sense of a door closing. And then Welles is gone. His voice, his image vanish. Stratten and Beatrice Nelson are in the darkness, outside the frame. They regard each other, then go their separate ways.)

21.

Music. Clip from The Lady From Shanghai. *An actress speaks her private thoughts out loud. An exposé. A scandal. The stories of Rita Hayworth, Dolores Del Rio, and Elsa Bannister blend into one. A funhouse of memories. Reflection upon reflection.*

ACTRESS: He cut her hair. He dyed it blond. He made her look—cold, hard. She always loved him. She couldn't understand how he could do that to her. All those other women. And the way everybody knew, how they all knew. The things people said. Private things. Even in the papers. How they talked about her, how they looked at her. People said he made her look ugly. He made what she did, who she was, he made it all seem so ugly. And a part of her believed them. She felt ashamed. At the end he walked away. He just kept walking. He left her alone in that shattered room. And she saw herself in his eyes, and she felt so ashamed. Even after, she couldn't help it. She thought of him. She kept hoping he'd come back. But then, of course, he never did.

(The clip ends. The film scholar appears. He's been watching. Thompson takes notes.)

FILM SCHOLAR: *Lady From Shanghai* was released in 1948. The studio re-edited the picture. They cut its running time by almost half. There are strange gaps in continuity, moments that simply don't make sense. Despite its flaws, it's still considered by many to be a masterpiece. The writer James Naremore pointed out that the mirror-maze sequence, which is also the grandest example of Welles's delight in movie illusionism, the gun battle among the mirrors—do you take cream in your coffee? The gun battle among the mirrors functions beautifully within the plot...

(The film scholar's voice fades away. Silence. Welles appears. He watches the film scholar and Thompson exit.)

22.

Welles is backstage. The University Theatre in Salt Lake City. May 1947. The theatre is empty. Enter Webber. He's been drinking. Webber and Welles are actors. They have scripts. They speak their lines.

WELLES: It makes me nervous not to be able to change anything. I think it comes from being in the theatre. You used to go to opening, then go backstage and change things, cut out bits, rewrite the ending.

WEBBER: Which one am I?

WELLES: The best friend.

WEBBER: All right.

WELLES: I'll get drunk, too, if you'd like, if it would do any good. It's a game, and I'm afraid I don't play it very well.

WEBBER: You talk about it all as if it doesn't matter. As long as I've known you, you used to talk about the work, how it mattered. You used to talk about making art. You used to talk about making something original and new.

WELLES: Aw, go on home.

WEBBER: I believed in you. You could persuade just about anyone to believe in you, love you even. Only it's love on your own terms. Something to be played your way, according to your rules.

WELLES: You're not drunk enough.

WEBBER: Drunk—What do you care?

WELLES: Stephen—

WEBBER: I've taken another job.

WELLES: You already have a job.

WEBBER: In Los Angeles. Working for Selznick.

WELLES: What about Mercury?

WEBBER: I think that ended a long time ago, don't you?

WELLES: I warn you, Stephen, you're not going to like Hollywood. They don't know anything about anything out there. They're vulgar and they hate art. Or maybe it's just artists they hate.

WEBBER: I'll take my chances. And you? What will you do?

WELLES: I'm going to Europe. Harry Kohn, RKO, they can all go to hell.

WEBBER: For how long?

WELLES: I don't know, I don't know for how long. There's nothing keeping me here anymore. I'm not sure there ever was. Stephen.

WEBBER: A toast. I want to make a toast. How do these lines go?

WELLES: To love on my terms. Those are the only terms anyone ever knows, his own.

(Webber exits. The sound of footsteps across a vast space. A door closes. Fade out.)

23.

Fade up. Backstage. Chaos. Late 1940s, early 1950s. Europe and North Africa. A movie version of an ancient play. The actors change into costumes. The film crew gets set up. Old photographs come to life.

WELLES: I think we tend to look back on the immediate past—the past that isn't history, but still a dim memory—as being faintly comic. It's an American attitude. I remember my parents looking at old pictures of themselves and laughing. One recognizes the impulse. One laughs at oneself. What else can one do? This next part takes place abroad: Rome, Mogador, Venice, Antibes. It features a cast of thousands. There's romance and intrigue. I play a multitude of roles: a Hun, a Nazi, a Moor. I even had time to write a play. It was called *The Unthinking Lobster*. No one remembers it; it's just as well.

(The theme from The Third Man *begins.)*

WELLES: Not that goddamn song again.

(Music continues. Welles and a foreign starlet. Harry's Bar in Rome, the Pam Pam in Antibes. Circa 1949. The band is playing the theme from The Third Man. *Reporters converge on Welles.)*

WELLES: If I have to hear that song one more time.

REPORTER #1: Mr. Welles.

REPORTER #2: Orson.

REPORTER #1: What are you working on these days?

WELLES: Shakespeare mostly.

REPORTER #1: And how do you find that?

WELLES: Invigorating.

REPORTER #2: Do you miss America?

WELLES: Not one bit.

REPORTER #1: How do you like the local weather?

WELLES: Enchanting.

REPORTER #1: Who's your friend?

REPORTER #2: Does she have a name?

REPORTER #1: Does she speak English?

REPORTER #2: Does she speak?

WELLES: She will.

(Lap dissolve.)

24.

1949-1955. Fast-forwarding through time. A montage of places, various film locations in Europe and Africa, a world of hotel rooms and restaurants. A chorus of overlapping PERSONALITIES: Michael MacLiammoir, Carol Reed, Alexander Korda, Laurence Olivier, Lea Padovani, Lady Diana Duff, Kenneth Tynan, Eartha Kitt, Brooks Atkinson, Walter Kerr, et al. Welles presides.

PERSONALITY #1: When we arrived in Morocco, there were four thousand Arab extras and not a one spoke English. The costumes were torture.

PERSONALITY #2: Welles had a Berber mistress.

PERSONALITY #1: It was 120 degrees by midday. We were miserable.

PERSONALITY #2: No one knew her name.

PERSONALITY #1: We stayed at the Beau Rivage Hotel. Orson said to order the most expensive things to eat so we'd all seem rich.

PERSONALITY #3: He and Hathaway fought night and day.

PERSONALITY #1: We had no money to pay.

PERSONALITY #4: One night, Orson sang a song in white pajamas.

PERSONALITY #2: Later, we came upon the idea of mandolins.

PERSONALITY #4: He said he'd wrote it when he was fourteen.

PERSONALITY #1: Robert was afraid of heights.

PERSONALITY #3: Michael was suffering from sun-blindness, and the wind was so damn strong. And then, of course, he kept changing Desdemonas.

PERSONALITY #2: First there was Lea, then Cecile—

PERSONALITY #5: Then Betsy—

ALL: Then Suzanne.

PERSONALITY #4: It was very jolly in the evenings.

PERSONALITY #1: We stayed at Casa Pilozzo.

PERSONALITY #4: We ate caviar and drank brandy.

PERSONALITY #1: Virginia and Charles came to visit.

PERSONALITY #4: Orson spoke about the Bhagavad Gita and W.C. Fields.

PERSONALITY #1: Little Christopher did imitations of the Barrymores.

PERSONALITY #5: Eventually, of course—

ALL: The money ran out.

WELLES: Arranging payment as fast as possible repeat as fast as possible.

PERSONALITY #3: Nobody saw Orson. He dropped out of sight.

PERSONALITY #2: He was spotted in Antibes and then Viterbo and then Tuscany and then Nice.

PERSONALITY #4: I saw them all in Venice: Orson and Suzanne in a gondola. Hilton was waving at me from above. I was in my own gondola. I wore a white mushroom hat. Later, Joe Cotten showed up at the villa, and we ate and ate.

PERSONALITY #5: We drank all night long. Orson ate lobster after lobster, and screamed at us the whole time about a shot he'd missed of the sunset, and what a terrible lot we were, all of us.

WELLES: I can't work this way. I refuse.

PERSONALITY #2: And then, of course—

ALL: The money ran out.

WELLES: I need 70,000 dollars. Leaving tomorrow. On my way to London. Will have your money when we meet in Rome. Arranging payment as fast as possible repeat as fast as possible.

PERSONALITY #3: He was staying at the Claridge.

PERSONALITY #1: Do you have any idea how much it costs to stay at the Claridge?

WELLES: I'm done with that. I'm onto something else. I've met this lovely black girl. She's just a tiny thing, and phenomenal, just phenomenal.

PERSONALITY #4: Eartha.

PERSONALITY #1: Eartha.

PERSONALITY #2: Eartha.

PERSONALITY #3: Her name was Eartha.

WELLES: Eartha will play Helen of Troy. Michael will play Algernon. I will play Lady Bracknell. I will also deliver a brief lecture on life.

PERSONALITY #4: We dined out at Bricktop's and Calabados. There was never anything between us, no matter what the papers said.

WELLES: I will also play Gloucester. I'll have a hunchback. You will play Henry. Later on, I'll perform magic tricks. Eartha will sing throughout.

PERSONALITY #5: Are you out of your mind?

WELLES: Of course I am, didn't you know?

PERSONALITY #1: We found him naked in bed, smoking a cigar and drinking a gin fizz.

WELLES: *Doctor Faustus*, not *Faust* goddamnit.

PERSONALITY #2: He meant Marlowe's. Not Goethe's. Orson hated Goethe.

WELLES: I despise Goethe.

PERSONALITY #4: Everywhere we went, they played that song from *The Third Man.*

WELLES: I hate the zither.

PERSONALITY #4: We toured all over Germany.

WELLES: I hate the Germans.

PERSONALITY #4: The Germans were perplexed.

WELLES: I'm done with that. I'm onto something else. We'll do *Othello.* We'll do *Othello* at the St. James. Olivier will produce. Peter will play Iago. Michael will not. I don't care what Michael thinks.

PERSONALITY #4: He kissed me one night on stage, and bit my lip so hard, I bled.

PERSONALITY #3: He had everything except the breath. He didn't go into training.

PERSONALITY #4: Another night, he almost strangled me. I think he's mad, I really do.

WELLES: I have just come from the St. James Theatre, where I have been murdering Desdemona—or Shakespeare, if you believe the papers.

PERSONALITY #5: He owes me $30,000.

PERSONALITY #4: He owes me $60,000.

PERSONALITY #2: The man owes me over $50,000.

PERSONALITY #3: He owes back taxes totalling $80,000.

PERSONALITY #1: He owes somewhere in the vicinity of $100,000.

PERSONALITY #5: $48,000.

PERSONALITY #2: $63,000.

PERSONALITY #3: $75,000.

WELLES: After *Othello,* I thought about doing *Julius Caesar, Don Quixote, Twelfth Night.* I thought about *Volpone* and *Earnest,* but ultimately I was persuaded to do *Lear.*
(*Lap dissolve: New York. 1955. Welles returns to America after years of living overseas. Opening night of* Lear. *Welles is center in a wheelchair. He is all of a sudden older and unwell. The world is a changed place. Time is passing quickly.*)

WELLES: Thou think'st 'tis much that this contentious storm
Invades us to the skin: so 'tis to thee;
But where the greater malady is fixed,
The lesser is scarce felt. Thou'dst shun a bear;
But if thy flight lay toward the roaring sea,
Thou'dst meet the bear i' th' mouth. When the mind's free,
The body's delicate. The tempest in my mind

Doth from my senses take all feeling else,
Save what beats there. Filial ingratitude,
Is it not as this mouth should tear this hand
For lifting food to't? But I will punish home.
No, I will weep no more. In such a night
To shut me out! Pour on, I will endure.
In such a night as this!
(The memory fades away.)

25.

Thompson and Webber. The film crew has vanished. Thompson and Webber are alone in a vast dark space full of ghosts. Welles moves across the soundstage, trapped within an ancient movie.

WEBBER: Afterwards, he went to Vegas, did his magic act at the Riviera; did a little Shakespeare, in between the card tricks. He made that movie, too, I forget the name. Paid for it all out of his own pocket, the filming stretched on for years, the actors got old, moved on. He never finished it. Leni was with him all that time towards the end. I think he made that last movie for her.

THOMPSON: That sounds like love.

Beatrice Nelson appears from out of the darkness. Welles sees her. She is a memory from a distant past. A ghost in the machine.

WEBBER: Oh, I don't know. I think it was something more like defiance. Or spite.

BEATRICE NELSON: 2X2L calling CQ.

WEBBER: What do you say after all to a world you don't recognize anymore, a world that seems suddenly alien and strange to you? What do you say to people who never knew who you were, people who have no idea who you are?

BEATRICE NELSON: 2X2L calling CQ.

WEBBER: What traces do you leave behind? What signs of life? What do you say before you go? At the end of the day, who will know you? Who will know what you really were?

BEATRICE NELSON: George.

WEBBER: You see, I don't think any one word can explain a man, all that he was. And facts, I think facts are less important than truth. Wait. Wait. Something has happened. Silence. That's odd.

BEATRICE NELSON: George Orson.

(Rewind.)

26.

Bernstein and Thompson. A silent interview in progress. We hear the click of Thompson's lighter. We hear Bernstein's laughter. A slow motion, mute and faraway. Leni Zadrov is moving backwards in time, back to the hotel room, back to the interview with Thompson. Time is moving backwards. A rush of memories. Welles tries to restore order, tries to be heard above the din. Beatrice Nelson appears.

WELLES: Look, I played the Clover Room at the Riviera, I made back everything I lost, no regrets, not a one. I did a ballet, I did *Lear*, I did a thriller called *Pay the Devil*. I'm always ready to change, that't the thing. I'm constantly reaching and fishing and hoping and trying and improvising and changing. One does what one needs to do. I have no modesty about these things. Let's keep focused on what really matters, alright, on the thing itself. Let's try to get into it. Everybody in the world is an actor. Conversing is acting. Man as a social animal is an actor; everything we do is a kind of performance. My point is that it's how you look at it, point of view. If you came to see Shakespeare—well, then you got something else, but if you came to see theater—well, you got that in spades, didn't you? Everything I do, you see, is a kind of theater, I'm a kind of theater unto myself, I'm always taking on a character, I'm always in character, there's no point where I'm not being someone else. You can call that a lie, if you want, a lie in service of the truth.

BEATRICE NELSON: George. George Orson.

WELLES: A truth. A memory. You see, you have to let it go. You have to.

(An ancient, black and white movie ends. Static, snow, the sound at the end of the tape. The living area of a hotel suite. A generic hotel on the outskirts of a city. Leni Zadrov and Thompson. Thompson stands by. The silent assistant turns the television off. Silence.)

ZADROV: He made so much, he did so much, but in the end, there was nothing left. Not even his own films. Somebody else always owned the rights. Why do you think he took on all those roles, the TV shows, the commercials? You think he wanted to?

THOMPSON: You're the one who knew him.

ZADROV: I don't know. Maybe he had the time of his life. He made a couple of great movies. Mostly, though, he did exactly what he wanted. How many people do you know who can say that? The last time I saw him, you know, we fought. We were staying in a hotel in Prague, and we had a terrible fight. I never saw him again.

27.

One last scene between Leni Zadrov and Orson Welles. A clip of The Trial. *A maze of shadows. They watch the movie. They are the movie.*

WELLES: I liked *The Trial.*

ZADROV: Did you?

WELLES: I may be the only one. I think Kafka is very amusing.

ZADROV: How can you say that?

WELLES: How can you not?

ZADROV: For me, I think the whole thing, it's very tragic.

WELLES: Well, you're wrong about that. See, he's not guilty, but he feels guilty. It's totally without meaning whether he's guilty or not. The point is that he feels guilty.

ZADROV: But why? Why does he feel guilty, if he did nothing wrong? He must've done something wrong. What did he do?

WELLES: You tell me.

ZADROV: I don't know. It seems so unjust, so cruel to me what happens to him, his fate.

WELLES: Unlucky maybe. I don't know about cruel. You'll have to take another look at it someday. Maybe you'll see things differently.

ZADROV: I saw him in the hotel room. It was the middle of the night. I heard the TV in the other room. He didn't know I was there. He was in his own world by then. He had been unwell for some time, and sad. He hid it well, he tried to, but you could see. He was unhappy.

(Echoes of A Touch of Evil. *The voice of Hank Quinlan. Welles transforms before our eyes.)*

WELLES: He felt guilty. He wears his guilt for all to see. He can't help it, it's his nature—

ZADROV: It was dark, but even so—

WELLES: Sloth, gluttony, vanity, pride—

ZADROV: He was watching one of his old movies with the sound turned down—

WELLES: He felt ashamed—

ZADROV: It was like a dream—

WELLES: His whole life, the man he was, the man he might have been, his legacy, the smallest thing—

ZADROV: And he was crying. I could see the tears. He was an old man. It was a movie he had made a lifetime ago. All the actors had grown old or died. The best parts had been cut, lost forever—

WELLES: It was like some terrible dream—

ZADROV: Don't tell me you're sorry.

WELLES: I'm not sorry. I'm not sorry for anything.

(Leni Zadrov turns and walks away. The sound of her footsteps as she walks down the hall. Eyes follow her as she goes.)

WELLES: Wait, Leni. Leni, don't go. Leni! Please don't go.

(Welles fills the stage with the machinery of filmmaking, all the objects in the great hall of Xanadu. A litany of names and titles begins, all the movies, all the roles. A lifetime of work, one man's legacy.)

FILM SCHOLAR: Citizen Kane, Journey Into Fear, The Magnificent Ambersons, It's All True, Jane Eyre, Follow the Boys, Tomorrow is Forever, The Stranger, Duel in the Sun, Black Magic, The Lady From Shanghai, The Third Man, The Black Rose, Return to Glennascaul, Lords of the Forest, Trent's Last Case, Napoleon, Othello, Mr. Arkadin, Trouble in the Glen, Moby Dick, Pay the Devil, The Vikings, The Long Hot Summer, Touch of Evil, The Roots of Heaven, Compulsion, High Journey, South Seas Adventure, David and Goliath, Ferry to Hong Kong, Austerlitz, The Crack in the Mirror, The Tartars, Lafayette, King of Kings, The Trial, River of the Ocean, The Finest Hours, The V.I.P.s, Rogopag, Chimes at Midnight, The Adventures of Marco Polo, Casino Royale, Is Paris Burning?, The Sailor From Gibraltar, A Man For All Seasons, I'll Never Forget What's 'is Name, Oedipus the King, The Last Roman, The Immortal Story, House of Cards, The Southern Star, 12 +1, Battle of Neretva, The Deep, Waterloo, The Kremlin Letter, Start the Revolution Without me, Catch-22, Ten Days Wonder, Don Quixote, A Safe Place, The Canterbury Tales, Sentinels of Silence, Sutjeska, Malpertius, F For Fake, The Other Side of the Wind.

28.

The projection room from the top of the play. Stratten lights a cigarette. Stratten and Thompson.

STRATTEN: When I think of Orson Welles, I think of Paul Masson wine. He was obese at this point. He could barely move. Oh, he still had that voice, that booming voice, but he was difficult. Some said lazy. Towards the end, nobody would hire him. He was a has-been. I saw him once on *The Merv Griffin Show*, laughing at some joke somebody made about his weight. He died in debt, you know. He owed just about everybody. And he never did finish that last movie of his. Just bits and pieces. It's tragic really when you stop and think about it. Such a waste. What did you find out about him? Anything?

THOMPSON: Not much really.

STRATTEN: Did you ever find out what it meant? Thorne, I mean.

THOMPSON: No. I never did.

STRATTEN: You know, there's a room somewhere—Art Institute of Chicago, I think—called the Thorne Room. I went there once when I was a kid. Picture frames all along the walls, and you'd go up close and look through the frame, and inside the frame, there'd be a whole entire world—a room in a house, say, a woman at the window from a long time ago, tiny and perfect, everything just like it was, the smallest thing, and I remember thinking how strange it was—What do I know? Sometimes I think I don't know anything. Keep asking questions, Thompson. Who knows what you'll find.

(Stratten and Thompson exit.)

29.

A soundstage in disrepair. An echo chamber. Fragments, pieces, puzzle pieces coming together. Welles is in the foreground. He has trouble breathing. His heart hurts.

BERNSTEIN: Hello.

WEBBER: Hello.

THOMPSON: That's it.

BERNSTEIN: Stand by.

(An echo of laughter, Leni Zadrov laughing.)

STRATTEN: I'll tell you Thompson, a man's dying words.

WEBBER: He was a strange, beautiful boy.

BERNSTEIN: One of the biggest.

THOMPSON: How about a photo Mr. Welles.

STRATTEN: Mr. Welles.

BERNSTEIN: Jack, how agrees the devil and thee about thy soul.

WEBBER: Orson and I, we started out together in the theater.

LENI ZADROV: He did so much, he made so much.

BERNSTEIN: Why then thou art damned for keeping thy word with the devil.

LENI ZADROV: A person is all things to all people.

THOMPSON: Genius.

LENI ZADROV: Welles is a genius.

STRATTEN: The man's a genius.

WEBBER: Genius.

LENI ZADROV: He's a genius.

BERNSTEIN: An absolute genius.

STRATTEN: Hit it Harry!

LENI ZADROV: I've flown around the world in a plane.

THOMPSON: You and Welles were close.

WEBBER: We were friends and then we weren't.

LENI ZADROV: The last time I saw him you know we fought. We were staying in a hotel in Prague. We had a terrible fight. I never saw him again.

BERNSTEIN: Excuse me, Mr. Welles.

WEBBER: Take a look at it Stephen, the biggest electric train set a boy ever had.

LENI ZADROV: Mr. Welles doesn't scare easy.

THOMPSON: Can you tell me anything about his life?

STRATTEN: Welcome to the RKO lot, Mr. Welles.

(The last magic trick. The stage is suddenly empty.)

WELLES: Ladies and gentlemen, this is Orson Welles, and I'm in trouble. When I was a much younger man, I had a show. It was called the *Mercury Wonder Show*. My friends and I, we performed feats of illusion, magic. This was before your time, but magic is timeless. It never gets old. It always begins and ends with the figure of the magician asking the audience to believe, if only for a moment, that the lady is floating in mid-air. To be a child again, to see with the eyes of a child.

30.

The sound of a radio. Light. A tiny box. Inside the box is a room. Inside the room is Beatrice Nelson. Orson Welles approaches her. In the background is a window. The month is May. Almost a century ago. Outside the window is a cherry blossom tree. White blossoms. As they fall, they look like snow. A voice-over.

THE YOUNG ORSON WELLES: Before the cylinder fell there was a general persuasion that through all the deep of space no life existed beyond the petty surface of our minute sphere. Now we see further. Dim and wonderful is the vision I have conjured up in my mind of life spreading slowly from this little seedbed of the solar system throughout the inanimate vastness of sidereal space. But that is a remote dream. It may be that the destruction of the Martians is only a reprieve. To them, and not to us, is the future ordained perhaps. Strange it now seems to sit in my peaceful study at Princeton writing down this last chapter of the record begun at a deserted farm in Grovers Mill. Strange to watch children playing in the streets. Strange to see young people strolling on the green, where the new spring grass heals the last black scars of a bruised earth. Strange to watch the sightseers enter the museum where the dissembled parts of a Martian machine are kept on public view. Strange when I recall the time when I first saw it, bright and clean-cut, hard, and silent, under the dawn of that last great day.

(A moment of dead air. A still from a memory. Ghosts in the machine. A frame within a frame.)

THE YOUNG ORSON WELLES: Ladies and gentleman, this was *War of the Worlds.* An original adaptation. My name was Orson Welles. Good night.

(Fade out.)

END OF PLAY

Arabian Nights
by David Ives

BIOGRAPHY

David Ives was born in Chicago and educated at Northwestern University and The Yale School of Drama. A 1995 Guggenheim Fellow in playwriting, he is probably best known for his evening of one-act comedies called *All in the Timing*. The show won the Outer Critics Circle Playwriting Award and was included in *The Best Plays of 1993-94*. Another evening of short comedies, *Mere Mortals*, enjoyed an extended off-Broadway run in 1997-98. Four of his short comedies have been included in the *Best Short Plays of the Year* volumes. Among his full-length plays are *Ancient History, Don Juan in Chicago*, and *The Red Address*.

HUMANA FESTIVAL PRODUCTION

Arabian Nights was commmissioned by Actors Theatre of Louisville and premiered at the Humana Festival of New American Plays in April 2000. It was directed by Jon Jory with the following cast:

Interpreter . . . . Ellen Lauren
Flora . . . . Gretchen Lee Krich
Norman. . . . . Will Bond

and the following production staff:

Scenic Designer . . . . Paul Owen
Costume Designer . . . . Kevin R. McLeod
Lighting Designer. . . . . Paul Werner
Sound Designer. Martin R. Desjardins
Properties Designer. . . . . Ben Hohman
Stage Manager . . . . Charles M. Turner III
Assistant Stage Manager . . . . Juliet Penna
Dramaturgs . . . . Amy Wegener & Kerry Mulvaney
Casting . . . . Laura Richin Casting

CHARACTERS

INTERPRETER: Wears loose colorful robes and sandals. May be played by a woman wearing a dark beard.

FLORA: Very ordinary.

NORMAN: Utterly normal. Carries a suitcase.

TIME & PLACE

Flora's shop. The present.

Ellen Lauren, Will Bond and Gretchen Lee Krich
in *Arabian Nights*

24th Annual Humana Festival of New American Plays
Actors Theatre of Louisville, 2000
photo by Richard Trigg

Arabian Nights

Up right, a freestanding, open doorway with a multi-colored bead curtain. Center, a small, plain wooden table with a white cloth. On it: an ornament, a stone, a gold ring, and a figure of a frog.

At lights up, Flora is at the table, dusting the objects with a featherduster. Through the bead curtain comes the Interpreter, leading in Norman, who carries a suitcase.

INTERPRETER: Right this way, sir, this way. The most beautiful shop in the world. All the wonders of the kingdom. For nothing! Nothing! I will interpret for you.

NORMAN: *(To Flora.)* Hello.

INTERPRETER: Hail, fair maid! says he.

FLORA: *(To Norman, putting the featherduster away.)* Good morning.

INTERPRETER: All praise to the highest, says she.

NORMAN: Do you...speak any English?

INTERPRETER: Do you...speak any English?

FLORA: *(She speaks perfect, unaccented English.)* Yes, I speak some English.

INTERPRETER: Indeed, sir, I can stammer out a broken song of pitiful, insufficient words.

NORMAN: Ah-ha.

INTERPRETER: Ah-ha.

NORMAN: Well...

INTERPRETER: A deep hole in the ground.

NORMAN: I...

INTERPRETER: *(Points to his eye.)* The organ of vision.

NORMAN: Ummm...

INTERPRETER: Ummm...

NORMAN: Listen.

INTERPRETER: Do you hear something?

(Interpreter and Flora listen for something.)

NORMAN: I'm sorry to rush in so late like this.

FLORA: No, please.

INTERPRETER: No, please.

NORMAN: But you see...

INTERPRETER: *(Points to his butt.)* But—*(Points to Flora.)*—you—*(Does binoculars with his hands.)*—see...

NORMAN: *(Looks at his watch.)* Darn...

INTERPRETER: *(Produces an hourglass from among his robes.)* How swiftly flow the sands of time!

NORMAN: I know this sounds crazy—

INTERPRETER: I know this sounds crazy—

NORMAN: I only have about ten minutes.

INTERPRETER: Soon the golden orb of heaven will cleave the house of the hedgehog.

NORMAN: I have to catch a plane.

INTERPRETER: I must clamber upon the flying corporate carpet and flap away from your kingdom.

NORMAN: Anyway, I want to find...

INTERPRETER: Anyway, I want to find...

FLORA: Yes?

INTERPRETER: Yes?

NORMAN: I guess you'd call it...

INTERPRETER: Something unparalleled! Something sublime!

NORMAN: A souvenir.

INTERPRETER: *(You're kidding.)* A *souvenir*...?!

NORMAN: Something to take with me.

INTERPRETER: A treasure!

FLORA: Any particular kind of thing?

INTERPRETER: Can the funicular hide the spring?

NORMAN: Excuse me?

INTERPRETER: Accuse me?

FLORA: How much did you want to spend?

INTERPRETER: How much did you want to spend?

NORMAN: It doesn't matter.

INTERPRETER: Let's haggle. I'm loaded!

FLORA: Is this for yourself?

INTERPRETER: Have you a mistress, a wife, a *hareem*?

NORMAN: No, this is for me.

INTERPRETER: Alas, a lad alone in all the world am I.

FLORA: Well…

INTERPRETER: A deep hole in the ground.

FLORA: I think I can help you.

INTERPRETER: Solitary sir, the maiden says, I look in your eyes and I see your soul shining there like a golden carp in an azure pool.

NORMAN: Really…?

INTERPRETER: Really. Now, in this brief moment, in the midst of this mirage called life, here on this tiny square of soil on the whirling earth, I feel the two of us joined by a crystal thread, your soul to my soul to yours.

NORMAN: You do?

INTERPRETER: You do?

FLORA: I do.

INTERPRETER: She does.

NORMAN: You know, I've been up and down this street every day…

INTERPRETER: Day and night I have walked the bazaar…

NORMAN: I sure wish I'd seen this place sooner.

INTERPRETER: Only so that I might see *you.*

FLORA: I've noticed you walking by.

INTERPRETER: How I pined for you to enter as you passed.

NORMAN: You did?

INTERPRETER: She did. She asks your name.

NORMAN: My name is Norman.

INTERPRETER: My name is Sinbad!

NORMAN: I'm here on some business.

INTERPRETER: I am the merchant son of a great prince, exiled from my land.

FLORA: Is that so.

INTERPRETER: Her name is Izthatso.

FLORA: People call me Flora.

INTERPRETER: But people call me Flora.

FLORA: With an "F."

INTERPRETER: With an "F."

NORMAN: I…

INTERPRETER: The organ of vision.

NORMAN: *(Looks at watch.) Darn* it…

INTERPRETER: *(Produces hourglass.) Darn* it…

NORMAN: Y'know, Flora…

INTERPRETER: Y'know, Flora.…

NORMAN: You shop and you shop…

INTERPRETER: We live our brief lives…

NORMAN: …you never seem to find that special thing you're shopping for.

INTERPRETER: …each day awaiting the dawn that will give us purpose, bring us happiness.

FLORA: That's so true.

INTERPRETER: That's so true.

NORMAN: Maybe what I'm looking for is right here.

INTERPRETER: Perhaps my dawn has come.

FLORA: Shhh!

INTERPRETER: Shhh!

FLORA: I thought I heard my father.

INTERPRETER: My father may be listening!

FLORA: It's almost time for his tea.

INTERPRETER: If he sees me talking to you, he'll cut your throat!

NORMAN and INTERPRETER: *(Simultaneous—as they pick up the suitcase together.)* Maybe I should be going…

FLORA: No—

INTERPRETER: No—

FLORA: He won't bother us.

INTERPRETER: Have mercy, good sir!

NORMAN: *(Hefts suitcase.)* I do have a plane to catch.

INTERPRETER: Take my suitcase.

(Flora takes the suitcase from him and sets it down.)

FLORA: There's plenty of time.

INTERPRETER: Keep your voice low.

FLORA: Shhh!

INTERPRETER: Shhh!

FLORA: I thought I heard him calling.

INTERPRETER: He's sharpening the blade.

(We hear the sound of a blade being sharpened.)

NORMAN: *(Cry of surprise.)*

INTERPRETER: *(Cry of surprise.)*

FLORA: He's watching old movies.

INTERPRETER: The old man is *mad.*

FLORA: Anyway, I'm sure I'll have something you'll like.

INTERPRETER: Act as if you're buying something.

NORMAN: What about these things right here?

INTERPRETER: What about these things right here?

FLORA: Maybe an ornament?

166 DAVID IVES

INTERPRETER: Can you conceive, prince, how lonely my life is?

FLORA: Or a stone?

INTERPRETER: It's as hard—and as cheap—as this stone.

FLORA: *(Gestures left.)* I have more in the back.

INTERPRETER: *(Gestures left.)* He keeps me locked in a tiny cell.

NORMAN: No. No.

INTERPRETER: Stay with me.

FLORA: Maybe…

INTERPRETER: What I long for…

FLORA: …a golden ring?

INTERPRETER: …is love. Golden love.

FLORA: If not a ring, maybe a figurine?

INTERPRETER: But my father has betrothed me to a man as ugly as this frog.

FLORA: Interested?

INTERPRETER: Would *you* marry this?

NORMAN: Not really.

INTERPRETER: Not really.

FLORA: I don't know what else I can show you.

INTERPRETER: I have nothing, sir. Nothing! Zip zero nada zilch!

NORMAN: My God, you're beautiful.

INTERPRETER: My God, you're beautiful.

FLORA: Excuse me?

INTERPRETER: Excuse me?

NORMAN: I'm sorry.

INTERPRETER: I'm sorry.

NORMAN: I don't usually say things like that.

INTERPRETER: I know I sound like a jerk.

NORMAN: Sometimes it's something so simple.

INTERPRETER: So complicated are the ways of kismet.

NORMAN: You walk into a shop…

INTERPRETER: I look at you…

NORMAN: …and everything's suddenly different, somehow.

INTERPRETER: …and my heart flutters inside me like a leaf of the perfumed gum tree at the scented bounce of bedspring.

FLORA: Really?

INTERPRETER: Really.

NORMAN: Now in this brief moment…

INTERPRETER: Now in this brief moment…

NORMAN: On this tiny patch of ground on the whirling earth…

INTERPRETER: In the midst of this mirage called life…

NORMAN: I feel us joined by a crystal thread, your soul to my soul to yours.

INTERPRETER: Etcetera, etcetera, etcetera.

FLORA: You do?

INTERPRETER: You do?

NORMAN: I…

INTERPRETER: The organ of vision.

NORMAN: …do.

INTERPRETER: He does.

NORMAN: How can I leave, now that I've seen you, met you, heard you?

INTERPRETER: How can I get on a plane?

NORMAN: Now that fate has brought me to this bazaar?

INTERPRETER: It's so bizarre. But fate has decreed that we must part.

NORMAN: *(Takes out an hourglass.)* O cruel fate! How swiftly flow the sands of time!

INTERPRETER: *(Looks at a watch.)* Shit…!

NORMAN: The stars have decreed we must part.

INTERPRETER: Look, I really gotta go.

NORMAN: *(Kisses Flora's hand.)* But I will return, O my florid queen!

INTERPRETER: Maybe I'll pass this way again sometime.

FLORA: I will wait for you, my Norman prince!

NORMAN: Izthatso.

FLORA: It *is* so! I will be yours and you will be mine and we will be each other's.

INTERPRETER: Maybe I'll have something you like.

NORMAN: Well…

INTERPRETER: A deep hole in the ground.

FLORA: Well…

INTERPRETER: With purest water at the bottom.

NORMAN: Salaam!

INTERPRETER: So long!

FLORA: Salaam!

INTERPRETER: So long! So long! So long!

NORMAN: Open, sesame!

 (Norman whirls out, followed by the Interpreter.)

FLORA: *(Sighs.)* Oh, well.

 (She takes out the featherduster—and it's been changed into a large red rose.) Shazam!

 (She starts to dust the objects with it. Blackout.)

END OF PLAY

Anton in Show Business

A Comedy

by Jane Martin

BIOGRAPHY

Jane Martin, a Kentuckian, first came to national attention for *Talking With*, a collection of monologues premiering in the 1982 Humana Festival. Since its New York premiere at the Manhattan Theatre Club in 1982, *Talking With* has been performed around the world, winning the Best Foreign Play of the Year award in Germany from *Theater Heute* magazine. Ms. Martin's *Keely and Du*, which premiered in the 1993 Humana Festival, was nominated for the Pulitzer Prize in drama and won the American Theatre Critics Association Award for Best New Play in 1994. Two years later, her play *Jack and Jill* premiered in the Humana Festival and won the American Theatre Critics Association Award for Best New Play in 1997. Her other work includes: *Mr. Bundy* (1998 Humana Festival), *Middle-Aged White Guys* (1995 Humana Festival), *Cementville* (1991 Humana Festival), and *Vital Signs* (1990 Humana Festival). Ms. Martin's work has been translated into Spanish, French, German, Dutch, Russian and several other languages.

HUMANA FESTIVAL PRODUCTION

Anton in Show Business premiered at the Humana Festival of New American Plays in March 2000. It was directed by Jon Jory with the following cast:

T-Anne, Andwyneth, Don Blount, and
Gate Manager . . . . Saidah Arrika Ekulona
Lisabette. . . . . Monica Koskey
Casey. . . . . Gretchen Lee Krich
Kate, Ben, Jackey, ... Annette Helde
Ralph, Wikéwitch, Joe Bob . . . . Chick Reid
Holly . . . . Caitlin Miller
Joby. . . . . Stacey Swift

and the following production staff:

Scenic Designer . . . . Paul Owen
Costume Designer . . . . Marcia Dixcy Jory
Lighting Designer . . . . Greg Sullivan
Sound Designer. . . . . Martin R. Desjardins
Properties Designer. . . . . Ben Hohman
Stage Manager . . . . Deb Acquavella
Assistant Stage Manager. . . . . Amber Martin
Dramaturg . . . . Michael Bigelow Dixon
Assistant Dramaturg. . . . . Ginna Hoben
Casting . . . . Laura Richin Casting

CHARACTERS

T-ANNE: The Stage Manager—also playing: Airport Announcer; Andwyneth; Don Blount; Gate Manager

ACTRESS #1: Kate; Ben; Jackey

ACTRESS #2: Ralph, Wikéwitch; Joe Bob

CASEY: 36 years old; tall, lean, plain

LISABETTE: 24 years old; charming and energetic

HOLLY: 30 years old. A drop-dead gorgeous TV star

JOBY: 26 years old. A recent graduate with an M.F.A. in dramaturgy

The play is performed by women in roles of both sexes.

SETTING

Various locations in New York and San Antonio in the present.

There is one intermission.

DIRECTOR'S NOTE

It is possible to use a bare stage and minimal furniture. Many costumes must be rigged for quick change. You need six female scene changers/dressers, who handle the furniture moves and quick changes. Costume changes were full and were not done in sight. All changes were possible with the given text. I strongly suggest that you have the scene changers in several rehearsals prior to tech. Actors continued to play during scene changes. Have fun!

Caitlin Miller, Monica Koskey, Annette Helde,
Saidah Arrika Ekulona, Chick Reid and Gretchen Lee Krich
in *Anton in Show Business*

24th Annual Humana Festival of New American Plays
Actors Theatre of Louisville, 2000
photo by Richard Trigg

Anton in Show Business

A bare stage. In the darkness, rolling thunder, and then suddenly cutting across it, lightning. The flashes illuminate a mysterious cloaked figure. Thunder. A special. The figure speaks.

T-ANNE: The American theatre's in a shitload of trouble. *(Flash, crash.)* That's why the stage is bare, and it's a cast of six, one non-union. *(Flash, crash.)* I'm T-Anne, the stage manager, but I'm also in the play. *(Flash.)* Like a lot of plays you've seen at the end of the 20th century, we all have to play a lot of parts to make the whole thing economically viable… *(Crash.)* …HOMAGE TO THORNTON WILDER. *(Flash, crash. She drops the cloak. She wears blue jeans, a T-shirt, many keys at her belt.)* The date is *(date)*, 2000, just before noon. Well, I'll show you a little bit about how our profession is laid out. Up around here are the Broadway theatres, sort of between 42nd and 52nd Street, we like to think that's the heart of everything. City of New York, State of New York, United States of America, the world, the galaxy, the universe. Down over here is Greenwich Village, around there we do off-Broadway, that's good too. Now Tribeca, Soho, Lower East Side, we call that the "downtown scene," off-off stuff. An incredibly colorful group of people who despise realism and have all won the Obie Award…that's good too. Beyond that, radiating out in all directions for thousands of miles is something called "regional theatre," which I understand once showed a lot of promise but has since degenerated into dying medieval fiefdoms and arrogant baronies producing small-cast comedies, cabaret musicals, mean-spirited new plays and the occasional deconstructed classic, which everybody hates. After that, moving west, we reach the burning, uninhabitable desert and its militias who don't go to plays, and beyond that, singing a siren call, the twin evil kingdoms of Flick and Tube, the bourne from which no traveler returns. Now back to New York, thank God. Let's see, the Empire State Building, the Statue of

Liberty and the Actors' Equity offices…that's our union. They make sure no more than 80% of our membership is out of work on any given day. And over there…yes, right over there is where we worship, yes sir, *The New York Times*. Well, that's about it. Now, with a short subway ride we get to one of the audition studios where producers and theatres come to find actors for their plays. Here's the front door, elevator up to the fifth floor, Studio C, where the San Antonio, Texas Actors Express has come to the big city to cast *The Three Sisters* by Anton Chekhov. He's Russian. At noon, you can always hear the actors doing their vocal warm-ups.

(Vocal warm-ups can be heard.)

Aya—there they are. Not much happens before noon. Theatre folks sleep late. So, another day's begun. There's Lisabette Cartwright walking into Studio C. She graduated from the SMU (*Southern Methodist*) drama department and began teaching third grade. Then she was invited all the way to New York for an audition because the producer once had her appendix removed by one of her uncles. Lisabette's really excited, and her mom, who is at this moment canning okra, is too. Over there is Casey Mulgraw, the one dressed in the skirt/pants, skirt/pants thing, a lot of people call her the Queen of off-off Broadway. She's a little hung over because she just celebrated the opening of her 200th play without ever having been paid a salary. She also has a yeast infection that is really pissing her off. In our town, we like to know the facts about everybody.

(NOTE: All scene and costume changes are done by six female "changers," dressed in a variety of contemporary styles, but all in black. T-Anne, the stage manager, moves to a small out-of-the-way table where she sits and follows the script. Three folding chairs are placed to create the waiting room of Studio C. Casey, a woman of 36, waits. Lisabette, 24, enters. She has a rolling suitcase.)

LISABETTE: Hi. *(Casey nods.)* Is this the Studio C waiting room for Actors Express? *(Casey nods.)* Three Sisters audition? *(Casey nods.)* Oh, my heavens, it's so humid! I feel like I'm oiled up for the beach or something. I surely admire your fortitude in wearing both skirt and pants. Bet you're auditioning for Olga, huh?

CASEY: Why? Because Olga is older and homely and a spinster and has no life of her own and thus has assumed the role of caregiver to her brother and it's usually thought to be the least interesting acting role of the *The Three Sisters*. Would that be it?

LISABETTE: Well, no, I…

CASEY: It's what you meant.

LISABETTE: I think I'll just start over. *(She does.)* Hi.

CASEY: Hi.

LISABETTE: I'm Lisabette Cartwright, from La Vernia, Texas. Graduated SMU but then I taught third grade for two years, bein' scared of an actor's life, and Maple Elementary loved me and wants me back anytime, but in a dream the Lord himself reaffirmed my calling so I made my comeback in *Fiddler on the Roof* but this is my first New York audition and I'm so jumpy my breasts bob even when I walk real slow. What's your name?

CASEY: Casey Mulgraw, one of my breasts had to be surgically removed because of a malignancy and I seem to be in remission but who knows how long that will last.

LISABETTE: Oh, my G-o-o-d-d-d!

CASEY: Want to do one more take?

LISABETTE: No, I would like you to forgive me for bein' such a dipshit, pardon the language, Jesus. I'm real sorry for your troubles and it looks to me like they did a real good match.

CASEY: *(Chuckles.)* And yes, I'm reading for Olga for the obvious reasons.

LISABETTE: Really, I think Olga is the most spiritual of all the sisters.

CASEY: Good try. You don't have a smoke by any chance?

LISABETTE: Ummmm, I don't.

CASEY: Cough drop?

LISABETTE: Beef jerky.

CASEY: No thanks.

LISABETTE: I'm auditioning for Masha.

CASEY: The dark, passionate, amoral poetess. I feel dark; men call me passionate; I'm definitely amoral, and I've actually had several poems published but they never, never, never let me read for that part.

LISABETTE: Because you're a little plain?

CASEY: Thank you for speaking the unspeakable.

LISABETTE: I did it again, huh? I'm, oh my, very nervous but that's just no excuse. I would like to say I'm in way over my head and could I have a hug?

CASEY: *(Not unkindly.)* If it's absolutely necessary.

(They hug. The stage manager enters to speak to the actors. A rolling door might divide the spaces. Behind her, a table with three chairs is set up as the audition room. Ralph Brightly, an English director, and Kate, the producer, are at the table. In a third chair, to the side, sits Holly Seabé, a TV goddess who is pre-cast as Irina and is helping audition.)

STAGE MANAGER: Ms. Todoravskia is ready to see you both.

CASEY: Both?

STAGE MANAGER: Both. Hustle it up, we're running behind.

LISABETTE: *(Still in the anteroom. To Casey.)* Do they usually see actors in groups?

CASEY: No. And we're not a group.

(Casey and Lisabette enter the audition room.)

KATE: *(Rising.)* Hi. I am Katrina Todoravskia, Producing Director of Actors Express. And you are?

LISABETTE: Me?

KATE: You.

LISABETTE: I'm sorry, I forgot the question.

CASEY: Your name.

LISABETTE: Oh, Lisabette Cartwright.

(Kate kisses Lisabette's hand extended for a shake.)

KATE: You are devastatingly beautiful. *(Turns to Casey.)* And I gather you're here to audition for Olga?

CASEY: How'd you guess?

KATE: You look like an Olga.

CASEY: Thanks.

KATE: This is the play's director, Ralph Brightly; he runs the Toads Hall Rep in London.

RALPH: *(Shaking hands.)* Well, a stone's throw outside, really. *(Shakes Lisabette's hand.)* Charmed. *(Shakes Casey's hand.)* Pleased.

KATE: *(Gesturing toward Holly.)* And this is…

LISABETTE: Oh my G-o-o-d-d, you're Holly Seabé. I can't believe it! Holly Seabé. I love your TV show! Your character is so kooky and glamorous. You have such great timing. I've learned practically everything I know about foreplay from that show. You are so liberated!

HOLLY: Thanks.

LISABETTE: Oh my God, pardon me Jesus, are you going to be in the play?

HOLLY: Irina.

LISABETTE: *(Clapping her hands.)* She's going to be in the play. This is way cool! *(To Casey.)* Isn't that cool?

CASEY: *(Smiling, but a bit reserved.)* Yes, cool.

HOLLY: Thanks.

LISABETTE: I am so stoked!

RALPH: Yes, well, off we go then. *Three Sisters*, as you know, by Anton

Pavlovitch himself. I'll just drop some breadcrumbs along the path before we hear you…

KATE: Running 40 minutes behind.

RALPH: Right. Straight along. Give you the gist in five words. Funny, funny, funny, funny, tragic.

CASEY: We're referring to *Three Sisters?*

RALPH: *The Three Sisters,* yes.

CASEY: Funny, funny, funny, funny, tragic?

RALPH: *Funny,* funny, funny, *funny,* tragic.

CASEY: Okay, I can do that.

LISABETTE: Do what?

CASEY: Show him that in our auditions.

LISABETTE: Gee, I didn't think it was funny.

RALPH: Precisely, that's to be our little revelation.

KATE: Forty minutes late.

RALPH: Right then, on we go.

(*A young woman in the audience rises and says:*)

JOBY: Excuse me.

RALPH: Let's get cracking.

JOBY: Excuse me.

(*The actors glance up, confused. The "director" tries to go on.*)

RALPH: It's Chekhov, don't you see, so we're certainly not ready to do text.

JOBY: (*From the audience.*) Excuse me.

(*The actors stop. They look to Kate.*)

KATE: Yes?

JOBY: Is the director…ummm…

RALPH: (*Supplying the character name.*) Ralph.

JOBY: Right, Ralph. Is it supposed to be a man played by a woman?

KATE: Yes. (*To Ralph.*) Go on.

JOBY: How come?

RALPH: You mean why am I playing a man?

JOBY: I mean what's the point?

RALPH: Could you possibly sit down and let us act?

KATE: Wait. (*To Joby.*) Hi.

JOBY: Hi.

KATE: What's your name?

JOBY: Joby. But I…

KATE: Joby, we want to thank you for coming to the theatre; we need young audiences.

RALPH: But…

KATE: Shhhh. Now you'll understand this as a woman, Joby…

RALPH: Could she please…

(Kate silences Ralph with a look.)

KATE: Eighty percent of the roles in the American theatre are played by men, and 90% of the directors are men. The point of having a male director played by a woman is to redress the former and satirize the latter. How's that?

JOBY: *(After a brief pause.)* Okay.

(She sits down. Kate nods at Ralph.)

RALPH: Right. Onward and upward, eh? *(He looks at Casey.)* What I'd like you to do, sweetie, is use only the word "tiddlypee" as text… *(He looks at Lisabette.)* And you, dear, will say only "tiddlypoo." With these words, we will now play the scene where Masha tells Olga she's leaving her husband Kulygin and leaving town with the soldier Vershinin.

CASEY: But there is no such scene.

RALPH: Yes, precisely.

CASEY: So why?

RALPH: *(Sweetly.)* You don't wish to audition?

CASEY: That's the answer to "why?"

RALPH: Look, dear…

(Lisabette, trying to circumvent the oncoming conflict, goes into the improvisation.)

LISABETTE: *(You wished to see me?)* Tiddlypoo, tiddlypoo?

CASEY: *(Is it true you and Vershinin are in love?)* Tiddlypee, tiddlypee, tiddlypee…tiddlypee?

LISABETTE: *(I am leaving Kulygin and going away with Vershinin.)* Tiddlypoo, tiddlypoo…tiddlypoo…tiddlypoo, tiddlypoo, tiddlypoo, tiddlypoo.

CASEY: *(If you go, what will happen to me?)* Tiddlypee…tiddlypee, tiddlypee, tiddlypee?

LISABETTE: *(You'll be fine.)* Tiddlypoo, tiddlypoo.

CASEY: *(To Ralph.)* How am I supposed to know what she's saying?

RALPH: Well, that would be the heart of the audition, wouldn't it?

(Casey tries once more.)

CASEY: *(If you go, we'll be left with Natasha!)* Tiddlypee, tiddlypee…tiddlypee, tiddlypee. *(She stops.)* Look, this is ridiculous.

RALPH: *(Coolly.)* Really?

CASEY: Well, yes, really. Can't we just do a scene using the script? I mean that would be sensible, right?

RALPH: Perhaps to an American actress, dear.

CASEY: *(Not happy.)* Ummmmmm…

LISABETTE: Oh, but this is fun. Don't you think it's fun? It's kind of interesting.

CASEY: *(Slow burn.)* American actress.

LISABETTE: *(Feeling the tension.)* Just really, really, really, really fun!

CASEY: *(Burning.)* You know, Ralph…dear…you Brits are arrogant, pompous, chauvinistic, smug, insufferable boors who take jobs from American actors and directors because of the toadying of the American press and the Anglophile American rich, and I've seen Chekhov done in London that really smelled up the place with its stiff-upper-lip, over practical, no-self-pity-or-despair-here-darling style that has nothing, nothing to do with Russian passion or spiritual darkness, so…

JOBY: Excuse me.

CASEY: *(Still on the emotional high.)* What?! What do you want?

KATE: Easy.

JOBY: Isn't this all just a little self-referential?

KATE: I'm sorry, Joby, but we are trying to perform a play and…

JOBY: I mean it's all just about the theatre. Isn't that a little precious?

KATE: Why?

JOBY: Well, theatre people talking about theatre.

KATE As opposed to theatre people talking about the international monetary fund or the cloning of sheep?

JOBY: Well, is theatre culturally important enough to be the subject of a play?

RALPH: Nice of you to buy a ticket.

JOBY: Actually, they're comps.

RALPH: Ah.

JOBY: I'd think your only hope is to work on a deeply personal and profoundly emotional level.

CASEY: Well, the thing about the Brits is very emotional.

RALPH: And plays aren't ordinarily deeply personal until after the exposition.

JOBY: Oh.

CASEY: Later on, the play takes hold, and there is devastating loss and a lot of really profound metaphors that will knock your socks off. I mean, knock your socks off!

JOBY: Oh.

CASEY: Okay?

JOBY: *(A brief pause.)* Fine.
　　　(She sits down.)

CASEY: *(Going back,)* ...with its stiff-upper-lip, over-practical, no-self-pity-or-despair-here-darling style that has nothing, nothing to do with Russian passion or spiritual darkness. So don't give me that American actress crap! *(A tense moment.)*

RALPH: Right. Nicely done. I think I've seen more than enough. Thanks ever so for coming in.

LISABETTE: We're finished?

RALPH: Lovely work, sweetie. *(Turning to Casey, smiling.)* And I quite agree with you, dear, when Americans do Chekhov, it's just awash in self-pity. *(Casey gives him the finger and stalks out.)*

LISABETTE: Well, anyway, this was my first professional audition, and it was really a lot of fun, and I want to thank you for calling me in and I really hope to work for you someday and... *(She begins to cry.)* ...and I'm sorry I'm crying. I didn't mean to cry, and I've never even been to London but...she's right, you're a real jerk.
(She runs out, leaving Ralph, Kate and Holly alone.)

RALPH: *(Ironically.)* Well, that was a breath of fresh air.

KATE: Ralph, I want to apologize to you as an American...

RALPH: No, no...

KATE: I've seen hundreds, thousands of auditions, and I never...

RALPH: No need, sweetie...

KATE: I mean, who do they think they are?

RALPH: Made their beds, haven't they? Fat chance they'll be getting any work from this old British fairy.
(Kate laughs appreciatively.)

HOLLY: I liked them. *(They turn to look at her.)* I've been treated like dirt in situations like this, but now I'm rich and famous and you need me so you're sort of shit out of luck, huh? So here's the deal: I liked them and I'm bored with auditions so they're over and those two are in our play.

RALPH: Miss Seabé, they do not have the requisite talent.

HOLLY: Well, neither do I so maybe nobody will notice. *(She starts to exit.)* One thing, though. The little sweet one from Texas should play Irina, and I'll play Masha. Oh, and the Olga...well, she's Olga. Tiddlypee, tiddlypoo.

RALPH: So, Kate, love, I gather that's the horse that pulls our custard wagon, eh?

KATE: Well...

RALPH: Not to worry. In the kingdom of the barbarians, shit tastes like veal.
(Lights change. Furniture is removed as Casey and Lisabette move into two specials, where they talk to their mothers on the "phone.")

LISABETTE: Ma? It's me, Lisabette…

CASEY: Mother, okay, don't go ballistic…

LISABETTE: I got it! I got it! I got it! I got the part!

CASEY: Yes, I know I'm 36 years old, and I still have $40,000 in student loans…

LISABETTE: Ma, Ma, wait, no, there's more…

CASEY: Yes, I would have to leave my day job…

LISABETTE: I'm gonna act with a TV star!

CASEY: Okay, the real deal…

LISABETTE: Holly Seabé! Yes! Me and Holly Seabé; can you believe it?

CASEY: Yes, it's kind of a crappy part; it's some hick town in Texas; the salary is like pesos; I'll lose my job; you won't have anybody to abuse but, lest we forget here, I'm supposed to be an actress!

LISABETTE: Ma, it's Chekhov!

CASEY: Mother…

LISABETTE: He's a Russian.

CASEY: Mother…

LISABETTE: No, it's beautiful and wise and sad, and I get to be a real professional!

CASEY: Screw you! Mother!

LISABETTE: Love you, Ma!

CASEY: *(Hanging up.)* Damnit!

LISABETTE: *(Hanging up.)* Yes!

(Two connected plane seats are brought on. Lisabette and Casey move to sit in them. We hear an airport announcement.)

GATE ANNOUNCER: Flight number 270 to San Antonio, Texas, gate 27B, boarding is now complete. Flight number 270. All passengers…

CASEY: My dad's great. I worked weekends for a thousand years in his hardware store.

LISABETTE: You are kidding!

CASEY: What kidding?

LISABETTE: My dad has a hardware store.

CASEY: Yeah?

LISABETTE: You sorted screws?

CASEY: Oh yeah. *(They smile.)* Your dad want you to run it?

LISABETTE: Me? No. He sold it. He works in a community center.

CASEY: Well, my dad wants me. I dream I take it over and I wake up, stapled to 3/4 inch plywood, screaming. Okay, the hardware connection.

LISABETTE: You're not married, right?

CASEY: I'm not married, right. You?

LISABETTE: I can't abide sex.

CASEY: Oh.

LISABETTE: Well, temporarily. I've kinda had some bad luck.

CASEY: Doesn't hold me back.

LISABETTE: I was kinda doin' it with my high school boyfriend in the back of his car, an' we were hit from behind by a drunk in a pickup.

CASEY: Ouch.

LISABETTE: They said they'd never seen that kind of whiplash.

CASEY: Sorry.

LISABETTE: Meanwhile, back at school I was kind of bein' forced into an affair by my history teacher an' just after that I was sort of halfway raped by a plumber.

CASEY: *(Horrified.)* Jesus.

LISABETTE: No, it wasn't too bad really. I had to deal, y'know? The only bad part was for three years I couldn't touch a man, even like a handshake, without throwing up. Projectile vomiting, so there were some awkward moments at parties.

CASEY: You're kidding me, right?

LISABETTE: No, really, it wasn't so bad. I'm over it, except really, really occasionally when I first meet people. How about your relationships?

CASEY: A lot of casual sex.

LISABETTE: Really.

CASEY: A lot. Always with members of the cast. And I've done 200 plays off-off.

LISABETTE: Wow.

CASEY: Outside of rehearsal, I'm actually a virgin.

LISABETTE: Wow.

CASEY: Of course, I'm always in rehearsal.

LISABETTE: Oh, I really respect that. I'm a virgin too. Except for being harassed, whiplashed, and on New Year's Eve.

(Holly enters from first class.)

CASEY: Hi.

LISABETTE: Oh my God.

HOLLY: I saw you guys when you came through first class.

LISABETTE: We walked right by you!?

HOLLY: No problem. I was enjoying some brain surgeon hitting on me.

LISABETTE: Excuse me, but...shoot...I just want to say that when Kate, the producer person, made me the offer...well...she said you had put in a word for us…me and Casey…Casey and I…God, I am such a hick, pardon me Jesus, anyway…thank you, thank you, thank you!

CASEY: It was really nice.

HOLLY: Well, hey, yeah I did, thanks but, you know, I was like nobody once too. Really down on the food chain like you guys…ummm…I won't even tell you the stuff I went through. Well, okay, the easy stuff was being told I had no talent like that director piranha said about you, right? And my deal was that talent isn't the point here…I mean, we're going to whatever Texas or wherever. Like, nobody who is anybody will see us or care. Maybe excepting my manager who has time for one client, me, and who would not care diddly dick if you guys had talent or not. *(A brief awkwardness.)* But the point is…you didn't think I meant you had no talent, did you?

CASEY: No, no.

LISABETTE: No, no.

HOLLY: Because you can understand I have no way of knowing that. I mean… tiddlypee, tiddlypoo.

LISABETTE: Right.

CASEY: Right.

HOLLY: My point is you guys were disrespected and he had to pay.

CASEY: You mean…

HOLLY: I mean, once they said you had no talent, I had to see you were hired.

LISABETTE: Wow.

HOLLY: Because I had that pulled on me, and now that will not happen in my presence. Like I'm the respect police.

CASEY: Thanks.

HOLLY: No problem. So I just wanted to shed a little light.

LISABETTE: That is really so nice.

CASEY: Just think, all of us have been told we have no talent.

HOLLY: Exactly!

CASEY: Well, that's something to build on.

HOLLY: Yeah, that's the other thing. We have to stick together down there in…

CASEY: Texas.

LISABETTE: Oh absolutely.

HOLLY: Because I have this intuition it's going to be like combat, but we stick together, we make them pay.

LISABETTE: Like we were three sisters.

HOLLY: That is so sweet and so right. That like zaps my guts.

CASEY: There's an empty seat.

HOLLY: Nah, I got to go back, I don't eat pretzels.

LISABETTE: We're talking about guys.

HOLLY: Them I eat. See you later.

(Holly leaves. Three folding chairs are set, facing two other chairs for the next scene. Please remember the changes are cinematic. We never stop or take the lights out for a change.)

T-ANNE: Please place your seats and tray tables in an upright position; we are beginning our descent into San Antonio.

(We are now in the rehearsal room on the first day. Kate, Casey, Holly, Lisabette and the new director, an African-American woman named Andwyneth Wyoré.)

KATE: *(Addressing them.)* Actors Express. Get it? Express? We are a serious the-atre. We are unique. What is our artistic policy? Well, I can state that policy clearly. We live these ideas. At Actors Express, we call them the Seven Virtues. Number one, we do plays that... *(She makes a complex gesture.)* Two: our style is surgically defined as... *(A series of sounds.)* And only that. Fourthly, multi-cultural new works from the classical repertoire that say to the audience... *(An even more complex gesture.)* So that, in summation, or seventh, we can say... *(She stares at the ceiling, thinking.)* and we say that with no fear of being misunderstood. Oh, I know, this policy makes us controversial. We offend, we pique, we challenge while at the same time bringing together, healing, and making our community one. In a nutshell. This unique mission has made us essential to San Antonio, not because...is there something out the window?

CASEY: Sorry.

KATE: Not because I have the best education money can buy...

LISABETTE: Wow.

KATE: Stanford, Harvard, Yale, but because... *(Holly is doctoring her lipstick.)* Holly, if you give this a chance, I think you'll find it's crucial to our work.

HOLLY: Stanford, Harvard, Yale...

KATE: Precisely.

HOLLY: *(Pointing at herself.)* Biddyup High, Biddyup, Nebraska.

KATE: But because...hear this...contemporary relevance.

CASEY: Contemporary relevance.

KATE: Contemporary relevance.

CASEY: Yes.

KATE: Our raison d'être! Does anyone find what I said moving? *(Lisabette raises her hand.)* Because I am moved, and it is central to our aesthetic.

(Lisabette applauds.) Now I wanted to meet with you, our three sisters, before the rest of our cast arrived, to bond as sisters and to achieve a... It's now my pleasure to introduce our director, Andwyneth Wyoré, Artistic Director of San Antonio's Black Rage Ensemble. We're involved in an exciting cultural exchange with Black Rage.

HOLLY: Doesn't that happen between countries?

KATE: Excuse me?

HOLLY: Cultural exchange?

ANDWYNETH: *(Chuckling.)* You got that right, girl.

KATE: Interestingly enough, Andwyneth also went to Stanford, Harvard, and Yale.

ANDWYNETH: 'Course I went free.

CASEY: What happened to the Brit?

KATE: Well, there were...

KATE/ANDWYNETH/HOLLY: Artistic differences.

ANDWYNETH: Uh-huh.

KATE: And I came to feel a sister...

ANDWYNETH: Girl, I'm not your sister. My momma see you, she faint, girl. She smack my daddy with an iron skillet! Huh-uh, baby, we got a little mutual use goin'. How about that? Down here in San Antonio you get some black people, some white people in the same room, there's always some foundation goes orgasmic. *(Cries deep in the act of sex.)* Multicultural! Multicultural! Yes! Yes!! Multicultural!! *(Back to her own voice.)* Pay a little rent, right? Suck a little green. Hey, I never did no white play, dig? Y'all a mystery to me, but I tell you one thing on Brother Chekhov, he just talk, talk, talk, talk, talk! Lord have mercy!

KATE: Well yes, but...

ANDWYNETH: Whine, whine, whine. Man, he got the self-pity diarrhea! Gushin' it out all over! Cut all that shit, X it out! Get down on the race question, down on the poverty question, get down on abuse of power, baby! No more, "Whine and dine with Brother Chekhov." Huh-uh. We gonna heat this sucker up! No script, huh-uh. I don't do script. Hell with that! What I see is a little white sisters thing, an' a black peasants thing. Little dance drama thing, little street corner doo-wap. *(Holly raises hand.)* S'up, girl?

HOLLY: I'm doing the script.

ANDWYNETH: You didn't follow the conversation?

HOLLY: Yeah, I can follow it, but I'm not doing that.

ANDWYNETH: Who the hell are you, girl?

HOLLY: You watch TV?

ANDWYNETH: Hell no, colored people all live in a cave.

HOLLY: I'm a big TV star.

ANDWYNETH: Well girl, you just pat yourself right on the back.

HOLLY: They begged me to come down here to wherever Texas to do a classic style play. I don't give a shit about the race question or the poverty question. I don't have those problems. I got the film problem. I need to do film. No film, no respect. It's kind of like the race problem only in show business.

ANDWYNETH: You crazy, huh?

HOLLY: Yeah. So the rap is, you do TV you can't act. So my manager says to go backdoor. Get a little respect. Chekhov, Shakespeare, that stuff gives you shine. So like then you're a classical actress with fabulous breasts, and you can segue into sci-fi, action, cop-schlock, meet-cute or any genre.

ANDWYNETH: Let's cut to the bottom line, sister.

HOLLY: I'm saying every syllable Chekhov wrote, slow and clear.

ANDWYNETH: See, you are so far from my trip I can't even find you on the map.

HOLLY: Ms. Wyoré, the real difference between the two of us isn't what you think.

ANDWYNETH: Well, little thing, you bring it on.

HOLLY: The real difference is, you're fired.

(Andwyneth looks at Kate.)

KATE: *(At a loss.)* Well…

HOLLY: Trust me.

ANDWYNETH: You are one straight-up, no kiddin' around, in-your-face, don't-misunderstand-me, bitch.

HOLLY: Sometimes, things just don't…work out.

ANDWYNETH: *(Focusing on Kate.)* What are you, invisible?

KATE: Ummmmm…

ANDWYNETH: She's the deal, or you're the deal?

(Holly also focuses on Kate.)

KATE: *(Finally, to Andwyneth.)* She's the deal.

ANDWYNETH: You get me down here, whip up a little money on my color, cast a buncha white girls an' then blow me off 'cause this prime-time toots shows up? *(To Kate.)* I'm gonna pin "racist" to your ass, Momma. They gonna burn you in the public square to get right with my people. There won't be nothin' left of you but little snowy white ashes, dig? You an' Chekhov is both toast!

(She exits.)

KATE: Ummm…if you'll excuse me.

(She exits to talk to Andwyneth. The sisters are silent for a moment.)

CASEY: Anyone want some Skittles?

LISABETTE: You just fired the director in front of the producer without asking.

HOLLY: I am saying the lines.

CASEY: She's saying the lines.

HOLLY: Directors are a very gray area for me. It has been my experience that they actually like to be fired because they suffer from severe performance anxiety. They have these pushy little egos but hardly any usable information, which makes them very sad and time-consuming. I wouldn't worry because after you fire them, they usually find successful careers on cruise ships where they are completely harmless.

LISABETTE: But to do that, is that ethical?

HOLLY: Lisabette, I like you. I do. You seem like a very nice person. I'm not a very nice person, but I can still appreciate one when I see her.

LISABETTE: Thanks.

HOLLY: In college plays, community stuff, arty nowheresville professional gigs like this, there is probably something called ethics, but up where the eagles fly and the wolves run, up where American presidents screw the actresses, there is only power. The ethics thing is a little foggy. Power, on the other hand, is clear, it's clear, it's understood. For a very short time, Lisabette, here in wherever-it-is Texas, you will fly with an eagle. Say whoosh.

LISABETTE: Whoosh.

HOLLY: Enjoy.

(At this moment, Ben Shipwright, a craggy actor, enters. He is playing Vershinin.)

BEN: Hello, ladies.

LISABETTE: Hi.

CASEY: Hi.

HOLLY: Hi.

BEN: Ben Shipwright. Gonna play Vershinin.

CASEY: Olga, the boring sister.

LISABETTE: Masha. But I can't shake your hand right now. I'll explain later.

HOLLY: Masha.

LISABETTE: You're playing Masha?

HOLLY: We'll talk. Where are you from, Ben?

BEN: Right around here. I do some acting but I actually make my living singing country.

LISABETTE: Oh my God, you're Ben Shipwright?

BEN: Yeah.

LISABETTE: Oh my God, I love your records!

HOLLY: You record?

BEN: Little bit.

LISABETTE: Little bit? This week he has two singles in Top 50 Country!

HOLLY: Really?

CASEY: Mazeltov.

BEN: *(To Holly and Casey.)* You girls from New York?

CASEY: Yeah.

HOLLY: L.A.

BEN: *(To Lisabette.)* Now I know you're a home girl.

LISABETTE: How do you know?

BEN: Well, you talk San Antonio and you listen to a bunch of no-good pickers like me.

HOLLY: Ben?

BEN: Yes ma'am.

HOLLY: This relationship thing that goes down between Masha and Vershinin? We probably should get together and talk that out.

BEN: Be my pleasure. I'll let y'all get settled.

(He starts to exit.)

HOLLY: Dinner?

BEN: I'm sorry, you speakin' to me?

HOLLY: I was speaking to you.

BEN: Well…ummm…I don't believe I caught your name.

HOLLY: Holly Seabé.

BEN: Well, Miss Seabé, I got me a couple of kids want me to barbecue some ribs tonight.

(Starts to exit.)

HOLLY: Drink later?

BEN: Well, ummm, no ma'am. No ma'am, I can't. No offense intended.

HOLLY: *(Smiling, but not pleased.)* Really?

BEN: No ma'am, I better not. My wife…

HOLLY: How old are your kids?

BEN: Four and seven. Seven and a half.

HOLLY: Won't they be asleep?

BEN: *(They regard each other.)* Just no-can-do, ma'am. *(Shakes her hand.)* Real pleased to meet you. Lookin' forward to rehearsal. Catch y'all later.

(He exits.)

LISABETTE: I don't think he knew who you were! Can you believe that? I mean, you are on the cover of TV Guide!

HOLLY: I'll have to buy him a copy.

LISABETTE: But, am I right or am I wrong, he is really cute!

CASEY: My take is if you... *(She indicates Holly.)* ...come on to a guy, looking the way you do, and he stiffs you while talking about his kids, he is *really* unavailable.

HOLLY: If I come on to a guy...and I'm not saying I did...that guy can kiss his previous life goodbye for as long as I find said guy entertaining. And on this I would be willing to wager some fairly serious money.

CASEY: I think serious money to me and serious money to you could be seriously different.

LISABETTE: But what about his wife and kids?

HOLLY and CASEY: Shhh.

HOLLY: Okay, forget the money thing. We'll bet hair. Loser shaves her head.

LISABETTE: Wow.

CASEY: You can't afford to shave your head.

HOLLY: I won't have to.

CASEY: The guy's straight from Norman Rockwell.

HOLLY: I could screw anybody Norman Rockwell ever drew.

LISABETTE: This is so yeasty!

CASEY: Let's get it on.

(She holds out her hand. Holly shakes it.)

HOLLY: He's going down.

LISABETTE: You aren't Baptist, huh?

HOLLY: Hey, Lisabette?

LISABETTE: Uh-huh?

HOLLY: I'm going to play Masha because it's the best part, and the most powerful person plays the best part. That's one of Hollywood's ten commandments. You'll play Irina, because I say so, but also because she's the youngest and you're the youngest and you would be really good doing her because you have yet to become a completely calcified diva.

LISABETTE: *(Not at all upset.)* Okay.

HOLLY: Everything's copasetic. Hey, let's go to the apartment hotel and get settled in fleabag hell and then find some cowboy dive with pine paneling and get unbelievably plotzed before tomorrow's first rehearsal, because I need to be hung over to face whatever director she digs up next.

(A scene change starts. Eventually, there will be two single beds, two chairs and a rolling door in place. This scene is played during the change.)

JOBY: *(From the audience.)* Excuse me. *(Scene change continues.)* Excuse me.

T-ANNE: What?

JOBY: Well, I…didn't you…

T-ANNE: Hey, spit it out; I'm busy.

JOBY: Well, didn't you consider that role offensive?

T-ANNE: Did you notice we're doing a scene change?

JOBY: Golly, as a person of color…

T-ANNE: You're a person of color?

JOBY: No, you are.

T-ANNE: Ooooo, I hate it when I forget.

JOBY: But, wasn't that… *(Whispers.)* …stereotyped behavior?

T-ANNE: *(Again stopping her work.)* Listen, I have to…all right, okay…listen, Babyface, I would like to do something, almost anything, where nice white people like you didn't feel like they had to defend me. Particularly… *(Whispers back.)* …in the middle of a scene change. *(Goes back to work.)*

JOBY: But it satirizes your political…

T-ANNE: Got to go.

JOBY: But, aren't you…

T-ANNE: No, I'm not. Want to know why?

JOBY: Oh, I do.

T-ANNE: 'Cause if I didn't do the plays that offended my color or politics or sex or religion or taste, I'd be shit out of work. Lights!
(She exits. The scene light snaps on. Joby is still standing.)

CASEY: *(To Joby, not unkindly.)* Sit down, Joby. *(Starting the scene.)* I am leveled by that last drink. I am, as my beloved father would say, schnockered. *(Sings.)* Tell me I can't sing Karaoke?

HOLLY: You can't sing Karaoke.

LISABETTE: This is so amazing, it's like a pajama party.

HOLLY: *(Patting her knee.)* It is a pajama party.

LISABETTE: I mean, here I am, just out of drama school, and I am completely drunk, talking with real actors in a real way, including a great actress of the stage and a great actress from TV, and it just makes me want to cry.

HOLLY: Don't cry. Where did the vodka go?

LISABETTE: Holly, can I ask you a question?

HOLLY: Here it is. *(Pours herself another drink.)*

LISABETTE: It's something about acting.

HOLLY: I don't know anything about acting.

LISABETTE: Okay then, have you had breast implants?

HOLLY: Yes.

LISABETTE: Yes?!

HOLLY: Yes.

CASEY: That actually makes me feel better.

HOLLY: I have had seventeen separate surgical procedures to make me the completely natural beauty you see before you. They have even reshaped my toes because I do a lot of swimsuit.

LISABETTE: Those are artificial toes?

HOLLY: They are not artificial, they have been slimmed.

CASEY: How much?

HOLLY: Altogether?

CASEY: For the toes?

HOLLY: Seventeen thousand dollars.

LISABETTE: Wow.

CASEY: How much would it take to make me beautiful?

HOLLY: You're serious?

CASEY: Yeah.

HOLLY: Take off the sweatshirt.

(She does.)

LISABETTE: But beauty is subjective.

HOLLY: Not in Hollywood. Stand up and turn around. Over here. Over here, over here. *(Casey does.)* Look at the ceiling. *(She does.)* Hold your arms out like wings. Look left. Look right. Okay. I could be off 10, even 15% here depending on bone and muscle structure, but my estimate would be $600,000.

CASEY: Go ahead, flatter me.

HOLLY: Oh, there are divas who have paid more, and the kicker is even then there's no guarantee the camera loves you.

LISABETTE: Oh my God.

HOLLY and CASEY: Pardon me Jesus.

CASEY: I'm giving it one more year.

(Refreshes her drink.)

LISABETTE: Give what?

CASEY: This. I don't have to put up with this hellish life. I have other skills.

HOLLY: Let me guess...

CASEY: For six years I worked in a slaughterhouse.

LISABETTE: No.

CASEY: Yeah.

LISABETTE: No way. You worked in your dad's hardware store.

CASEY: That was earlier. Where's the chocolates?

HOLLY: *(Handing her the box.)* There's only creams left.

CASEY: I took the slaughterhouse job because it paid more than waitressing, and I could cut the pigs' throats at night, which left my days free to audition.

HOLLY: Was there a lot of blood?

CASEY: Gouts.

HOLLY: I hate blood.

LISABETTE: I faint. I fainted the first time I had my period.

CASEY: I mean, look at us. Holly's the Frankenstein monster. You teach third grade. I support myself as a murderess from midnight to dawn so I can do godawful plays for free in black box theatres built into linen closets in welfare hotels. This is a career in the arts in America.

LISABETTE: But now we get to do Chekhov! It's like lacework. It's beautiful and delicate and demands everything. Everything! It's unbearably sweet and sad and painful, just like our lives.

HOLLY: Don't you love her.

CASEY: Plus I get a paycheck so my mother will think acting is actually a job.

LISABETTE: No, but it's Chekhov!

CASEY: As long as it pays the bills.

LISABETTE: That's so cynical.

CASEY: Lisabette, sweetie, I'm not cynical. Look at me. I'm like a beating heart you can hold in your hand. I just happen to live in a country where they give people who do what I do endless shit.

LISABETTE: But why can't it be beautiful? I want it to be beautiful.

CASEY: Lisabette, you're drunk.

LISABETTE: I am, I'm really drunk. But the three of us are so sad, right? I mean, I'm sad because I'm hopelessly naïve and have absolutely no idea what will become of me, like I'm running down the railway tracks and the train is coming. *(To Casey.)* And you're sad because you're hoping against hope when you really probably know there is no hope. *(To Holly.)* And you're sad because…why are you sad, I forget?

HOLLY: I am sad because that beautiful country singer dissed me, and now I'm going to have to make him pay, and that'll make me feel badly about myself, and that'll put me back in therapy which means I have to switch therapists because my last one is too busy writing screenplays.

LISABETTE: See, Chekhov knows us.

CASEY: *(Nodding.)* 'Fraid so.

LISABETTE: To Chekhov.

(There is a knock on the door.)

LISABETTE: Who is it?

KATE: *(Outside.)* Lisabette? It's Kate. Kate Todoravskia. I wondered if you would like to drink red wine with me and make love?

LISABETTE: *(Sotto voice to the sisters.)* Oh my God.

KATE: I find you unbearably beautiful. I can't think, I can't eat. I want to produce *Romeo and Juliet* for you.

LISABETTE: *(To the sisters.)* What do I do?

(Holly beckons her over and whispers.)

KATE: I just want to hold you. You could move into my apartment. I have a satellite dish.

LISABETTE: Kate?

KATE: *(Still outside.)* Yes?

LISABETTE: It's a little awkward because I'm in here having sex with Holly.

(She mouths "Pardon me Jesus" to the ceiling.)

KATE: With Holly?

HOLLY: With Holly.

KATE: Oh...never mind...goodbye.

(They wait as Kate's footsteps recede.)

CASEY: Now that's Chekhov.

LISABETTE: Thank you, thank you, thank you!

HOLLY: No problem.

LISABETTE: *(Turning to Casey, meaning Kate's crush.)* Did you know that?

(Casey indicates "yes.")

HOLLY: Hey, Lisabette.

LISABETTE: What?

HOLLY: In my world, you'd be right there looking at her satellite dish.

(A change now moves from the apartment to a circle of folding chairs. It takes place during the opening half of Kate's speech.)

KATE: Dearest friends. Dearest, dearest actors. You may wonder why at this our first rehearsal I have spoken of my childhood for three hours. Why, I have told you of my Mother, the only American killed by prairie dogs, of my Father whose love of literature inspired him to inscribe 3 chapters of Tolstoy's *War and Peace* on the convex side of a single contact lens which was then tragically lost at Daytona Beach. These then are the threads with which I wove my love of the Russian Classics, and then carried in my heart here to San Antonio…San Antonio is to Houston as rural Russia is to Moscow. The sisters of San Antonio, their hearts beat with this play. We know what it is to be isolated, vulgarized, we know what it is to work! This play runs in our veins. Its pain is our pain. The pain of the women of San Antonio. So I say to you, on the brink of rehearsal, the final lines of Chekhov's Texas play, *The Three Sisters*, "In a little while we shall know why we live and why we suffer!"

(Applause from those gathered.)

CASEY: But that's not the final line, right?

KATE: I was speaking metaphorically.

CASEY: Because the final line is, "If only we knew."

KATE: Yes, Casey, that is the final line. Thank you.

CASEY: Said twice.

KATE: I'd like to move on if that's all right?

CASEY: Hey, it's your theatre.

KATE: Thank you. Thank you. And now it is my extraordinary pleasure to introduce our fabulous director, Wikéwitch Konalkvis, a fellow Pole and recent émigré who has directed seventy-one Chekhov productions and…

WIKÉWITCH: Seventy-two.

KATE: …Seventy-two productions and…

WIKÉWITCH: No, you are right, seventy-one.

KATE: …Seventy-one productions and…

WIKÉWITCH: Every one jewel. Make beating heart of Chekhov.

KATE: …and I just want to say…

WIKÉWITCH: Make beautiful from the pain of love this life which is like some…

KATE: …he is so…

WIKÉWITCH: You, I know, will play Olga. You have pain. Have loss. Radiating of loss. Good. Good Olga.

KATE: I just want to say, and I'm likely to get a little emotional…

HOLLY: Could we go around the room and meet the other actors?

KATE: Oh.

HOLLY: So we like know who we are. Like we were beginning a process.

KATE: Absolutely.

HOLLY: Holly Seabé, which probably goes without saying, Masha.

CASEY: Casey Mulgraw, radiating of loss, Olga.

LISABETTE: Lisabette Cartwright, Irina.

(Now T-Anne moves from chair to chair, being all the other actors.)

GUNTER: Gunter Sinsel, Solyony.

ALLEN: Allen Greif, thrilled to be Andrey.

JAMES: James George, the hapless Tusenbach.

WIKÉWITCH: *(Ferocious.)* Not hapless!

JAMES: The definitely-not-hapless Tusenbach.

(T-Anne indicates it would take too much time to do every introduction.)

T-ANNE: *(On book.)* Talk, talk, talk, talk, talk, talk, talk, talk, talk. Introductions over.

WIKÉWITCH: Okay, now I talk...

KATE: Could I...

WIKÉWITCH: You are going to speak of deep love you feel for Chekhov...

KATE: Yes, because when I was 15...

WIKÉWITCH: Stop! This love for Chekhov is like American fantasy. You make God from Chekhov. You say Chekhov, bullshit, Chekhov, bullshit, Chekhov, bullshit, bullshit, bullshit. From God we can't make play. From God we make worship. Worship makes boring play. You want to know in this room who is God? Who is God here?

LISABETTE: *(A guess.)* You are?

WIKÉWITCH: This is very intelligent young actress. God in theatre is interpretation of play. I, Wikéwitch, make interpretation.... In this room, in this time, I, Wikéwitch, will be God.

JOBY: Excuse me.

WIKÉWITCH: This is audience. Audience is talking!

JOBY: I mean, this is driving me crazy! This is the whole problem with 20th century theatre. This is part of the reason nobody wants to buy a ticket. We used to get stories; now we get "interpretations." The director is not God!

WIKÉWITCH: I am God.

JOBY: You are not God!

CASEY: Joby...

JOBY: What?!

CASEY: A character is talking.

JOBY: I know a character is talking, so?

CASEY: Who says it's the author's view?

WIKÉWITCH: *(Triumphantly.)* You are making interpretation!

JOBY: I don't care whose view it is, it's pernicious.

WIKÉWITCH: You are being God. Who gave you this position?

JOBY: I have a ticket!

WIKÉWITCH: If I do not make interpretation, you cannot make interpretation of my interpretation. You are secondary! I am artist! I fuck you with my art and you cry out.

JOBY: What the hell are you talking about?

WIKÉWITCH: Sit down, little audience, I give you *Three Sisters*. From big soul.

CASEY: *(Trying to calm her.)* Joby…

JOBY: I have never heard such unadulterated…

CASEY: Joby…

JOBY: Sit here and listen to…

CASEY: Joby! *(Joby stops talking.)* Not now.

JOBY: Then "now" what?

CASEY: You are the audience, Joby. If you talk to us all the time, you become an actor, and then you would have to come down here. Do you want to come down here?

(Joby, still upset, stands in silence for a moment, then, making a decision, sits back down. Don Blount enters.)

KATE: Don!

DON: Running a little late.

KATE: Don Blount, everybody, Vice President for Grants and Contributions at Albert & Sons Tobacco, our wonderful corporate sponsor.

DON: Don't mean to interrupt. Please go on with the Art.

KATE: Thanks Don. Now, we have the opportunity to make Chekhov with… *(Indicating Wikéwitch.)* this fine artist…

WIKÉWITCH: Great artist.

KATE: Great artist, and I feel deeply, even profoundly, that…

DON: *(Back in the scene.)* Could I just say a couple of things… *(Taps watch.)*

WIKÉWITCH: Okay. I pee now.

DON: …because, uh…well, I'm not part of your world…I'm a businessman. I actually have things to do.

KATE: Oh, Don, absolutely. Don Blount, everybody. Our underwriter.

DON: This is really a…revelation…for me to get to see what art's really all about. It's just that, uh… *(Taps watch.)* So I wanted to say that Albert & Sons Tobacco is really pleased to make this gift to the community of …*Four Sisters*… *(Casey holds up three fingers.)* Three Sisters. Sorry. Because Albert & Sons Tobacco International…we're in 130 countries, but we feel our role in this community is to…

CASEY: Kill people.

DON: Excuse me.

CASEY: Your role is to kill people, to target children and African Americans and to seek profit independent of any ethics or morality.

KATE: Oh dear.

CASEY: And by involving yourself in the arts who have no money and have no alternative to taking your minuscule handout, you hope to give the impression that you are on the side of life, when actually you are merchants of death.

DON: *(Pause.)* Thank you so much for the feedback. Albert & Sons respects others and their disparate and useful points of view. But in closing, I will say to you personally that if you take money from us it is disingenuous to make a pretense of morality and that historically, insofar as I understand it, actors were traditionally pickpockets, whores, and parasites on the body politic. Of course, given that your very profession is pretense, I still have the pleasure of enjoying your morality as entertainment. *(Taps watch.)* Got to go. Good luck with however many sisters you've got.
(He leaves. There is a stunned moment. Lights down.)

END OF ACT ONE

ACT TWO

The act opens with a bare stage, one folding chair and an inch-high, two-foot square box that Holly stands on while being fitted for her dress as Masha.

JACKEY: *(The costume designer.)* Baby-darlin'-honey-dear, your luscious body is a costume designer's dream! You have proportions goin' on like Greek statuary on a good day! Oh, my goodness! Your "out arm center back to wrist bent" is a world-class pisser. Your "shoulder point to mid-bust to center waist" is to die for, and your "depth of crotch and nipple to nipple" would turn Cleopatra mauve with envy. Golly-goodness-gracious, darlin', you are Masha the bomb!

HOLLY: But this is like, "Why have a body?"

JACKEY : Well, a little draggy, but 1901, if you see what I mean?

HOLLY: I am not going out there dressed up like a funeral cake. This would be, in fact, a good dress for somebody ugly. I mean, Olga might look like this, sure.

JACKEY: Au contraire, my goddess, au contraire. Every man in that audience is gonna hafta keep his program over his lap.

HOLLY: Ugly does not enhance luscious. People who wear ugly become ugly. Are we trying to make me ugly? I am not here to suffer the revenge of the ugly Texans. And I am not beautiful in this dress!
(Wikéwitch enters.)

WIKÉWITCH: Okay, okay. So. Masha is great beauty, yes? But is hiding. Hide-and-go-seek-Masha.

HOLLY: The west coast, we don't hide it. All right, a slit—waist to floor—let a little leg out.

JACKEY: 1901, honeydoll, no tits, no slits.

WIKÉWITCH: Repress. Very constrict. Very dark. This is sex for brain peoples.

HOLLY: Brain peoples. Reality check, all right?

JACKEY: (Working.) Ooooo, reality, I don't live there.

HOLLY: I spent $114,000 on my legs. I was in rehab for three months with animal, killer, monster rehab nurses in the Dominican Republic. An Internet survey shows that my legs alone, without the rest of me, have nineteen million fans. I either have legs or I walk. (Jackey has his head in his hands.) Jackey, will you stop crying. Every time we have a fitting, you weep.

JACKEY: You think I want to make women ugly because I'm a gay man.

HOLLY: Oh, please.

JACKEY: You think I'm hostile because you make millions, and I do consignment store windows.

HOLLY: Okay, all right, I'm going to try something completely new for me. I'm going to try compromise.

WIKÉWITCH: No compromise.

JACKEY: I love compromise.

HOLLY: Everybody listening? Floor length/see-thru.

WIKÉWITCH: I am in madhouse.

JACKEY: Well, lil' darlin', you would look delicious, but I keep rememberin' what you said the day you got here as to how the play was about like a tidal wave of vulgarity sweepin' everything good and beautiful away, which just made me bawl like a baby, and how the vulgarity of the rich was not to see the desperate need of the poor, and how the vulgarity of the poor was to be blind to beauty, and the vulgarity of the intellectual was to separate thought from action. So that everyone in the play was as different as they could be but in this funny way they all shared the same despair.

HOLLY: When did I say that?

JACKEY: Well, it was such a pretty thought, you are such a talk-diva, baby love. But it made me think maybe Masha could be this little simplicity in the sea of vulgarity and get all the attention, an' reviews, an' applause, applause, applause.

HOLLY: Well, if I said that, that's what we should do.

WIKÉWITCH: *(To Jackey.)* You are God in other form.

JACKEY: *(Sweetly.)* Well, she said.

HOLLY: No more talking!!! The dress rocks. I gotta book to make rehearsal.

(The scene now transitions into rehearsal. At first we see only the director because Holly has a costume change.)

WIKÉWITCH: Okay. Okay. Please stopping. Good. Okay. Leave brain. Brain no more. Brain outside, art inside. What you are doing in this time? Hah? Okay, good. Is very clear, is very smart, is very beautiful, is very professional. But is not art. No more professional. No good to Chekhov, this professional. No, no, no, no, no, no, no! Peel off skin. Rip open body. Lungs, liver, spleen. Okay. Begin.

HOLLY/MASHA: "I don't know. I don't know. Of course, being used to something means a lot. For example…"

WIKÉWITCH: *(Interrupting.)* You say line.

HOLLY/MASHA: *(Confused.)* I did.

WIKÉWITCH: Yes, you say "you don't know."

HOLLY/MASHA: I know the line.

WIKÉWITCH: You don't know!

HOLLY/MASHA: I just said it!

WIKÉWITCH: Saying is not being.

HOLLY: What are you talking about?

WIKÉWITCH: Look, little television actress, Masha say, "I don't know," but you don't know what this is not to know, so you just say line. So this little thing, this "I don't know" is dead, and more you say, you go from corpse to corpse over this dead Chekhov. You make graveyard of scene by just say lines. No good. Okay. Her father, military man, is dead. Real corpse, not acting corpse. Since that moment, this Masha lives, imbeciles all around, peasant idiots, animals, mud, stupidity. Peasant thirsty for drink, they spit in hand, like spit for drink. Only soldiers, like father, have brain. She is thirsty for brain. She says soldiers honorable, educated, worthwhile. Vershinin is soldier. His soul is dead. He knows soldier is animal too. He says this. How can she bear this? This is break her heart. He says this before scene. It is like stone. Like stone. You understand? She says, "I don't know." Yes! This is heart bleeding. Yes! Now you say.

HOLLY: I don't know.

WIKÉWITCH: No.

HOLLY: I don't know.

WIKÉWITCH: No!

HOLLY: What the hell do you want?

WIKÉWITCH: I want you to *be* line, not *say* line!

HOLLY: I don't know!

WIKÉWITCH: No.

HOLLY: I don't know.

WIKÉWITCH: No!

HOLLY: You think I know what the hell you mean but I'm telling you *I don't know!*

WIKÉWITCH: Yes! *Now* you know!

HOLLY: What?!

WIKÉWITCH: What you don't know! Chekhov is back from dead!

(*A pause.*)

HOLLY: Okay, I get it.

WIKÉWITCH: You get it.

HOLLY: Yes.

WIKÉWITCH: One line. Twenty minutes. You get one scene, I'm dead from old age.

HOLLY: I really get it.

WIKÉWITCH: Enough. Rehearse. Say "I don't know."

HOLLY: *I don't know.*

WIKÉWITCH: Okay. Next line.

(*There are now a series of short Ben/Holly scenes with minimal furniture being brought in and out during a continuous flow.*)

BEN: Hey.

HOLLY: Hi.

BEN: Ummmm.

HOLLY: Ummmmm?

BEN: Coffee?

HOLLY: Sure.

(*Chairs are placed under them and a table between them.*)

BEN: I held that kiss too long.

HOLLY: I noticed.

BEN: That was unprofessional.

HOLLY: Nice tongue, though.

BEN: Ma'am, I never meant…

HOLLY: You did.

BEN: I have to go.

(He moves away from the table.)

HOLLY: Ben?

BEN: Yeah?

HOLLY: You kiss your wife like that?

(They meet outside rehearsal.)

HOLLY: What the hell's going on in rehearsal?

BEN: Please don't call me at home.

HOLLY: When we're doing the scene, don't avoid the kiss and then say, "Kiss. Kiss over." I feel like I'm in middle school.

BEN: That scene is driving me crazy.

HOLLY: Why is that?

BEN: You know perfectly well why.

HOLLY: Yeah. I do.

BEN: I am married. I have two kids.

HOLLY: I have a live-in lover.

BEN: My wife is ill.

HOLLY: My lover's an ex-convict.

BEN: The kids are waiting for me to come.

HOLLY: Me too. All right, Ben. Come over in the morning.

(A rolling door moves on. Ben knocks. Holly opens it. He steps in and immediately kisses her. They start ripping off clothes. Dialogue along this vein ensues.)

HOLLY: My neck. Yes. Yes! My mouth.

BEN: Oh God.

HOLLY: *(While being kissed, she is trying to undo his belt.)* Belt.

BEN: Belt.

(She keeps trying.)

HOLLY: Can't. Ouch. Hate that belt.

(She steps back and takes her blouse off over her head. He is working on the belt.)

BEN: Beautiful. Goddamnit, you're beautiful!

HOLLY: I know. *(Trying to undo his buttons.)* Hate these buttons.

BEN: Boots.

HOLLY: *(Pulling his pants down.)* Screw the boots!

JOBY: Excuse me.

BEN: *(Freezes. Pants around his ankles.)* Yes, Joby, we've missed you.

JOBY: I don't think this love story is necessary.

HOLLY: Does anybody have any Tylenol?

(T-Anne brings her some.)

BEN: The Ben/Holly relationship is a crucial parallel to Masha and Vershinin in *The Three Sisters*.

JOBY: I never read *The Three Sisters*.

HOLLY: Shut up. I'm a character, and you're a character, and I'm cutting your character's lines!

(He kisses her more roughly. They freeze. The lights change. It's now post-coital. Ben pulls up his pants.)

BEN: You were incredible.

HOLLY: Lots of practice.

BEN: What in the hell did you say that for?

HOLLY: Because it's true. It doesn't mean I didn't like it.

BEN: I'm not kidding around here, Holly.

HOLLY: Okay. It was my first time.

(The scene breaks up. Two period chairs and a standing lamp become the set for rehearsal.)

HOLLY/MASHA: What a noise the stove's making. The wind was...line?

T-ANNE: (Prompting.) Moaning in the chimney.

HOLLY/MASHA: ...moaning in the chimney just before Father died.

T-ANNE: The same sound exactly.

HOLLY/MASHA: The same sound exactly.

BEN/VERSHININ: Are you superstitious?

HOLLY/MASHA: Yes.

BEN/VERSHININ: Strange. (Kisses her hand.) You magnificent, magical woman. Magnificent, magical! It's dark in here but I can see the shining of your eyes.

HOLLY/MASHA: There's more light over here...

BEN/VERSHININ: I'm in love, I'm in love, I'm in love...

(He stops.)

T-ANNE: (Prompting.) In love with your eyes, with the way you move.

BEN: (Out of scene.) I don't want to do this.

HOLLY: (Out of scene.) Are you?

BEN: Am I what?

HOLLY: In love?

T-ANNE: (Prompting.) In love with your eyes, with...

HOLLY: Can it, okay? You are or you aren't.

BEN: I have a real life. I can hurt real people here.

HOLLY: And what am I, animation? You think I'm not susceptible? Hey, man, three years ago, I'm involved with a guy commits suicide jumping off the Golden Gate Bridge in a wedding dress. Two years ago, the guy I'm living with whacks me, breaks my jaw so I couldn't work for three weeks and they almost pulled the show. Right now, as we speak, my significant other is an actor who has an immobilizing drinking problem mainly because in high school he murdered his prom date and served eleven years. You see why I might be susceptible to some ordinary, straight-up guy? Okay, it's mutual.

(Light comes up on Joby. Holly sees it.)

JOBY: Excuse me.

HOLLY: Don't even think about it!

(Holly leaves. Furniture is struck. An exercycle and some mats become the gym.)

CASEY: So, the casting agent says to me, "You're not right for it; you're a character woman." I die. My blood congeals. Fissures appear. It's the actresses' death knell. I go through menopause in five seconds. All fluids dry. I become the Mojave Desert. Character woman! I, who have screwed every leading man on the East Coast, become their mother. Vertigo. I scream out in a silent, unattending universe: "I'm too young to be a character woman!" and the echo replies, rolling out of infinite space: "They want to see you for the funny aunt at the wedding!"

(She ritually disembowels herself. Holly enters in exercise clothes. All three begin to work out; Holly particularly exercises fiercely.)

CASEY: Bad day?

HOLLY: Bad day.

LISABETTE: Bad day.

CASEY: Bad day.

(They exercise.)

CASEY: Why does every actor in America go to the gym?

HOLLY: Because it's a beauty contest, not a profession.

(They exercise.)

LISABETTE: Damn it to hell! *(She drops the weights.)* Wikéwitch called me dense as a turkey, an' I'm a lot smarter than a turkey. An' then he picked on me for three hours an' I cried an' he patted me on my shoulder an' I threw up all over him. Then I ran out an' tripped over the doorjamb an' cracked a tooth an' I could just spit fire an' eat broke glass.

CASEY: *(Exercising.)* He called you a turkey?

LISABETTE: He didn't call me a turkey. He said I had the brain of a turkey.

HOLLY: Wikéwitch is a tyrannical, woman-hating buttwipe, but he seems to know what he's doing.

(They exercise.)

HOLLY: Meanwhile, my boyfriend has just been arrested for sexually soliciting a seven-foot transsexual on Hollywood Blvd. who turned out to be a policewoman on stilts, so *People* magazine called me for a quote.

(They exercise.)

CASEY: What'd you say?

HOLLY: I said it just showed he missed me.

(They exercise.)

CASEY: Play's going pretty well. *(They exercise.)* Whattayathink? *(They exercise.)* Play's going pretty well.

HOLLY: I wouldn't know, I've never done a play.

(Casey and Lisabette stop exercising.)

CASEY: You are kidding? Are you kidding?

HOLLY: From high school to TV…well, I was in one play, but I had to leave to get an abortion. One play and one porn flick.

LISABETTE: You didn't do a porn flick!?

HOLLY: *(Still exercising.)* Yeah.

CASEY: Tell.

HOLLY: Actually I got fired.

LISABETTE: How do you get fired from a porn flick?

HOLLY: I came. Joking. I got fired because I started crying uncontrollably on camera. It depressed the porn divas so they dumped me.

LISABETTE: Why were you crying?

HOLLY: Because I came. First time. Consider those implications.

(They all exercise.)

LISABETTE: What if it were good?

CASEY: What?

LISABETTE: You know.

CASEY: Our little Russian skit? The Sisters Three?

LISABETTE: I mean, what if it were *really* good? Really. Really, really good. Could we? You're good. You're both good. We could do something good. Could we do something good? It could be good. It could be really, really good. Could it? Be good?

CASEY: I once believed I could be very good. I wanted to be so concentrated, so compressed, so vivid and present and skilful and heartfelt that anyone watching me would literally burst into flame. Combust.

LISABETTE: That kills me. I want that. Did you ever do it? Did it ever happen?

CASEY: No.

LISABETTE: But maybe we could do that? What would happen if we did that?

HOLLY: Nobody would care.

LISABETTE: That's so cold. How can you say that? It could change people's lives.

CASEY: God love you, Lisabette, two months later the audience can't remember the name of the play.

LISABETTE: *I don't believe that. I don't believe that.*

CASEY: Has anybody you know to be a sentient being ever walked up to you and said the play changed their life? No, fine, okay. You know who is changed by Chekhov? Me. I finish a play, it's like, "Get me an exorcist!" He eats my life. He chews me up. He spits me out. I'm like bleeding from Chekhov. The audience? Who knows what their deal is? They come from the mists; they return to the mist. They cough, they sneeze, they sleep, they unwrap little hard candies, and then they head for their cars during the curtain call. And once, once I would like to step out and say to the ones who are up the aisles while we take the bows, "Hey! Excuse me! Could you show a little mercy because I just left it all out here on the stage and even if you don't have the foggiest notion what it was or what it meant, could you have the common courtesy to leave your goddamn cars in the garage for another forty seconds and give me a little hand for twenty years of work!" ·

JOBY: That is unmitigated hogwash!

HOLLY: Oh, please…

JOBY: I don't cough or sleep or unwrap little candies, I come to feel. *(She taps her head and chest.)* Here and here. Because if I'm ever going to understand my own life, it will have to be through feeling, and my own life and experience isn't big enough so I come for enlargement. Plus I want the highest quality moments for my life I can get, and you're supposed to provide them, though you usually don't, so when I write my review…

CASEY: Hold it.

JOBY: …I need to point out whether there is any enlargement…

HOLLY: Your review?

JOBY: …to be had by the audience…

CASEY: You're a critic.

JOBY: …in this particular experience!

CASEY: You have been interrupting us all night…

JOBY: I am part of the process.

CASEY: After the play, not during the play.

JOBY: After the play I'm not part of the process. After the play you revile and dismiss me. Some of you claim you don't even read reviews, which is a complete joke!

CASEY: I don't read reviews.

JOBY: You do.

CASEY: Don't.

JOBY: Do.

CASEY: Don't.

JOBY: Do.

CASEY: Okay, sometimes.

JOBY: Hah!

CASEY: Look, we only put up with you because half our audience is three months from the nursing home.

HOLLY: I can't believe it—a critic!?

JOBY: Well…

HOLLY: How are we doing so far?

JOBY: Well, it's definitely interesting, sometimes amusing, well-paced, but a very uneasy mix of…

LISABETTE: Stop! Not while we're doing it! Critics are gods to me. I completely measure my self-worth by my reviews.

HOLLY: Who do you write for?

JOBY: *(A pause.)* I don't want to talk about it.
(She sits down.)

CASEY: That is completely unfair. We have to go on here. Do we have to be afraid of you or not?

JOBY: It doesn't matter who I write for; it matters what I perceive.

CASEY: Joby, even you don't believe that. Don't tell me there isn't a critical hierarchy when you would poison your colleagues for the six best jobs.

JOBY: Not my job.

CASEY: Who do you write for, Joby?

JOBY: Bargain Mart Suburban Shoppers Guide.

CASEY: *(Turning back to the stage.)* She's nobody, let's act.

JOBY: I am not nobody!

CASEY: *(Referring back.)* I didn't mean you personally, Joby.
(Joby sits down. The actresses exercise.)

LISABETTE: What was wrong with your day, Casey?

CASEY: Forget it.

LISABETTE: We told you.

CASEY: Forget it.

LISABETTE: We're not important enough to tell?

(They exercise a moment in silence.)

CASEY: I felt a lump in the shower. I saw a doctor. She wants to do a biopsy.

HOLLY: When?

CASEY: On the day off.

LISABETTE: Oh my God.

(Casey exercises. Lisabette is frozen. Holly stops exercising, stands and walks over to Casey, who keeps working out.)

HOLLY: *(Standing above her.)* Stop. *(Casey does. Holly puts out her hand.)* Get off. *(Casey does.)* Hug me. *(Casey does.)*

BEN: Excuse me?

LISABETTE: Yes?

BEN: It's Ben.

HOLLY: Come in.

(He does.)

BEN: I left my wife.

(A moment.)

CASEY: Well, either way I lose my hair.

(Holly and Casey exit. The gym is struck and a desk and two chairs are brought on for Don Blount's office.)

DON: Don Blount of Albert & Sons Tobacco calling for Martha Graham. Then why is it called the Martha Graham Dance Company? Oh. No, I knew that. Little joke. Listen, the grant's in the mail. Yes. Well, it's our pleasure to support a dance company of your caliber, and if you might find an opportunity to mention to the chairman of your board that we'd be thrilled if she'd tell her brother the congressman to stop sodomizing the tobacco industry just because he's personally in the pocket of the HMO's, I think you'd find your grant is definitely renewable. My pleasure.

(Don hangs up the phone, picks it back up and dials.)

Mom, it's Don. Your son Don. I need the favor, Mom. I know we did it yesterday, but I'm feeling a little alienated...a little remote. Wonderful. Good. I knew I could count on you, Momma. Ready? All right, light it up, Mom. Inhale, Mom. Would I encourage you to smoke if there was any danger? That's right, I wouldn't. I would never harm my mom. I must be a good person if I would never harm my mom. If I'm a good person, it must be all right to do what I do. Thanks, I feel a lot better. Put it out now, Momma. Everything's all right. I feel damn good. Go back on the oxygen, Ma. See you Sunday.

(Kate enters Albert & Sons. Don rises, smiling and affable.)

DON: Ms. Todoravskia, it's really nice of you to come over on short notice.

KATE: No, I've been wanting to...

DON: Can I get you something?

KATE: Well...

DON: At this level in the executive suite, we could fly in crabs' legs from Iceland. Just kidding. But in Iceland the crabs have pneumonia. Wouldn't affect their legs though. Just kidding. Tea, coffee, soft drink, bottled water, mixed drinks of all kinds, munchies, brownies my mother sends in... *(Does his Dracula imitation.)* Cigarette?!

KATE: No, I...

DON: You know, Kate...may I call you Kate? Nice dress, by the way. I deal with a lot of artists, and usually they look like they bought their clothes from the llama shop in Costa Rica.

KATE: Well, I...

DON: I can't tell you how impressed I was by that rehearsal of whatsit you let me see.

KATE: *Three Sisters.*

DON: Well, it just seemed like a metaphor for the lives we all lead, don't you think?

KATE: Well I...

DON: Plus it confirmed my every doubt about corporate investment in Russia. In that way it was very personal for me.

KATE: I'm glad that you...

DON: So it's a real downer to have to pull the funding. Oh, I think we also have fruit juices.

KATE: The funding.

DON: The funding. In a way here, Ms. Todoravskia, I have to tell you I personally blew it. I've only been in Grants and Contributions with Albert & Sons for a couple of months—before that, they let me do real work—just kidding, and I didn't realize when I gave you the okay that there had been a policy change up top.

KATE: Do you mean...

DON: Let me just wrap this up and then we'll relate. We had sort of turned our contribution policy on a dime based on the fact that all this tobacco legislation, politically motivated lawsuits, advertising restrictions have made it clear to us that our market focus in the future will be overseas where they just plain old like a good smoke. Plus their life expectancy is so low that we don't really constitute a health hazard. Hah! Just kidding. Just kidding. And it's in those communities in our target market we'll be looking to leverage our contributions. So the bad news is that I didn't have the authority to give you the money. I hope this won't inconvenience you?

KATE: But you did authorize it.

DON: *(Smiling.)* Poof.

KATE: But we're in the middle of the work.

DON: Poof.

KATE: We will have to default on the salaries and the Board will fire me.

DON: You know, I'm very interested in artists and how they function, and a little research shows an overwhelming percentage of the best work didn't have grants. As far as I can see, good art is almost invariably a product of good old-fashioned adversity and rage. Anger is the engine of art, so in an odd way this is a good situation for you. You don't want to be the lap dog of big tobacco. We're the bad guys. Great art is a personal passion, not a grant. Ms. Todoravskia, Albert & Sons Tobacco is sorry to defund you, but that doesn't mean we aren't proud to fuel your anger.

KATE: I cannot believe…

DON: I'm afraid that's all the time I have for you. I do however want to make a $75 personal contribution to your theatre. If you wonder about the cost basis, it's the same amount I give to public radio, which I actually use. *(She takes the envelope. He heads back for his desk.)* Oh, listen, I wonder if you have Holly Seabé's phone number?

(Office is struck. The girls are talking—one seated. Kate enters with her suitcase.)

KATE: Hi.

(She puts down her suitcase.)

LISABETTE: Hi.

CASEY: Hi.

HOLLY: Hi.

KATE: I, uh…are my eyes red? *(Furious.)* I hate it when my eyes are red!! Sorry, I'm sorry. Look, I want to…uh…tell you how proud…proud I am of you… *(She pauses on the brink of something. It explodes.)* To hell with everybody!! Okay, that feels better…umm, it was very emotional to see this great play being so well done in our little theatre that has…struggled and…held on by its fingernails…believe me…for all these years. When I settled here, having attended Stanford, Harvard and Yale, I hoped…I hoped!!…well, those rehearsals were what I hoped for as an artist. They surpassed my hopes. It's one hell of a time to be fired, I'll tell you that.

LISABETTE: Oh my God…

KATE: Albert & Sons removed the funding.

CASEY: Oh God.

KATE: And when I told Joe Bob Mattingly, the Chairman of our Board of Directors, he said…

JOE BOB: *(From somewhere out in the house.)* Damn woman! You got no more sense than a hog on ice! I been pourin' my money an' the money of my friends down your double-talk rathole since Jesus was a pup, so my wife could drag me down here to see plays nobody can understand with a buncha people I would never invite to dinner, on the basis it creates some quality of life I'm supposed to have since I figgered out how to make some money. Half the time, that stuff doesn't have a story, and it's been five years since you done one takes place in a kitchen, which is the kind all of us like. The rest of the time it's about how rich people is bad and Democrats is good and white people is stupid and homosexuals have more fun an' we should get rid of the corporations an' eat grass an' then, by God, you wonder why you don't have a big audience! Now you just blew 15% of your budget 'cause you riled up the tobacco interests, plus you got the colored rattlin' on my cage, an' as of this precise minute, you are out of luck, out of work an' outta San Antonio, Texas. See, I am closin' us down, lockin' the door, an' then, by God, we can go back to hittin' each other up to give to the United Way where it will, by God, do some poor handicap some actual, measurable good, an' I won't have to hear anybody say "aesthetic" from one year to the goddamned next! Now, vaya con Dios, darlin'.

JOE BOB and KATE: You got three minutes to clean out your desk.

(He disappears. Kate speaks to Casey.)

KATE: So that's it. They said if I was out of the city before five o'clock I'd get six months' severance and my plane ticket. What, do you suppose, I thought I was doing here? Making theatre because… See I just can't remember. Well, I guess nobody told us everything has a purpose.

CASEY: Man cannot live by bread alone.

KATE: No, he needs salsa. *(Shakes Casey's hand.)* Actually, I think I hate theatre. It makes you think it was about something when it was actually only about yourself. It fascinates you. It seduces you. It leaves you penniless by the side of the road. Screw Thespis! *(She looks at the women.)* Run for your lives.

    (She exits. The women look at each other.)

LISABETTE: Goodness gracious. *(Wipes tear.)*

CASEY: You okay?

LISABETTE: I guess.

JOBY: *(From audience.)* Don't let it get too sentimental.

CASEY: *(Without looking up.)* Thanks for the tip. *(Turns to Holly.)* So that this doesn't get too sentimental, why don't you pay for the production? You have the money.

HOLLY: Why would I do that?

CASEY: Self-interest?

HOLLY: Ah.

CASEY: You want the credit. You don't like to be pushed around. You're secretly thrilled you're good in the part. Based on proving you can act, you might get a film where you kept your clothes on. And I could use the distraction from the fact the biopsy was positive.

HOLLY: That's not too sentimental. Anything else?

CASEY: No, that's about it.

HOLLY: *(Seeing Ben enter.)* Hi.

BEN: Stay.

HOLLY: *(Turns to Lisabette.)* And you, little one?

LISABETTE: It might make you happy.

    (Holly chuckles.)

HOLLY: Well, that aside, why not?

CASEY: You'll pay to get us open?

HOLLY: I'll get us open.

LISABETTE: No way?

HOLLY: They screwed with us, now they lose.

LISABETTE: You really mean it?

HOLLY: I don't want to talk about it, I want to do it.

    (At this point, Wikéwitch walks in with his suitcase.)

WIKÉWITCH: So. Is not to be. Okay. I put life in small suitcase. You. You. You. On we go, yes? Is hard to tell what is good, what is bad. Everything is doorway to something else. *(Shaking hands.)* Little Irina, okay, goodbye. Olga. Olga, she goes on. Vershinin. He finds another girl next town. *(To Holly.)* Like cat you land on feet, yes?

CASEY: It's not over.

WIKÉWITCH: No?

CASEY: We have the money. We can open.

WIKÉWITCH: Where is money?

HOLLY: Here is money.

WIKÉWITCH: Ah. Is for what?

LISABETTE: So we can do your beautiful play.

WIKÉWITCH: Ah. Okay, okay. Honorable sisters and Lieutenant Colonel. Okay. I wake, wake, wake. No sleeping. Okay. I get up, pack suitcase, close suitcase. Knock, knock, knock. Theatre producer says no more money. Dead Chekhov. Okay. Bye-bye. Money, money, money. But, dear American actors, before knock-knock, I am pack. So why is this? Because work is finish. When do Chekhov, now, now, now, young, middle, old. So much you can do, only what you know. No more. Then wait for life to teach. You are sweet young people, but what I know… *(Points to head.)* …you cannot do. What for I do this? No sleep, no sleep. We must be a little realistic in this time. For you, Chekhov is fantasy. For me, life. You have nice, small talent. We can do together baby-Chekhov. Okay, but I have…short time…short time now…no sleep…no time for baby-Chekhov…I must take small suitcase, find big souls to do play, so I don't die with this Chekhov in my head. This you understand or not understand?

HOLLY: We're not good enough.

WIKÉWITCH: You do not understand. OK. Bye-bye. *(Goes to exit and turns back.)* You are good enough to do the Chekhov you are good enough to do. But is not good enough. *(He tips his hat and is gone.)*

LISABETTE: See, I've always been terrified that some guy dressed in black would show up and tell me I'm not good enough.

HOLLY: Yeah, but what he said was:

CASEY and HOLLY: You just have to do the Chekhov you're good enough to do.

LISABETTE: He did say that.

HOLLY: Okay. We'll do the Chekhov we can do.

LISABETTE: Really?

HOLLY: Really.

LISABETTE: Yes! Oh yes! *(To Casey.)* Can you believe this? Can we please work on the last scene? *(She picks up the script.)* I want to work on the last scene.

HOLLY: Where from?

LISABETTE: The band. Ta ra ra boom de ay.

CASEY: We're over here.

HOLLY/MASHA: "Oh, but listen to the band! They're leaving us."

T-ANNE: *(Entering.)* Sorry. Sorry to interrupt. Phone for you, Holly.

HOLLY: Take the message.

(She turns back to the scene.)

T-ANNE: Dreamworks.

(A moment.)

HOLLY: *(To the others.)* I'll be right back.

(She goes.)

LISABETTE: What's Dreamworks?

CASEY: Who are you? What planet do you live on? Spielberg.

LISABETTE: Oh, you mean…

T-ANNE: *(As a stage manager, cutting to another place in the text.)* Talk, talk, talk, talk, talk, talk, talk. Holly comes back.

(She does.)

HOLLY: I got a film.

CASEY: You are kidding?

(Holly shakes her head. No, she's not kidding.)

LISABETTE: That is great! That is so exciting! What is it! I never heard anybody say that, "I got a film." I was right here when you said it!

CASEY: When?

LISABETTE: What when?

CASEY: *(Directly to Holly.)* When film?

HOLLY: Now. Yesterday. I'm replacing somebody who walked.

LISABETTE: Now?

HOLLY: They want me on a flight in ninety minutes. Jesus, I gotta pack. Rental car? How will I get rid of the rental car. Damn it, my dogs? How the hell am I going to do that? I'm supposed to film tonight.

CASEY: How long?

HOLLY: One month, L.A.; one month, Thailand. I mean, the part is dogmeat. Girlfriend stuff. Two scenes naked, three scenes I listen to the guy talk, one scene I get crushed by pythons. Two months I say a dozen sentences. Listen, I am…I am sorry, I am really sorry, but I am really happy…bad for you, good for me…me, me, me…and I can't even pretend I'm anything but euphoric! Kill me, I'm horrible! Gotta go, gotta go.

(She starts to race out.)

BEN: I'll come with.

HOLLY: Damn.

BEN: I don't have anything here. I got rid of everything here. You're it.

HOLLY: You just don't have a clue who you got mixed up with, do you?

BEN: I love you.

HOLLY: I got the call. We've just been fooling around while I waited for the call.

BEN: I'll just come out and hang.

HOLLY: Oh Ben. You just don't get it. This is the shot. You are a very sweet cowboy, but it makes you, don't you see, completely disposable, babe. Trust me, you don't want to hang around Malibu while I give head for billing. This is it. I will take no prisoners. You have to blow me off. You know what? *(She kisses his cheek.)* Go back to your wife. Sorry to be the meat grinder. It's just the way it plays out. *(Looks at him.)* I got a couple minutes, tell me to go screw myself. *(He shakes his head.)* Okay. *(She kisses him.)* Bye L. *(Hugs Lisabette. Appraises Casey.)* More I see of you, you could probably get it done for a hundred thousand. *(Casey chuckles; they hug.)* Anything I can do, you call me. We almost made it, huh?

CASEY: Almost.

HOLLY: I'm no surprise to you guys, I know that. Gotta go. Want to know the really worst part? I-am-so-happy!

(She leaves.)

CASEY: You okay, Ben?

(He nods yes.)

LISABETTE: *(Concerned.)* What will you do?

(He shakes his head "I don't know.")

CASEY: She was really beautiful, huh? *(He nods yes.)* Kind of like really sexy Russian roulette, right? Only you're alive.

BEN: *(A pained smile.)* Thanks.

(He exits.)

LISABETTE: What will we do?

CASEY: When the play's over, you pack.

LISABETTE: I live here.

CASEY: Then I will allow you to skip the packing.

LISABETTE: What will you do?

CASEY: What will I do? Oh, probably get my other breast lopped off, and then I think I will try to accept that you don't necessarily get to do what you want to do. I will try to be a grown-up about that. And after I'm a grown-up, I will try to like doing the things grown-ups like to do. Right now, I'm thinking hardware store. I am worried, however, that I will make a lousy grown-up and that I will cry a lot and be depressed.

LISABETTE: Oh God.

CASEY: Can I tell you something about theatre?

LISABETTE: Sure.

CASEY: Never ask an out-of-work actress what's next.

LISABETTE: Okay.

CASEY: *(Giving her a hug.)* Pardon you Jesus.

(Chair is struck. An airplane gate table is rolled in, as well as three waiting room chairs that move as a unit. Holly enters with luggage.)

AIRPORT ANNOUNCER: Because of weather, the following flights have been canceled or rescheduled: Flight #1726 to Los Angeles, Flight #343 to Dallas/Ft. Worth, Flight #2121 to Seattle, Flight #1643 to San Francisco... *(Holly begins talking to a gate check-in person, overlapping the flight cancellations.)*

HOLLY: No, you don't understand, I have to be in L.A. by 6 P.M.

GATE MANAGER: Ma'am, we have weather cancellations or long delays on everything going west.

HOLLY: You said that. I am a famous television star who is shooting a movie at 7 P.M. tonight.

GATE MANAGER: Wow, what movie?

HOLLY: Get me on a plane!

GATE MANAGER: Ma'am. Weather is weather, ma'am. There is nothing flying.

HOLLY: *(Overlapping his speech.)* And if I'm not there for the shoot, I will lose the most important job of my career!

GATE MANAGER: I can get you on Flight #1077 arriving L.A. 7:30 A.M. tomorrow.

HOLLY: Too late.

GATE MANAGER: All I've got.

HOLLY: Look, is there a VIP lounge?

GATE MANAGER: Sure.

HOLLY: Is there a sofa in it?

GATE MANAGER: Absolutely.

HOLLY: I'll fuck you for a flight.

GATE MANAGER: You are one sad chick, and I don't have a plane.

HOLLY: *(Apoplectic.)* I'll have your job, do you understand me?!

GATE MANAGER: *(Gently.)* No, you won't, ma'am.

(He exits.)

HOLLY: *(Utter frustration.)* Arrghrrrahhhhh! *(Smashes the bag down, kicks it, throws an enraged fit. She then sits with her head in her hands in a row of gate seating. Casey enters with her bag. Lisabette tags along.)*

CASEY: Holly? *(Holly rocks, keening.)* What's the deal?

LISABETTE: Are you okay?

HOLLY: Do I look like I'm okay?

LISABETTE: Oh no, what is it?

CASEY: Holly? *(Holly, crying, doesn't look up.)* What's the deal?

LISABETTE: What, what is it?

HOLLY: My flight's canceled, nobody's flying. I called my agent, he says they'll replace me.

LISABETTE: Oh no.

CASEY: You can't connect through another city?

HOLLY: You can't land on the West Coast. I'm cursed. It's my karma.

(She leans on Casey who now sits beside her.)

LISABETTE: I drove Casey out for her New York flight. We thought we'd check to see if you left.

HOLLY: No, I haven't left! You can't see I haven't left? I can't take this, I can't, I'll kill myself. *(A band is heard in the distance.)* No planes! It's like some incredibly murderous cosmic joke. *(The band's sound intrudes.)* What the hell is that?

CASEY: There's some high school band playing in the terminal.

HOLLY: Does anybody have a goddamn Kleenex? That was my last Kleenex. My life is like a nightmare. I'm a nightmare. *(She blows her nose.)* What happened to Ben?

CASEY: He threw his stuff in his car and drove to Nashville. Said Texas was over, acting was over, his marriage was over and you were over, the end.

HOLLY: Eat me!

(She puts her head back in her hands. Silence, except for the band. Lisabette makes the connection with the last scene in The Three Sisters *and sings softly.)*

LISABETTE: Ta-ra-ra boom-de-ay, ta-ra-ra boom-de-ay.

HOLLY: Oh please.

(Casey wipes at her eyes with another Kleenex.)

LISABETTE: (Quoting.) "Let them have their little cry. Doesn't matter, does it?" *(They are in the familiar tableau. Holly and Lisabette sitting, Casey behind them. She looks at Holly.)* Your line.

HOLLY: So?

CASEY: *(A pause.)* It is, it's your line.

HOLLY: Do I give a damn?

CASEY: Yeah, you do.

HOLLY: "Listen. Hear how the band plays. They are leaving us. One has already gone, gone forever, and we are alone, left behind to start life again. We have to live; we must live."

LISABETTE: "A time will come when everyone knows what it was all for and why we suffer. There will be no secrets, but meantime we must live; we must work, only work! Tomorrow I set out alone. I'll teach in a school and give the whole of my own life to those who can make some use of it. Now it's autumn, but winter will come, covering everything with snow, and I will work; I will work."

CASEY: "The music plays so gaily, vigorously, as if it wants itself to live. Oh, my God. Time will pass, and then we shall be gone forever. They will forget us, our faces, voices, even how many of us there were. But our sufferings will become joy for those who live after us. A season of happiness and peace, and we who lived now will be blessed and thought of kindly. Oh, dear sisters, our life is still not finished. We will live. The music plays so bravely, so joyfully, as if in another moment we shall know why we live and why we suffer. If we could only know, if we could only know!"

(A moment held in the traditional pose, and then Casey and Holly leave the stage. Everyone has gone except Lisabette. She looks up in the audience and speaks to Joby.)

LISABETTE: So how did we do?

JOBY: Oh fine. Not bad. Is it over?

LISABETTE: Sort of. I mean I'm the only one left. Their planes left.

JOBY: But not really.

LISABETTE: No, not really. I mean, in the play they left.

JOBY: They don't give me much space in the paper. I'm kind of between the car ads and the pet ads.

LISABETTE: I didn't have a lot of lines either. Not like a lead character or anything.

JOBY: You were good though, with what you had.

LISABETTE: Thanks. And?

JOBY: Oh. Well I…okay umm. So I would say…it played _(the time)_ , you know _(the date)_, at _(the place)_ , and umm…a seriocomic, ummm, look at the creative drive and how the culture and, like, human frailty warp that, make it less pure…almost ludicrous, maybe breaks it…umm, calls into question whether it's kind of over for the theatre…you know. Pretty good acting and everything…minimal set. I guess my question would be if plays, doing plays, doesn't speak to the culture, then examining why, or satirizing why, is kind of beating a dead horse…from the inside. So, uh, anyway, I only have about a hundred words to say that. You were good.

LISABETTE: Wow.

JOBY: Yeah. I could send you a copy.

LISABETTE: Thanks.

JOBY: I mean, I'm not a real critic...yet.

LISABETTE: Oh, you will be.

JOBY: Yeah. I don't know.

LISABETTE: Really.

JOBY: Yeah. Anyway. Bye.

LISABETTE: Bye.

JOBY: Bye.

(Joby leaves. Airport is struck. T-Anne enters and sets a ghost light.)

T-ANNE: 'Night, baby.

LISABETTE: 'Night. *(Lisabette remains in a single light. She looks around her.)* Wow. Crazy. It's so stupid, but I love to act. It always feels like anything could happen. That something wonderful could happen. It's just people, you know, just people doing it and watching it, but I think everybody hopes that it might turn out to be something more than that. Like people buy a ticket to the lottery, only this has more...heart to it. And most times, it doesn't turn out any better than the lottery, but sometimes...my dad runs a community center, and back in the day they did this play called *Raisin in the Sun*, just about a black family or something, and it was just people doing it. He said there was a grocery guy and a car mechanic, a waitress, but the whole thing had like...I don't know...aura, and people wanted to be there...so much that when they would practice at night, 'cause everybody had jobs, they had to open the doors at the center and hundreds of black people would just show up, show up for the play practice. They brought kids, they brought dinner, old people in wheelchairs, and they would hang around the whole time, kids running up and down, until the actors went home, night after night at practice, and when they finished, these people would stick around and they would line up outside like a...reception line...like a wedding...and the actors would walk down that line... "How you doin'? How you doin'?" shaking hands, pattin' on the kids, and the people would give them pies and yard flowers, and then the audience and the actors would all walk out, in the pitch dark, to the parking lot together. Nobody knew exactly what it was or why it happened. Some day I'd like to be in a play like that. I would. So I guess I'll go on...keep trying...what do you think? Could happen. Maybe. Maybe not. *(She looks at the audience.)* Well, you came tonight anyway. *(Blackout.)*

END OF PLAY

Big Love
by Charles L. Mee

BIOGRAPHY

Charles L. Mee's plays include *The Berlin Circle, Orestes, Vienna: Lusthaus, The Investigation of the Murder in El Salvador, Another Person Is a Foreign Country* and *Time to Burn.* His plays have been performed in New York, Washington, Los Angeles, and elsewhere in the United States, as well as in Venice, Vienna, Paris and other cities in Europe. Among his books are *Meeting at Potsdam, The Marshall Plan* and *The End of Order.* His books have been selections of Book of the Month Club, the Literary Guild, and the History Book Club, and have been published in England, France, Germany, Italy, Argentina, Japan, Holland, Poland, Turkey, Yugoslavia, Israel and the United States. His autobiography, *A Nearly Normal Life,* was published in 1999.

HUMANA FESTIVAL PRODUCTION

Big Love was commissioned by Actors Theatre of Louisville with support from the National Endowment for the Arts. It premiered at the Humana Festival of New American Plays in March 2000. It was directed by Les Waters with the following cast:

Lydia . . . . Carolyn Baeumler
Giuliano. . . . . Tony Speciale
Olympia. . . . . Aimee Guillot
Thyona. . . . . Karenjune Sanchez
Bella/Eleanor . . . . Lauren Klein
Piero/Leo . . . . Fred Major
Nikos . . . . T Ryder Smith
Constantine . . . . Mark Zeisler
Oed . . . . Jeff Jenkins
Extra Brides . . . . Pascaline Bellegarde, Aimée Hayes
Extra Grooms . . . . Dano Madden, Matt Zehnder

and the following production staff:

Scenic Designer . . . . Paul Owen
Costume Designer . . . . Marcia Dixcy Jory
Lighting Designer . . . . Greg Sullivan
Sound Designer . . . . Malcolm Nicholls
Properties Designer. . . . . Ben Hohman
Stage Manager . . . . Alyssa Hoggatt
Assistant Stage Manager. Kathy Preher
Movement Supervisor . . . . Jean Isaacs
Dramaturg . . . . Michael Bigelow Dixon
Assistant Dramaturgs . . . . Kelly Lea Miller, Kerry Mulvaney
Casting . . . . Laura Richin Casting

CHARACTERS

LYDIA

OLYMPIA

THYONA

BELLA/ELEANOR

PIERO/LEO

GIULIANO

CONSTANTINE

NIKOS

OED

SETTING

A villa on the coast of Italy. The present.

AUTHOR'S NOTE

This play, written in celebration of the millennium, is inspired by what some believe to be the earliest surviving play of the western world, *The Suppliant Women* by Aeschylus. It is also inspired by, or takes texts from, Valerie Solanus, Maureen Stanton, Lisa St Aubin de Teran, Sei Shonagon, Eleanor Clark, Barbara Grizzuti Harrison, Kate Simon, and Laurie Williams, among others. Charles L. Mee's work is made possible by the support of Richard B. Fisher and Jeanne Donovan Fisher.

Karenjune Sanchez, Carolyn Baeumler and Aimee Guillot
in *Big Love*

24th Annual Humana Festival of New American Plays
Actors Theatre of Louisville, 2000
photo by Richard Trigg

Big Love

Blackout.
Full volume: wedding processional music:
the triumphant music at the end of Scene 13, Act III,
of Mozart's Marriage of Figaro.
Lydia walks up the aisle,
looking somewhat disoriented,
carrying a wedding bouquet,
in a white wedding dress that is disheveled,
a little torn in places, dirty in spots.
She steps up onto the stage,
goes to the bathtub,
drops the bouquet on the floor,
takes off all her clothes,
or simply walks out of them,
steps into the tub,
leans her head back against the rim, exhausted,
and closes her eyes,
her arms thrown back out of the tub as though she were crucified,
as we listen to the music finish playing.
Now, quietly, sweetly, restfully,
Pachelbel's Canon in D
is heard,
and Giuliano steps onto the stage,
a glass of wine in his hand.
He is a young Italian man, handsome, agreeable,
weak and useless.
He seems a little surprised to see Lydia there
apparently napping in the tub.
This is Italy:
rose and white.
If Emanuel Ungaro had a villa on the west coast of Italy, this would be it:
we are outdoors,

on the terrace or in the garden,
facing the ocean:
wrought iron
white muslin
flowers
a tree
an arbor
an outdoor dinner table with chairs for six
a white marble balustrade
elegant
simple
basic
eternal.
But the setting for the piece should not be real, or naturalistic.
It should not be a set for the piece to play within
but rather something against which the piece can resonate:
something on the order of a bathtub, 100 olive trees,
and 300 wine glasses half-full of red wine.
More an installation than a set.
It is midsummer evening—the long, long golden twilight.
Giuliano and Lydia speak, quietly, and with many silences between their words,
as the music continues under the dialogue.
[Note: there are lots of Italians in this play,
but I don't think the actors should speak in Italian accents
any more than they would if they were doing Romeo and Juliet
or The Merchant of Venice.*]*

GIULIANO: Hello.
   [She opens her eyes.]
LYDIA: Hello.
GIULIANO: I'm Giuliano.
LYDIA: Hello, Giuliano
GIULIANO: And you are…
LYDIA: Lydia.
GIULIANO: Lydia.
   I don't think we've met.
LYDIA: No.
GIULIANO: You've just—arrived.

LYDIA: Yes.

GIULIANO: That's your boat offshore?

LYDIA: Yes.

GIULIANO: A big boat.

LYDIA: Well...it belongs to my family.

GIULIANO: You've come for the weekend?

LYDIA: Yes, oh, yes, at least.

GIULIANO: You're friends of my sister.

LYDIA: Your sister?

GIULIANO: My uncle?

LYDIA: Your uncle?

    [Silence.]

GIULIANO: I don't mean to be rude, but...

    [With a smile.]

    who was it invited you?

LYDIA: Invited us?

GIULIANO: You didn't come to the party?

    You mean: you're not a guest.

LYDIA: Oh, you mean, this is your home.

    I'm in your home.

GIULIANO: Yes.

    Well, it's my uncle's house.

LYDIA: It's so big.

    I thought it was a hotel.

GIULIANO: We have a big family.

LYDIA: I'm sorry I just...

GIULIANO: It's OK.

    Where do you come from?

LYDIA: Greece.

GIULIANO: Greece. You mean

    just now?

LYDIA: Yes.

    My sisters and I.

    We were to be married to our cousins, and

    well, we didn't want to, but

    we had to, so

    when the wedding day came

    we just got on our boat and left

so

here we are.

GIULIANO: Just like that.

LYDIA: Yes.

GIULIANO: Just walked away from the altar
and sailed away from Greece.

LYDIA: Yes.

Where are we?

GIULIANO: Italy.

This is Italy.

LYDIA: Oh. Italy.

I love Italy.

GIULIANO: It's...well...yes. So do I.

And your sisters are still on the boat?

LYDIA: Yes, most of them.

We came...

[Looking around.]

at least, some of us came ashore.

There are fifty of us all together.

GIULIANO: Fifteen?

LYDIA: Fifty.

Fifty sisters.

GIULIANO: [Laughing awkwardly.]

I...

I don't think even I know anyone who has fifty sisters.

And you were all to get married?

LYDIA: Yes.

GIULIANO: To your cousins?

LYDIA: Yes.

We're looking for asylum.

We want to be taken in here

so we don't have to marry our cousins.

GIULIANO: You want to be taken in as immigrants?

LYDIA: As refugees.

GIULIANO: Refugees.

LYDIA: Yes.

GIULIANO: From...

LYDIA: From Greece.

GIULIANO: I mean, from, you know:

   political oppression, or war…

LYDIA: Or kidnapping. Or rape.

GIULIANO: From rape.

LYDIA: By our cousins.

GIULIANO: Well, marriage really.

LYDIA: Not if we can help it.

   [Silence.]

GIULIANO: I see.

LYDIA: You seem like a good person, Giuliano.

   We need your help.

   [Silence.]

GIULIANO: I think you should talk to my uncle.

   Piero, he has…connections.

   Just stay right here.

   If you'll wait here,

   I'll bring him out.

LYDIA: Thank you.

   [The conversation ends just a few moments
   before the end of the 4:58 of the Pachelbel Canon in D;
   Giuliano leaves, and
   she weeps and weeps while the music finishes
   and the Pachelbel segues into another musical piece,
   a contemporary song
   about freedom and making one's own life,
   a song of triumph and liberation;
   and, as the intro to this song plays,
   two more young women in wedding dresses enter:
   Olympia and Thyona.
   Their wedding dresses, too, are of course white,
   but in different styles,
   and in varying states of disrepair—
   torn or dirty or wrinkled.
   Olympia carries the broken heel of a high-heeled shoe,
   and she walks, up and down, in a single shoe.
   The women enter without ceremony,
   dragging in a huge steamer trunk,
   struggling with it.

Or else they have a matching set of luggage,
eight pieces or more, that they wrestle onto the stage,
and they peel off, one by one, exhausted or exasperated with the luggage,
giving up on it.

Olympia goes to the bathtub,
pulls up her dress and sits on the edge
with her feet in the tub
and sings with all her heart.
Thyona, meanwhile, unpacks wedding gifts from the trunk—
plates and glasses and cups and saucers,
and—to set the scene for what kind of a play this is,
that it is not a text with brief dances and other physical activities
added to it, but rather a piece in which
the physical activities and the text are equally important to the experience—
she hurls the plates and cups and glasses with all her force against the wall
shattering them into a million bits.
Olympia sings a song of coming through trials to triumph.

Lydia joins in singing with Olympia on the choruses;
finally Thyona joins in the singing, too.
Bella, an old Italian woman in black dress and babushka
with a basket of tomatoes, comes out before the song ends;
she drags out a simple wooden chair and a folding card table with her,
which she sets up noisily.]

BELLA: Scusi, eh?

[And she sits and starts sorting through her tomatoes,
putting the nice ones to one side,
shining them a bit first on her apron.
Bella looks up at the young women.]

BELLA: So.

This is your wedding day?

LYDIA: No.

BELLA: You are trying on your dresses

because your wedding day is coming soon.

LYDIA: No.

THYONA: No, we're not getting married.

BELLA: You have been married already.

OLYMPIA: No.

BELLA: So, it's none of my business.
And yet, I can tell you
marriage is a wonderful thing.
Imagine that:
No husbands.
At your age.
And children.
When I was your age already I had three sons.
Now, I have thirteen sons.

LYDIA: Thirteen sons.

BELLA: My oldest, that's Piero,
he stays home here with his mother.
He's a good boy.
*[She puts one polished tomato carefully, lovingly to one side,
as though it were her own baby.]*
But too old for you.

LYDIA: We were hoping to meet Piero. We wanted to…

BELLA: *[Ignoring Lydia, continuing.]*
My second son, Paolo,
he lives just next door
a doctor
he takes good care of people here in town
[Another polished tomato placed lovingly to one side.]
Married.
Five children.
A good boy.
Paolo, he is Giuliano's father.
You met Giuliano?

LYDIA: Yes, and he said we might be able to meet…

BELLA: *[Ignoring Lydia, continuing.]*
My third son, he's in business here in the town,
visits me every week
every Sunday without fail
a good boy.
Also married,
four children.
[Another polished tomato tenderly to one side.]

LYDIA: Excuse me, but…
BELLA: My fourth son
    he was a sweet child
    cherubic
    such little cheeks
    such a tender boy
    a sunny disposition
    [She puts another tomato to one side,
    but too close to the edge so that it
    "accidentally" rolls off the table to the ground,
    where it splats.]
LYDIA: Oh.
BELLA: he joined the church.
    [She looks at the splatted tomato for a moment,
    then resumes.]
    My fifth son
    he also went into business here in town
    [She starts to put the polished tomato carefully to one side.]
    but then he got involved with certain business associates…
    [She moves her hand out over open space,
    pauses a moment,
    then drops the tomato with a splat to the ground.]
    My sixth son
    he's married to a German girl.
    [Splat.]
    My seventh son
    he went to America
    [Splat.]
    took his younger brother
    [Splat.]
    and then, two years later,
    they sent for their brother Guido,
    and he went to America, too.
    [Splat.]
    My tenth son,
    he became a politician.
    [She holds the tomato out over the ground for several moments,
    in deep anguish,
    then shrugs, and splats it.]

230   CHARLES L. MEE

LYDIA: Excuse me, but…

BELLA: My eleventh son
    he is on television
    on a soap opera
    with the stories of love affairs
    and godknows whatnot
    [She starts to drop another tomato to the ground,
    thinks better of it,
    puts it on the table.]
    he's not killing people.

LYDIA: No.

BELLA: My twelfth son
    he's not killing anyone either
    but he has his love affairs
    he argues all the time with his wife
    he keeps her like a tramp
    he spends all his money
    going here and there for soccer games
    [She starts to drop another tomato.]
    but,
    a good man is hard to find.
    [Thinks better of it, starts to put it with the others she has saved.]

OLYMPIA: That's so true.

BELLA: Still, he's always getting into fights
    he comes home in the middle of the night
    [Starts to drop it again.]
    nobody's perfect

THYONA: No.

BELLA: *[She saves the tomato.]*
    he loves his children.
    [She saves it.]

LYDIA: That's a good thing.

BELLA: My youngest son
    he likes to ride the motorcycles
    he likes to be in Rome
    with the young movie actresses
    and the parties
    [She starts to splat another tomato,

then takes it back and puts it gently on the table.]
he's my baby.

LYDIA: I see.

BELLA: So, what do I have left?
Now you see why I love my Piero so much,
and want to protect him,
my first born,
who is too old for you.
[Silence.]
You're staying for dinner?

LYDIA: We haven't been invited.
*[The uncle, Piero, comes out of the house,
a glass of wine in his hand.]*

BELLA: Piero,
you should make them stay for dinner.
They're good girls.
[Bella gathers her tomatoes into her apron.]
I never had daughters.
Imagine that.
[Bella leaves.]

PIERO: Giuliano,
mi dispiacce, ma…
[Piero shrugs.]

GIULIANO: Si. Fa niente.
*[Giuliano picks up a pail and rag
and cleans up the mess Bella has made.
Piero speaks to the young women with great warmth,
a welcoming manner, relaxed, a sense of playfulness.
There might be music under this scene,
maybe Molloy's* Love's Old Sweet Song
or some champagne music from inside the house.]

PIERO: May I offer you something?

LYDIA: No, thank you.

PIERO: A glass of wine?

OLYMPIA and THYONA:
No, thank you.

PIERO: Coffee? Tea?

LYDIA: No thanks.

PIERO: Something to eat?

LYDIA: No, thank you.

OLYMPIA: Actually,

    I don't know how to say this,

    I don't want to complain

    but you don't seem to have a lot of products.

PIERO: Products?

OLYMPIA: Soaps, you know, and creams,

    things like,

LYDIA: Olympia…

OLYMPIA: You know, we've been travelling,

    and when you've been travelling

    you hope at the end of the journey that you might find

    some, like,

    Oil of Olay Moisturizing Body Wash

    or like

    John Frieda Sheer Blonde Shampoo and Conditioner for Highlighted Blondes.

LYDIA: Olympia…

OLYMPIA: I know this is not a hotel, so you wouldn't have everything,

    but maybe some Estēe Lauder 24 Karat Color Golden Body Creme with

        Sunblock,

    or Fetish Go Glitter Body Art in Soiree,

LYDIA: Olympia…

OLYMPIA: or some Prescriptives Uplift Eye Cream: firming,

    Mac lip gloss in Pink Poodle

    just

    some things to make a woman feel

    you know

    fresh

LYDIA: Olympia….

PIERO: I am afraid I don't know about these things,

    but I'll ask Giuliano to go out and see what he can find.

OLYMPIA: Thank you.

LYDIA: Olympia…

    Really we were mostly hoping to ask you to just: take us in.

PIERO: Take you in?

LYDIA: Your nephew Giuliano says you have some connections.

PIERO: Oh?

LYDIA: And that you can help us.

PIERO: Well, of course, this is a country where people know one another
and, Giuliano is right, sometimes these connections can be useful.
If, for example,
you were a member of my family,
certainly I would just take you in.
But
[He shrugs.]
I don't know you.

LYDIA: [Thinking quickly.]
Oh. But.
We are related.
I mean, you know: in some way.
Our people came from Greece to Sicily a long time ago
and to Siracusa
and from Siracusa to Taormina and to the Golfo di Sant'Eufemia
and from there up the coast of Italy to where we are now.
So we are probably members of the same family you and I.

PIERO: [Amused.]
Descended from Zeus, you mean.

OLYMPIA: Yes. We're all sort of goddesses in a way.

PIERO: Indeed. It's very enticing to recover a family connection to Zeus.
And, where is your father, meanwhile?
Is he not able to take care of you?

LYDIA: Our father signed a wedding contract to give us away.

PIERO: To your cousins from Greece.

THYONA: From America.
They went from Greece to America,
and now they're rich
and they think they can come back
and take whatever they want.

PIERO: And the courts in your country:
will they enforce such a contract?

LYDIA: It's an old contract. It seems they will.
We have nothing against men—

OLYMPIA: Not all of us.

LYDIA: but what these men have in mind is not usual.

THYONA: Or else
all too usual.

[Silence.]

PIERO: You know, as it happens, I have some houseguests here for the weekend
and I would be delighted if you would all join us for dinner,
stay the night if you like
until you get your bearings
but really
as for the difficulties you find yourselves in
disagreeable as they are
and as much as I would like to help
this is not my business.

THYONA: Whose business is it
if not yours?
You're a human being.

OLYMPIA: And a relative.

PIERO: A relative.

THYONA: This is a crisis.

PIERO: And yet…
You know, I am not the Red Cross.

THYONA: And so?

PIERO: So, to be frank,
I can't take in every refugee who comes into my garden.

OLYMPIA: Why not?

PIERO: Because the next thing I know I would have a refugee camp here in my
home.
I'd have a house full of Kosovars and Ibo and Tootsies
boat people from China and godknows whatall.

OLYMPIA: That would be nice.

PIERO: I don't think I can open my doors to the whole world.

OLYMPIA: Look at you, you're a rich person.

PIERO: OK. Well, then,
what if I were to say, yes, I can do my part,
in fact, I'm not a bad person entirely,
some people think of me even as a generous person,
and I can help,
but why should I help you?
Shouldn't I rather look around at the world and say:
no, not these people perhaps
but someone else has the greater claim on my attention.

LYDIA: But we are here.

PIERO: Yes?

LYDIA: We are here on your terrace.

Why do you look for someone else?

Look for someone else, too, if you want,

but we are here.

PIERO: And yet I know nothing about this dispute.

I don't know whether these fellows have some rights, too.

What shall I do if they come to me

and say you've abducted our women

give us our women

or we'll shoot you?

LYDIA: Shoot you?

PIERO: What do I know?

I don't know what sort of fellows they are.

I should put myself, perhaps my life on the line—

knowing nothing—

and also the life of my nephew

my brother next door

my brother's sons

people the same as you who just want to enjoy their own lives

take a stroll or play a game of cards

listen to their children play their violins

my niece next door, she plays the piano

Brahms and Bach.

I put their lives on the line

for what?

To save you whom

I've never met before?

I don't know what this is about

why would I do this?

LYDIA: Because it's right.

PIERO: I understand it may be right,

but one doesn't always go around doing what's right.

I've never heard of such a thing.

The world is a complicated place.

[Silence.]

OLYMPIA: It's not that no one's never said no to me,

but I don't think I've ever asked a guy to save me

in a situation like this
and had him say no.

THYONA: There is only one question to ask:
do we want to marry them or not?
No, we don't.
Are you going to let them
drag us away from your house
and do whatever they want with us?
Think of it this way:
if you don't take us in,
my sisters and I will hang ourselves here on your terrace:
fifty dead women hanging in front of your house.

PIERO: Hang yourselves?

THYONA: What choice do we have?
No one will help us. No one.
[Silence.]

LYDIA: Shall we ask your mother what she thinks would be right?

PIERO: You're right.
Of course.
You're right.
I beg your pardon.
Of course I'll take you in.
I don't know what I was thinking.

LYDIA: Thank you.

PIERO: I beg your pardon, really.
I wasn't quite absorbing what it was you were saying.
I'll tell my mother
you will stay for dinner,
and then we'll talk and see what's to be done.
Please, make yourselves at home.
And if there's anything at all you want, please ask.
[He leaves.]

OLYMPIA: Now you see, there are men who are kind and decent.

THYONA: Not so kind and decent
if he's not threatened with some kind of scandal of
dead women hanging off his house.

OLYMPIA: I liked him.
You should give a person the benefit of the doubt.

THYONA: You think you found this man's good side.

   Men don't have a good side.

OLYMPIA: I've known men who have a good side, Thyona.

LYDIA: I've known men you could sit with after dinner

      in front of the fireplace

      and just listen to the timbre of their voices

      and hear the gentleness in it

      and the carefulness

OLYMPIA: I've known men who think,

      oh,

      a woman,

      I'd like to take care of her

      not in any way that he thinks he is superior and has control

      but in the way that he understands

      a woman is a different sort of person

      and precious because of that

      vulnerable in certain ways because of that

      in ways that he isn't

      although he might be vulnerable in other ways

      because of his stuff that he has

      and that he treasures what a woman has

      and thinks, oh, if only I could be close to her

      and feel what she feels

      and see the world as she sees it

      how much richer my life would be

      and so, because of that, he thinks,

      oh, a woman,

      I can really respect her

      and love her

      for who she really is

THYONA: I know a man who will say I want to take care of you

      because he means he wants to use you for a while

      and while he's using you

      so you don't notice what he's doing

      he'll take care of you as if you were a new car

      before he decides to trade you in.

LYDIA: I've known men like that, too.

      But not all men are necessarily the same.

      Sometimes you can hear the whole man just in his voice

238   CHARLES L. MEE

how deep it is or how frightened
where it stops to think
and how complex and supple and sure it is
OLYMPIA: you can hear the strength in it
and you can know that you're safe
THYONA: The male
the male is a biological accident
an incomplete female
the product of a damaged gene
a half-dead lump of flesh
trapped in a twilight zone somewhere between apes and humans
always looking obsessively for some woman
LYDIA: That's maybe a little bit extreme.
THYONA: any woman
because he thinks if he can make some connection with a woman
that will make him a whole human being!
But it won't. It never will.
Boy babies should be flushed down the toilet at birth.
LYDIA: I know how you feel, Thyona.
OLYMPIA: I've felt that way myself sometimes.
LYDIA: Still, this man who doesn't even know us
who owes us nothing
doesn't know what he risks by offering us a place to stay.
There are places in the world
where refugees are taken in
out of generosity
and often these are men who do the taking in
because people have the capacity for goodness
and there could be a world where people care for one another
[As the speech goes on,
it is joined by the sound of a helicopter overhead
which grows louder and louder,
drowning out Lydia's words even as she goes on shouting them
until the helicopter is deafening
and wind is whipping everyone around so they have to fight to stand up.
Again: the over-the-top extremity of this physical world,
like Thyona throwing plates just when she enters—
should establish the kind of physical piece this is.]

where men are good to women
and there is not a men's history
and a separate women's history
but a human history
where we are all together
and support one another
nurture one another
[Stanley's Trumpet Tune *joins the deafening helicopter noise.]*
honor one another's differences
and learn to live together
in common justice
reconciling our differences in peaceful conversation
reaching out with goodwill towards another
[A loudspeaker says:
"STAND BACK. STAND BACK.
STAND AWAY FROM THE HELICOPTER."]
not trying to obliterate those who are not as we are
but learning to understand
learning to take deep pleasure
in the enormous variety of creatures
[She is on the ground toward the end of this speech,
her head lifted up to the sky as she shouts her words
until
finally, she is hunkered down on stage,
her hands over her head;
the helicopter engine is turned off,
and the noise recedes,
and Stanley's Trumpet Tune *concludes;*
she lifts her head to see that
three guys have entered: Nikos, Constantine, and Oed;
they wear tuxedoes with flowers in their buttonholes
underneath flight suits,
and, as they enter, they are removing their ultra-high-tech flying helmets.]
Oh, Nikos,
you found us.
NIKOS: Lydia, why did you run away from us?
LYDIA: What?
NIKOS: We were waiting for you at the church.

THYONA: You can't force us to marry you, Nikos.

NIKOS: Force you?

We thought you were coming.

OLYMPIA: Why should we come?

OED: Because we were getting married.

THYONA: We never agreed to marry you.

NIKOS: We have a prenuptial agreement, Lydia.

CONSTANTINE: We have a deal.

THYONA: We never had a deal with you, Constantine.

CONSTANTINE: Your father made a deal with my father

before you were born, Thyona.

You are engaged to me,

and I am going to marry you.

THYONA: This is from the Dark Ages.

NIKOS: Well, if there was some misunderstanding…

THYONA: There was no misunderstanding.

We are not marrying you.

CONSTANTINE: There is a contract involved here.

NIKOS: My brothers and I, we've counted on this all our lives.

And, plus, I thought it would be kind of neat:

a big wedding, fifty brides and fifty grooms,

a real event.

CONSTANTINE: And we never agreed to release you from your promise.

THYONA: Why not?

CONSTANTINE: Because I am a traditional person, Thyona.

I want a traditional marriage,

a traditional wife.

That's the way it is.

THYONA: It's a different world now, Constantine.

You can't just marry someone against their will

because there's been some kind of family understanding.

CONSTANTINE: What do you think?

You think you live in a world nowadays where

you can throw out a promise

just because you don't feel like keeping it?

Just because

drugs are rife

gambling is legal

medicine is euthanasia

birth is abortion

homosexuality is the norm

pornography is piped into everybody's home on the internet

now you think you can do whatever you want

whenever you want to do it

no matter what the law might say?

I don't accept that.

Sometimes I like to lie down at night

with my arms around someone

and KNOW she is there for me

know this gives her pleasure—

my arms around her

her back to me

my stomach pressed against her back

my face buried in her hair

one hand on her stomach

feeling at peace.

That's my plan

to have that.

I'll have my bride.

If I have to have her arms tied behind her back

and dragged to me

I'll have her back.

What is it you women want

you want to be strung up with hoods and gags and blindfolds

stretched out on a board with weights on your chest

you want me to sew your legs to the bed

and pour gasoline on you

and light you on fire

is that what I have to do to keep you?

[Silence.]

NIKOS: Lydia,

isn't this your wedding dress?

LYDIA: Yes.

NIKOS: It seems you were ready to get married.

CONSTANTINE: The future is going to happen, Thyona,

whether you like it or not.

You say, you don't want to be taken against your will.

People are taken against their will every day.

Do you want tomorrow to come?

Do you want to live in the future?

Never mind. You can't stop the clock.

Tomorrow will take today by force

whether you like it or not.

Time itself is an act of rape.

Life is rape.

No one asks to be born.

No one asks to die.

We are all taken by force, all the time.

You make the best of it.

You do what you have to do.

OLYMPIA: We have an uncle here, Constantine,

and he is going to take care of us.

CONSTANTINE: I am an American now, Olympia.

I'm not afraid of your uncle.

Do you watch television?

Do you see what happens when Americans want something?

[The uncle has entered.]

PIERO: Excuse me.

I am Piero. This is my home.

And you would be the cousins of these young women?

NIKOS: We're engaged to be married.

PIERO: I understand the women are no longer interested.

CONSTANTINE : We are not here to negotiate.

PIERO: That's a forthright position.

I like to know where I stand when I deal with a man.

But, before we talk, let me welcome you properly.

Why don't you come into the house with me,

and have a glass of something.

What's your favorite cigar?

Do you like a Cuban?

A Vegas Robaina?

A Partagas?

Is it...?

CONSTANTINE: Constantine.

PIERO: Constantine. And you are…?

OED: Oed.

PIERO: And…

NIKOS: Nikos.

PIERO: Nikos. Come with me.

We'll have a glass of something,

have a smoke,

get things sorted out.

NIKOS: I'd like that.

PIERO: Excuse us, ladies.

Come with me.

[He leads them out.]

THYONA: That bastard!

What did I tell you?

OLYMPIA: He's going to solve it peacefully.

THYONA: He's giving in, don't you get it?

These men and their deals.

LYDIA: Right.

You could be right.

OLYMPIA: I don't think he would do that.

THYONA: These men can talk a good game,

but when push comes to shove, they're weak right to the core.

OLYMPIA: Except for Constantine.

THYONA: And except for me.

I haven't given in either.

This game isn't over till someone lies on the ground

with the flesh pulled off their bones.

MEN.

You think you can do whatever you want with me, think again.

you think that I'm so delicate?

you think you have to care for me?

You throw me to the ground

you think I break?

[She throws herself to the ground.]

you think I can't get up again?

you think I can't get up again?

[She gets up.]

you think I need a man to save my life?

[She throws herself to the ground again.]
I don't need a man!
I don't need a man!
[She gets up and throws herself to the ground again and again as she yells.]
These men can fuck themselves!
these men are leeches
these men are parasites
these rapists,
these politicians,
these Breadwinners,
[She is throwing herself to the ground over and over,
letting her loose limbs hit the ground with the rattle of a skeleton's bones,
her head lolling over and hitting the ground with a thwack,
rolling over, bones banging the ground,
back to her feet,
and throwing herself to the ground again in the same way over and over
music kicks in over this—
maybe J.S. Bach's "Sleepers Awake!" from Cantata No. 140
and, as she hits the ground over and over,
repeating her same litany as she does,
Olympia watches her
and then she joins in,
and starts throwing herself to the ground synchronously
so that it is a choreographed piece
of the two women throwing themselves to the ground,
rolling around, flailing on the ground,
banging angrily on the ground,
rising again and again.]
THYONA: *[Yelling.]*
these cheap pikers,
these welchers,
these liars,
these double dealers,
flim-flam artists,
litterbugs,
psychiatrists!
[And now Olympia starts to yell, too,
simultaneously with Thyona, on top of her words,
as both of them continue to throw themselves to the ground over and over.]

OLYMPIA: These men!
  These men!
  All I wanted was a man who could be gentle
  a man who likes to cuddle
  a man who likes to talk
  a man who likes to listen
THYONA: Men who speak when they have nothing to say!
  These men should be eliminated!
  These men should be snuffed out!
  Who needs a man?
  Who needs a man?
  I'll make it on my own.
  I'm an autonomous person!
  I'm an independent person!
  I can do what I want!
  I can be who I am!
OLYMPIA: [Still yelling simultaneously with Thyona.]
  And I don't think it's wrong
  to lie in the bath
  and curl my hair
  and paint my nails
  to like my clothes
  and think they're sexy
  and wear short skirts
  that blow up in the wind
  I don't think it's wrong
  for a man to love me
  to like to touch me
  and listen to me
  and talk to me
  and write me notes
  and give me flowers
  because I like men
  I like men
  And, I like to be submissive.
  [And, finally, Lydia joins in, too,
  until all three women are yelling their words
  over the loud music
  and throwing themselves to the ground over and over.]

LYDIA: Why can't a man
　　　be more like a woman?
　　　Plainspoken and forthright.
　　　Honest and clear.
　　　Able to process.
　　　To deal with his feelings.
　　　To speak from the heart
　　　to say what he means.
　　　Because if he can
　　　I don't have a grudge
　　　or something against him
　　　we couldn't work out.
　　　I think it's wrong
　　　to make sweeping judgments
　　　write off a whole sex
　　　the way men do to women
　　　we could talk to each other
　　　person to person
　　　get along with each other
　　　then we could go deep
　　　to what a man or a woman
　　　really can be
　　　deep down to the mysteries
　　　of being alive
　　　of knowing ourselves
　　　to know what it is
　　　to live life on earth
　　　[The women work themselves, still in choreographed sync,
　　　to a state of total exhaustion
　　　until one by one, they sprawl on chairs, panting.
　　　Giuliano comes in with an armload of wedding gifts
　　　which he begins unwrapping and holding up for everyone to see:
　　　there could be many pots and pans,
　　　14 toasters, carving knives, lingerie—
　　　or it could be all sex equipment: dildos,
　　　dominatrix costumes, ropes, handcuffs, chains,
　　　bondage equipment of all sorts.
　　　Bella enters with him,
　　　also carrying gifts.]

GIULIANO: The wedding presents have come
    now that everyone knows where to find you.
    Frankly, I've never seen so many gifts
    so much silver
    so many white things
    so much satin ribbon.
    Do you think
    we could save the ribbon?
    Because
    I wouldn't mind having the ribbon
    I haven't taken any yet
    I was going to ask you
    if you don't want it
    because I have a collection of Barbies and Kens
    and this ribbon would go with the whole ensemble
    so perfectly
    this ensemble that I have
    they are all arrayed together with their hands up in the air
    because they are doing the firewalking ceremony
    and Barbie has her pink feather boa
    and her lime green outfit with the flowers at the waist
    and the gold bow at the bodice
    and Ken is doing the Lambada
    so of course they all have mai tais
    and they're just having a wonderful time
    and their convertible is parked nearby
    so you know they can take off to see the sunset any time they want
    and when people come over and see my collection
    they just say wow
    because
    because they can't believe I've just done it
    but I think if that's who you are
    you should just be who you are
    whatever that is
    just do who you are
    because that's why we're here
    and if it's you
    it can't be wrong.

Some people like to be taken forcibly.
If that's what they like, then that's okay.
And if not, then not.
I myself happen to like it.
To have somebody grab me.
Hold me down.
To know they have to have me
no matter what.
It's not everyone's cup of tea.
Everyone should be free to choose for themselves.

OLYMPIA: *[Picking up one of the wedding gifts.]*
Plus some of these things are nice.
Can we keep them?

THYONA: No, Olympia.
Not if you aren't getting married.

OLYMPIA: Maybe we should think about it.
Some people go on honeymoons, too.

LYDIA: Olympia.

OLYMPIA: They go to places where there are hammocks and white sand
and people hold them by the waist
and lift them up out of the water
splashing and laughing
and they dive underwater
without the tops to their swimming suits
and the sun sets
and people drink things through straws

LYDIA: Olympia…

OLYMPIA: and they listen to the waves
and even make love in the afternoon
and even be submissive
because, to me,
submission is giving up your body,
and your soul and your mind and your heart and your emotions
and everything
to a someone who can accept all the responsibilities that go with that.
And I enjoy the freedom that submission gives me,
allowing my mind to go completely free.
I like to be tickled and tortured

and I like to scream and scream
and feel helpless
and be totally controlled
and see how good that makes someone else feel
It is for me the most natural high.
And the most intense natural high.
I like to be bound up tight.
I like to be manhandled.
It is so much better than taking drugs,
because you can imagine so much
it just sets you entirely free
you can just relax and enjoy yourself
and feel alive and free inside.

LYDIA: I think we're losing the point.
Like
shouldn't we be leaving?

THYONA: You don't think they'll follow us now wherever we go?
They found us here.
They'll find us anywhere.
Now we have to stand our ground
and meet them face to face.

BELLA: I had a man once
I was walking along the Appia Antica
and he came along on his motor scooter
and offered me a ride.
A skinny, ugly fellow with dark hair
and skin so sleek and smooth
I wanted to put my hands on it.
I got on the back of his motor scooter
and ten minutes later
we were in bed together at his mother's house
and I married him
and we had our boys.
All his life he worked
giving the gift of his labor to me
and to our children
he died of a heart attack
while he was out among the trees

harvesting the olives
and
if he came along now
I would get on the scooter again just like the first time.
[Bella plumks down the wedding gifts she was carrying and goes out.
By this time Giuliano is sitting at the piano
and he plays and sings a medley of love songs
or parts of love songs.]

[Two more house guests enter,
Eleanor and Leo,
with arms full of wedding gifts.
She is English; he is Italian.]

ELEANOR: Look, we have more presents.

Are these things for you girls?

THYONA: We're not accepting gifts.

ELEANOR: Not accepting gifts?

Whoever heard of such a thing?

Oh, Leo, these girls!

I suppose they're nervous before the wedding!

LYDIA: We are not nervous.

It's like Thyona says.

We don't want wedding presents!

OLYMPIA: Yet.

ELEANOR: Oh, darling, don't say that.

There are so few occasions

when people give you things

and things are good!

LEO: A bottle of champagne.

Good food.

ELEANOR: A handsome man.

A sunny day.

Life's pleasures,

you can't have too many really.

LEO: When you are young, you think nothing of it.

But the older you get

the more you think: oh, god, let me have more pleasures!

ELEANOR: Don't take me away from the blessed earth

and all its joys.

A swim in the afternoon.
Sex.
A man with a nice nose
a good pair of shoulders
sky blue eyes—
[Remembering Leo.]
or chocolate brown eyes!

THYONA: Who are you?

ELEANOR: House guests, dear.
Guests of Piero.
And you're the brides?

THYONA: No.

OLYMPIA: We're still sort of thinking about it.

ELEANOR: How exciting for Piero to have a wedding for us.
To me, it just makes a perfect weekend.

LEO: I myself always say:
you need to embrace life.

ELEANOR: You need to let it in through every pore.

LEO: We come this way but once
this brief, brief time on earth
we need to suck it in.
The key thing is
you'll be wanting to let go of fear

ELEANOR: throw yourself into life

LEO: put all your fears and pain in a garbage can
and attach the garbage can to a yellow balloon
filled with helium
and let it go!

ELEANOR: This has to stop!

LEO: Love,
love touches,
love fondles,
love listens to its own needs.

ELEANOR: Love goes beyond hope.

LEO: Hope is a beginning.
Love is forever.

OLYMPIA: Yes.
This is how I feel.

LEO: We are on a fantastic journey, all of us.
    Every day is new.
    Every experience is new.
    Every person is new.
THYONA: What is it with you Italian guys?
    You spout this kind of bullshit
    and all you're ever thinking is,
    if I keep up this line of chatter,
    can I pinch some woman's butt?
ELEANOR: Isn't that the truth?
    And if you smile
    or simply return a look with a look
    you find you've sealed your fate
    you've fallen into life way over your head
    nothing is held back
    like a Roman fountain
    all splash and burble
    and you find yourself carried off
    or even to walk through a crowd
    you're in constant contact
    with all sorts of elbows and knees
    and souls and buttocks
    touching and rubbing
    everything that in another minute will all be naked.
    I just think everything is shocking in Italy,
    and I'm not a puritan
    I mean, of course, I am a puritan,
    but that's what I love about Italy,
    because here, I am not a puritan.
    I am alive. I love life. I take it in,
    its tomatoes, its sunshine,
LEO: its olive oil,
ELEANOR: its paintings, its men
LEO: everything is as though a giant mother
    were squashing you to her breast.
ELEANOR: In Italy, to go out
    is to come home.
OLYMPIA: I'd like to take it in.
    You know, I wouldn't mind, like,

going swimming even.

Plus guys.

I don't have a problem with guys.

THYONA: I don't have a problem with guys either.

This is not about sunshine and olive oil.

This is about guys hauling you off to their cave.

LYDIA: *[To Leo.]*

Still.

You remind me of my father.

So kind and gentle.

So full of enthusiasm.

[Music.

Handel's Air from Water Music, Suite No. 1.

Lydia and Leo dance,

a long, long, slow, intimate, heartbreaking father/daughter dance.

The others are all silent,

respectful of the moment.

They stand watching.

And when the dance is ended,

and the music stops,

there is a moment of silence before Giuliano speaks

meditatively—

or, if it seems good, Giuliano can start speaking while they are still dancing.]

GIULIANO: I knew a man once

so kind and generous.

I was a boy

I was on a train going to Brindisi

and he said, I'm going to marry you.

I was so surprised.

He came out of nowhere.

There was such a crowd on the train

and nothing to eat

and he shared his picnic basket with me.

He asked how far I was going.

To Rome, I said.

No, no, he said,

you can't get off so soon,

you need to go with me to Bologna.

He wouldn't hear of my getting off in Rome
or he would get off, too, and meet my family.
He would buy me from them.
He wanted to know, what would it take.
He gave me a pocket watch
and a silk scarf
and a little statue of a saint
he had picked up in Morocco.
He quoted Dante to me
and sang bits of Verdi and Puccini.
He was trying everything he knew
to make me laugh and enjoy myself.
But, finally,
he seemed so insistent
that I grew frightened of him.
I thought he might be insane.
He never touched me,
but he made me promise, finally,
that I would come to Bologna in two weeks time
after I had seen my family.
I promised him,
because I thought he might not let me get off the train
unless I promised,
although, of course,
I never intended to keep my promise.
He gave me his address, which of course I threw away,
it seemed dangerous to me to keep it,
and I gave a false address to him.
And when I got off the train,
I saw that he was weeping.
And I've often thought,
oh, well,
maybe he really did love me
maybe that was my chance
and I ran away from it
because
I didn't know it at the time.
OLYMPIA: I think,
    for me,

there's nothing quite like it
when you know a person is attracted to you
and you look into his eyes and see your own reflection
through the tears of joy in his eyes,
as you've always wanted to see yourself,
and never have since you were a child
just sharing the daily things with another person
knowing you can count on him
having him tell me how he feels deep inside,
And I know he loves me all the time
when he purrs when I wake him up in the morning
hugging me all day
treating me as though I were precious.

THYONA: You are a twit.

OLYMPIA: I am not.

THYONA: I'll tell you something, Olympia.
You're the kind of person
who ends up in the bottom of a ravine somewhere
with your underpants over your head.
I'm trying to save your neck
and you don't even get it!

OLYMPIA: Oh!
What did I say wrong?

THYONA: Do you think I like feeling this way?
do you think it feels good to feel bad all the time
do you think I wouldn't rather just be a nice, happy
well-adjusted seeming person
who can just take it as it comes and like it?
But I can't just not be honest.
Do you think that makes me happy?
To spend my whole life on earth
the only life I'm going to have
feeling angry?
[She turns and runs out.]

OLYMPIA: Thyona!
[She runs after Thyona;
Nikos enters, shyly, stands to one side.
Eleanor and Leo hold a moment, seeing Nikos and Lydia looking at each other.]

ELEANOR: Come, Leo.

> Let's leave them alone.
>
> *[Eleanor and Leo leave.]*

NIKOS: I'm sorry

> for the way Constantine seemed a little rude.
> Well,
> I shouldn't put it all on him.
> I'm sorry for the way that we've behaved.

LYDIA: Thank you for saying so, Nikos.

NIKOS: I thought,

> I've always liked you, Lydia
> seeing you with your sisters
> sometimes in the summers
> when our families would get together at the beach.
> I thought you were fun, and funny
> and really good at volleyball

LYDIA: Volleyball?

NIKOS: which I thought showed you have a

> well,
> a natural grace
> and beauty
> and a lot of energy.

LYDIA: Oh.

NIKOS: And it's not that I thought I fell in love with you at the time

> or that I've been like a stalker or something in the background
> all these years.

LYDIA: No, I never…

NIKOS: But really, over the years,

> I've thought back from time to time
> how good it felt just to be around you.

LYDIA: Oh.

NIKOS: And so I thought: well, maybe this is an okay way

> to have a marriage

LYDIA: A marriage.

NIKOS: to start out

> not in a romantic way, but
> as a friendship

LYDIA: Oh.

NIKOS: because I admire you
and I thought perhaps this might grow into
something deeper
and longer lasting
LYDIA: Oh.
NIKOS: but maybe this isn't quite the thing you want
and really I don't want to force myself on you
you should be free to choose
I mean: obviously.
LYDIA: Thank you.
NIKOS: Although I think I should say
what began as friendship for me
and a sort of distant, even inattentive regard
has grown into a passion already
LYDIA: A passion.
NIKOS: I don't know how
or where it came from, or when
but somehow the more I felt this admiration
and, well, pleasure in you
LYDIA: Pleasure.
NIKOS: seeing you become the person that you are
I think a thoughtful person and smart
and it seems to me funny and warm
LYDIA: Funny.
NIKOS: and passionate, I mean about the things
I heard you talk about in school
a movie or playing the piano
I saw you one night at a cafe by the harbor
drinking almond nectar
and I saw that happiness made you raucous.
And I myself don't want to have a relationship
that's cool or distant
I want a love really that's all-consuming
that consumes my whole life
LYDIA: Your whole life.
NIKOS: and the longer the sense of you has lived with me
the more it has grown into a longing for you
so I wish you'd consider

maybe not marriage
because it's true you hardly know me
but a kind of courtship
LYDIA: A courtship.
NIKOS: or, maybe you'd just I don't know
go sailing with me or see a movie
LYDIA: Gee, Nikos,
you seem to talk a lot.
NIKOS: I talk too much.
I'm sorry.
LYDIA: Sometimes it seems to me
men get all caught up
in what they're doing
and they forget to take a moment
and look around
and see what effect they're having
on other people.
NIKOS: That's true.
LYDIA: They get on a roll.
NIKOS: I do that sometimes.
I wish I didn't.
But I get started on a sentence,
and that leads to another sentence,
and then, the first thing I know,
I'm just trying to work it through,
the logic of it,
follow it through to the end
because I think,
if I stop,
or if I don't get through to the end
before someone interrupts me
they won't understand what I'm saying
and what I'm saying isn't necessarily wrong—
it might be, but not necessarily,
and if it is, I'll be glad to be corrected,
or change my mind—
but if I get stopped along the way
I get confused

I don't remember where I was
or how to get back to the end of what I was saying.
LYDIA: I understand.
NIKOS: And I think sometimes I scare people
    because of it
    they think I'm so, like determined
    just barging ahead—
    not really a sensitive person,
    whereas, in truth,
    I am.
LYDIA: I know.
    Do you know about dreams?
NIKOS: Well, I have dreams.
LYDIA: But do you know what they mean?
NIKOS: I don't know. Maybe.
LYDIA: I had this dream
    I was going to a wedding
    of these old friends of mine
    and part of the wedding—uh, sort of event—
    was an enormous pond that they had built,
    and I was late getting to the wedding
    so I got someone to airlift me in,
    and I dove into the pond but,
    when I landed in the water,
    the walls of the pond collapsed and it drained out
    and 1500 fish died,
    and everyone was looking for survivors
    but I had to leave to take Yeltsin to the Museum of Modern Art,
    because I had to get to the gym.

    So, when I took him in to one of the exhibits
    and turned around to hug him goodbye,
    he turned to my mother and said,
    "Wow, look at that Julian Schnabel bridge."
    There was an enormous sterling silver bridge
    designed by Julian Schnabel.
    So I walked my mother into the water to say goodbye to her,
    and this immense 25-story high tidal wave crashed over me

and threw me up over the Julian Schnabel bridge
and then I was completely alone in the middle of the ocean
until I realized:
I had the cell phone tucked into my undies.
So I phoned Olympia to come and get me,
and she said, oh, perfect, I'll send Chopin—
which is the name of her dog—
I'll send Chopin over in the car,
and then would you take him for a walk
and leave the car on 8th Avenue?
What do you think of that?

NIKOS: Well,
    I think things happen so suddenly sometimes.

LYDIA: Sometimes people don't want to fall in love.
    Because when you love someone
    it's too late to set conditions.
    You can't say
    I'll love you if you do this
    or I'll love you if you change that
    because you can't help yourself
    and then you have to live
    with whoever it is you fall in love with
    however they are
    and just put up with the difficulties you've made for yourself
    because true love has no conditions.
    That's why it's so awful to fall in love.
    [The heartbreaking music of the Largo
    from Bach's "Air on the G-string"
    and after a moment,
    Lydia and Nikos dance—a long, long, sweet dance.
    And then, when they stop at last:]

LYDIA: What would you like to do with me?

NIKOS: I'd like to kiss you.

LYDIA: Kiss you? But I don't even know you.

NIKOS: Well, if you'd kiss me, then you'd know me.
    [They kiss;
    they part;
    she looks at him,
    and then she turns and runs out.]

NIKOS: Oh.

    God.

    God.

    Goddammit.

    [He throws himself to the ground.]

    Goddammit!

    [He gets up;

    Constantine enters, sees Nikos;

    Nikos whirls and throws himself to the ground again.]

NIKOS: Goddammit.

CONSTANTINE: Goddammit.

    [Nikos gets up;

    Constantine saunters over to stand next to Nikos.]

CONSTANTINE: This is how it is.

NIKOS: Yes, this is how it is.

    Goddammit!

    [Nikos throws himself to the ground again;

    Constantine hesitates a moment; then throws himself to the ground, too,

    in imitation of Nikos—not that he, Constantine, has any particular agenda

    about it.

    Music.

    Marc-Antoine Charpentier's Prelude to Te Deum *at full volume*

    so that hardly any of the following words can be heard.

    Oed enters; he sees Nikos and Constantine continue to throw themselves to the

    ground over and over as they talk/shout.]

NIKOS: When I was a boy I thought

    I had it made.

    My coach said to me

    you could be good.

CONSTANTINE: damned good

NIKOS: I had the instincts.

    I could hit the ball.

CONSTANTINE: I could hit the ball.

NIKOS: I could run.

CONSTANTINE: I could run

NIKOS: My dad played football.

CONSTANTINE: My dad played football.

[Working along at this kind of rhythm
Constantine repeats the words of Nikos that appear in bold type;
and sometimes he can take just one thought, such as "jerk" or "big man"
and keep yelling it over and over while Nikos goes on with the rest of what he
   is saying;
or sometimes he says it simultaneously or nearly simultaneously with Nikos;
and, pretty soon,
Oed joins in,
yelling out the words and phrases that are in boldface
sometimes simultaneously with Nikos and Constantine,
or at different moments,
so it is a chaos of three talking at once,
but we can hear it because it is the same phrase repeated.]
Then everybody told me
you're just a jerk
this macho stuff
big man
bullshit
and then I thought
my instincts are off
my instincts are all off
[He's starting to cry now.]
I thought: **girls will like this**
but they didn't
so I hung out with **these guys**
it wasn't what I had in mind
and **all the fun had gone**
pretty soon **I couldn't hit**
I couldn't catch
I was slowing down
[Now all three men are throwing themselves to the ground
over and over and over
in synchronization,
while they yell the dialogue,
now Constantine and Nikos picking up phrases from Oed to repeat;
although, with the music deafening now,
we can't hear more than occasional words or phrases.]

OED: *[Shouting, as the action continues.]*

You should have gone to your dad
you think no one could understand
but you can talk about these things
to other men
because, these men,
they understand
because this is **what it is to be a man**
men know about this
because **they have gone through it**
and **they remember**
they know the pain,
they don't want to talk about it
they try to hide it
but if you open up to them
they'll open up right back

[Oed rips off his shirt and throws it to the floor, picks up circular saw blades, one after another, from a pile of saw blades, and hurls them across the stage so they stick in the side of another building that has been wheeled into place, yelling, for no good reason other than that he has gotten himself worked up; he is hopping mad, throwing a saw blade, then jumping into the air and stomping back down on the ground and yelling.

Constantine cuts out of the synchronized collapsing and starts jumping up in the air and landing with apparent full force on Nikos's splayed body, as Nikos rolls over and over on the stage, and Constantine yells, on top of the other yelling.]

CONSTANTINE: Girls are socialized
so they want a man to be older
take charge
have money
have status
while they play hard to get
and boys are taught to feel stupid
feel inferior
not as smart as girls
then hormones happen
a boy wants a girl
she plays hard to get
so a boy learns to

talk big
develop a line
take all the risk
hit on women
not take the answer no
look for younger women
go for status jobs
how do the women
handle men like this?
they get more hostile
more aloof
they wear high heels
they diet too much
they hate themselves
they blame the men
the men hate them
it's a vicious circle
it's a vicious circle
so fuck these women
fuck these women

NIKOS: *[Continuing simultaneously with Constantine, as the action continues.]*

I said to my dad
I don't want to do this
this isn't me
I felt so ashamed
He said, what do you mean?
your friends out there
they're doing it
they like it
just get in there
don't be afraid
you can't get hurt
if you get hurt
it doesn't matter
that's how it is
you pick yourself up get on with it
what do you care
because you belong

but I never did belong
it never was for me
Little League never was for me
[The music is drowning out all the speech
and finally, it comes to an end.
Silence.
The men stand panting, embarrassed, looking at one another.
Constantine and Nikos are weeping.
Oed snatches up his shirt from the ground and struts out in a huff.
Constantine kicks the ground over and over—releasing the last spasms of rage,
     like little aftershocks, to finally settle down.
Nikos watches him.
Finally, Constantine speaks very quietly.]
CONSTANTINE : People think
    it's hard to be a woman;
    but it's not easy
    to be a man,
    the expectations people have
    that a man should be a civilized person
    of course I think everyone should be civilized
    men and women both
    but when push comes to shove
    say you have some bad people
    who are invading your country
    raping your own wives and daughters
    and now we see:
    this happens all the time
    all around the world
    and then a person wants a man
    who can defend his home
    you can say, yes, it was men who started this
    there's no such thing as good guys and bad guys
    only guys
    and they kill people
    but if you are a man who doesn't want to be a bad guy
    and you try not to be a bad guy
    it doesn't matter
    because even if it is possible to be good

and you are good
when push comes to shove
and people need defending
then no one wants a good guy any more
then they want a man who can fuck someone up
who can go to his target like a bullet
burst all bonds
his blood hot
howling up the bank
rage in his heart
screaming
with every urge to vomit
the ground moving beneath his feet
the earth alive with pounding
the cry hammering in his heart
like tanked up motors turned loose
with no brakes to hold them

this noxious world

and then when it's over
suddenly
when this impulse isn't called for any longer
a man is expected to put it away
carry on with life
as though he didn't have such impulses
or to know that, if he does
he is a despicable person
and so it may be that when a man turns this violence on a woman
in her bedroom
or in the midst of war
slamming her down, hitting her,
he should be esteemed for this
for informing her
about what it is that civilization really contains
the impulse to hurt side by side with the gentleness
the use of force as well as tenderness
the presence of coercion and necessity

because it has just been a luxury for her really
not to have to act on this impulse or even feel it
to let a man do it for her
so that she can stand aside and deplore it
whereas in reality
it is an inextricable part of the civilization in which she lives
on which she depends
that provides her a long life, longer usually than her husband,
and food and clothes
dining out in restaurants
and going on vacations to the oceanside
so that when a man turns it against her
he is showing her a different sort of civilized behavior really
that she should know and feel intimately
as he does
to know the truth of how it is to live on earth
to know this is part not just of him
but also of her life
not go through life denying it
pretending it belongs to another
rather knowing it as her own
feeling it as her own
feeling it as a part of life as intense as love
as lovely in its way as kindness
because to know this pain
is to know the whole of life
before we die
and not just some pretty piece of it
to know who we are
both of us together
this is a gift that a man can give a woman.
[Constantine finally leaves—pushing Nikos on his way out.
Nikos hustles to catch up to Constantine, and gives him a shove.
Constantine shoves back.
They leave shoving one another back and forth.
Eleanor enters, with Olympia helping her,
carrying a huge wedding cake.]
ELEANOR: Let's put it here, dear,
over here.

OLYMPIA: Does it have candles?

ELEANOR: Usually it has a little bride and groom on top
  but this time we need fifty little brides and fifty little grooms
  so we will have them all around on all the different tiers
  and it will be like a huge party
  like Carnival.

OLYMPIA: I would like candles.

ELEANOR: Oh, candles. You want candles.
  Of course, you'll have candles if you want them.
  [Thyona enters.]

THYONA: We don't want a cake.
  What are you doing, Olympia,
  helping with this cake?
  [Lydia enters.]

LYDIA: Did someone order a cake?

ELEANOR: It was delivered to the house.

LYDIA: I thought there were some conversations to be had.

THYONA: What's going on?

LYDIA: Things are moving awfully fast.

PIERO: *[Entering with a glass of brandy in hand.]*
  I ordered the cake.
  Thank you, Eleanor.

ELEANOR: Any time, dear.
  I'm just going to get some candles for the cake.
  [She leaves.]

THYONA: So.
  You gave in to them, didn't you?

PIERO: I thought I might be able to strike an accommodation
  with your cousins.

THYONA: An accommodation?

PIERO: In the world I come from
  it's not always all or nothing.
  Men learn to compromise all the time.
  After all we have to go on living in the same world together.

THYONA: So you get up every morning and say
  who can I compromise with today?
  Surely there's a sociopath somewhere who wants to make a deal.

PIERO: [Ignoring her.]

> Frankly, I could see why you wouldn't want to accept
> the proposal of your cousins
> 50 grooms for 50 brides
> in its entirety.
> But it seemed to me that this young man, Nikos,
> was not such a bad a fellow after all.

THYONA: They're all the same
> just different manners.

PIERO: [Ignoring her still.]

> And I thought it might be
> that there could be one or two others like Nikos,
> and, that, if one were to find them,
> there might be some room to negotiate.

THYONA: To negotiate?

PIERO: To see whether there might be one or two natural alliances.

OLYMPIA: I'd like to love the person that I marry.

PIERO: Yes, we all would. To be sure.

> And sometimes we do—at first.
> Sometimes it lasts a little bit.

OLYMPIA: I know people who have loved one another
> all their lives.

PIERO: I do, too.

> And yet, it's very rare.
> For the rest of us,
> we make do.

THYONA: Maybe some of us don't want to be married at all.

PIERO: I thought that could be an option, too.

> And yet,
> for some of you—
> having a family is something you might long for as much as I do.
> To be close for all your lives
> to another human being
> and to the children that you have together
> coming through pleasures and pain over the years
> that bring you closer together
> closer to knowing the deepest truth of life
> that life is nothing for us

but an experience we share with others.

And, if we want our experience of life to be deep
and passionate,

to have a sense of its unfolding over many years

to be in touch with the whole of it

as we grow old,

some of us will welcome a lifelong marriage.

THYONA: What are you saying?

PIERO: It seemed to me

you might say to these fellows,

look, the deal as a whole is no good,

but we'll take 50% of you

or 10%.

THYONA: What?

PIERO: Of the fifty of you young women,

I felt sure there must be some

who still wished to be married to these young men.

And that was the accommodation I tried to arrange.

THYONA: Take 50%. Take 10%.

This is insane.

What is this?

We'll make some package deal?

LYDIA: Is Nikos part of this?

THYONA: And what about Constantine?

Is he part of the deal?

Am I part of the deal or not?

PIERO: We didn't get that far.

THYONA: Didn't get that far?

How long does it take to get that far?

These men think they can do anything.

OLYMPIA: I'm not afraid of men, Thyona.

In fact, I kind of like them.

THYONA: So?

OLYMPIA: Maybe you think I shouldn't play their game, but

I think I'm not a helpless victim.

When I put on a short skirt and paint my toenails

and dye my hair

I don't think that I'm a twit.

I think men know what I'm doing
and they think it's fun
and I think it's fun, too,
and I think I'm an equal
in the game we play.
I wouldn't mind some sort of negotiation.
THYONA: We don't accept your deal.
You can tell these men we don't accept it.
What we would accept is
if these men like
they can come to us one by one
and beg us to marry them
give each one of us time to make up our minds
postpone the wedding day
let us consider and reconsider
let us think about it when we are on our own ground
when we are strong and they are weak
let us come to them one by one
and say freely if we want to marry them
otherwise there's nothing to be said
OLYMPIA: Except…
THYONA: Nothing.
We reject your offer.
LYDIA: Thyona…
THYONA: I speak for all of us.
LYDIA: Thyona…
PIERO: I'm sorry to tell you
what I have been saying,
this is only the accommodation I was trying to work out.
In fact, Constantine won't have it either,
and he speaks for all your cousins.
Your cousins will marry you
whether you want to marry them or not.
None of you has a choice.
[Silence.]
LYDIA: And Nikos?
What did Nikos have to say?
PIERO: He let his brother speak for him.

LYDIA: Oh.

THYONA: Isn't this just what I said?

LYDIA: Yes.

> *[Silence;*
> *then, defeated, to Piero.]*
> Well, this is why we came to you.
> Thank God
> we were lucky enough to come here.
> Thank God we found you.

PIERO: I wish, in fact, you had found someone else.

> Because I can't protect you.

THYONA: What?

PIERO: I can't put my home at risk

> my home and my family.
> My nephew.
> The daughters of my brother.
> I can't do it.
> I'm sorry.
> For me, that never was an option.
> The wedding will take place today.
> The arrangements have been made.
> *[He leaves;*
> *silence.]*

OLYMPIA: Who am I supposed to marry, then?

> This is no different than it would be
> if we were lying in our beds
> and soldiers came through the door
> and took whoever it was they wanted.
> I'm not going to do this.

LYDIA: What choice do you have?

THYONA: What choice do you have

> if your father won't protect you
> the law will not protect you
> you flee to another country
> and some man will not protect you
> what is left?
> Nothing except to protect yourself.
> *[Silence.]*

We have no country.
We have become our own country now
where we make the laws ourselves.

LYDIA: Right.

OLYMPIA: Right.

THYONA: And when these men take us to bed
on our wedding night
these men who left us no choice
these men who force themselves on us
we will kill them
one by one.

LYDIA: What?

OLYMPIA: Kill them?

LYDIA: Kill them?

OLYMPIA: I can't kill them.
Are you crazy?

THYONA: Would you kill them if they were soldiers
coming through your bedroom door?

OLYMPIA: Of course I would.
But to kill them.

LYDIA: We can't kill them.

THYONA: What other choice do you have?
What choice did they give you
but to stop them
the only way they will be stopped.

LYDIA: But to kill them?
At the least maybe we don't want to kill them all.

OLYMPIA: Maybe some of them are good.

THYONA: None of them are good.

LYDIA: How can you say that?

THYONA: Here's how you can tell:
none of them objected to Constantine,
not one of them stood up against him and said:
No, Constantine,
let's take this deal,
or let's at least negotiate,
let's talk to these sisters and see if one or two of them wants to marry us
and let the rest go free

let those go free who don't want to marry.

Take the risk that some of us will be rejected.

No, no one stood up against him.

All his brothers are his silent partners.

Would you want to live with someone

who just gives in like this?

Would you ever be safe with a person as weak as this?

A pretty talker who paves the way for a rapist.

[Silence.]

LYDIA: No.

THYONA: They have all gone along with this.

They have made their decision.

And now there is no one to protect us but ourselves.

The only question is:

Will you protect yourself

and protect your sisters?

[Silence.]

OLYMPIA: Lydia?

Lydia?

LYDIA: Yes.

THYONA: Olympia?

OLYMPIA: Yes.

THYONA: We have a pact then.

Not one groom will live through his wedding night,

not one.

Are we agreed?

LYDIA: Yes.

OLYMPIA: Yes.

[Eleanor enters.]

ELEANOR: I'm going to help you girls get dressed

for the wedding.

[Through the following,

Eleanor helps the women get into their petticoats and dresses,

veils and garters and shoes

and powder and lipstick and rouge.

As the brides dress to kill,

sweet music plays,

J.S. Bach's Air on the G String, *from Orchestral Suite No. 3 in D,*

while Giuliano,
who at first has helped Eleanor bring in clothes for the brides,
goes off on his own transvestite solo dance.]

OLYMPIA: Nothing seems to be working out.

I was hoping for a wedding dress from Monique Lhuillier,
but back home in Greece,
all I could find was an Alvina Valenta,
not even a Vera Wang
and I'd been planning all my life
or most of it
for something with little spaghetti straps
and some lace right on the bodice
and little lace flowers just where the straps join the bodice
and people said sometimes you just have to settle
but I don't want to
I don't think I have to settle
I don't see why
at least on my wedding day
I can't have things exactly the way I want them!

ELEANOR: Never mind, dear.

You're going to love the way you look
by the time we're finished.
What lovely faces you all have
I think myself
if I'd had such a complexion
I'd have been married seven times by now.
What I always say is:
if both of you are physically fit
you should lie face downward on the bed
legs hanging over the edge
and let him help you raise your legs
and wrap them around his waist or shoulders
or if you like
you can start on the floor
and let him lift your ankles
while you walk around the floor on your hands
because I think you'll find
this makes for very deep penetration—
some say the very deepest.

LYDIA: Everything is moving so fucking fast.

ELEANOR: Now, I suppose you might be saying to yourselves
   before we make the final decision,
   let's ask ourselves:
   Do we have similar backgrounds?
   Do we agree on our religious beliefs?
   Do we have the same ideals and standards and tastes?
   Are we real friends?
   Do we have a real happiness in being together,
   Talking, or just doing nothing together?
   Do we have a feeling of paired unity?
   [The wedding music begins at full volume:
   Wagner's "Wedding March" from Lohengrin.
   In stately fashion
   the grooms enter in a line, wearing tuxedoes:
   fifty grooms, led by Constantine and Nikos.
   And our three brides take their places
   and they are followed by their
   forty-seven sisters, all in wedding dresses,
   who enter in a stately manner.
   Finally,
   Eleanor cuts the wedding cake
   and hands a piece of cake to Olympia
   who feeds it to Oed,
   crushing it playfully into his mouth;
   he smiles at this,
   takes her in his arms
   and dances with her.
   Lydia does the same with the cake with Nikos,
   and they dance.
   Thyona does the same,
   and then takes Constantine by the back of the head
   and pushes his head down into the cake.
   Constantine retaliates by picking Thyona up
   and shoving her head-first into the wedding cake.
   She recovers and wrestles him head-first into the cake.
   He takes off his jacket
   as though to start a real fight with her.

She pulls up her wedding dress
to show her bare butt to him
and to do a seductive-hostile butt dance
while she faces upstage.
The music segues into the exuberant party music
of Handel's "Arrival of the Queen of Sheba" from Solomon.
Constantine, taking Thyona's dance as a seductive challenge,
undoes his tie,
unbuttons his shirt,
and joins the dance with Thyona.
As her dance gets increasingly lewd and hostile
he takes off his shirt
and then his shoes
and then his pants
until he is doing a complete, abandoned striptease
while the others have moved into throwing themselves to the floor
and throwing themselves down on top of one another
or throwing one another to the floor
and then jumping on the one who lies there
—as the music segues into the wild, violent, Dionysian
Widor's "Toccata" from Organ Symphony No. 5—
and, of all the brides and grooms, some are
burning themselves with cigarettes
lighting their hands on fire and standing with their hands burning
throwing plates and smashing them
throwing kitchen knives
taking huge bites of food
and having to spit it out at once, vomiting.
Not these things necessarily, but things like these, things as extreme as these:
one groom lying across two chairs—his head on one, his feet on the other,
dropping bowling balls on his stomach and letting them roll onto the floor;
one groom on his back on the ground,
a board filled with nails resting on his naked chest;
another groom putting an anvil on the board,
and then hammering the anvil with a sledgehammer;
one groom with his feet locked into moon boots nailed to the ground
and he is rocking violently back and forth;
one bride slamming her head repeatedly in a door;

Eleanor screaming, running from side to side, and smashing plates and cups.
Some of the wedding guests are enjoying themselves;
so that, as at any wedding reception,
there is also joy, and warm sentiment, and sentimentality,
people happy,
young people in love,
quiet conversations, laughter,
older people remembering happy times.
If there is a cast of hundreds,
Leo can re-appear as a character now
and dance with the brides, one after another,
as though he is their father.
It may be that Constantine is the groom who should
have his feet in the moon boots
so that he is naked now, rocking back and forth violently,
when Thyona
comes to him with a kitchen knife
and stabs him in the heart
so that blood floods over his chest and stomach
and onto her white dress
and the other brides pull out kitchen knives
and murder their husbands, one by one,
all of them splashing their white wedding dresses with blood
and one of the men circling round and round the stage
holding his crotch
and he, too, bleeds and bleeds,
circling dizzily,
finally coming to his knees,
continuing on his knees.
And, all this while,
Lydia and Nikos are off to one side
making love.

(NOTE: for the small cast—nine actors—production of the play
there can be three grooms and three brides;
and the murders occur sequentially,
so that with each murder,
the bride drags the groom offstage

as another bride enters with her groom and stabs him;
in this way,
the murders can occur over and over in pairs.
Note also:
while the Widor may be the best music for the cast of one hundred,
the small-cast production
might need a more controlled music to go with the more ritualized
murders,
so we might think of having Bella singing Ave Maria
or Handel's "Pena tiranna" from Amadigi.*)*

A little before the music ends,
all the violent action on stage has subsided.
Thyona drags Constantine's body downstage
and throws it into the orchestra pit
(or else, a trap door opens, she dumps him in the hole,
and the trap door accommodatingly closes again).
People lie or sprawl, exhausted.
Only Lydia and Nikos are moving, gently,
with one another.
Piero enters—with Guiliano—
a cup of espresso in his hand,
and walks among the bodies,
in shock and dismay.
Bella enters from the other side.
People begin to stir.]

PIERO: Guiliano, mi dispiacce, ma…
   [He gestures to the carnage.]
GUILIANO: Si, si. Lascia me.
   [He starts to pick things up.]
BELLA: Piero
   you should have stopped this.
PIERO: What
   what could I have done?
THYONA: Lydia!
   Lydia!
   Who is that with you?
   [All eyes turn to Lydia and Nikos.]

LYDIA: This is Nikos,
  my husband.
THYONA: Your husband?
LYDIA: Yes.
THYONA: You broke your word?
LYDIA: I love him, Thyona.
OLYMPIA: We had an agreement, Lydia.
LYDIA: I couldn't do it.
THYONA: We all agreed together what we had to do
  however hard it was
  we made a promise to each other, to stand by one another.
  We didn't know when the moment came
  whether these men might have turned on us
  and even killed us.
  And then you go behind our backs—
  you decide all on your own—
  to take just what you want—throw away our pact,
  forget the only thing
  we had finally to protect us,
  and put all our lives at risk?
LYDIA: I love him!
  I love him!
THYONA: You can't love a person in this world
  when everyone else might be hurt, or worse
  choose your selfish choice
  and let everyone else go to hell.
LYDIA: I'm sorry, Thyona.
  I couldn't help myself.
THYONA: You're sorry?
  In any civilized society
  you would be put on trial.
LYDIA: Put on trial?
THYONA: And hanged probably.
OLYMPIA: Hanged?
THYONA: Or electrocuted.
LYDIA: Electrocuted!
PIERO: Now. Now. Let's just stop where we are.
THYONA: We are not finished here.

PIERO: Let's just slow things down.

    Everyone deserves a fair trial, after all.

THYONA : Right. Good.

    We'll put Lydia on trial.

    And we will be the jury.

PIERO: Wait a minute. Wait a minute. The what?

BELLA: And I will be the judge.

    [Silence.]

PIERO: The judge?

THYONA: You?

BELLA: Yes.

    Who else?

LYDIA: Yes. Good. Okay.

    I agree to that. Fine.

OLYMPIA: I agree to that, too.

THYONA: All right, then

    Betrayal is the charge.

    She broke her promise

    We have no country to protect us, no laws

    so we made our own law

    our own country

    our last refuge.

    What Lydia did, in any other country,

    would be treason.

LYDIA: I love him.

    I have nothing more to say.

    If we live in a world where it is not possible

    to love another person

    I don't want to live.

THYONA: All this talk of love.

    You think I'm not capable of love, too?

    But in the real world,

    if there is no justice

    there can be no love

    because there can be no love

    that is not freely offered

    and it cannot be free

    unless every person has equal standing

and so
the first order of business is to make a just society.
You wish there would be love and mercy and compassion
But first comes justice,
and if there is no justice
then those who are being taken advantage of
have every right
to take their oppressors
to take those who stand in their way
and drive them across the fields
like frightened horses
to set fire to their houses
to ruin everything that comes to hand
to hurl their corpses into wells
where once there were houses
to leave rubble
smoldering woodpiles
to leave shattered stones,
empty streets,
and silence
no living thing
no bird, no animal
no dogs,
no children,
not one stone left standing on another,
rather a wilderness of stones
and see if finally then
a lesson has been learned.
Because there are times
when this is justified
there are times, though you may not like it,
when this is all that human beings may rightly do and to shrink from it
is to be less than human.

LYDIA: You know, everything you say may be right, Thyona,
    but I have to ask myself,
    if it is
    then why don't I feel good about it?
    I have to somehow go on my gut instincts

because sometimes
you can convince yourself in your mind
about the rightness of a thing
and you try to find fault with your reasoning
but you can't
because
however you turn it over in your mind
it comes out right
and so you have to think:
I'm just a completely unreasonable person
I know it's right but I don't think it is
or I think it's right but I know it isn't
and you could end up thinking
you're just a moron
or an emotional person
or some sort of deficient sort of thing
but really there are some things
when you want to know the truth of them
you have to use your whole person
you have to use not just your mind and your feelings
but your neurons or your cells or whatever
your whole body
to make some decisions
because they are too complicated for just your mind
or even just your mind and feelings
they need to be considered in some larger way
and in the largest way of all
I know in my bones
that I have to go with my heart
or whatever it is
I have to go with my whole being
when it says I love him and he loves me
and nothing else matters
even if other things do matter even quite a lot
even if I'm doing this in the midst of everyone getting killed
I can't help myself
and I don't think I should.
Probably this is how people end up marrying Nazis
but I can't help it.

THYONA: You should.

You should.

LYDIA: I couldn't!

OLYMPIA: If I'd known it was okay to do what you did,

I might have loved someone, too.

I was just

I know everyone says this

but the truth is

I was just following orders in a way.

I should kill myself probably

now that I see the kind of person that I am.

BELLA: That's enough now.

That's enough.

I'm ready with my verdict.

This is what I have to say.

[Silence.]

You did a dreadful thing, you women, when you killed these men.

What could be worse than to take another's life?

And yet, I have to ask, what else could you have done?

You came to us,

to my family and to me,

your last chance,

to help you, and we failed you.

We share the blame with you.

Now, Piero, it will be your job

to keep all this out of the hands of courts and judges.

That much you can do.

You women made your own laws because you had no others to protect you.

And Lydia, in her betrayal of your pact,

imperilled all of you.

I understand what you say.

And yet,

you can't condemn your sister.

No matter what.

She chose love.

She reached out

she found another person—

and she embraced him.

[Thyona turns her back
and takes several steps to the side, facing away.
Bella continues her argument, to persuade Thyona and Olympia.]
She couldn't know
when she reached out
whether she would find someone good or bad,
whether she chose wrong
whether all the hopes of her childhood for true love and tenderness
for a soulmate for all her life
were destined for disillusion.
Still, she reached out.
And, if we cannot embrace another
what hope do we have of life?
What hope is there to survive at all?
[Spoken out, as though from a judge's bench.]
This is why: love trumps all.
Love is the highest law.
It can be bound by no other.
Love of another human being—
man or woman—
it cannot be wrong.
Does this mean every woman must get married?
Not at all.
A woman might want another woman;
sometimes a man prefers a man.
But to love:
this cannot be wrong.
So Lydia: she cannot be condemned.
And that's the end of it.
And as for you,
there will be no punishment for you either,
even though you may have done wrong,
there will be no justice.
For the sake of healing
for the sake of life itself
for life to go on
there will be no justice.
You will live now like so many others

among neighbors who know you did wrong
and who may feel
you have some punishment coming to you,
who may burn with bitterness for some years
feeling you should have paid for your crimes,
but that will be their job to settle that bitterness in their hearts.
And now,
you girls,
alone in the world,
what will you do now?
I have to tell you, I wish you would stay on here with me.
I would take you in and care for you
as my own daughters.
That would make me happy.
[Thyona turns back to face her,
and she speaks to Thyona]
I like a strong woman.
[And then to Olympia.]
And I like a woman who sticks with her sister.
You'll see,
one day you'll find a good man.
Or not.
A woman doesn't always need a man.
I myself, I no longer need a man—
except, of course, my son Piero,
who stays with me forever,
and Giuliano, who takes such good care of me.
For we all live together
and come to embrace
the splendid variety of life on earth
good and bad
sweet and sour
take it for what it is: the glory of life.
We know life is going to bring us
cruelty as well as kindness
heartache, and much worse, as well as joy.
This is why at weddings
everybody cries

out of happiness and sorrow
regret and hope combined.
Because, in the end,
of all human qualities, the greatest is sympathy—
GIULIANO: for clouds even
BELLA: or snow
GIULIANO: for meadows
for the banks of ditches
BELLA: for turf bogs
or rotten wood
for wet ravines
GIULIANO: silk stockings
buttons
BELLA: birds' nests
hummingbirds
GIULIANO: prisms
BELLA: jasmine
GIULIANO: orange flower water
BELLA: lessons for the flute
GIULIANO: a quill pen
BELLA: a red umbrella
GIULIANO: some faded thing
BELLA: handkerchiefs made of lawn
GIULIANO: of cambric
BELLA: of Irish linen
GIULIANO: of Chinese silk
BELLA: seagulls
the white of an egg
GIULIANO: an earth worm in vinegar
BELLA: an earth worm in honey
GIULIANO: the bark of an elm
BELLA: the ash of an old shoe
driftwood
dog's blood
GIULIANO: the dung beetle
BELLA: goat dung
GIULIANO: a mouse cut in two
BELLA: an earthen cup
a child eating strawberries

GIULIANO: beach parsley

BELLA: wet lips

GIULIANO: club moss

BELLA: In spring the dawn.
    In summer the nights.
    In autumn the evenings.

GIULIANO: In winter the early mornings
    the burning firewood
    piles of white ashes
    the ground white with frost

BELLA: spring water welling up

GIULIANO: the hum of the insects
    the human voice

BELLA: piano virtuosos
    orchestras

GIULIANO: the pear tree

BELLA: The sunlight you see in water as you pour it from a pitcher into a bowl.

GIULIANO: The earth itself.

BELLA: Dirt.

    [Here comes, immediately, at full volume,
    Mendelssohn's "Wedding March" from Midsummer Night's Dream.
    Lydia and Nikos kiss
    and a hundred flashbulbs go off for a wedding picture.
    A receiving line
    is instantly constituted,
    and Lydia and Nikos make their way down the line—
    all the guests kissing the bride and shaking the groom's hand
    and talking among themselves and fussing with their clothes.
    Nikos stops for an earnest conversation with Piero—
    which we cannot hear at all over the music—
    about how sometimes men don't even want to get married
    because they find it hard enough getting through the day on their own
    all by themselves, and the burdens of life are so heavy and the demands so great
    they think: how can I take on the responsibility of someone else, too,
    not that they would take on the responsibility entirely, but to the extent they
    do,
    because they have made a promise to see life through together
    and sometimes a man could just cry, things seem so hard,

but when you fall in love, what choice do you have?
At the last moment,
everyone turns front,
a hundred flash cameras go off again,
the family photo is taken.]

OLYMPIA: Lydia! Lydia! Throw your bouquet!
[Lydia throws her bouquet into the audience.
Booming music.]

OLYMPIA: And your garter! Your garter!
[Lydia pulls up her dress.
Nikos takes her garter
and throws that into the audience.
Everyone throws rice.
Lydia and Nikos, the bride and groom,
exit up the center aisle to the music.
Nikos's clothing is disheveled,
and he looks sheepish and uncertain,
even frightened, maybe even filled with foreboding—
in fact, they both look shellshocked and devastated—
as Nikos exits up the aisle with Lydia.
Fireworks.]

END OF PLAY

Touch
by Toni Press-Coffman
Conceived by Toni Press-Coffman and
Jonathan Ingbretson

This play is dedicated to the memory and inspired by the spirit of Jason Ingbretson.

BIOGRAPHY

Toni Press-Coffman was born and raised in the Bronx, New York. The author of twenty plays, which have been produced throughout the country, she was recently awarded one of ten NEA/TCG Playwright Residencies. Created with a grant from Arizona Commission on the Arts, *Touch* has won four playwriting contests and had its first production at Damesrocket Theater in Tucson, Arizona. It was subsequently produced as the winner of the South Carolina Playwrights Festival/Trustus New Play Award and the Festival of Emerging American Theatre Contest at the Phoenix Theatre in Indianapolis. *Touch* will be presented at the Women's International Theatre Conference in Athens in October, 2000. Ms. Press-Coffman has had work developed at the O'Neill National Playwrights Conference, the Sundance Institute, Midwest Professional Playwrights Laboratory and Minneapolis's Playwrights' Center. Her play *Stand* received the Brodkin Award, given annually to support the career of an O'Neill playwright. The recipient of many other grants and awards, Ms. Press-Coffman lives, writes, performs, and teaches theatre in Tucson, Arizona.

HUMANA FESTIVAL PRODUCTION

Touch premiered at the Humana Festival of New American Plays in March 2000. It was directed by Mladen Kiselov with the following cast:

Kyle Kalke . . . . Stephen Kunken
Bennie Locasto . . . . Dominic Fumusa
Serena . . . . Kaili Vernoff
Kathleen . . . . Joanna Glushak

and the following production staff:

Scenic Designer . . . . Paul Owen
Costume Designer . . . . James Schuette
Lighting Designer . . . . Mimi Jordan Sherin
Sound Designer . . . . Martin R. Desjardins
Properties Designer . . . . Mark Walston
Stage Manager . . . . Juliet Penna
Assistant Stage Manager . . . . Charles M. Turner III
Dramaturg . . . . Amy Wegener
Assistant Dramaturg . . . . Ginna Hoben
Casting . . . . Laura Richin Casting

FIRST PRODUCTION

Touch was originally produced in April-May 1999 at Damesrocket Theater in Tucson, Arizona. It was directed by Caroline Reed with the following cast:

Kyle Kalke . . . . Jonathan Ingbretson
Bennie Locasto . . . . Patrick Burke
Serena . . . . Christina Walker
Kathleen. . . . . Erika Cossitt

and the following production staff:

Production Manager. . . . . David Walker
Scenic and Costume Designer . . . . Susan Rojas
Lighting Designer . . . . Norm Testa
Sound Designer . . . . Chris Babbie
Stage Manager . . . . William Barrett

CHARACTERS

KYLE KALKE: An astronomer in his late twenties.

BENNIE LOCASTO: A doctor in his late twenties. Kyle's best friend.

SERENA: Kyle's sister-in-law, in her thirties.

KATHLEEN: A prostitute, about 35.

TIME & PLACE

The play is set in Kyle's mind and the places he conjures there.

Every cubic inch of space is a miracle.
—Walt Whitman

Dominic Fumusa and Stephen Kunken
in *Touch*

24th Annual Humana Festival of New American Plays
Actors Theatre of Louisville, 2000
photo by Richard Trigg

Touch

ACT I

Kyle is alone on the stage, which is bare—except for perhaps a chair or two—throughout the play, except occasionally when a specific set piece or prop is referred to in the script.

KYLE: I was taking physics. I was taking physics again is what I mean. My freshman year I took biology and chemistry and physics. My sophomore year I took advanced biology and physics again because there's nothing else in high school. *(Beat.)* Earth science. Which I skipped. I wasn't sure about my career yet, although I was leaning toward the planets and the stars even then. Zoe told me later I was leaning toward the cosmos. That was one of her ways, that way of making me feel like the tiniest thing was full of meaning. I thought that—a person thinks inside that—the things that attract him are significant things, except a person doesn't expect another person to think so. Ever. I kept taking physics because that's all that was offered. Chemistry doesn't work more than once, what you need for chemistry is a higher level class, but somehow with physics, you can take it over and over and over and over and the world keeps opening. High school didn't offer astronomy. That's what I would have been taking had it been offered. Instead I was taking physics for the fourth year in a row, and that's where I saw her for the first time.

She looked into the room. Peeked in. The teacher asked her whether he could help her, and then she stepped in, looking all around the room. She was wearing orange pants and a strange hat and a lot of make-up. *(Beat.)* Zoe had huge eyes. Gigantic. And she always wore bright green or dark brown or lavender eye shadow and that made her eyes seem even larger than they actually were. And they were so big to begin with that as she looked around the room, her eyes reminded me of the heavens. Which I had already come to love. I was thinking hard about how a person's physical features could cause me to reflect on planetary bodies, when she said,

"Jesus," and started laughing. I looked straight at her, and she said, "This is a science class." *(He thinks. Then he laughs.)* I laughed. I think now how odd that I laughed about science, since science was everything I loved from the time I was small, but I did. When I laughed, she glanced at me. No one else had laughed, no one else had grasped that she had stepped into an entirely foreign world. The wonderful thing was that she wasn't afraid of what was foreign to her. She fixed her glance on me for a second or maybe two seconds, only it felt like much longer. Then she said, "I am so in the wrong room," and turned around and walked out the door. I didn't think. Which had rarely—maybe never—happened before. I literally jumped to my feet and went after her. I followed her out into the hall and stood outside my physics classroom watching her. The bell sounded for class to start, but I didn't budge. Zoe caused me to be late to class for the first time in my life.

Then it was every day. Every day. I arrived at school and I looked for her. Before then, I had arrived at school maybe a minute before the first bell because I didn't hang out. Because I grew up in the desert—it's hard to hang out in such heat. Well, other kids did it, but I didn't hang out with my friends because I had no friends. *(Beat.)* That's not true. I have a friend from childhood. Bennie Locasto. His mother always corrected me when I called him Bennie because she hated if people did not call him by his full name, which is Benjamin. But Bennie liked his nickname, and I wanted to please him because he was my friend. Bennie went to a private high school, where I wished I could go because the private high school did offer astronomy, but my parents couldn't afford it. Since Bennie didn't go to my high school, I had no reason to come to school early to hang out. Except I came early the day after Zoe visited my physics class. Because I wanted to find her. It was easy. She had on another hat. That's another thing about Zoe. Another way she had. She owned a couple dozen hats, one stranger than the next. Which I liked. I found her and all I did was look at her. She wasn't beautiful in the way a lot of people think is beautiful. She wasn't skinny. She wasn't fat, but she wasn't skinny. She had a face that was falling in on itself. Flattened out. Hollow. And the eyes. What I mean is she was beyond gorgeous. It was impossible to stop looking at her once I started. I would come to school early, I would find her, and I would look at her until the bell. I dreamed of her at night and did nothing but look at her at school. I looked and looked and looked and looked and looked and looked at her. *(Pause, then a gigantic grin.)* Astounding. She looked back. I'd been coming to school early every morning for at least a week. I don't know how long she'd been looking back, but she did tell me later that it took me a while to notice. She used to say that for a scientist, for a person who does painstaking research, I didn't notice much besides what's in the sky. I suppose I notice things best through a telescope, or with a magnifying glass. Except I noticed Zoe. Which I now believe was a miracle. And I finally noticed her looking back at me. First I could not believe it. But she made it clear. When she saw me realizing she was looking back, she waved. Not in a cute way at all, not in a dopey way. In an excited way. *(Almost to himself.)* Zoe was excited that I was looking at her.

I was always an in-the-shadows person, never in the forefront, not often in the light. That follows because I was attracted to the night sky early on. And to being alone. I enjoyed solitude. Like John Keats. The only poet. Boundless understanding of the universe. *(A smile, then another beat.)* Even after I realized Zoe was looking back, I didn't know what to do. She was always surrounded by people. Most of them were guys. Although she had a lot of girlfriends too. And they'd squeal and laugh. Zoe was noisy. One morning, one of her admirers knocked her hat off her head. A straw hat with a giant-sized, rose-like silk flower attached to the band. The weather was tranquil, so the hat didn't go very far. She ran after it and scooped it up and put it on her head and then in one motion, she stood up straight, walked across the quad and spoke to me. As though it was natural to walk across practically the entire campus in order to speak to a guy you'd never met. Which for Zoe it was. "I found out your name you know." That's what she said. "I found out your name you know." I said, "How'd you do that?" I was trying to keep the thrill out of my voice. I had let go of the idea that I was ever going to be cool, so I didn't go for cool. I was trying more for calm. *(Beat.)* She'd asked my physics teacher my name. I got very happy thinking about her approaching the physics teacher, inquiring about my name. *(Beat.)* "Kyle Kalke. Right?" That's what she said.

Now the guys backed off. She made it clear to them. Come to think of it, that was another way she had. She had a way of making things clear. There was never any confusion about what Zoe felt or thought. "This is

Kyle," she said. "He's with me." *(Big grin.)* The next day was the first time I kissed her. After school, she walked out to my car with me. We stood near my car, talking and mostly laughing. She said, "Don't science guys kiss girls?" I couldn't possibly have kissed a person faster. Which still surprises me when I think about it because I had not kissed a girl very often. Twice to be exact, in the ninth grade. The girl was my lab partner and we got the highest grade on our experiment, so I kissed her to congratulate her and then I kissed her again, because I—I just liked the way it felt. Which was a completely different situation. With Zoe, I didn't think, there was no worry about whether it would go well. There was her and me, all over each other in the parking lot. Boy.

We got married the Christmas after high school graduation. December 22. Winter solstice. Our decision to marry made our parents insane. Mine told me I didn't have to marry the first young woman I dated and that there was a lot of time to fall in love with other women. *(Beat, some anger comes in here.)* It was like they didn't even know me. It was like they thought I was going to marry Zoe out of fear of never falling in love again. Which is an insult to her that I still haven't forgiven them for. Tell me I'm too young to marry. Tell me you're afraid I won't go to college and fulfill my dreams if I marry. But don't tell me I'm marrying Zoe out of fear, don't hurt me by implying that I don't love Zoe. Goddammit. I loved her so Goddamn much. *(Beat.)* Her folks and her older brother and sister just thought I was—odd. I could understand why they would think so, since Zoe was so vibrant, while I was much more introverted. That's changed about me—Zoe reached in there. I let her. She reached in and coaxed more of me out into the light. *(He thinks for a long time. He wants to stop thinking. He pushes the thoughts he doesn't want out—struggles to keep his composure. He does it.)* Um. *(Beat.)* I understood her family's attitude toward me, but it was not understandable to Zoe. She called a family meeting the night before our wedding and told them that they all had to take back what they said and they all had to apologize to me and not together, and not with a card, separately and in person. She told them that once the wedding was over, she would not speak to them until they did that. *(Beat.)* They did it. Each one of her family members apologized to me in person. Except her brother called me on the phone. Zoe thought I shouldn't accept that, but I did. I tried to explain to her how amazing and extraordinary it was that he called me, how so many people's families might say all right. Fine. Don't speak to us.

We had our honeymoon in New York City. The honeymoon was beautiful beyond imagining. By the time we planned the honeymoon, I trusted her so much that when she suggested New York City, I just said yes. I didn't worry about the size of the city or the number of people or getting mugged or lost. I said yes. *(Beat.)* The entire week, snow kept falling and freezing over. The ice on the ground kept cracking and spreading apart. Snowdrifts appeared in unlikely places. The air was cold. Simply that. Cold. We took every cent of our wedding gift money and stayed in an expensive beautiful classy hotel. Zoe found a hotel that had a telescope on its roof so we ran up there every night, we literally ran up the stairs. *(Beat.)* We made love and then watched the snow fall onto our balcony. Zoe wanted to make love on our balcony in the snow, but I said that was too much. I couldn't help thinking if we did that we'd both catch pneumonia. I know sometimes I'm too much the scientist, but I made it up to her. I brought Keats and read to her. She was surprised, she kept giggling. She applauded after every poem. I believed—probably up to the minute I packed him—that how I felt about Keats was too private to share with anyone. Even Zoe. As I was reading, I was thinking, God, maybe nothing is too private to share with Zoe. *(Beat.)* Everyone else in the city wore scarves and earmuffs but Zoe wore her hats. I wore an overcoat that I borrowed from my father. It was a little bit too big. It was brown and big and warm and one night I took Zoe for a walk through Central Park. I wore the overcoat and she wore a deep blue hat, soft, with a narrow burgundy brim. Lots of ice floes. The sky was an exquisite color, for which there is no word. Blue-ish, slate gray-ish, luminous. It's possible that night walking with my wife through the gleam of Central Park, the thousands of muted lights just beyond our reach, was the happiest of my life.

We both went to college. I majored in Astronomy, Zoe majored in— um—. She kept changing her mind. *(He thinks.)* I can't—. I can't remember what she settled on. *(Upset.)* Why can't I remember that? *(Composes himself.)* For the first time, I lived in a world populated by people besides Mom, Dad, and Bennie Locasto. Zoe had a large and—eclectic—collection of friends. Collection is exactly the word, too. We would have gatherings at our apartment. Bennie would come. Zoe's sister Serena would come. The sister of the guy who helps us do our taxes would come. Zoe's manicurist would come. One of the other research assistants from school would come. Some guy Zoe met in the parking lot of the supermarket changing a flat tire a couple years earlier would come. We'd put on music. We'd order Chinese food. We'd talk about—God—everything. God, yeah. Politics. The dangerous subjects, we didn't care, we'd just talk about them. A lot of nights like that Zoe would suddenly look at me and tell me she loved me, from across the room or in the kitchen or wherever she was. She'd walk over to me and sit on me, not on my lap so much. All around me. She'd say, "I love you, Kyle." And she'd kiss me. For a long time. In front of company. *(Beat.)* There is just no way to explain how that felt.

It's true we had bad moments. We had dozens of arguments about astrology. I would tell her that I was a scientist and that astrology was make believe, that it was not scientific. The first time we had this conversation, she asked me didn't I think there was such a thing as the spirit and I said yes, of course. Although I'd never thought about it before and I wasn't actually sure what she meant. She told me I was being a prig. Which hurt my feelings. She said, "Don't you have a wild and crazy bone in your entire body, Kyle?" *(Beat.)* She knew I did. *(Beat.)* I said, "Well, I just know what I know. And I know astrology is just a game. It's just something people do for fun. And why do it, because what's real and true is so much more fantastically beautiful?" *(Pause.)* She breathed hard. I could tell she was trying not to be angry anymore. She breathed and breathed and breathed and breathed and breathed. She took five minutes maybe. Zoe could do that. She could take five minutes and then feel better. *(Pause.)* Not always. Zoe had a terrible jealous streak. At one point, she became convinced I was falling in love with one of her friends. Which was not true. Not even a little bit. But one night, this woman—Sherry—I hate even saying her name—Sherry and I were laughing together in the living room while Zoe and some other people were in the kitchen playing cards. Zoe was something of a card shark, actually. I was laughing so hard—and I think it was because I'd drunk a lot more beer than I'm used to, I think I'd drunk four beers—that I fell off my chair onto the floor, which made a big banging noise so Zoe ran in from the other room calling my name and there I was flat on my back howling with laughter and Sherry had slid down to the floor with me and parts of us were touching each other. Zoe said, "What's so goddamn funny, Kyle?" I sat up fast. I was shocked by the tone in her voice. A long time passed in the silence. Then Zoe said, and this was even more shocking, Zoe said to Sherry, "You have to go." The other guests left too, in silence. After we were alone, the silence continued and continued and continued. It was eerie. Finally, I said, "Please, Zoe, tell me what's wrong." *(Beat.)* Well, she did. She started talking fast, so quietly, I could hardly hear her, I had to stand so close to her to hear her. Because Zoe's voice was so high, what came out of her was like a squeaky hiss. Like how a snake might sound if it could talk. Zoe talked about how Sherry looked, about how her body was different from Zoe's, about how I must be bored with the same body all the time. Then she said why couldn't I tell Sherry to keep her hands off me? Didn't I notice how she was constantly touching me? The truth is, she did touch me a lot, and I did notice, but I pretended she did that to everybody. Tell her to keep her hands off you. Tell her to keep her fucking hands off you. Tell her not to touch you, Kyle. *(Beat.)* Why do you keep inviting her to come over here, Zoe? What is that, some kind of test? I like to be touched. So? I am not going to tell her not to touch me, you want her to stop touching me, you tell her, goddammit. *(He breathes hard. He takes some time to calm down. Then softly.)* Goddammit. *(Beat.)* The argument went on for hours, into the middle of the night, until Zoe and I were both exhausted. We made love through the exhaustion. *(Quietly.)* Violently. *(Beat.)* I was enraged. I think Zoe was grateful for my rage. Even though it made her cry.

For the next few days, thinking about it would make me shake. Zoe would say, "What, Kyle?" She knew what. She knew I was thinking about having sex with my wife while she wept and the harder she cried, the more I made the sex hurt. One night—maybe a week later—I lay on our bed in the dark and Zoe came in and leaned against the bedroom door and said if I wanted to be with this other woman, why didn't I just admit it and stop—she said, "and stop torturing me." She used those words. Stop—torturing—me. *(He shivers. This is an extraordinarily unpleasant memory for him.)* I got up—furious—and went to her and took her in my arms and shouted no, no. I held her hard against me, shaking. She stood steadfastly in my grip and repeated my name over and over. Over, over, over, over, over and over. *(Beat.)* Kyle. *(Beat.)* That much love—what Zoe and I felt together—that has a—dangerous—side.

After Zoe and I married, I still enjoyed solitude. I figured out how to be with people and still live as much in my thoughts as I needed to. For example, Bennie Locasto and I started camping together. Bennie had been trying to convince me to do this for years, but I was stubborn about it. Which now seems foolish because after all, in the desert the earth and the sky become one at night. Zoe would say, "Go camping. Go. Go. Go. Go." So I'd bring a Walkman and I'd bring Keats and I'd wear the same clothes for four days and Bennie'd take care of the food. Bennie's a good cook. When we camped, he could make coffee that tasted like something. We'd walk at night—after dinner—covered by the night sky and whatever in it was showing itself just then and talk, sometimes until daybreak. But other times he'd leave me alone, so I could have everything—I could have his company and I could have solitude. *(Beat.)* I found that I had a feeling of contentment with Bennie. When I was near him, I felt that peacefulness that comes from being in the same room with someone who knows you well. Calm. *(Beat.)* Calm. *(Beat.)* Calm. There's a link between Bennie—those walks, that talking, that love we first felt as kids—and my work. There's a relationship between Bennie being in the world and how deeply I probe, how profoundly I allow myself to explore the hundreds of unanswered questions I'm confronted with each day.

When I was finishing my doctorate, sometimes I was at school long past midnight, so immersed in my work that at certain moments I would have been hard pressed to remember my name. I am capable of looking through a telescope for many, many, many hours uninterrupted. My colleagues at school thought I was ridiculous, attaching an eyepiece to a two-meter telescope, because we do almost all our work with computers now. Now we can take photographs of space from space—they're breathtaking, sometimes so breathtaking I can't sleep. But my own eyes on the telescope, it's still true that nothing compares to that. It's like I am walking along the precipice of discovery the way I walked along the edge of the curb as a child, arms outstretched, keeping my balance with difficulty and knowing that at the end of the block lays an unparalleled feeling of accomplishment. I believe we who live on earth are not the only prescient beings in the universe. It is that belief that helped me begin to understand what Zoe meant by the spirit. The billions of galaxies, the thousands and thousands and thousands of unknowns about atmospheric conditions in those galaxies, the mind-boggling infinite number of possibilities—those are the places—the galaxies, all of them, those are the places where science and the spirit meet.

A month before our sixth anniversary, Zoe went out one night and didn't come back. She and I gave Thanksgiving. A couple of years after we got married, we'd started doing that. Our people used it as a day to acknowledge our anniversary too. Each year we hosted Thanksgiving dinner, our guests surprised us with something to celebrate our marriage. I can imagine the convoluted train of phone calls between Bennie and my mom and my mom and Zoe's mom and Zoe's sister and Zoe's brother and our tax guy and his sister, and between one of my colleagues from the observatory and Zoe's manicurist, and then somehow back again to Bennie. That last Thanksgiving, they did a little performance. "Kyle and Zoe in Love." After we ate, they acted out a little play of how we met and how we fell in love—according to them—and our trip to New York and how we act at home alone, which for having to imagine it, they got pretty well. My father played me and Zoe's mom played her. A couple of times they'd get to the part where—if one thing led to another—kissing would happen and *(He's amazed.)* my mom yelled out, "Don't you dare" to my dad. Zoe and I laughed and laughed.

"Kyle and Zoe in Love" was their last anniversary gift to us. The year before that they gave us a photograph of Central Park in winter taken by someone named Adolf Fassbender. He took it on Christmas Eve of 1932. *(Beat.)* In 1932, Central Park looked exactly the way it looked on our honeymoon sixty years later. The year before that—. *(Beat.)* The year before the photograph—it was framed, and I think it was expensive. I don't know how they afforded it. *(Beat.)* The year before that—. I can't remember. *(He hits something, hard.)* Dammit.

Zoe was sitting on a big red pillow in our living room, her cheeks were red too because she'd drunk quite a bit of wine. People kissed us as they left. People kissed Zoe. Her mom kissed each of her cheeks and Zoe threw back her head and through this completely radiant smile told her mother, "You make a great me." Then she said, "I'm so happy you realize how I feel about Kyle now." *(Beat, it's starting to get him, but he wards it off.)* By ten or so it was just us and Bennie and Serena. Zoe decided we had to have this coffee drink she liked to make, with Triple Sec and whipping cream, only we had no whipping cream and Zoe said she'd go to the twenty-four-hour market to get some. I only listened vaguely, Bennie and Serena and I were arguing about—Jesus Christ—we were arguing about whether there should be condom dispensers on high school campuses. We were all pretty heated, Serena was blasting me because I told her she was being a real girl about it. Serena told Zoe to wait, she'd go with her, but Zoe said no, Serena should stay, she'd be right back. *(Beat.)* She grabbed her purse. *(Beat.)* She put on her black leather hat. *(Beat.)* She kissed me. *(Beat, tears come up.)* Thank fucking God. *(He composes himself.)* She left. *(Kyle pauses for a long time. A light comes up on Bennie, somewhere else on the stage.)*

KYLE: Forty-five minutes after she left, her sister asked—um—how far away the market was anyway. Forty-five minutes. Which is impossible. My wife went to the grocery store to buy one item, I let her go, late at night, by herself—

BENNIE: Stop that.

KYLE: *(He is not registering Bennie.)* —and she's gone forty-five fucking minutes and even then I don't notice. Her sister notices. Which is unforgivable.

BENNIE: No, Kyle.

KYLE: Because that is a long goddamn time, and in that time—

BENNIE: Don't do this to yourself.

KYLE: —I could have—(done something to help her)

BENNIE: No, you couldn't.

KYLE: I should have—(gone to the grocery store myself)

BENNIE: No. *(Beat.)* Please, Kyle.

KYLE: After that—after Serena noticed Zoe wasn't coming home—I was delirious with worry.

BENNIE: Second intersection after Benson, take a left? Stay here near the phone. *(Beat.)* Kyle, stay here with Serena.

KYLE: When he came back without her, I already knew.

BENNIE: *(Softly.)* Your car's still in the supermarket parking lot.

KYLE: Maybe not that she was—

BENNIE: But Zoe's not there.

KYLE: —maybe not that she was dead. *(He stops. Big breath.)* I knew that she was at least badly hurt because I knew Zoe. *(Beat.)* I knew Zoe. *(Beat.)* I knew her. I knew Zoe. *(He can't help it. He starts to sob. He stops, abruptly. He blows his nose.)* I knew Zoe would not stay away and not call. I knew she was hurt and I knew I could have gone to the grocery store.

BENNIE: That does not help. That's not going to make them look for her any faster.

KYLE: The police wouldn't look for her until she was missing for twenty-four hours. A detective asked me who she might have—he said split with.

BENNIE: Police are cold, Kyle. They're cold. It' s nothing personal.

KYLE: Bennie said it was nothing personal. *(He turns furiously to Bennie.)* She's hurt, she's hurt and this fuck—

BENNIE: You be calm.

KYLE: *(Registers this, tries to calm down.)* Who might your wife, the person you care about most in the world, the only woman you've ever loved, have split with? Nothing personal. *(Beat.)* I tried to explain that Zoe did not mince words, Zoe always said exactly what was on her mind, no exceptions whatsoever, including sorry Kyle, I love somebody else, I'm leaving. That's what she would have done, she would not have just—split. My wife would not have done that.

BENNIE: It has nothing to do with Zoe, Kyle. Police always ask that first thing.

KYLE: I told the detective about Zoe. I talked and talked and talked and talked and talked.

BENNIE: Kyle, listen.

KYLE: *(Pleading with the cop.)* Our car is still in the parking lot, doesn't that tell you something? *(Beat.)* It told him that whoever she left me for picked her up in the supermarket parking lot. *(Beat.)* Nothing registered. He was going to wait twenty-four hours.

BENNIE: Kyle, I think we should call the hospitals.

KYLE: Bennie insisted we call the hospitals. He actually did it himself, he called the hospital where he worked first and then he put the word out to the others. Nobody had her. *(Beat.)* I'm so grateful he was with me all twenty-four of those hours. Which lasted forever. Which continue still.

BENNIE: Let me give you something to help you sleep.

KYLE: I don't want to sleep. I want Zoe. *(Beat.)* I refused to sleep at first. I felt that if she was hurt or scared, then I should stay awake because there was no other way to help her.

BENNIE: There's nothing you can do for her.

KYLE: *(To Bennie.)* Fuck you. *(Pause.)* Will you take Serena home?

BENNIE: No. Not unless you come with us.

KYLE: I'm not leaving, what if Zoe calls?

BENNIE: It's almost dawn. Serena needs to go home, someone should talk to Zoe's parents.

KYLE: I can't do that.

BENNIE: I know. But Serena needs to tell them, so put on a jacket, let's do it. *(Beat.)* I am not going to leave you here alone, Kyle, so either you get your jacket and come with me or I hold you down and inject you with something that will knock you out. What's it going to be?

KYLE: *(After a pause.)* I didn't sleep until much later. When she died. Which I didn't know at the time, but my body would not shut down until hers did. Then I slept.

BENNIE: Pretty much I was devastated when Kyle met Zoe. I wasn't exactly like Kyle, you know, I had a couple other friends and a big Italian family and all, but Kyle and me—we were in each other's blood. He didn't know it like I knew it because he could do being alone so much better than I could. That's why even though we're both scientists, I did medicine and he did astronomy. It's like, I wanted to be with people, I wanted to fix what was broken in them, I wanted to make them well. Kyle and I used to talk about how people were broken in their—just in their humanity like. But he retreated to something he thought was more vast than human nature and more powerful, something that would take him out of harm's way. We started out as two little science kids and we fought off the ridicule of pretty much everybody together. But he got to be a science nerd and I got more and more Italian—I don't know how else to say that, but it's like I got darker, and louder, and more in the world, and Kyle receded. So not only was I devastated when Kyle met Zoe, the devastation took me completely by surprise. It's like—Kyle was mine. Not in a—you know—not like a sex thing mine, not like that, just plain Kyle was mine. I counted on it. So here I was so much more worldly than him and here he was with this astonishing woman. Zoe wasn't very pretty, except she had a great body, but she had like constant energy, and there were times every ounce of that huge energy was aimed right at Kyle. So who wouldn't be envious? She was a kook too which was surprising in and of itself, because I never thought Kyle would go for that kind of wackiness, except now I realize he used to say stuff to me about his work like he loved looking at this or that configuration in the sky because there was something wacky about it. I'd be like, what, wacky in the sky, what's that mean? I swear, I never heard him laugh the way Zoe made him laugh. And strange? Vice versa too. He could totally crack that woman up. Maybe that was it, you know? Maybe I was jealous because I thought I knew all about Kyle, but she showed me how I didn't. The poetry, for example, that's another thing I didn't know until after he married Zoe.

KYLE: It's not poetry. It's Keats.

BENNIE: Oh, Keats is not poetry?

KYLE: Ha ha, Bennie.

BENNIE: So what about it?

KYLE: Keats is all of poetry. Which is narrow-minded, but that doesn't matter to me.

BENNIE: But what about it? Keats. What about him?

KYLE: Why don't you read him and see for yourself?

BENNIE: Kyle, I'm a college graduate, all right? I've read Keats.

KYLE: *(Beat.)* You have?

BENNIE: Yeah. Didn't make an impression.

KYLE: I knew you'd act like this.

BENNIE: Jesus, you sound like a ten-year-old.

KYLE: Bennie, shut up.

BENNIE: Okay, listen. Just tell me this one part, all right? Why the hell are you reading Keats on the sly? Why are you sneaking around reading Beauty is Truth under the covers like it was *Penthouse* or something?

KYLE: *(Beat.)* I thought it didn't make an impression.

BENNIE: He had me there, I have to admit. Why lie to your best friend? Why not tell him yeah, I like that Beauty is Truth line, yeah, the poem about the woman whose brothers kill her lover brought tears to my eyes? What am I afraid of? What the fuck are we afraid of?

KYLE: Try to tell me something about how I'm going to live without Zoe. *(Beat.)* Please, Bennie. *(Pause, very quietly.)* This is where you're supposed to say you don't know that yet, Kyle. *(Beat.)* This is where reassurance is supposed to come in. This is where you're supposed to tell me not to lose hope. Come on Bennie, tell me not to lose hope. *(Beat.)* Well, you're right. If she could have come home, she would have. If she could have called, she would have, you know that just as well as I do, right?

(There is loud, repeated knocking, then banging.)

KYLE: I knew something was off by the way they shouted open up, it's the police, and banged and banged on my door. Like I was a criminal they'd finally ferreted out after a long search. Like I had been on the FBI's most wanted list for months. Like when Zoe's folks reported her missing that was the first they'd heard of it. I stood in the middle of the room and I didn't want to go to the door because I was terrified they were going to tell me she was dead. Which I already knew. It was early in the morning two days after Thanksgiving and I couldn't move and I couldn't speak. I breathed as deeply and as regularly as I could. Which is something Zoe always did and it seemed to calm her down, so I did that.

BENNIE: I'm going to let them in, okay? Okay, Kyle?

KYLE: After a couple minutes, Bennie made a move to the door but he had no chance to open it. After refusing to search for her until a day and a half after she disappeared, the police came to our apartment and broke the door down. Two policemen kicked down the door and rushed me, guns drawn.

BENNIE: What the fuck are you doing?

KYLE: I breathed. *(Beat.)* I breathed.

(Bennie moves in front of Kyle, stretches his arms out as though to shield him.)

BENNIE: Kyle was amazing. He just stood there, like he was in a trance. The cops started asking him all these—really stupid—questions. Kyle didn't speak. He kept—breathing. Every time they asked him where was he when she disappeared or some stupid shit like where was he born or did they have a lease on their apartment, he'd close his eyes. And breathe. And when it was quiet, he'd open his eyes. The cops finally said would he come down to the station? Kyle didn't move or answer them. He closed his eyes. The cops put cuffs on him. *(To the cops.)* Jesus, don't do that to him.

KYLE: They took me to the police station in handcuffs and when they pulled me out of the back seat of the car, I realized that they thought I had killed Zoe, and then made her disappear.

BENNIE: You guys are lunatics. I was with Kyle the night she disappeared, and so was Zoe's sister. I brought him down to report her missing. He tried to convince you to start the search right away, but—(you guys wouldn't listen)

KYLE: The police told us the bad guys always did that. They told us the bad guys contacted the police immediately to make it look good, to put them off the scent. They told us it didn't matter that I was at home, people killed other people all the time and never left the house. There was no why or how mentioned, just a pattern these cases always followed and they were not going to be fooled this time. So why didn't I just not waste all of our time? Where's Zoe?

BENNIE: Kyle wouldn't speak to them. Now and then, he actually smiled, like when they asked him where Zoe was.

KYLE: Where's Zoe?

BENNIE: They were such morons, I damn near got myself arrested.

KYLE: When it got too loud—Bennie's Italian, so he can get loud—I closed my eyes. Open or closed, I imagined Sagittarius. I happen to be very well acquainted with that constellation and suddenly, after all my lecturing her about astrology is just a game, it had meaning to me that Sagittarius was Zoe's sun sign. Picturing Sagittarius filled my mind all the way up, Sagittarius has so much to offer, there are so many places to look. Which is true about each constellation, but that night I knew this one particularly well. I soared into the Lagoon Nebula, thinking—God, thinking happily—about the river of dust that intersects it, thinking about—no, seeing—millions and millions of stars being born within the nebula, and the nebula surrounded by Sagittarius. *(A smile.)* Zoe said Sag. She'd say, "I'm a Sag," and she'd pretend to be shooting an arrow, and she'd be angry at me—no matter how many times I said it so that she should have known it, when I'd say the constellation Sagittarius has nothing to do with arrows or centaurs, it's shaped like a teapot.

BENNIE: What?

KYLE: I said that out loud.

BENNIE: Keep not saying anything, okay, Kyle? No telling what these idiots are likely to do. You don't want them rounding up a straitjacket.

KYLE: Do you think I care? Let them put me in a straitjacket. Go ahead. A straitjacket would be fine.

BENNIE: Shut up.

KYLE: Fine.

BENNIE: You're in shock, you don't know what you're saying.

KYLE: In shock? Why? Is Zoe dead? Did they find her? Is she dead?

BENNIE: No, they didn't find her.

(A pause.)

KYLE: They have to find her.

BENNIE: They'll find her.

KYLE: They think they're going to find her by making me confess.

(Kyle goes to Bennie, and touches him.)

KYLE: Bennie, God, they have to find her.

(Bennie puts his arms around Kyle.)

BENNIE: I know. *(Silence for a moment, Kyle in Bennie's arms. Then they separate.)* I don't know what this kind of screw-up is called—officially—in police enforcement circles. The cops who came to the door were under the impression Kyle had been questioned a lot of times before. They were under the impression that he was a suspect, only he wasn't. When I asked where they got that idea, one of them kept saying, "I read it." He couldn't say where he read it, or who gave him bad information. Nobody could explain anything. One of those coincidences—what's that called?—when exactly what has to happen to make something right happens.

(Lights up on Serena somewhere on the stage.)

SERENA: Synchronicity.

(Bennie glances at Serena.)

BENNIE: Zoe's family arrived at the police station, just because they couldn't stand to sit at home and wait. They saw Kyle being questioned pretty hard. They were furious and incoherent. Serena kept yelling at the cop—you—(stupid fuck)

SERENA: You stupid fuck, you stupid fuck, you stupid fuck.

BENNIE: She kept it up until her father told her to stop shouting and act like a lady.

SERENA: *(Under Bennie's line above.)* You stupid fuck, you stupid fuck, you stupid fuck. *(Pause, she looks at Kyle.)* Kyle? *(Beat, then to Bennie.)* What's he doing?

BENNIE: At that moment, the detective—the one we talked to Thanksgiving night—came from around some corner and realized for the first time that Kyle was even there. When he found out the police had taken Kyle out of his place in handcuffs, he flipped. Man, he was mad.

KYLE: I was too focused on the Lagoon Nebula to speak to anyone. *(Beat.)* I don't know how I got home.

BENNIE: I took Kyle home in a cab.

KYLE: The search began, the newspaper ran pictures of Zoe in her leather hat.

BENNIE: Zoe's picture was all over the television for a couple days.

SERENA: I went to Mom and Dad's after school each day and finally had to forbid them to turn on the television. I called the police every day.

KYLE: Bennie called the police every day.

BENNIE: Every day I called the police to find out their progress.

SERENA: Our hope dwindled. We began to focus our hope on the police finding—if that was the truth of it—finding her body. *(Beat.)* Kyle refused to speak to us.

BENNIE: Serena, he's not refusing. He just can't. He's in shock.

KYLE: Find her.

BENNIE: Some days he can't speak at all.

KYLE: Find her.

BENNIE: Except to say—to the sky—

KYLE: Find her.

BENNIE: He goes to work.

KYLE: Find her. Find her.

BENNIE: He started working crazy hours.

KYLE: Find her. *(Light out on Serena.)*

BENNIE: I was tormented trying to figure out how to take care of him. I was tormented because I knew I couldn't take care of him. Something had happened to him that couldn't be smoothed over, talked out, medicated, surgically removed, forgotten. Something as dark and infinite as the night sky he loved so much had happened to him. I was nothing. I was a bug. I was an irritant. Kyle suffered.

KYLE: I started working again immediately. Some days during the next two weeks, I worked sixteen hours. Some days twenty. The department was in the middle of the chaos of a typical power struggle—whose work had more funding, whose work had less. I grabbed a tiny piece of the work to take off into a corner. Triton. One of Neptune's moons, all ice, the coolest place in our solar system. Which is an illusion because beneath the frozen surface the rocky core is producing heat. Yeah. Radioactive heat deep down in the core. Triton's surface makes it appear to be something it in fact is not. Which is not exactly a big surprise. *(Beat.)* The heat turns some of the ice to gas and then—finally—when the pressure has built to the point at which it is unbearable—an explosion of gas and debris breaks through the frozen surface, rising five miles into space, into the thin, thin atmosphere surrounding Neptune and her moons, like a gigantic geyser. *(Beat, eyes closed.)* Which is so beautiful that for a split second I feel like I will burst into tears the way the geyser explodes through Triton's smooth surface. *(Beat.)* Then that feeling flees and is replaced by no feeling. Again. I keep working. I don't focus on what I'm looking for. I don't care what I'm looking for. I only care to keep working. Could I compile enough of those milliseconds to create a full minute of feeling? *(A phone is ringing.)* I don't know. I don't care. Triton is all ice. It isn't. It seems to be. It isn't. I don't care.

BENNIE: Kyle. The phone.

KYLE: I don't care whose project gets cut.

BENNIE: Should I answer it? *(Silence, then answering the phone.)* Hello. *(Beat, then to Kyle.)* Gone.

KYLE: I don't care whether there is anything left worth knowing about the cosmos.

BENNIE: You don't.

KYLE: No.

BENNIE: Jesus. Kyle.

KYLE: *(Vacantly.)* What?

(The phone rings. Twice. Three times.)

BENNIE: *(After a look at Kyle, answering.)* Hello. *(Pause.)* Yeah, he is. Kyle? *(Pause.)* This guy found Zoe's purse. *(Beat.)* He's on the Navajo reservation.

(Kyle looks at Bennie for several seconds. He walks toward Bennie, his breathing getting increasingly heavy. As he arrives at Bennie, he stands nearly hyperventilating. Bennie touches him gently. Kyle starts to cry. In a minute, he composes himself.)

KYLE: *(On the phone.)* Yes? *(Beat.)* Yes, this is Zoe Kalke's home. I'm her husband. *(Quickly.)* Did you find my wife? *(A pause, as Kyle listens.)* Yes. *(Pause, listens.)* Yes, may I come now? *(Beat.)* Don't worry about that.

(Kyle is done talking on the phone. He steps away from Bennie.)

Sixteen days after Thanksgiving, a man's dog found Zoe's bag buried in his yard. Up at the Southeast corner of the Navajo reservation. Schoolteacher. Um. He searched and found—just beyond his property—a pile of rocks. *(Beat.)* A big pile of rocks, all sizes and—. And the Navajo believe it will harm them to come in contact with a dead body, and—and he sensed she was there but he didn't want to uncover her for—survival—uh—spiritual— reasons. *(Beat.)* He thought of involving the police but—well, the tribal police are Navajo and he didn't want them to have to—touch her. And then he was afraid the regular police might find a way to harass him about it. *(Beat.)* So he thought if he called her number, that might help him decide what was best. I told him I'd come immediately.

BENNIE: Now? That's a five or six hour drive, we'll get there in the middle of the night.

KYLE: *(Overlap.)* He said the sooner the better. He thinks she's under those rocks and he wants her out of there. I promised him no police.

BENNIE: I've got to call the hospital. Then we'll go. Give me five minutes, all right?

KYLE: All right.

(Light up on the rocks. Kyle and Bennie move toward them, Kyle clutching Zoe's bag. He stops, stares at the bag.)

BENNIE: Jesus, it's freezing up here.

(Kyle extends the purse to Bennie.)

KYLE: Will you hold this?

(Bennie moves toward the rocks.)

BENNIE: *(Removing a large, heavy rock.)* I'm going to do this.

KYLE: *(Alarmed.)* NO.

(Kyle drops Zoe's bag and rushes to the rocks. He starts to take rocks off the pile.)

BENNIE: Let me do this, Kyle. *(He takes Kyle by the shoulders.)* Let me do this for you. *(Kyle drops to his knees, then sits back on them. Bennie follows.)*

BENNIE: Let me.

KYLE: I am thinking thoughts that must be worse than the truth. *(Pause.)* Bennie, I want her to have died quickly. *(After a couple beats in which Bennie looks at the rock pile, and Kyle looks up into the sky.)* Let's wait another minute.

BENNIE: All right.

KYLE: *(Pointing to the sky.)* Look. Here the ground acts like a telescope and the heavens are unobstructed by concrete and artificial light fixtures. Look. What the eye can see is quadrupled here. *(Beat.)* I'd like to live here.

BENNIE: Not enough people for me.

KYLE: Zoe thought the same thing, that she needed to be near people.

(A pause.)

BENNIE: Love endures all things.

KYLE: What?

BENNIE: Love endures all things. *(Beat.)* It's from the Bible.

KYLE: You surprised me.

BENNIE: You don't remember what a teetotaling Bible-thumper my mom is?

KYLE: Yes. I do.

BENNIE: Man. Those Sunday mornings.

KYLE: Be grateful you're not a Methodist or a Lutheran. Then she would have sent you to teen meetings on Saturdays too. *(Beat.)* I envied kids who went to those teen meetings.

BENNIE: Me too.

KYLE: I envied everyone.

BENNIE: And then everyone envied you.

KYLE: Yes. *(Beat.)* Bennie? *(Beat.)* I'm going to have to look at her.

BENNIE: I know you are. I know you, Kyle.

KYLE: Okay.

BENNIE: Look, I brought something.

(Kyle looks at him. Bennie pulls a very small book out of his pocket, gives it to Kyle.)

KYLE: This is Keats?

BENNIE: Yeah, you know, a small—abridged—Keats. *(Bennie turns the pages.)* I'm gonna do this. *(Points to a poem.)* You read. *(Bennie gets up, goes to the rocks.)* Read.

KYLE: Okay.

(Bennie starts removing rocks. Bennie stops.)

BENNIE: Read.

KYLE: *(Reading.)* "After dark vapours have oppress'd our plains
For a long dreary season, comes a day
Born of the gentle South—"
(Pause. Bennie keeps removing rocks.)

BENNIE: Don't stop.

KYLE: You don't stop.

BENNIE: I won't.

KYLE: Okay. *(Reading.)* "—comes a day
Born of the gentle South and clears away
From the sick heavens all unseemly stains."
(Pause.) That's nice, Bennie.
(Bennie has taken off nearly all the rocks—enough so he sees Zoe. He reacts to seeing her. He lifts Zoe's hat out of the shallow grave, brushes dirt off it, then puts it back, as Kyle keeps reading.)

KYLE: *(Reading.)*
"The anxious month, relieved of its pains
Takes as a long-lost right the feel of May;
The eyelids of the passing coolness play
Like rose leaves with the drip of summer rain."
(Bennie finishes as Kyle reads. He looks at Zoe's body for a long minute. He is a doctor, so he looks at her with more than one intention. Then he turns to Kyle.)

KYLE: *(Reading.)* "The calmest thoughts come round us."
(Kyle stops reading as he hears Bennie step toward him. Kyle continues to face front. As Bennie moves to him, Kyle lifts an arm in the air. Bennie takes his hand. Kyle struggles to keep his breath even. He starts to shake.)

KYLE: All right.

BENNIE: We found her. Zoe is here. Zoe is dead.
(After a pause, Kyle makes a movement as though he's going to stand.)

BENNIE: Wait. I'll tell you what you're going to see. *(Beat.)* Her clothes are laid on top of her body.

KYLE: She has no clothes on.

BENNIE: No. *(Beat.)* She's cut.

KYLE: In the face?

BENNIE: Yeah. Her shoulders are bruised.
(Pause.)

KYLE: Okay.

BENNIE: There's something else.

KYLE: What?

BENNIE: There's something—weird. Remarkable.

KYLE: What?

BENNIE: *(Pulling on Kyle's arm to invite him up.)* Look.
  (Kyle stands and crosses to Zoe. He looks at her, gulping in large breaths of air as he does. A beat or two, then, not taking his eyes off her—)

KYLE: Is she smiling?

BENNIE: That's what it looks like.

KYLE: Could it be just—a—an—anomaly? Could it have happened after she died?

BENNIE: Maybe. *(Pause.)* I'm going to see if this guy will give us a blanket.
  (Kyle ignores him. Bennie exits. Kyle kneels beside Zoe, looking at her intently. He lifts each article of her clothing out of the grave, then looks and looks at her.)

KYLE: Zoe, are you smiling?
  (Lights out. End of Act I.)

ACT II

Kyle on stage. Bennie some distance from him.

KYLE: Any time I wanted, I could annoy Zoe by bringing up the Big Bang. Married people enjoy annoying one another from time to time, I don't know why. Sometimes I felt frustrated, or I felt unsettled, some small something would be gnawing at me and somehow the way I diminished that gnawing thing was to annoy Zoe. I had several tried and true ways to do that. We both did. But there was one failsafe, one subject that I could rely on absolutely to annoy her. Which was the Big Bang. Partly I brought it up because I was annoyed that she would not—comprehend it. She refused. I'd find a way to get it into the conversation—yes, from one infinitely dense, infinitely minute, infinitely hot point of pure energy, fueled by some unimaginable force, exploded the universe and absolutely everything in it. Bang. I think it was the word "some" that got her. Some force? What force? Before that bang, nothing. Imagine nothing. She'd tell me I wasn't answering her question and scold me for the hundredth time about refusing to admit the spirit into my life. Maybe that was it. Maybe I felt so bereft of spirit that I wanted her to talk about it, and I knew the Big Bang could get us there.

BENNIE: Stop.

KYLE: Zoe and I were equal then. She had the spirit, and I had the Big Bang.

BENNIE: Stop talking about the Big Bang.

KYLE: Yes. From a pinprick of burning density emerged everything in the heavens and all of life. Which is the wrong subject. *(Beat.)* Who cut her, Bennie? *(No answer.)* Do you know the second law of thermodynamics, Bennie?

BENNIE: No, I do not know the second law of thermodynamics.

KYLE: Yes you do.

BENNIE: Okay I do.

KYLE: The amount of disorder in a closed system—which is entropy—can only grow with time.

BENNIE: I don't want to talk about—(entropy)

KYLE: Random chaos—entropy—like a black hole—always increases.

BENNIE: I don't care.

KYLE: You don't want to talk about the Big Bang? Let's talk about black holes.

BENNIE: No, Kyle.

KYLE: Which swallow everything that crosses their path. I mean everything. The supermarket swallowed Zoe. Or maybe her car swallowed her. Or— you know what?

BENNIE: *(Reluctantly.)* What?

KYLE: Maybe her heart. Maybe Zoe got swallowed by her great big, ever-expanding, loaded with the spirit heart.

BENNIE: I know what you've been doing.

KYLE: What? Grieving? *(Beat.)* What? Working?

BENNIE: You have not made one inquiry since the police started trying to find out who killed her.

KYLE: *(Beat.)* I ask you.

BENNIE: In three weeks, you have not called the police to see what they've discovered.

KYLE: What have they discovered?

BENNIE: More than one person was involved. They think two.

KYLE: They think two different men raped my wife?

BENNIE: Yeah.

KYLE: *(Swallows hard.)* See, you told me. Which I prefer. I prefer not to think about the police and their investigation. I prefer to think about black holes. I'm not confident they will find the men who hurt Zoe and thinking about that is—. I prefer to think about that in the abstract. I prefer thinking about black holes.

BENNIE: You haven't seen Zoe's family. Serena wants to see you.

KYLE: No.

BENNIE: Why?

KYLE: I can't.

BENNIE: Why? *(Beat.)* I know why. *(Beat.)* I know what you're doing, Kyle. *(Beat.)* Last night wasn't the first time, was it?

KYLE: How do you know? *(Beat.)* Did you follow me?

BENNIE: How many times?

KYLE: You're following me?

BENNIE: Goddammit.

KYLE: Four.

BENNIE: You've been with her four times? Jesus. In three weeks?

KYLE: It's my money.

BENNIE: Oh, well, that's different. I thought you knocked over a Quik Mart to get the money.

KYLE: Shut up.

BENNIE: What are you doing?

KYLE: You know what I'm doing, remember?

BENNIE: Is it the same one every time at least?

(Lights up on Kathleen somewhere else on the stage. She is perhaps 35.)

KYLE: Yes. She thinks I'm weird.

BENNIE: So do I.

KYLE: She calls me John Sky. The John part's just—she calls all of us John.

BENNIE: What? You gonna tell me now you and this whore stargaze together?

KATHLEEN: The first time, he sits on a chair in the hotel room for—Christ— for ten minutes maybe, and I start to take my clothes off but I notice he's someplace else, on another planet maybe, so I say, because some of them do this, I say *(She turns to Kyle.)* No sex?

KYLE: Yes. Sex.

KATHLEEN: Oh, you want me to do it. *(Beat.)* I figure out he wants me to undress him because some of them like that. Men are such babies. So I walk over there, to the chair where he's sitting, and I reach for his belt and he stands up like somebody shot at him, fast and scared, and tells me not to touch him.

KYLE: *(Soft.)* Don't touch me.

KATHLEEN: We've got a problem here. *(Pause.)* You know a way to have sex without touching, because I can do a lot of things but having sex without touching is not one I've attempted.

KYLE: I want to take off my clothes myself.

TOUCH 317

KATHLEEN: He turns out the light. Lots of them turn out the light of course because they know they're bad boys. I figure he's ashamed, that's the going thing. Ashamed of what he's doing or ashamed of his body. Both. So before he gets naked I tell him he has to use a condom. That seems to really shake him up.

KYLE: *(Shaken.)* I don't have a—. I don't have one.

KATHLEEN: Then no intercourse. What do you want instead?

KYLE: No. I don't want anything instead. That's what I want.

KATHLEEN: Well, I don't do intercourse without a condom. It's dangerous.

KYLE: I don't mind that.

KATHLEEN: You go ahead and have a death wish, I have no problem with that. I do not have a death wish, so no condom, no intercourse. You want to die, do it on your own time.

KYLE: All right. *(Beat.)* I'll get one. *(Pause.)* Will you wait here?

KATHLEEN: Yes. *(Beat.)* Of course I will. But if we're longer than a half hour it's more money. *(Beat.)* So then he gives me more money.

KYLE: Will you wait?

KATHLEEN: Yeah, I'll wait. *(Beat.)* So then he starts to leave, but he comes right back.

KYLE: I can't buy a condom.

KATHLEEN: Well, I don't have one. I should. Sometimes I do. Right now I don't. So what do you want instead?

KYLE: Will you go get one? *(Quickly.)* I'll give you the money.

KATHLEEN: He did. Then he said—

KYLE: I can't buy a condom. I don't want to explain why.

KATHLEEN: Don't bother. I'll be back in a minute, they've got them in a dispenser in the ladies' room.

KYLE: When she got back, I was already undressed and in bed.

BENNIE: You're going to have to explain this to me, Kyle.

KYLE: I'll explain. I'll explain. The first time, I was walking near downtown, I wasn't watching where I was walking, I just walked and walked and walked and walked and walked. I've been doing it every night since we found Zoe. After work, so it's already late, that night it was midnight. And she approaches me and asks me if she can help me. And I look at her wearing a bright red extremely short dress and black stockings and those big square heels on her shoes. Which all looks almost like Zoe. *(Beat.)* Which makes me want to kill her. I look at her and I think she's going to take a step back because of the way I look at her. Her eyes get bigger.

Which also makes me think of Zoe. Again, I have an impulse to—. I want to kill her. I'm standing in the street feeling murderous toward this prostitute, thinking about stabbing and stabbing and stabbing her and I know she doesn't deserve it. *(Beat.)* She holds her ground. *(Beat.)* I realize I'm excited. My body. My body is excited. I pull some bills out of my wallet and put them in her hand and ask her if it's enough and she counts it and says yeah, come on, so I do. Suddenly I stop thinking this woman doesn't deserve to live if Zoe is dead and start thinking my life depends on having sex with her.

BENNIE: Are you not alarmed that you wanted to hurt this woman?

KYLE: No. That feeling went away.

BENNIE: Suppose it comes back.

KYLE: No. It won't.

BENNIE: How can you be sure of that?

KYLE: *(Comes in on "sure.")* Because I told you the feeling turned into another feeling. I told you that.

BENNIE: An urgent need to have sex with a prostitute.

KYLE: Sex. Yes. I told you.

BENNIE: Christ, Kyle, God knows what diseases she has.

KYLE: You are not listening.

BENNIE: So you had the good fortune to get hit on by one of the three prostitutes in the city who's clean. You didn't know that going in.

KYLE: She said no kissing.

KATHLEEN: I don't kiss johns on the first date.

KYLE: I don't want to kiss you. Just sex.

KATHLEEN: The next time, he found me. A week later maybe. Right before Christmas.

KYLE: It was our wedding anniversary. Winter solstice.

KATHLEEN: He went up ahead of me and when I got there, he was looking out the open window with binoculars. *(To Kyle.)* Hey, close the window.

KYLE: Sorry. I'm an astronomer.

KATHLEEN: Whatever. *(Beat.)* Then he gave me a couple dozen condoms. *(To Kyle.)* This must mean I'm going to see a lot of you?

KYLE: No, you—. I don't know. I got them and you can use them whenever you want. Not just with me, with anyone.

KATHLEEN: *(Beat.)* Thank you. *(Beat.)* It wasn't a diamond bracelet, but as gifts go, it was a good one. *(Beat.)* Should I turn out the light?

KYLE: Please.

BENNIE: Thanks, Kyle, I don't need any more details.

KYLE: That time before I left I asked if I should tell her my name.

KATHLEEN: I know your name. Your name is John Sky.

BENNIE: You've got to stop.

KYLE: Why? I feel happy when I'm—(with her)

BENNIE: You feel happy? She's a hooker.

KYLE: Not because of her. Because I can feel my body working again. Because I can feel myself making and expending energy again. Because when I'm lost inside this woman's body, I don't think about who killed Zoe. I don't think about how much pain she might have been in before she died. I don't think about why she was smiling. Which I think about nonstop.

BENNIE: Are you telling me there's nothing else that could—?

KYLE: Could what?

BENNIE: Help.

(A pause. Kyle is thinking.)

KYLE: Maybe a green flash. *(Quickly.)* Just as the sun sets, the atmosphere acts as a prism—

BENNIE: Stop it.

KYLE: *(Continued.)* —separating the sun's light into its component colors, and the last of those colors is an infinitesimally small patch—not a patch— flash, of course—flash of green.

BENNIE: Either you need to have sex with a prostitute or you need to see something no one's ever seen?

KYLE: The green flash has been seen. *(Beat.)* Not by me. *(Beat.)* But it happens at that wonderful time day turns to night and so I've always thought I should see it. I want to see it. I'm entitled to see it. *(Beat.)* It would make me feel—something—for a few minutes.

BENNIE: Kyle, you should stop with this hooker.

KYLE: Bennie, don't tell me what to do. You've been telling me what to do since we were kids. Now stop. *You* stop.

BENNIE: *(Comes in after "kids.")* What the hell are you talking about? I have not.

KYLE: You have too. I haven't been doing it, but you've been telling me.

BENNIE: I had to. Left alone, you would have—you never even went to a movie I didn't drag you to.

KYLE: So what?

BENNIE: It was all I could do to get you to come outdoors in the daytime, for God's sake.

KYLE: But you insisted. Which is my point.

BENNIE: What? You're rebelling? What am I, your father?

KYLE: I want to see this woman.

BENNIE: You're not seeing a woman, Kyle. You're—(having sex with a hooker)

KYLE: I want to fuck this woman. Which I have to pay her money for. Which I want to pay her money for. Is that better? I'm not pretending anything here, Bennie. I'm not delusional.

BENNIE: Listen to yourself.

KYLE: What? Listen to myself say I want to fuck a woman? It feels good, fucking her feels good, saying it to you feels good.

BENNIE: And don't worry about the consequences?

KYLE: She makes me use a condom, all right?

BENNIE: *(Pissed.)* I'm not talking about the health consequences and you damn well know it. I mean the consequences to your—

KYLE: Spirit? You taking over where Zoe left off? *(Enraged.)* Don't. I want this woman's body. FUCK THE CONSEQUENCES. *(Kyle stops, surprised by his fury. He breathes. He breathes. Several beats.)* Bennie. It feels like finding high ground and looking up into a black sky that is at the same time so so so so brilliant with bits of light. I like the immersion. I like the intensity. I like the dark, and then the brief flash of brilliance. *(Pause.)* I need to do this. I tried to explain why. Leave me alone.

BENNIE: *(Beat.)* Okay, look. I'm sorry. I apologize. I don't know a damn thing about this. I have no Zoe, I've never had a Zoe, I don't know a fucking thing, okay? I'm sorry.

KYLE: That's okay.

BENNIE: I'm just going to keep calling the cops and telling them I'm you and finding out what's doing. Right?

KYLE: I'd be grateful.

KATHLEEN: The time after that, he sat by the window again. *(Beat.)* Go ahead. Open it.

KYLE: Thanks.

KATHLEEN: You're welcome.

KYLE: Would you like to see Jupiter?

KATHLEEN: Out the window?

KYLE: Yes. Look.

(Kyle hands her binoculars. Kathleen looks out the window.)

KATHLEEN: Do I see it?

(Kyle leans over her, then points.)

KYLE: There. Look.

(Pause.)

KATHLEEN: That's Jupiter.

KYLE: It is.

KATHLEEN: It looks small.

KYLE: It's the biggest planet in our solar system.

KATHLEEN: Oh.

KYLE: I'll bring you a picture next time. When I was a teenager, I saw five of the planets aligned in the sky. *(Beat.)* You see them, Bennie?

BENNIE: Man.

KYLE: Yeah.

BENNIE: Wait, I only see four of them. Where's Mercury?

KYLE: Find it in the telescope first. Do you see it?

BENNIE: No. *(Quickly.)* Yeah.

KYLE: Okay, now look without the telescope. *(Beat.)* You see it? You see it?

BENNIE: I see all five of them.

KYLE: Jesus. Jesus. Jesus. Jesus.

BENNIE: You better calm down, Kyle.

KYLE: Are you crazy? Calm down? I bet this is better than having sex.

BENNIE: Right.

KYLE: For excitement I mean.

BENNIE: Kyle. I bet not.

KYLE: *(Still looking up at the sky.)* Well. I'm never going to know.

BENNIE: You've got to get out of the house, that's all. You've got to come with me to some of the parties at school.

KYLE: No money for college, remember? It's straight A's or not enough financial aid and no college.

BENNIE: Hey, buddy, you can go to a party and make straight A's, I'm making straight A's and it's harder to do at my school.

KYLE: You're taking easier classes though.

BENNIE: No I'm not.

KYLE: *(Beat.)* You haven't, have you? Had sex?

BENNIE: Yeah, right.

KYLE: You would have told me.

BENNIE: I'll call you first thing.

KYLE: I bet this is better.

KATHLEEN: Five planets at one time. That must have been something.

KYLE: It was.

KATHLEEN: *(After a pause.)* Did she leave you? *(Pause.)* Is she dead?

KYLE: Yes. Which is the same old tired story to you, right?

KATHLEEN: I don't know the story. *(Quickly, quietly.)* I don't want to know the story. I don't have to know the story to know it's not old or tired if it's your story. *(Beat.)* We're going to have to speed this up.

KYLE: Do you want to see Betelgeuse?

KATHLEEN: Who?

KYLE: It's a giant red star in Orion's shoulder.

KATHLEEN: Red?

KYLE: You maybe couldn't tell it was red at first. But if you practiced looking up into the sky, it would happen. You could see it red. We'd have to go up on the roof.

KATHLEEN: Your time's almost up.

KYLE: I'm good for it.

KATHLEEN: *(A smile.)* Yeah, I know. *(Beat.)* Let's not. *(Beat.)* He gave me more money immediately. *(To Kyle.)* John Sky. I'll kiss you if you want.

KYLE: No. Just—. No. Turn out the light.

KATHLEEN: Right. Take off your clothes.

(Lights out on Kathleen.)

BENNIE: Serena's coming over.

KYLE: No, Bennie.

BENNIE: Are you going to avoid seeing Zoe's family forever?

KYLE: Forever? It's been five weeks since—. Thanksgiving.

BENNIE: It's New Year's Eve. Serena called, she's upset—Zoe's birthday, your anniversary—.

KYLE: I know what month it is.

BENNIE: Then Christmas. She wants to see you.

KYLE: I have plans.

BENNIE: You were just there last night.

KYLE: I can't see Serena yet.

BENNIE: She loves you, Kyle.

KYLE: *(Closes his eyes.)* I know that. *(He opens his eyes.)* Zoe was her baby sister. *(Pause.)* I can't face Serena's sadness.

(Lights up on Serena somewhere on the stage. Kyle crosses to Kathleen's part of the stage and waits for her. Serena crosses to Bennie, carrying champagne, puts it down somewhere on the stage. Serena is agitated; she looks around the room. Bennie watches her. She paces.)

SERENA: Is he hiding somewhere in the house?

BENNIE: No. *(Beat.)* He's out.

SERENA: He's been out for six weeks.

BENNIE: I tried, you know, to get him to see you.

SERENA: I appreciate it. Clearly he's being as dismissive of you as he is of me.

BENNIE: I don't want you to take it personally. He won't see anyone, you know, he won't even see his parents.

SERENA: I suppose I should disabuse myself of the idea that Kyle and I could help each other with this.

KYLE: Bennie tells me I should let him help me. I should let Serena help me. I should let my parents help me. Which I would like to do. All right. Help me. *(Pause.)* What's our goal, though?

BENNIE: I've been thinking, what am I trying to help him do anyway? Forget he loved Zoe? Forget Zoe ever lived? *(Sees Serena react to this.)* Sorry. *(Beat.)* But there is something—something not so good about that idea of helping. Do you know what I mean? Something—I don't know, something—

SERENA: Pernicious.

BENNIE: *(A grin.)* That might be it.

SERENA: Dangerous but insidiously—secretly—dangerous. Undermining in a subtle way. Imposing.

BENNIE: That one word means all that?

SERENA: Don't get me started on words. They're profoundly beautiful. Every one of them.

BENNIE: You sound like Kyle. You know, he's got this thing for Keats.

SERENA: Zoe told me that. Don't tell anyone, she said, as though she was revealing something about their sex life. She whispered, Kyle's a Keats freak. *(Bennie laughs.)* I prefer T.S. Eliot—ultimately—but he's right. There's something exquisite about Keats.

KYLE/SERENA: *(Reciting.)* "Bold Lover, never, never canst thou kiss,
Though winning near the goal—"

SERENA: *(To Bennie.)* You know this poem?

BENNIE: No. *(Beat.)* Well, maybe a little, like I read it in high school or something. *(He hands her a book of Keats' poems.)* Here you go, knock yourself out.

(Serena thumbs through the book.)

KYLE: *(Still reciting.)*
"—yet do not grieve;
She cannot fade, though thou hast not thy bliss—"
Those lovers have that one moment. Which is eternal. That's the goal. To become one of those lovers. To chase Zoe around and around and around

and around and never catch her, but keep smiling because I can see her running ahead of me, just out of my reach, and I am filled with anticipation and—. I am filled with hope. *(Beat.)* How's that for a goal?

SERENA: *(Closing the book.)* You don't like poetry?

BENNIE: I didn't say that.

SERENA: I cannot comprehend how anyone could not like poetry. I love words, I eat words, I sleep words.

BENNIE: That's why you're a teacher.

SERENA: Actually, I chose my profession because of Zoe.

BENNIE: How's that?

SERENA: I made the decision to teach young children when I was twelve, on Zoe's first day of kindergarten. That first day was terrifying for her. I met her at the bus at noon and she walked down the steps on tiptoe—on tiptoe—Zoe!—looking like she'd been struck by lightning. She jumped into my arms, really frightened. I said to myself, small children need someone wonderful at school every day. I'm wonderful. How about me?

BENNIE: That confidence pulled you right along I bet.

SERENA: Confidence is one of the few things the three of us have in common—Trevor, Zoe and I. We were undeterred by any so-called obstacle in our path.

BENNIE: Indestructible.

SERENA: Well.

BENNIE: Fuck.

SERENA: Never mind. You must be tired of watching everything you say.

BENNIE: Yeah, I'm exhausted by Kyle's pain. Poor Bennie, you know?

SERENA: Indeed. Poor Bennie.

BENNIE: So, otherwise—aside from the confidence—you're all pretty different?

SERENA: We had our tempers in common too. Not Trevor. He's always been patient, soft-spoken. But Zoe and I both have terrible tempers. And God, she could lose her temper about absolutely anything on earth. When we were choosing bridesmaids' dresses for Trevor's wedding, the one Zoe wanted was a color euphemistically called sunflower, which in fact was a stark yellow that teetered dangerously toward orange. It was beyond hideous—it was revolting. Looking at it actually made me queasy. When I objected—on the grounds that if I wore that dress I was bound to vomit at some point during the ceremony—Zoe became hysterical—she was trying the dress on, I refused to go anywhere near it—telling me that I was denigrating her taste in clothing.

BENNIE: Denigrating?

SERENA: She said putting down. Actually, she shouted.

BENNIE: Whereas you make it a policy to shout only in police stations.

SERENA: Anyway. She said I was putting down her taste in clothing. I preferred a dress that was a light lilac color, for which she accused me of behaving in my usual drab way. Drab. Just because a person doesn't constantly go out in public wearing purple thigh-high hose does not make her drab. *(Beat.)* I have a lingering image of Zoe in that hose and a white sundress and a polka dot hat. Do you remember that polka dot hat?

BENNIE: Who could forget that hat? Big purple and blue dots?

SERENA: Blue? I hope Zoe's not listening. Turquoise.

BENNIE: Turquoise. Of course.

SERENA: I loved that hat. After you found her, I decided to ask Kyle if I could have it. Except Kyle won't see me, or talk to me. *(Serena starts to cry. A few beats; she composes herself.)* It's like they both died. *(Beat.)* It's after eleven. Where the hell is he?

BENNIE: Who knows? *(Quickly.)* Maybe—did you see the moon tonight? Maybe he's at the observatory—you know—observing—um—the moon.

SERENA: What's going on, Bennie? Where is he?

BENNIE: No, I don't know for sure. I just thought—did you see the moon? Really. Look out the window.

SERENA: *(Looks out the window, after a beat.)* Spectacular moon, huh? *(Beat.)* The children and I had a wonderful time with the moon right before Christmas break. We had spent the entire week with the word lunatic. They especially loved that I asked them to show me the way a lunatic behaves.

BENNIE: Then you talked about the moon.

SERENA: Yes. Draw the moon. Tell me how you feel when you look at the moon.

KYLE: *(Looking up.)* I don't like it full.

SERENA: I asked them do you get that lunatic feeling when you look at the moon?

KYLE: The full moon's light obscures most of the other bodies in the sky. Which I hate.

SERENA: We have a code now. That's one of the things they like most about words—codemaking. I say, "What's the problem, Tom? Are you feeling like a lunatic?"

KYLE: Zoe used to say—but what about that gorgeous light, sweetheart? *(Beat.)* What about that gorgeous light, sweetheart?

SERENA: One of the students told me the moon made him feel like dancing, but unfettered dancing, he said, and alone. No partner. He said he could look up and see his silhouette reflected on the surface of the moon.

BENNIE: He did not.

SERENA: That's what he said. Fourth grader.

BENNIE: He said unfettered?

SERENA: He meant unfettered.

BENNIE: But he couldn't have seen—. That silhouette part couldn't be true.

SERENA: Sure it's true. Remember when you were nine?

BENNIE: I never felt like that. Kyle did, I think.

> (A pause. Kyle continues to look up at the sky through this scene. Serena pours herself a glass of champagne and drinks it.)

SERENA: It's New Year's Eve. Do you want champagne?

BENNIE: Always. Do you want music?

SERENA: Yes.

> (Serena pours Bennie a glass of champagne, and another for herself.)

BENNIE: Kyle's collection is small.

SERENA: That shouldn't pose a problem. Zoe's was huge.

BENNIE: He put all her stuff in storage.

SERENA: (Beat.) Good for him.

BENNIE: You know? I'll ask him about the hat. I mean, I'll tell him you want the hat with the polka dots.

SERENA: Thanks, Bennie.

BENNIE: If he doesn't want to go through her things, I can do it. That hat won't be hard to find.

SERENA: Why have I not realized before how much I like you?

BENNIE: Yeah, dammit.

SERENA: All these years, I've thought of you as an extension of Kyle. By God, I think I've taken you for granted, Benjamin.

BENNIE: Oh, God, nobody calls me that except my whacked-out, religious fanatic mother.

SERENA: Nevertheless, nice name.

BENNIE: How about your name? Serena.

SERENA: What?

BENNIE: I mean your name. It's so beautiful.

SERENA: Thank you.

BENNIE: I mean, just the way it sounds coming out of my mouth. Serena.

SERENA: See what I mean about words?

> (A pause.)

BENNIE: Okay, let's get the music going. Kyle's got like fifty CDs, but they're all by the same four artists. Kyle's very loyal. He's got Eric Clapton. In his astonishing number of incarnations. This guy played with all kinds of rock groups before he—(went solo)

SERENA: No. Eric Clapton's child fell out a window. He makes me think of death.

BENNIE: Oh. Yeah.

SERENA: And I think about death enough.

BENNIE: No problem. Keith Jarrett?

SERENA: The grunting pianist.

BENNIE: Nix. Pat Benatar?

SERENA: Kyle likes Pat Benatar?

BENNIE: He'd never admit it, but I think he masturbated to Pat Benatar as a child.

SERENA: That settles that.

BENNIE: Kyle likes passion. *(Beat.)* And finally—so you better like this one—

SERENA: I like Pat Benatar and Eric Clapton. That Derek and the Dominoes album. Wow.

BENNIE: "Layla."

SERENA: Yes. "Layla." We listened to it here in this room quite a lot, I think.

BENNIE: Yup. They both love it. *(Beat.)* Okay, last, but I hope most, John Klemmer.

SERENA: Don't know him.

BENNIE: Jazz saxophone.

SERENA: That sounds good. *(Beat.)* You know what, Benjamin?

BENNIE: What?

SERENA: I'm glad Kyle's not here.

(A couple beats, then John Klemmer's "Touch" comes up.)

BENNIE: *(Holding out his hand to her.)* Could I interest you in a little unfettered dancing?

(Serena gives Bennie her hand. He takes her in his arms, and they dance. Their dancing is close and romantic. The lights go out on them.)

KYLE: *(After a pause.)* The brightest light ever seen from earth—at least in recorded history—was the light from a supernova in Lupus the Wolf, May 1, 1006. When a dying star explodes, its light is so great that it outshines its entire galaxy. Which is as it should be, a final burst of blazing, all-encompassing light and then nothing, then death. *(Beat.)* Zoe wouldn't buy the Big Bang no matter how many ways I tried to convince her, but the spilling of stardust following a supernova—that idea thrilled her. She'd look out our window all of a sudden and yell, I want to see a supernova

NOW. I'd tell her a supernova only occurs about every fifty years per galaxy and since one occurred in our galaxy in the seventies, there probably won't be another until she's an old lady. *(Abrupt stop, then after a beat.)* Which isn't a hard and fast rule. Nothing in science is hard and fast. Zoe'd say of course not, how could it be? Have faith she'd tell me. *(Pause.)* After a supernova, all the tiny bits of elements, all the particles, scatter throughout the galaxy. Billions of years ago, that—what should we call it?—heavenly debris—fell to earth, covered the earth. Which is why life on earth shares a portion of its elemental make-up with the stars. Which is why, for instance, human beings' bodies contain traces of iron—residue from stars exploding four billion years ago.

(Lights up on Kathleen.)

KATHLEEN: You're not serious. You and I are made of the same stuff as stars.

KYLE: Not entirely. Not in the same proportion. But yes.

KATHLEEN: I didn't know that.

KYLE: Yes.

KATHLEEN: But the last explosion was 1006?

KYLE: Not the last. The brightest. The most gorgeous.

KATHLEEN: Uh huh. *(Picking up a photograph.)* And this is Jupiter.

KYLE: Yes.

KATHLEEN: Thank you for bringing it.

KYLE: I told you I would.

KATHLEEN: Yeah, well. That usually doesn't mean shit. *(She looks at the picture.)* That's quite a profession you've got yourself.

(Silence. She looks at him.)

KYLE: This is quite a profession too. Yours.

KATHLEEN: *(A smile.)* John Sky, you are unique.

KYLE: Everyone is unique.

KATHLEEN: You'd be surprised at how predictable the folks who travel in and out of this room are. Believe me, you're the first who's given me a photograph of Jupiter, or any other planet.

KYLE: They couldn't be more dissimilar—our professions.

KATHLEEN: *(A moment's thought.)* Right.

KYLE: When I leave here, I think about the amount of trust a person has to have to do this.

KATHLEEN: Are you kidding?

KYLE: No, I—. No. In yourself. In other people. That you can handle them. That they'll let you.

KATHLEEN: I think of it more like being a restaurant worker. Here's all the items, what can I get you?

KYLE: And the amount of—of—patience—it must take. *(He shudders.)* People. Constantly.

KATHLEEN: I'm filling in? Until you can tolerate real people? *(Kyle turns away from her.)* I don't mind. That's part of my job description—not to mind anything. *(She looks at her watch.)* We better get started. I have an appointment in about an hour.

KYLE: Oh.

KATHLEEN: New Year's Eve.

KYLE: I'm sorry.

(She reaches toward him, touches his cheek. He allows it for a split second, then turns his head away.)

KATHLEEN: Don't be sorry, okay? *(Quiet.)* Do you want to take off your clothes?

KYLE: *(Near tears.)* Yes. All right?

KATHLEEN: Yeah. *(She turns out the light.)* I hope she loved you with her whole heart.

KYLE: She did.

(Light up on Kyle.)

Sometimes that's a comfort, knowing how much Zoe loved me. Sometimes I fall asleep knowing I was loved deeply. I can't say I feel happy at that moment of drifting off. But I feel comforted. By knowing that if I never feel joy again, I was loved by Zoe. Passionately. The thing about passion is that it's easy to recall. I try not to recall it because as comforting as it is to know how deeply Zoe loved me, it is equally discomforting to recall her passion. I fight off that recollection but sometimes I lose the fight. I can't ward off a few seconds of feeling Zoe's passion. Which I pay for. For the thrill of those seconds, for the quick breath, for the moan, for the response my body makes to that conjuring, I pay with the next moment of hollowness that is so complete that I believe I know how it feels to be dead. Not dead with Zoe. Dead alone. Which Isaac Newton warned me about. For every action, an equal and opposite reaction. Passion countered by the void. *(Pause.)* I felt protected from these thoughts in that hotel room. Which is why I kept going to her. Once—maybe twice—a week.

KATHLEEN: He was still coming regularly when the cactus bloomed.

KYLE: I couldn't possibly have gotten through the winter otherwise.

KATHLEEN: Now and then I tried to touch him. I mean tenderly—instead of just lying naked beneath him, I'd try to touch his face or even just his hand.

KYLE: No. *(Beat.)* Please. No.

KATHLEEN: Your call, John Sky.

KYLE: But she kept trying—just occasionally.

KATHLEEN: I kept trying. I couldn't stop myself.

KYLE: Then in the summer, early in July, the police arrested two men for rape, and when the police searched their van, they found pictures. *(Beat.)* Of Zoe. *(Beat.)* I suppose I should be grateful that these criminals were so stupid. The police called me at work, and I went down there. I should have asked Bennie to go with me, but I didn't. *(Beat.)* She was alive in the pictures. *(Beat.)* She didn't look hurt, but she wasn't smiling.

KATHLEEN: Something the matter? *(Kyle doesn't reply.)* John Sky, you've been coming here a long time. *(Beat.)* I think something's wrong.

KYLE: So what?

KATHLEEN: So nothing. What's wrong?

KYLE: What the fuck difference does it make to you? You are not a friend of mine. *(Beat.)* I didn't mean to insult you.

KATHLEEN: You didn't insult me for God's sake. You're right, we're not friends. We're business associates, so if we were business associates on Wall Street and you were paying me to—say—buy stocks for you, and you came to a business appointment looking more like shit than usual, I'd ask what was wrong.

KYLE: The police arrested the men who murdered my wife.

KATHLEEN: Murdered?

KYLE: My wife was raped and murdered.

KATHLEEN: The cops found the guys who did it?

KYLE: Yes. *(Beat.)* I didn't see them. *(Beat.)* I couldn't look at them. I'm not sure I'll ever be able to bring myself to look at them.

KATHLEEN: I hope the state of Arizona executes them on my behalf if you don't mind my saying so.

KYLE: No. I don't mind you saying so. *(Quiet, but intense.)* I hope they're young and attractive and every murdering creep in prison fucks them first.

KATHLEEN: You sure that's what you want to wish for?

KYLE: Yeah. I'm sure.

(Kyle closes his eyes, breathes hard.)

KATHLEEN: *(After a couple beats, as Kyle continues to breathe deeply.)* I've been meaning to confess something to you. *(He waits, keeps breathing.)* I've been looking at Betelgeuse. I've been practicing like you suggested, so my eyes could become accustomed and I could see its real color. *(He keeps breathing.)* I couldn't at first, like you predicted. And I'm kind of a perfectionist so I was pissed off and wouldn't try again for a week or so and then I did, but it still looked white. *(Beat.)* I kept trying and gradually it started to look peach-colored, you know, compared to stars near it. Except I bought a book, a kind of catalogue of all the stars.

KYLE: *Cycle of Celestial Objects.*

KATHLEEN: Yes. And then once I looked at the star list, I realized how the stars are not near each other at all. *(Kathleen moves to Kyle. She starts to unbutton his shirt.)* So I mean I compared Betelgeuse to stars that appear to be near it. *(His shirt is unbuttoned. She opens it and bends down and kisses his chest. Kyle gasps.)* That's when it looked more like a peach color than white. Then—.

(She strokes his chest.)

KYLE: *(Responding to her touch.)* Oh.

KATHLEEN: Then it began to look orange. So I know— *(She continues to touch his chest, arms, face. He continues to respond.)* —if I keep looking, if I keep trying, just like you told me, I'll see it red and true. *(Kyle opens his eyes. He wraps his arms around her, pulls her against him. Kathleen pulls back a little bit so she can kiss him. Kyle gives himself over to this kiss completely. The kiss is long and intense. It ends naturally. Kyle steps back. He walks over to the bed and sits on it, shaking, overwhelmed by the passion he is feeling.)* Do you want me to turn out the light?

KYLE: No. I can't stay.

(Kyle stands up and tries to give Kathleen some money.)

KATHLEEN: You paid me already.

KYLE: Oh.

KATHLEEN: So stay.

KYLE: *(To Kathleen, not looking at her.)* That felt wonderful.

KATHLEEN: So stay.

KYLE: But I can't do it that way.

KATHLEEN: We'll do it any way you want. *(Beat.)* Hey, turn around. What, you can't look at me all of a sudden?

(Kyle turns to her. A couple beats, then he takes her in his arms and kisses her passionately. She returns his passion. They continue to kiss and touch each other. A couple beats after this starts to happen, Serena enters and Bennie takes Serena in his arms. They kiss each other over and over again. As lights dim on Kyle and Kathleen, Kyle extricates himself from their embrace. He steps into his own light. Bennie and Serena continue to kiss and touch each other, but nearly in black.)

KYLE: I wanted to give over to her. I wanted to give over to her hands and her mouth because everywhere I felt them, I felt awakened, I felt excited. I felt myself move beyond the physical—no, move through the physical—and I felt my heart beat. Then I heard her desire.

KATHLEEN: *(In the dark.)* Do that. Yes. God, please do that.

KYLE: I heard her pleasure.

KATHLEEN: *(In the dark.)* Like that. Just like that.

KYLE: Then I took a breath.

KATHLEEN: *(In the dark.)* Please.

KYLE: Then I thought a moment.

KATHLEEN: Please.

KYLE: Then I left my body completely. *(Pause.)* Then nothing. *(Pause.)* I couldn't feel her anymore. I left her, and went to Bennie's. I did what I always did at Bennie's. I knocked—rather, I tapped—on the door and walked in.

(Lights up full on Bennie and Serena. Serena's blouse should be off or open. She and Bennie are sexually engaged in some way—he is kissing her breast perhaps. Kyle stands still and looks at them. He steps further into the room, not taking his eyes off them. After a few seconds, Serena opens her eyes and see him.)

SERENA: Oh my God. *(Bennie holds her close.)*

BENNIE: Jesus Christ, Kyle.

KYLE: Jesus Christ what? Jesus Christ I caught you?

BENNIE: Caught me? No, you didn't catch me, I'm not a kindergarten kid.

(Pause. Kyle moves around the room, agitated.)

SERENA: Hello, Kyle.

KYLE: I wish you'd get dressed.

SERENA: That's a good idea.

(Kyle looks away as Serena puts on or buttons her blouse. She smoothes her hair.)

SERENA: I'm dressed.

KYLE: You're Zoe's sister.

SERENA: And here I thought you'd forgotten.

(Kyle turns to her.)

KYLE: No. *(Pause.)* What is this?

SERENA: What does it look like?

KYLE: It looks like my best friend is fucking my dead wife's sister and hiding it from me.

SERENA: That's what it is.

KYLE: How long have you two been—um—

SERENA: Together?

KYLE: Yes.

SERENA: Since New Year's Eve.

KYLE: *(To Bennie.)* You've been fucking Zoe's sister since New Year's Eve?

BENNIE: Kyle, watch your mouth.

SERENA: No. *(To Kyle.)* That's right. We've been fucking since December 31. We drank champagne, we listened to John Klemmer. We made love on your sofa. Then we—

KYLE: I get the picture.

SERENA: *(Continuing.)* —took a couple of breaths, and then we made love on your living room floor.

(Kyle bangs his fist against a piece of furniture—maybe something falls off it and breaks.)

KYLE: Enough.

BENNIE: *(Gesturing to Serena to shush.)* Sit down, Kyle.

KYLE: No.

BENNIE: Sit down. I'll get you a beer or something.

KYLE: I don't want to sit down. I don't want a beer. I want an explanation.

BENNIE: You want an explanation?

KYLE: I gave you an explanation.

BENNIE: You're comparing my feeling for Serena with your going to a whore?

SERENA: What?

KYLE: *(Overlap.)* No, I couldn't be doing that because I don't know anything about your feeling for Serena.

SERENA: You went to a prostitute?

KYLE: Not went. Still.

SERENA: How often?

KYLE: Often.

SERENA: Is that in honor of Zoe's memory, Kyle?

BENNIE: Shh. Serena.

KYLE: *(Overlap.)* Yes. It is.

SERENA: How respectful.

KYLE: *(Now he's really furious.)* Are you saying I don't respect Zoe? How can you say—how can you think—I would do anything disrespectful of Zoe?

SERENA: Tell me, Kyle. How is going to a whore respecting Zoe?

BENNIE: Come on, Serena.

(During the next speech, Kyle closes his eyes and starts to breathe.)

SERENA: That one's too hard? Then tell me something else. How is banishing her family from your life respecting her, Kyle? You think she's up in heaven smiling down at you while you ignore her mother and her father, while you refuse to see Trevor and me, while you pretend none of us has any pain or ever loved you, and while you instead take your grief to a prostitute and pay her to alleviate it?

BENNIE: Sweetheart—

SERENA: Alleviate it for—how long does it take, Kyle? Ten minutes? Five? Yes, I'm certain Zoe's spirit is out there thrilled, she's not just smiling down on you, I'm sure she's not just smiling —

BENNIE: Stop, Serena.

SERENA: No, I'm certain she's grinning broadly, grinning from ear to ear.

BENNIE: Shut up.

SERENA: Yes, she's delighted—don't maintain contact with anyone who loved me, dearest. No. Find a woman for hire and pay her twenty-five bucks to let you stick it in.

BENNIE: God.

(Silence. Serena moves to Kyle and speaks quietly, but intensely.)

SERENA: I don't know where the hell you are, but open your eyes and come back here because I am not going to allow you to ignore me anymore.

(Kyle opens his eyes. He and Serena stand very close to one another, looking at each other directly, intensely. A couple beats.)

KYLE: Zoe was smiling when we found her.

(Serena turns to Bennie, surprised.)

BENNIE: She was.

(Serena looks back to Kyle.)

KYLE: That's first. You should know that. *(Pause.)* Second. It costs more than twenty-five dollars.

(Serena tries to stop herself, but she laughs.)

BENNIE: *(Also laughing.)* No cheap whore for Kyle.

KYLE: She's worth it. She's a nice woman. *(Pause, then to Bennie.)* You didn't want me to know.

BENNIE: You didn't want to know.

KYLE: You called Serena sweetheart.

BENNIE: Yeah.

(Long pause.)

KYLE: The police caught them. The men who killed Zoe.

BENNIE: What? When?

SERENA: Definitely?

KYLE: Yes.

(Serena moves to Kyle and puts her arms around him. They hold each other hard. A telephone ringing can be heard faintly.)

KYLE: Yes. Definitely.

(As Kyle moves out of this scene, the telephone rings loudly and repeatedly. It is several days later.)

KYLE: *(Into a telephone.)* Hello.

(Lights up on Kathleen.)

KYLE: She knew my real name all along. She looked through my wallet early on. For a second, I was disoriented hearing her voice on the telephone. Even though she said—

KATHLEEN: John Sky, I'm hurt.

KYLE: One of the other customers had cut her. *(To Kathleen.)* God, call an ambulance.

KATHLEEN: I can't call an ambulance. If I call an ambulance, I can't work out of this hotel anymore.

KYLE: I'm coming. All right? Jesus Christ, I'm coming. *(Beat.)* It was near dawn.

KATHLEEN: Who the hell is this?

BENNIE: I'm a doctor.

KATHLEEN: *(Frightened.)* I'm cut everywhere.

BENNIE: Nowhere vital. Whoever did this wasn't very good at it. Let's get her to the hospital.

(Kyle picks up Kathleen and carries her.)

KYLE: I carried her out to my car. She kept saying, over and over again—

KATHLEEN: I can walk.

KYLE: *(Overlap.)* —that she could walk. *(To Kathleen.)* You're not walking.

KATHLEEN: And I'm not dying, right?

KYLE: You're not dying.

KATHLEEN: Your friend said I'm not dying.

KYLE: You are not dying. *(Kyle puts her down in a hospital bed.)* By the time I got her to the hospital the sun was up. I left her in Bennie's hands because I had to—. I went to the jail. *(Beat.)* I returned to Kathleen the next day and saw her in the daylight for the first time.

(Lights change. It's the next day.)

KYLE: Hello.

KATHLEEN: Hello. *(Points to TV.)* I've been watching public television. Guess why?

KYLE: Why?

KATHLEEN: Because they're showing a program about your profession. A series of programs. I wrote down the other days and times. You've hooked me, John Sky.

KYLE: Oh, yeah?

KATHLEEN: Okay, I guess that was an odd way to put that. I've been very entertained listening to several scientists explain why they believe there's life elsewhere in the universe. They're not a bunch of kooks—well, who's to say who's a kook? They're well-respected astronomers from what I could tell, and they believe this with all their hearts.

KYLE: So do I.

KATHLEEN: Do you really?

KYLE: I do.

KATHLEEN: Would you put that in the miracle category?

KYLE: What miracle category?

KATHLEEN: Hey. I depend on your refreshing lack of cynicism.

KYLE: I think—. You shouldn't.

KATHLEEN: I stand warned. *(Beat.)* Your friend stopped by to see me. Dr. Locasto.

KYLE: Bennie.

KATHLEEN: He says I'll only have to be here another day or so. How much do you think that psycho john is going to wind up costing me?

KYLE: I think you should call the police.

KATHLEEN: Call the police? I can't call the police.

KYLE: You need protection. *(Beat.)* Your job is dangerous.

KATHLEEN: News flash. Lots of men come to women for hire and throw their feelings around the room.

KYLE: No. I mean—. Could you tell? When he first got there?

KATHLEEN: No, if I could tell, I wouldn't—(have let him in.)

KYLE: Because there is no way to tell. Because, see, you think there are no feelings. You think you're dead inside.

KATHLEEN: Please don't compare yourself to this guy.

KYLE: Please call the police. *(Beat.)* They confessed.

KATHLEEN: The men who killed your wife?

KYLE: Zoe. I went to the jail this morning, and I made myself look at them. I looked hard. I looked for an eternity. I looked and looked and looked and looked and looked.

KATHLEEN: *(Pause.)* If I see him again, I'll call the police.

KYLE: Promise me that.

KATHLEEN: I promise. *(Beat.)* So what kind of hospital bill do you think I'm looking at?

KYLE: I'll take care of it.

KATHLEEN: No you will not.

KYLE: I'll take it out in trade.

(Pause.)

KATHLEEN: I don't think you will, John Sky. *(Pause.)* I don't want you to pay my hospital bill. Do you think I'd do this work if I wasn't making a good living? *(Slight awkward pause.)* Listen. *(Beat.)* Kyle. *(Beat, then she takes his hand.)* Everything's dangerous.

KYLE: I'm going on a vacation in November. Which terrifies me. The thought of not working sixteen hours a day is terrifying. But I'm going. I'm going to Hawaii, with Bennie and—. With Bennie and his—lover.

KATHLEEN: You going to bask in the sun?

KYLE: That would be a first. *(Beat.)* I should go.

KATHLEEN: You have another appointment?

KYLE: I'm going to the prison to visit the men who killed my wife.

KATHLEEN: You saw them already. Isn't that what you wanted—to be able to look at them?

KYLE: I want them to look back.

KATHLEEN: *(Pause.)* I'm not quitting until I see that star red.

KYLE: It's very beautiful when you see its true color.

KATHLEEN: I'm counting on it. I have a feeling you wouldn't lie to me.

KYLE: No.

KATHLEEN: *(Beat.)* I'm tired.

KYLE: I'm grateful for your being so—

KATHLEEN: Don't tell me. Trusting and patient.

KYLE: *(A smile.)* I was going to say forbearing.

KATHLEEN: You were going to say forbearing.

KYLE: I owe you—(so much. I don't know where to start.)

KATHLEEN: Stop. *(Beat.)* I need to sleep, okay?

KYLE: Yes, you should get some sleep. I'll—

KATHLEEN: Send me a postcard.

KYLE: Having a terrible time. The sun's always in my eyes.

(Kyle exits, raising his hand "goodbye" as he goes. Lights out on Kathleen.)

KYLE: I talked to each one of them separately. Each one could have said no, but each one agreed to speak to me. Which I didn't understand at first, but now I think it was Zoe. Zoe was smiling. Zoe was telling me I am dying, Kyle. It's what my life is now. I'm dying. *(Kyle stops, and closes his eyes and breathes. He opens his eyes.)* The first one said no, he didn't notice she was smiling. He was young, still a teenager. *(Beat.)* She said if one of them would stay there with her until she died, she would like that. *(Beat, he can hardly say this.)* She would be grateful. *(Beat.)* Zoe hated to be alone. This kid was spooked by that. He told me he didn't know why, but he grabbed her purse and ran with it. He had killed before, but he didn't want to be there when Zoe died. So the other one stayed with her. He was closer to her age—mid-twenties. *(Kyle closes his eyes and breathes. His measured breath becomes more shallow, becomes panting. He opens his eyes.)* When he came into the visiting room, he sat down, rigid, and fixed his gaze on me. He didn't speak. *(He takes a deep breath, like he did then.)* I asked him if he noticed she was smiling and he said yes. *(Pause, like he's waiting for more, like he did then.)* I asked him was she scared and he said yes. *(Beat.)* But as she faded, she seemed less and less so. He leaned toward me, and said her smiling made him furious and he asked her what the hell was so funny. She said, "Funny?" *(Beat.)* He sat back again, straight in his chair. And he stared. He looked—right—through—me. *(Pause.)* I asked if she spoke my name. He said no. He said he didn't want to piss me off but she was "one weird chick." Because as she lay dying, she mumbled something about the stars. *(Kyle closes his eyes and breathes. He opens them abruptly.)* GODDAMMIT, KEEP YOUR EYES OPEN. KEEP THEM OPEN. *(Beat.)* She died. *(He breathes, but his eyes are open. He becomes frenetic.)* I spoke to her murderer. I said to her murderer, whether or not there is life in some other galaxy, Zoe's huge heart notwithstanding, regardless of Triton's beauty, no goddamn matter how much she loved me or what shape Sagittarius is, she fucking died. He said you're crazy too, buddy. I banged the telephone on the Plexiglas separating me from him. I said did you touch her? *(He closes his eyes, opens them.)* Keep them open, Kyle. *(Beat.)* Did you touch her while she was dying? And there it was. He flinched. He looked at me. DID YOU FUCKING TOUCH HER? *(Beat.)* She—uh—she reached her hand out to me, he said. She reached for me. *(Beat.)* Yeah. I let her touch me. *(Kyle stops, cries, breathes, waits.)* I said—. I said—. We met in my physics class. *(Pause, then lights change. It is just before dusk, in Hawaii. Serena—wearing Zoe's polka dot hat—and Bennie walk together. Kyle follows more slowly, behind them.)*

SERENA: Benjamin, why do I continue to let you talk me into accompanying you to these movies?

BENNIE: They're exciting. Right, Kyle?

SERENA: Every character in it had a severe case of testosterone poisoning.

BENNIE: What about that Penelope Ann Miller?

SERENA: I said character. Penelope Ann Miller played a stick figure with breasts.

KYLE: Small ones.

BENNIE: Come on, she's beautiful.

KYLE: Not my type.

SERENA: Good for you, Kyle.

BENNIE: *(Joking.)* Maybe you're marrying the wrong guy. *(Several beats.)* Sorry, Kyle. *(Beat.)* We're getting married.

KYLE: I figured that out.

BENNIE: We were going to tell you.

KYLE: Relax.

SERENA: He proposed the night we arrived. You know what he did?

BENNIE: Serena.

KYLE: It's okay.

BENNIE: No, it's probably not something you want to hear.

KYLE: *(Overlap, to Serena.)* What?

SERENA: He read a poem. Then he asked me to marry him.

KYLE: Who wrote the poem?

BENNIE: T.S. Eliot.

KYLE: Good. Because Keats is mine.

BENNIE: Oh, Keats is yours.

KYLE: Correct.

BENNIE: You own Keats.

KYLE: Yes, because you claimed he didn't make an impression. Remember that?
(An awkward pause.)

KYLE: *(A big breath.)* Congratulations.

SERENA: Thank you, Kyle.
(Serena kisses Bennie. Kyle moves away from them.)

SERENA: We should get ready for dinner.
(Serena exits, followed more slowly by Bennie. Kyle looks at the sun going down. As the sun's light separates, he stands completely still and watches. As Bennie exits, we and Kyle see a flash of green.)

KYLE: OH MY GOD. *(Kyle jumps up and down, like a cheerleader.)* OH GOD, OH GOD, OH GOD, OH GOD, OH GOD.

(Bennie re-enters at the end of Kyle's line. Kyle falls to his knees, overwhelmed by his feelings. Pause, as they both look up into the sky.)

KYLE: Did you see it?

BENNIE: Green flash?

KYLE: Green flash.

BENNIE: No. I missed it.

KYLE: *(Near tears, he looks at Bennie.)* The possibility exists that I will live to see a supernova. Do you know that?

BENNIE: I believe you, Kyle.

KYLE: Go ahead to dinner, Bennie. I'll be right behind you. *(Bennie exits. Kyle looks after him for a moment, then back up into the darkening sky.)* According to scientific projections, it should be thirty more years before that incredible light, that most brilliant light imaginable, that gorgeous light, blankets the sky, but the truth is, it could happen next year. It could happen next week. It could happen tomorrow. It could happen tonight after dinner.

(Kyle keeps looking up at the heavens. The lights come up brilliantly and then go out.)

END OF PLAY

Standard Time

a short drama

by Naomi Wallace

BIOGRAPHY

Naomi Wallace's play *The Trestle at Pope Lick Creek* premiered at the 1998 Humana Festival, and her Obie Award-winning play *One Flea Spare* had its American premiere in the 1996 Humana Festival. A published poet in both England and the United States, she has received grants from The Kentucky Foundation for Women, The Kentucky Arts Council, and a 1997 NEA grant for poetry. Her film *Lawn Dogs*, produced by Duncan Kenworthy, opened successfully in Great Britain, moved to the U.S. and has won numerous film awards. At present, Ms. Wallace is under commission by the Royal Shakespeare Company, the Public Theater, Toledo Films and Dog Star Productions. She was a 1999 recipient of the prestigious MacArthur Fellowship, popularly known as the "genius award."

HUMANA FESTIVAL PRODUCTION

Standard Time premiered at the Humana Festival of New American Plays in April 2000. It was directed by Michael Bigelow Dixon with the following cast:

Young man . . . . Jason Cornwell

and the following production staff:

Scenic Designer . . . . Paul Owen
Costume Designer . . . . Kevin R. McLeod
Lighting Designer. . . . . Paul Werner
Sound Designer. . . . . Martin R. Desjardins
Properties Designer. . . . . Ben Hohman
Stage Manager . . . . Charles M. Turner III
Assistant Stage Manager . . . . Juliet Penna
Dramaturgs. . . . . Brandi Harrison, Ginna Hoben
Casting . . . . Laura Richin Casting

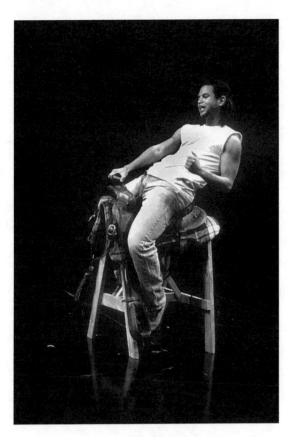

Jason Cornwell
in *Standard Time*

24th Annual Humana Festival of New American Plays
Actors Theatre of Louisville, 2000
photo by Richard Trigg

Standard Time

A working-class man, perhaps nineteen, on a bare stage, in a cell or room of confinement. The only object is a saddle on the stage floor, covered with a cloth so that its shape is not discernible. He is flipping a coin, slowly, casually.

I wanted her car because I needed to steal because I wanted *(Flips the coin, catches it.)* money because money is—yeah, they say—power and power is a garden, is a tree that never stops, is a field you can't get to the end of and I never had anything beautiful in my life. *(Flips the coin, catches it.)* But her. Flip a nickel. Catch it on your tongue. *(He does so.)* It's got a tang; that was her mouth.

(He spits the coin out into his hand, studies it a moment.)

And Tally's mouth made me think on money. Always there but not there. You could touch it but you just couldn't keep it. Every time I opened my hand it was gone. The money. The money I didn't have and her mouth, well, it was hers and it went where she went.

(Lets the coin drop.)

I couldn't keep track of it.

We were seventeen. Tally's car was the only thing that could stop and go in our town, and when Tally was mine it was our car together. It was a wreck but we rode it. Didn't have a back seat so we didn't need one. We threw down a sheet of plastic and piled it with dirt to keep the rear low so we could floor it. And the wind from the open windows took ahold of our throats and made us gag with the thrust of it. In through our mouths and out through our ass, at 85 miles per hour, blasting us clean.

(Uncovers the saddle, sits astride it.)

And one night Tally stole a saddle from a saddlery barn on the Pop-side of town and we strapped it to the roof of her car and while she drove, I rode, with the wind brushing my teeth into the kind of smile I couldn't make on my own. I was the Marlboro Man and I swept over that highway like I was sweeping plains while the other cars scattered like cattle in front of my wheels.

We were just kids. Kids. You know what that means? But we still couldn't stop being junk. That's what they called us in our hometown: J-town junk. And we didn't have a future cause we didn't have a dime but when we were driving we were nothing if not cold, hard cash, banking on the next turn to give us a spin and send us into America. Because that's where we wanted to be. Inside America. Where the sky is red and the heart is blue with the boast of it. And where your pockets are full. Yeah, where your pockets are full.

But that's where we couldn't get.

(Gets off the saddle.)

And then one day, it could have been any day just riding around wasn't enough because even the Marlboro man needs some spare change. And my ass was getting sore from the speed of it all and down below me Tally was rolling up the windows 'cause it had started to rain and then one, two, three, the colors just washed out of me and I was an idiot on a wet saddle, tied to the top of a wreck and the grass was starting to grow up through the dirt in the back seat of the car.

And then. Well. And then that's how the story goes if it goes at all. I took a breath or two. Tally must have done the same and then we weren't. Girlfriend and boyfriend. She turned around. Took a step. I missed one and it was over. And we passed the way days pass and it was another season by then, somewhere between August and waking up alone and that was it: she was gone. Her mouth was gone. The money none of us had was gone.

Time passed. That's what they say. Time passed. And I got to thinking that maybe it wasn't time passing but me, and I didn't even know it.

Days and months and pieces of things, they kept on passing. And every time I looked in the mirror it was her mouth I saw on my face, instead of my own. But when I touched it, touched myself, she was gone.

And so one night, it could of been any night, I needed her car. These are the facts: I went to her house. I hadn't been there in months. I said: Give me your car. She wouldn't let me have it at first. Then. Well, then she did.

The order. Of how it happened. Well, that was out. That's been out ever since, but when I said give me the car she just said: *You used to say my name like whiskey, like a light switch. Like a key.*

I said: I need the car. Tally said: *You would cover me in leaves up to my neck; you would never leave me.*

I said: This isn't about you and me. This is about ignition. This is about contact and speed and I need the car to get there by midnight. It's a lot of miles to drive but it's just up the road and the map's between my eyes and I know I can get there.

Tally kissed me then. Her mouth was cold like a piece of the river. And for a second I remembered: the books we'd opened at school, what we'd wanted for our lives, how a door swings open before it swings shut. And then she said. Tally said: We're already dead, when I showed her the gun. And she was right.

I never got to the Five Star—You're going the wrong way!—Never got to the steal. She wouldn't let me. She wouldn't let me drive—You're going the wrong way!—She drove the car out into a field. *(Quietly.)* You're going the wrong way.

We were parked now just a few feet from the river. It had started to snow. It was August and there's no such thing as snow in August in our town and there never has been. But it started to snow. Tally got out of the car. I stayed inside. I watched through the windshield. She threw the keys into the river. And they were gone. I remember. I remember thinking. How big that car was when I sat inside it without her. How it would never move again. And all I needed was a little piece of cut metal, a thing that small was all I needed to turn the whole thing over, to start it up again.

These are the facts: I got out of the car. Tally was standing there looking at the river like it was going to look back. She was covered in snow. I came up behind her. The snow all around us. The snow passing all around us like time and we stood still. I wiped the snow from my mouth but I couldn't feel my mouth. I touched my face but I couldn't feel my face. And I kept touching my face, trying to get the feel back into it. Tally, she said: *Yes.* Tally, with her back to me, she couldn't even see me behind her. She said: *Yes.* I wasn't touching her. I was touching myself. But she said: *Don't stop touching me.*

And then I didn't know anymore. I just had no idea. I stood there. Stood there in that spot like I'd been standing there all my life. In front of me the snow covered her hair. She raised her hand to brush the snow off her hair and I felt her hand on the back of my head. She wasn't near enough to touch me but I felt her hand on the back of my head. And I just didn't know anymore. I said I love you and I pulled the trigger.

I didn't want her dead. I didn't want. Her dead. How many times do I have to say it? I wanted to get there. I wanted to get there. I wanted to get there and lay down and rest with a big, hot sun inside my chest and never be wanting again. *(Beat.)* I didn't want her dead. I just. Wanted the car.

(He slowly, gently turns the saddle onto its back so that it lies upside down. He moves away from it and turns away. Then he turns back to look at the saddle, lying on its back on the empty stage.)

Those are the facts. Those are the facts of love.

END OF PLAY

Back Story
Based on characters created by
Joan Ackermann

A dramatic anthology by

Joan Ackermann, Courtney Baron, Neena Beber,

Constance Congdon, Jon Klein, Shirley Lauro,

Craig Lucas, Eduardo Machado, Donald Margulies,

Jane Martin, Susan Miller, John Olive, Tanya Palmer,

David Rambo, Edwin Sanchez, Adele Edling Shank,

Mayo Simon and Val Smith

The Making of *Back Story*

"What's the character's back story?" This question is a familiar one for actors working to build a psychologically complex role out of the clues provided in a dramatic text. By imagining the character's past, or what has happened outside of the immediate action represented in the play, the actor strives to find ways of informing, deepening, and rendering immediate the moments revealed onstage.

But consider what could happen to the way we think about creating characters if this process were reversed: what if a richly detailed character history—or the intertwined histories of two characters, say a brother and sister in their early twenties—became the imaginative impetus for not just one, but a multitude of playwrights and their texts? And what if these varied perspectives could come together to make one theatrical event?

These questions are at the heart of the challenge embraced by *Back Story*, an experiment based on a tale penned by Joan Ackermann. Ackermann's wonderfully textured and suggestive story details the adventures and misadventures of Ainsley and Ethan Belcher of Pittsfield, Massachusetts, siblings whose close relationship evolves throughout their lifetimes and reaches a pivotal moment in the year 2000. Using this narrative as a springboard, Ackermann and seventeen other talented dramatists wrote three scenes and sixteen monologues for Ainsley and Ethan. For the Humana Festival premiere of *Back Story*, the siblings were portrayed by eleven men and eleven women in Actors Theatre's 1999-2000 Apprentice Acting Company (though they could be played by as few as two actors). The spirit of collaboration inherent in the project extended to the direction of the festival production as well: *Back Story* was staged by five directors, working together to discover the larger portrait created by so many authorial (and actors') voices and styles.

This collaborative process began with the creation of the text, which required some logistical planning in order to build upon the rich foundation provided by Joan Ackermann's story. In addition to this narrative, Ackermann had been commissioned to write the first monologue and last scene of the play, which provided "bookends" for the other pieces. The rest of the playwrights, who had agreed to write either a two-minute monologue or a six-minute scene, received copies of the story, and were invited to contact us with several "moments" in the narrative that they would be interested in exploring. Over the course of several weeks, we spoke with each writer about these choices and their ideas, and coordinated their selections so that we could "cover" as much of the back story as possible, encouraging variety while also ensuring some sense of progression through time and events for both Ethan and Ainsley.

In general, we hypothesized that successful pieces would expand upon a "moment" in the story in some depth, rather than simply relating information from the story. There were a few basic guidelines as well: 1) The details of a piece could not contradict details in the story, 2) Moments from the past had to be explored actively in the present, since actors in their twenties could not plausibly play children or young teenagers, and 3) There could not be too many pieces using the same modes of address (writing a letter, for example). The playwrights generously shared their own questions and ideas about the process with us, which helped us to address many complications early on. Once everyone had "dibs" on a chunk of the story, they set out to compose their pieces.

When the first drafts began to pour into the literary office, we were delighted to discover that there was great variety in the work—the pieces ranged from outrageously funny to lyrical to philosophical in tone, and were as different as the actors who would eventually perform them. But already, a thematic coherence began to emerge. Certain images or ideas became motifs in several pieces, and the authors had developed some of the major currents in Ethan and Ainsley's relationship: the loss of a father who goes on a fishing trip to Alaska and never returns, Ainsley's self-sacrifice in her devotion to Ethan and her relationship with music, Ethan's entrepreneurial spirit and "uncontrolled velocity." Of course, there were some rewrites and cuts to coordinate and small contradictions to iron out, and many of the pieces continued to be refined throughout the rehearsal process. But somehow, in pursuing their own passions in depth, the playwrights had been able to hop onto the same wavelength while remaining wildly diverse.

The next step was to ponder how we could thread together these individual parts to shape the whole event. So we began an ongoing discussion about the order of the scenes and monologues: What kind of trajectory were the characters following together? What were Ethan's and Ainsley's individual "arcs" through the event? In what ways would chronology be important? How would some pieces set up information that would inform others? How could we vary the energy and tone of the work while building a set of impressions that would create a story?

Rehearsals began at odd hours and in odd corners of the building, with a weekly read-through (and later, run-throughs) so that everyone could chart

Back Story's progress. We heard several running orders for the pieces, settling on the performance order you see in this volume after much discussion and debate. The directors worked on transitions in order to make the show as seamless as possible, and fruitful questions continued to sharpen our collective sense of the characters, both as individual constructs and in relationship with each other. Many minds continued to strive to create a unified experience.

When audiences came to see the five performances scheduled during the Humana Festival, they were faced with a choice which would impact their experience: to read Ackermann's story beforehand, or to see the play without the benefit of having already digested the narrative upon which its many parts are based. We don't know which is the preferable choice, but we think that they deliver different kinds of pleasures. On the one hand, reading the story allows one to see how it has been adapted and to appreciate the authors' varying approaches; on the other, seeing the performance without this preparation allows an encounter with the characters which (we think) holds together on its own terms. In other words, if the back story is a colorful, high-resolution map of these characters' lives, then the play *Back Story* travels through an exploration of "stops," impressions, and turning-points in their journey.

—*Dramaturgs Amy Wegener and Michael Bigelow Dixon*

BIOGRAPHIES

Joan Ackermann is Co-Artistic Director of Mixed Company in Great Barrington, Massachusetts, a year-round theatre now in its eighteenth year. Her plays include *Zara Spook and Other Lures* (1990 Humana Festival of New American Plays), *Stanton's Garage* (1993 Humana Festival), *The Batting Cage* (1996 Humana Festival), *Don't Ride the Clutch, Yonder Peasant, Bed and Breakfast, The Light of His Eye, Rescuing Greenland, Off the Map, My New York Hit, Marcus is Walking* and her most recent play, *Isabella*, a musical for which she composed the music. Before writing plays, she was a journalist for ten years and wrote for *Sports Illustrated, Time, The Atlantic, Esquire, GQ, Audubon, New York* and other magazines.

Courtney Baron's ten-minute play *The Blue Room* premiered at the 1999 Humana Festival. Other productions include *Dear Anton* (Chekhov Now Festival), *You Are Not Forgotten* (workshop at the Royal Court Theatre, London), *Dream of Heaven and Hell* (Walkerspace, New York), *The Good Night* (Theatre for the New City, New York), *Love as a Science* (Seattle Fringe Festival), *Clip* (Frontera Fest) and *The White Girl and the Sheep* (Theatre Three, Dallas). In 1998, Ms. Baron received her M.F.A. from the Columbia University Playwriting Program.

Neena Beber was most recently at Actors Theatre of Louisville with her ten-minute play *Misreadings* (included in Best American Short Plays, 1996-97). *A Common Vision* and *The Brief but Exemplary Life of the Living Goddess* both premiered at the Magic Theatre; *Tomorrowland* at New Georges and subsequently Theatre J in Washington, D.C.; *Failure to Thrive* at Padua Hills Playwrights Festival. One-acts *Adaptive Ruse, Departures* and *Sensation(s)* at HB Playwrights Foundation; *Acts of Desire*, collected shorts, Watermark Theatre. Her new plays *Thirst* and *Hard Feelings* were developed at Ojai Playwrights Conference, Williamstown Theatre Festival, Otterbein and the Public Theater's New Work Now. Additional credits include an Amblin Commission from Playwrights Horizons, A.S.K. Exchange to The Royal Court, and a Distinguished Alumni Award from New York University's Tisch School of the Arts. Ms. Beber holds a B.A. from Harvard. *Bad Dates*, a film, is based on her one-act play, *Food*. Ms. Beber is a member of New Dramatists.

Constance Congdon's works include *Tales of the Lost Formicans*, which premiered at the Humana Festival and has had more than a hundred productions, *Lips, So Far, Losing Father's Body, Dark Bridge Mountain, The Automata Pietà, Casanova*, which premiered at the New York Shakespeare Festival, and *Dog Opera*, which was commissioned by the New York Shakespeare Festival. Ms. Congdon also wrote the libretto for a new opera by Peter Gordon, *The Strange*

Life of Ivan Osokin, as well as libretti for two operas by Ron Perera, *S., The Yellow Wallpaper*. She has written seven plays for the Children's Theatre of Minneapolis. A collection of Ms. Congdon's plays is published by the Theatre Communications Group, Inc. Other plays include *Native American, No Mercy, The Gilded Age*, and *One Day Earlier* (a companion piece for *No Mercy*). Ms. Congdon's plays have been produced in Moscow, Helsinki, Hong Kong, Edinburgh and London, as well as in over fifty regional and university theaters in the U.S.

Jon Klein is the author of twenty produced plays, which have been produced off-Broadway and at such major regional theatres as South Coast Repertory, Arena Stage, Alley Theatre, Alliance Theatre, Center Stage and A Contemporary Theatre. Actors Theatre of Louisville productions include *Betty the Yeti* and *T Bone N Weasel* (HBO New Plays USA Award; film version on TNT). Other plays: *Dimly Perceived Threats to the System, Octopus, Peoria, Four Our Fathers, Southern Cross* and *Losing It* (Dramatists Guild/CBS New Play Award). Stage adaptations: Stendhal's *The Red and the Black*, two *Hardy Boys* adventures and *Bunnicula*. Upcoming productions: *The Einstein Project* (co-author Paul D'Andrea) at the Berkshire Theatre Festival and *Punch in America* (musical with Chris Jeffries), co-produced by Woolly Mammoth, Illusion Theatre and The Empty Space.

Shirley Lauro most recently premiered *A Piece of My Heart* at Actors Theatre of Louisville, which won The Kitteredge Award and Barbara Deming Prize, and was a finalist for the Susan Smith Blackburn Prize. More than one hundred subsequent productions of *A Piece of My Heart* followed, including Manhattan Theatre Club, Stamford Theatre Works, International City Theatre, Bailiwick Repertory, a South African premiere which Ms. Lauro attended sponsored by the U.S.I.A. & Natal Performing Arts Council. Other Actors Theatre premieres: *The Coal Diamond* (Heideman Award), *Nothing Immediate* and *Sunday Go To Meetin'*. Broadway: Tony-nominated *Open Admissions*, recipient of Dramatists Guild's Hull Warriner Award, *The New York Times* "10 Best Plays of the Year" list. *Open Admissions* was adapted by Ms. Lauro for a CBS Special starring Jane Alexander. Off-Broadway: *The Contest*. Latest Play: *The Last Trial of Clarence Darrow*, EST Octoberfest '99. Major fellowships: The Guggenheim, NEA, N.Y. Foundation for the Arts.

Craig Lucas is the author of plays (*Stranger, The Dying Gaul, God's Heart, Prelude to a Kiss, Blue Window, Reckless, Missing Persons*), movies (*Longtime Companion, Prelude to a Kiss, Reckless, Blue Window*), opera libretti (*Orpheus In Love*), musical books (*Three Postcards, Marry Me A Little*), and essays. He has received the Outer Critics Circle, Burns Mantle Best Muscial, Drama-

Logue, Obie, George and Elisabeth Marton, L.A. Drama Critics, GLAAD Media, Sundance Audience and Villager Awards, as well as a Tony nomination and three Drama Desk nominations. He has been a Pulitzer finalist and is the recipient of Guggenheim, Rockefeller and NEA/TCG fellowships along with play commissions from South Coast Repertory, Hartford Stage and Actors Theatre of Louisville.

Eduardo Machado is the author of over twenty-five plays and several translations, including *Cuba and the Night, Stevie Wants to Play the Blues, A Burning Beach, Why to Refuse* and *Broken Eggs.* His plays have been produced in regional theaters all over the country, New York City and London. Some of these theaters include The Williamstown Theatre Festival, The Long Wharf Theater, The Mark Taper Forum, Actors Theatre of Louisville, The Ensemble Studio Theater, The American Place Theater, El Repertorio Español, The Los Angeles Theater Center, and The New Mexico Repertory. Mr. Machado has recently completed writing and directing his first feature-length film, *Exiles in New York,* which premiered at The Santa Barbara Film Festival, AFI Film Festival and Festival International Del Nuevo Cine Latino Americano. Other film credits include two movies for HBO, *China Rio's* and *Her Name Was Lupe.*

Donald Margulies is a familiar name at Actors Theatre of Louisville, where two of his plays, *Dinner with Friends* and *July 7, 1994,* debuted at previous Humana Festivals. His plays include *Collected Stories* (Los Angeles Drama Critics' Circle Award, Pulitzer Prize finalist), *The Model Apartment* (Obie Award, Drama-Logue Award), *Sight Unseen* (Obie Award, Dramatists Guild/Hull-Warriner Award, Pulitzer Prize finalist, a Burns Mantle "Best Play"), *The Loman Family Picnic* (a Burns Mantle "Best Play"), *Found a Peanut, Pitching to the Star* and *What's Wrong With This Picture?* His adaptation of Sholem Asch's Yiddish classic, *God of Vengeance,* recently premiered at A Contemporary Theatre in Seattle. He was awarded the 2000 Pulitzer Prize for Drama for *Dinner with Friends.* He is a member of the council of The Dramatists Guild of America. Mr. Margulies lives with his wife and son in New Haven, Connecticut, where he teaches playwriting at Yale University.

Jane Martin returned to Actors Theatre with her latest play, *Anton in Show Business,* following her premiere of *Mr. Bundy* in the 22nd Humana Festival. Ms. Martin, a Kentuckian, first came to national attention for *Talking With,* a collection of monologues premiering in the 1982 Humana Festival. Since its New York premiere at the Manhattan Theatre Club in 1982, *Talking With* has been performed around the world, winning the Best Foreign Play of the Year award in Germany from *Theater Heute* magazine. Ms. Martin's *Keely and Du,* which premiered in the 1993 Humana Festival, was nominated for the

Pulitzer Prize and won the American Theatre Critics Association Award for Best New Play in 1994. Her play *Jack and Jill* premiered in the 1996 Humana Festival and won the American Theatre Critics Association Award in 1997. Her other work includes: *Middle-Aged White Guys* (1995 Humana Festival), *Cementville* (1991 Humana Festival) and *Vital Signs* (1990 Humana Festival). Ms. Martin's work has been translated into Spanish, French, German, Dutch, Russian and several other languages.

Susan Miller won her second Obie and The Susan Smith Blackburn Prize for her one-woman play, *My Left Breast*, which premiered in the Humana Festival. She has since performed it in theatres around the country. *Nasty Rumors and Final Remarks, Cross Country, Flux, For Dear Life, Confessions of a Female Disorder*, and *It's Our Town, Too*, were produced by The Mark Taper Forum, O'Neill National Playwrights Conference, Second Stage, Trinity Repertory, Naked Angels, and The Public Theater. She received the Publishing Triangle's Robert Chessley Lifetime Achievement Award in Playwriting. Ms. Miller, a Yaddo Fellow, has also received NEA and Rockefeller Grants. She just completed a new play, *A Map of Doubt and Rescue*. She has written screenplays for Disney, Warner Bros., Universal, and Fox 2000, among others.

John Olive's Actors Theatre of Louisville productions include *Clara's Play, Killers* and *Evelyn and the Polka King*. Other plays include *Standing on my Knees, Minnesota Moon, The Voice of the Prairie* and *The Aspern Papers*. Mr. Olive's work has been widely produced. His most recent play, *The Summer Moon*, won a 1997 Kennedy Center Award for Drama, premiered in 1998 at A Contemporary Theatre in Seattle, and played in 1999 at South Coast Repertory. A film adaptation of the play, by ShadowCatcher Entertainment, is in development. Mr. Olive has written screenplays and teleplays for Disney, Amblin Entertainment, MGM/UA and Lorimar, among others. Mr. Olive lives in Minneapolis with his wife Mary and their son Michael.

Tanya Palmer is a playwright, dramaturg and educator living and working in Toronto, Canada. Her most recent play, *Nauvoo*, has been workshopped at York University. Previous work includes *Alone*, workshopped at Here Theatre in New York City and The Wilton Project in Los Angeles and produced at The Montreal Fringe Festival in 1997. *Fatherland* was produced at Hangar Theatre as part of The Drama League's New Directors project. A ten-minute play, *Body Talk*, was produced as part of Actors Theatre of Louisville's 1994 Winter Showcase and later published in *American Voice*. Tanya was a literary management intern at Actors Theatre during the 1994-95 season, and recently received an M.F.A. in Playwriting at York University.

David Rambo's play *God's Man in Texas* received its world premiere at the 1999 Humana Festival, followed by productions at the Warehouse Theatre, Hippodrome, Florida Stage, Northlight Theatre, Stages Repertory and the Old Globe. Other plays include *Speaky-Spikey-Spokey*, presented at the Ashland New Plays Festival in Oregon, where he has been playwright-in-residence for the last two years—and a farce, *There's No Place Like House*, which enjoyed a long run in Los Angeles. He is the author of several screenplays and freelance theatre journalism. He is a member of The Dramatists Guild.

Edwin Sanchez's notable productions include *Icarus* produced by Actors Theatre of Louisville as part of the Humana Festival and by San Jose Repertory; *Barefoot Boy With Shoes On*, at Primary Stages in New York as part of their 1999-2000 season; and *Unmerciful Good Fortune* (AT&T On Stage New Play Award, Nominee Best New Play—Jeff Award), co-produced by Northlight Theatre and Victory Gardens Theater of Chicago. Other productions include *Clean* (Kennedy Center Fund for New American Plays winner) produced by Hartford Stage Company where it was nominated by the American Theater Critics Association for its annual New Play Award. Mr. Sanchez is a member of The Dramatists Guild and New Dramatists.

Adele Edling Shank has been at Actors Theatre of Louisville with *Sunset/Sunrise* (co-winner of the Great American Play Contest) and *Sand Castles*, two of her California Plays. Other full-length plays include *Winterplay, Stuck: A Freeway Comedy, The Grass House* and *Tumbleweed* (California Plays); *War Horses, Rocks in Her Pocket, With Allison's Eyes, The Wives of the Magi* (a play for December) and *Sex Slaves*. Recently her play *Dry Smoke* was made into a chamber opera (music by Victor Kioulaphides) and her adaptation of *Stuck: A Freeway Comedy* was produced by Slovak Radio. Currently, she is working on a film adaptation of *With Allison's Eyes*. Ms. Shank has received numerous awards, including Rockefeller and NEA Playwriting grants. She is Head of Playwriting at the University of California, San Diego and is an editor of *Theatre Forum* magazine.

Mayo Simon's plays have been produced in many theaters in the United States and Europe. These productions include *Walking to Waldheim* (Lincoln Center, New York), *L.A. Under Siege* (Mark Taper Forum), *A Rich Full Life* (Los Angeles Theatre Center), *These Men* (Magic Theatre, San Francisco), *Elaine's Daughter* (Actors Theatre of Louisville, Philadelphia Theatre Company), *The Old Lady's Guide to Survival* (Actors Theatre of Louisville, Pittsburgh Public Theater, Lambs Club Theater, New York), and *Split* (Aurora Theatre Company, Berkeley, California). Mr. Simon's plays have also been produced in England, Ireland, Germany, Norway, Sweden, Denmark and Italy. They are published by the Dramatic Publishing Company.

Val Smith is the author of numerous plays which have been published and produced nationally. Her first full-length drama, *The Gamblers*, won the Playhouse on the Square's Mid-South Playwright's Competition, and was produced at American Stage Theatre in New Jersey in 1992. Her second full-length, *Ain't We Got Fun*, was commissioned and produced by Actors Theatre of Louisville in the 1993 Classics in Context Festival—The Roaring Twenties. She is the recipient of awards from the Kentucky Women's Foundation and the Kentucky Arts Council. Her most recent full-length play, *Marguerite Bonet*, is published in *Best Plays by Women of 1998*. Her ten-minute play *Meow* premiered in the 1998 Humana Festival.

HUMANA FESTIVAL PRODUCTION

Back Story was commissioned by Actors Theatre of Louisville and premiered at the Humana Festival of New American Plays in March 2000. It was directed by Pascaline Bellegarde, Aimée Hayes, Dano Madden, Meredith McDonough and Sullivan Canaday White with the following cast:

Ethan . . . . Phil Bolin, Cary Calebs, Patrick
Dall'Occhio, Jeff Jenkins, Tom Johnson,
Cabe McCarty, Tom Moglia, Stephen Sislen,
Mark Watson, Zach Welsheimer, Travis York

Ainsley . . . . Shawna Joy Anderson, Molly M.
Binder, Rachel Burttram, Christy Collier,
Samantha Desz, Melody G. Fenster, Aimeé
Kleisner, Kimberly Megna, Holly W. Sims,
Heather Springsteen, Jessica Wortham

and the following production staff:

Scenic Designer . . . . Paul Owen
Costume Designer . . . . Kevin McLeod
Lighting Designer . . . . Greg Sullivan
Sound Designer . . . . Darron L. West
Properties Designer . . . . Mark Walston
Stage Manager . . . . Amber D. Martin
Dramaturgs . . . . Michael Bigelow Dixon & Amy Wegener
Assistant Dramaturg . . . . Kerry Mulvaney

CHARACTERS

ETHAN BELCHER
AINSLEY BELCHER

Back Story

The story by Joan Ackermann

Part I

When Ethan Belcher was nearly born during a blizzard at three in the morning in the back of his father's van en route to Hillcrest Hospital in Pittsfield, Mass., his sister Ainsley chopped her toe off with a snow shovel on their front porch. She was two and a half years old, barefoot in six inches of soft snow, clad only in a motley colored hand-crocheted jersey with an unfinished right arm. Left in the care of her Great Aunt Lou, who collapsed to sleep on the broken recliner after all the drama with the jumper cables and the van had fishtailed out the driveway, Ainsley had bolted out the front door.

She could hear Lou's fitful snoring as she stood perched on the top of eight steps. The strangled sounds of tortured breathing almost supported her tiny frame as she swayed in the cold night air, blinking at updrafts of snow in the lights from the street lamps, the tears on her face slowly freezing over. Ainsley had screamed, howled with wild blue-faced uncharacteristic force to be taken to the hospital with her parents. "It's the baby," Lou had cooed, following the toddler around, attempting to calm her hysteria as Gloria and Jim hunted desperately for a flashlight. "It's all right, sweetie. The baby is coming." But Lou was only throwing fuel on the flames. Ainsley's awareness that the baby was coming was keener than anyone's in the family, including her mother Gloria, who was now cursing her husband as he ruefully tried to dig the van out of a snowdrift.

If Ainsley had been aware that the brown van which bore the chipped letters "Belcher Electric" had skidded off the road at the bottom of the hill, she might have jumped from the lip of the porch down into the night to rescue her baby brother. As it was, Reuben, their sixty-year-old tenant, discovered Ainsley crouched on the porch with the five-foot shovel when he staggered home from a late night of drinking. He had the presence of mind to find her toe, frozen and preserved in the snow. Reuben was the only one in that household to realize that Ainsley's accident with the snow shovel was a mission derailed. He alone saw her intention had been to clear the way for the baby's arrival.

And so it was that Ainsley Belcher arrived at the hospital after all, in time to be there for her younger brother. As the last stitch was sewn into place on her tiny foot, a barely coherent Reuben holding her hand, she heard Ethan's first cries from down the hall. It was not the last time she would sacrifice some part of her self in his behalf. Nor was it the last time that he would arrive late, that his movement would unleash havoc and drama, and that he would be unaware of his sister's efforts.

They all stayed in the hospital that night, the bad weather preventing travel. Long after Gloria, Jim and Reuben had escaped their disjointed lives in deep slumber, Ainsley remained awake on a cot in the hall, listening for every sound from the baby. As Ethan blindly waved tiny punches in the air, his body involuntarily twitched in her direction, turned by the sound of her small voice, singing to him.

Part II

In the summer of '81, Jim Belcher took off for a two-week fishing trip in Alaska. Ainsley was seven and Ethan was five. Gloria had just been promoted to dining room manager at Captain Toss's seafood restaurant and was in unusually good spirits, frosting her hair and buying short suits at Filene's Basement at the Holyoke Mall. Even at home her gait had a gyrating spring to it, as if her backside were still the viewing target of a counter full of lunching tradesmen. She cheerfully helped Jim pack for his lifelong dream trip. Bought him a quilted reversible jacket. Hand warmers. When the family loaded him and his poles onto the Bonanza bus for New York City, not even Jim, embarrassed by unexpected tears, had an inkling he wasn't coming back.

Reuben, the Belchers' tenant, introduced Ainsley to the clarinet that summer. For thirty years he had played with the Boston Symphony Orchestra before a complete physical and mental breakdown had broken him permanently. She would lay the instrument flat on his bed with the mouthpiece hanging over the edge and toot into it, standing, playing an open G while he sat in an unraveling rattan chair and mumbled encouragement. Outside, Ethan would throw up gravel. Every now and then a small white piece would sail through the open window and Ainsley would go down to keep him company.

Like a goat, Ethan had eradicated any sign of greenery in the fenced-in yard. Possessed of a mind that was a train yard of derailing and colliding engines, his body had its own uncontrolled velocity. His ability to effect total change on his surroundings in seconds was noteworthy for one so small. At five, he was forbidden from the local supermarket. An electrician's son, he aimed for current, plugging in and turning on anything that bore a cord. The Doberman next door lost all control of its bladder when in view of the tow-headed boy. Only Ainsley could contain and calm her brother. Her love for him was predicated on a need so great, she was not to be budged from it. She forgave him for putting her hamster in the freezer. (He said he thought it would hibernate.) For washing all her stickers in the bathtub.

By the fall of '81, Gloria's bright spirits had dimmed, her backside uncoiled. She was working twelve-hour days and had exchanged her high heels for sneakers. Jim's last card, a picture of disoriented caribou grouped by the pipeline, offered one sentence expressing a need for time to think. She was rarely home and when she was, she slept. The household subsisted on a steady seafood diet from the restaurant—coquilles St. Jacques for breakfast, clam chowder for snack. Great Aunt Lou did the housekeeping, moving with the Hoover slowly, steadily, from room to room and floor to floor like a sea snail in an aquarium, sucking up debris.

The day before he was to enter kindergarten, Ethan disappeared. Ainsley found him after midnight buried in the back of the cake room. A professional cake decorator, Great Aunt Lou had saved every cake that hadn't sold or been picked up. The sewing room on the third floor had become storage for hundreds of cakes in white boxes, some as old as thirty years, sculptures of hardened wedding cakes, Fourth of July cakes, ornate icing designs now rigid as set plaster. After Ainsley had helped Ethan crawl out, she tucked him into bed with the three clam shells he had guarded from dinner the day before.

It was chilly that night. A frost was predicted. She closed the window down hard on the rake rigged out the window with a twenty-foot piece of string tied at the tip. "I'm fishing for daddy!!" Ethan would wail at Gloria every time she tried to take it down. Cold wind ripped through the room in the crack past the rake handle, as Ainsley burrowed deep in her bed. She pictured her father on an ice floe, with a polar bear, surrounded by time to think. Ethan's eyes were closed and twitching. His fearful dread of his imminent academic career was in fact wholly justified, in actuality not an unadmirable indication of self-knowledge and awareness of his own limitations.

Part III

By the time Ethan dropped out of high school the day he turned sixteen, he had four business cards—one for a lawn mowing business, a bicycle messenger service, a VCR and television repair service, and a "Pittsfield, the Heart of the Berkshires" information hot line. Pittsfield was more the liver of the Berkshires with the General Electric plant pumping the bile, and Ethan rarely received calls on his hot line, but his other endeavors turned over handy profits. His sixteenth year he made more money than his mother who now worked the night shift at Dunkin Donuts. The used scuba diving gear he'd invested in to retrieve golf balls from a pond across from the golf course had been paid off twice over just from the sale of the balls. (Though he'd nearly drowned on a moonless night when his tank was empty and he was full of beer, unable to tell which way was up. His friend Willis hauled him out.)

He went through a tour-guiding period, bicycling fifteen miles down to Stockbridge to give tours at the Norman Rockwell Museum (Gloria used to take her children there after Jim left, feeling both comforted and shattered by the heartwarming scenes of domestic normalcy); to Lenox, to guide visitors at Chesterwood, home of sculptor Daniel French (he was seduced by a trustee in French's studio who later accused him of chipping the plaster model of the Lincoln Memorial when in fact she had flailed it over); and to Pittsfield's own Arrowhead, home of Herman Melville. Ethan had a gift for memorizing large chunks of text which proved useful because he was never able to learn to read well. Ainsley, who had read him thousands of pages since childhood, read him all the literature of these establishments, and he repeated it verbatim with a great charm and grin that endeared him to vacationing New Yorkers. He enhanced his tours with wildly creative and interesting lies.

When he was fired from Arrowhead for adamantly arguing against the in-house speculation that it was the distant rounded form of Mt. Greylock, seen from the second story window, that had inspired Melville to write a book about a whale there ("Oh, and the fact that he had been on several whaling expeditions had *nothing* to do with his choice of subject?"), he gave up tour-guiding. The money wasn't that great, and Willis had stopped trying to commit suicide and was now fooling around with computers. They joined forces.

Whereas Ethan's energies were manic and outwardly directed, Ainsley's were ingrown and unprofitable. As an adolescent, she drifted in a perpetual haze of longing, finding some release in her journal, the occasional poem. She was an unremarkable student, slipping by her teachers unnoticed, aiming primarily for invisibility. Only when defending her brother did her will surge to the forefront. At fourteen, she railed at the teacher who had scrawled the word "moron" on one of his rare attempts at writing. In a jailhouse in Danville, New Hampshire, she gave the cop such a headache he let Ethan out of his cell. (He'd been arrested for hitchhiking and drinking under age. She'd borrowed Reuben's car to drive up and retrieve him.) She went to the house of the thirteen-year-old kid who was supplying Ethan with pot and acid, and smacked him out of that inclination. Only once did she have a major run-in with her mother, over something inconsequential. It was a token gesture of rage; for the most part, her mother was too deflated to engage in battle. Her sad face already declared, "I have lost."

Throughout her childhood and adolescence, Reuben occasionally took Ainsley to Saturday morning rehearsals at Tanglewood, summer home of the Boston Symphony Orchestra. Several of the musicians remembered Reuben, he'd been first clarinetist, including visiting conductor Leonard Bernstein who kissed the back of Ainsley's hand. Bernstein was her first love; tanned, aged, Byronic. She sat, eleven years old, transfixed—pigeons cooing above in the open-aired shed—and stared at his impassioned conducting, his expressive hands, his long white hair. At home, she practiced the clarinet shut up in the cake room, imagining him conducting her in Beethoven's *Ode to Joy*.

In high school, Ainsley joined the track team and was startled to break a short distance record in her first meet. But she preferred long distance, running the old logging roads up October Mountain, the smell of wet decaying leaves underfoot, the descent in the dark as the days grew shorter. She eventually quit the team because everyone pressed her to compete and she really didn't want to. Her best friend Helena (whose parents owned Sophia's, a Greek restaurant where Ainsley bussed tables) talked her into joining the school band. Ainsley's bruising crush on the unattainable Mr. Harnette, the music teacher whose witty sarcasm took her breath away, caused far more pain than pleasure. Her junior year, after Helena had graduated and gone off to Smith College, he encouraged Ainsley to take up the oboe. It was a life-changing event. The instrument—which Mr. Harnette rented for her with his own money (the band lacked an oboist and funds)—answered her soul's cry for reciprocity. She gave it her breath and it responded; spoke back to her in plaintive harrowing notes. Mossy night sounds from deep moonlit forests. It was harder to play than the clarinet, the reed more complex and strange. She'd stare at it by candlelight as it soaked upside down in a glass of water.

She practiced night and day, playing woodwind duets with Reuben, who was gaining weight from all the boxes of Dunkin Donuts. The old Doberman next door (who had survived being run over by Ethan's Suburban; he'd apologized to the Grundys), hid in the basement from the unbearable strains. Ainsley composed her own music, traveled boldly and instinctively into uncharted territory. Her new-found voice brought her ashore. By the time she was nineteen, her haze had lifted. Her force field repolarized, she became visible, attractive; acquired sardonic wit. She was accepted at the Boston Conservatory of Music (Mr. Harnette, who, unbeknownst to Ainsley, was deeply in love with her, arranged the audition), but she declined their offer of admission.

In the spring of her senior year, she lost her virginity to an Appalachian Trail thru-hiker who lost his heart to her and wanted to quit the trail, but she levelheadedly convinced him to continue. She'd picked him up hitchhiking into town to buy groceries and he'd hung around for a month. After he left, every few weeks she'd send a package of chocolate and Little Debbies to the next P.O. on the list he'd given her of post offices that dotted his route down to Springer Mountain. She addressed the packages to his trail name, Mango Madness.

After high school, she worked first at General Electric, then at Grossman's Lumber, then at Canyon Ranch, a forty-million-dollar health spa where, as a program coordinator, she set up individual programs for guests (including Barbra Streisand who changed her massage appointment every ten seconds), and then back at Grossman's Lumber where she dated the yard foreman. At home, Great Aunt Lou was bedridden, but Reuben, now eighty-three and recharged by playing duets with Ainsley, joined the community orchestra and was making an effort to comb his hair and to remember to wear his dentures. Gloria was running her own video store, set up in business by Ethan, who was making excellent money installing and servicing computers with Willis.

On Thanksgiving morning in the year 2000, Ethan told Ainsley that his eighteen-year-old girlfriend Kimmy was pregnant and asked her what they should do. Ainsley said that Kimmy should move in with them and have the baby there. Gloria, after her initial shock, grimaced but then warmed to the idea. That evening, with Great Aunt Lou halfheartedly protesting from the second floor, the three of them cleared out the cake room to be the baby's room. They pitched the white boxes out the window and swept the oak floor, exposed for the first time in nearly fifty years. Later, after everyone had gone to bed—Reuben, with bad indigestion from the creamed onions—Ainsley and Ethan sat down at the kitchen table and wrote their father Jim a letter, advising him he was going to be a grandfather and sending congratulations.

The cast of
Back Story

24th Annual Humana Festival of New American Plays
Actors Theatre of Louisville, 2000
photo by Richard Trigg

Back Story

A Dramatic Anthology

Time to Think
by Joan Ackermann

Ainsley, age eighteen, enters, wearing an unbuttoned winter coat, sorrel snow boots, a scarf around her neck.

AINSLEY: August twentieth, the summer I was seven, my dad was supposed to come home from a fishing trip in Alaska. He didn't. Some time around the middle of September we got a postcard from him saying he needed time to think. That was all he wrote. "I need time to think."
(Yelling upstairs.) Ethan! We're leaving in two minutes!
My mother was in no mood to explain what his message meant, and I couldn't figure it out. "Time to think." When I was seven, all I *had* was time. If only I could have given some to my dad. The fact that he *never* came home created a whole lot of more time. Time to miss him. Time to try to figure out why he couldn't just come back and think in Pittsfield, Mass.
(Yelling up.) I'm not kidding! Ethan!
   (She does the buttons up on her coat and whips her scarf around.)
I wondered, was there a particular quality to time in Alaska that made him need to do his thinking there? I knew he was in a *different* time. My mother said we couldn't call him first thing in the morning because he'd still be asleep. That in itself was weird. Being an electrician, he was always up hours before the rest of us, at the crack of dawn, fooling with his tools in the back of his van. Belcher Electric. It was disconcerting, actually, to wake up and know he was still asleep. The problem was we were always ahead of him, at any point in the day. In some ways that made us older than him. Less protected.

(She takes a wool hat out of a pocket. Pulls it on. Takes out mittens and puts them on. Glances upstairs.)

The postcard was a picture of a bunch of depressed caribou hanging out by the pipeline in winter. My little brother thought they were Santa's reindeer. I knew they were not. Santa's reindeer were happier. Santa's reindeer were going places. These caribou weren't going anywhere. I taped them up over my bed. I wondered why he'd picked this particular picture for his message. Was he there, with those caribou? Was he planning to stay with them, and think? The key question was, was he thinking about us? Was he thinking about me? *(Pause.)* If he'd chosen a different card it would have been better. And maybe he was wildly happy.

(Yelling up…) Okay I'm leaving! Bye! *(Pause.)* You're walking! Enjoy the freezing rain! *(Pause.)*

People always say, oh how sad, you grew up without a father, your dad left you. It's really not so bad. I don't hold it against him, I really don't. He did what he had to do. And I admire him for that. Probably, at first, he did need time to think. Time to figure out he didn't want to come back. *(Pause.)* Honestly…? I don't think about him any more. I don't have the time. *(Pause.)*

(Yelling up…) Ethan!

(She doesn't move. Waits for him, all bundled up, still thinking…)

Good Morning to the Horse
by Craig Lucas

Ainsley and Ethan.

AINSLEY: *(Reading from a brochure.)* "—the view out his bedroom window was like seeing 'out of a port-hole of a ship in the Atlantic.' His study he described as his 'ship's cabin,' and when the wind woke him at night he imagined 'there was too much sail on the house.'" ...*(Looks up to Ethan.)* ... Shall I read it again?

ETHAN: *(Headshake: No.)* Mm-mm.

AINSLEY: You have it memorized.

ETHAN: *(A nod: Yes.)* Mm-hm.

AINSLEY: You do not!

ETHAN: *(Quickly, no effort.)* "Melville claimed that the countryside itself had 'a sort of sea-feeling' ...in a letter to his friend Evert Duyckinck, Melville said the view out his bedroom window was like seeing 'out of a port-hole of a ship in the Atlantic.' His study he described as his 'ship's cabin,' and when the wind woke him at night he imagined 'there was too much sail on the house.'"

AINSLEY: How do you do that?...Sooooooo what did he compare his study to?

ETHAN: *(Quickly murmuring through the spiel once more to find the answer, nearly inaudible except for the end.)* "His study he described as his—ship's cabin!!"

AINSLEY: Amazing. Okay, go back, how much did he pay for the house?

ETHAN: Heeee—*(Remembers something.)* Oh. Oh. Wait. There's, here in the index, a bunch of references to the house.

(Ethan retrieves an enormous book.)

AINSLEY: *Herman Melville!* Did you, what?, borrow this?

ETHAN: I bought it.

AINSLEY: Have you ever even bought a book before?

ETHAN: Here's a letter where he describes his working day, after he moves into the house, read this, I can surprise them with this information. During the tour.

AINSLEY: Well, I don't think they expect new guides to be able to rattle off whole letters by Melville.

ETHAN: It refers to the house.

AINSLEY: Even so. Wouldn't it be better to just read the book and call upon the general flavor of things?

ETHAN: Read.

AINSLEY: Why don't you like to read? I love it. *(A little pause, starts to read.)* "Do you want to know how I pass my time?—I rise at—"

ETHAN: You know why? I mean, what. I know what I don't like about reading.

AINSLEY: What?

ETHAN: That it makes things seem like they have a shape.

AINSLEY: What do you mean?

ETHAN: Like things are actually building up to certain events and then other things happen as a result of that annnnd…

AINSLEY: But they do.

ETHAN: Yeah, but it doesn't feel that way when it's happening, it only has a shape when you look back over it or retell it and by then it's too late.

AINSLEY: Too late…?

ETHAN: To do anything, it's already written in stone. When you would need the book is before it happened, not after. What's the big deal, somebody spent their life studying about Herman Melville, everybody knows he's great now, but if somebody could have seen that then they could have recorded a whole helluva lot more about what was going on and it would have helped Herman to know that he was going to write a great book and people would someday appreciate it.

AINSLEY: Maybe not. Maybe he needed not to know. Or maybe he knew.

(Ethan shakes his head.)

AINSLEY: You don't know.

ETHAN: It's always a lie, 'cause life doesn't feel like it has a shape, life feels like it has no shape, like its only shape and purpose is to foil and scare you and muddle—but books, in books it's like—Life, okay, I mean, life is like, "Oh no!, the car doesn't start. What do I do? Ugh, it's too long to walk, it's raining, I guess I have to bike to Arrowhead for my first day on my new job which I really need." Then: "Oh no!, somebody splashed mud on my new suit while I was bicycling. Oh no!, they're probably gonna fire me, I hope they don't, maybe I shouuuuuuuld quick run into the bathroom even though I'm a little bit late and wash this mud off, should I? Shouldn't I? I have no idea, I don't know the end, if I had the book!, but okay, I think I will." And then you get it all out, no mudstains, hooray!!! And they fire you for being late, so you SHOULDN'T have washed the mud out, it was time they were worried about, of course not mud, time...

AINSLEY: Everyone's always worried about time. *(Little pause.)* Are you worried they're going to fire you your first day?

ETHAN: And then you get home and Oh no! another gas bill. I forgot about the gas bill!

AINSLEY: *(Sniffing.)* Speaking of...

ETHAN: Sorry.

(She swats him.)

ETHAN: The book about all that, describing the rain and the deep, sensual, life-be-deepening color of the mud—

AINSLEY: Be-deepening?

ETHAN: *(Over her.)* —and the pounding heart and the sinking spirit when the bill, GAS bill, get it!?!, the symbolism, gas, it's worthless!, AND all books are about bad things happening to people, there are no books in which good and kind people meet and fall in love and raise healthy and respectful and talented and hardworking children and everyone lives into old age.... If a book isn't going to help you with the here and now and it is going to be all that work.... Read.

AINSLEY: You want them all to be happy?... *(Reading.)* "Do you want to know how I pass my time? —I rise at eight—thereabouts—& go to my barn—say good-morning to the horse, & give him his breakfast. (It goes to my heart to give him a cold one, but it can't be helped.) Then, pay a visit to my cow—cut up a pumpkin or two for her, & stand by to see her eat it—for it's a pleasant sight to see a cow move her jaws—she does it so mildly & with such a sanctity. —My breakfast over, I—" *(Stops.)* What?

ETHAN: He wrote that!

AINSLEY: I know.

ETHAN: No. He was worried about giving the horse cold food, and he died thinking *Moby-Dick* was a failure. Penniless. Completely forgotten.

AINSLEY: How do you—? Did you study it in high school?

ETHAN: It's in, right in there.

AINSLEY: You read this...whole book?

ETHAN: *(Over slightly.)* Bits. The end.

AINSLEY: You just read the end?

ETHAN: I always do that.

AINSLEY: Why?

ETHAN: I-I-I-I *(Note: the word "I" is drawn out as he debates whether or not he wants to reveal this about himself.)* check it first before I start to…you know…care about the characters so it won't break my heart when it comes around at the end. If it's…. Go on.

AINSLEY: *(Resumes reading.)* "I go to my workroom & light my fire—then spread my manuscript on the table—take one business squint at it, & fall to with a will. At 2 and a half P.M. I hear a preconcerted knock at my door, which serves to wean me effectively from my writing, however interested I may be … My evenings I spend in a sort of a mesmeric state in my room—not being able to read—only now & then skimming some large printed book."

(Pause.)

ETHAN: Books. *(Pause.)* You see? *(Stands abruptly, wipes his eye as if something got caught in it as he walks out.)* I gotta pee. *(Silence.)*

What Became of the Polar Bear?
by Mayo Simon

Ethan is heard offstage, approaching with a tour group: "...If you'll all just come this way. Watch your step, please."

Ethan enters speaking in his "tour voice" to the imaginary tour group.

ETHAN: In the summer of 1850, Herman Melville, seeking a quiet place to work, bought this eighteenth-century farmhouse in the town of Pittsfield which was then home to such famous literary figures such as Fanny Kemble, Oliver Wendell Holmes, James Russell Lowell, and in Lenox, less than six miles away, Nathaniel Hawthorne. I can repeat that in German. Spanish? French? Serbo-Croatian? Okay, everybody into Herman's study. If you look out the window you can see—Mount Greylock! You'll notice the top of the mountain is shaped like the head of a huge whale. This is the view, ladies and gentlemen, that became the inspiration for Melville's greatest novel, *Moby-Dick*!

    (Quietly.)

If you believe that, you'll believe anything. Now, you want to hear the real story of how Melville got the idea for *Moby-Dick*?

    (Motions people to gather around him.)

They don't like me to talk about this—too controversial. But you've been such a good group...

    (Looks around, then continues.)

Herman Melville was a harpooner on a whaling ship for two years. Started in the South Seas, ended up in the Gulf of Alaska. One foggy morning, as the ship is maneuvering around the ice floes where the whales hang out, Melville spies what's left of a fishing boat. Whales get a kick out of ramming boats, so Herman's on the lookout. Sure enough, coming out of the fog, he sees something. It's not a whale. It's...a man...on an ice floe...fishing. Name's Belcher—same name as mine—common name. And on that floe is also...a polar bear. Melville hails the man: "Avast, have you seen a great white whale?" They look at each other, Melville the harpooner, and Belcher, owner and manager of Belcher Electric. Then, as though he's come to some secret and profound conclusion about life, the man raises his arms and...takes off! Actually, a huge whale has crashed up from under the ice, lifting the man high in the air. Melville watches as the whale, with a giant splash, flops down in the water. The man flops down on the whale's back. The whale, with Belcher on his back, dives into the fog and disappears. Awesome. Melville is too stunned to throw the harpoon. Instead, he decides to write a book. It's all in one of Melville's letters to Hawthorne. You can look it up. What's that? What became of the polar bear? Strange you should ask because I ask the same question every night.... What became of him?... That concludes the tour. The gift shop is down the steps and to the right.

The Reluctant Instrument
by Neena Beber

AINSLEY: I learned how to kiss on the clarinet…but I learned how to love on the oboe.

(Ainsley takes out an oboe and blows into it. Nothing, no sound.)

Unrequited love, my specialty.

Mr. Harnette wants me to play the oboe, I don't know why. Mr. Harnette wants to torture me. The oboe is a complex, difficult instrument. It requires the smallest of breaths. Too much, and the sound is an embarrassment: overeager and desperate. The oboe requires passion, but also control. Force, but also delicacy.

Mr. Harnette knows: the oboe is the perfect instrument for one doing her best to disappear. When I play, I make myself small and contained. I try to become invisible, to hide inside the sounds as if they belong to someone else.

(Again Ainsley starts to play, but changes her mind.)

I don't think I'll ever get it right.

Mr. Harnette makes music. Mr. Harnette has gray eyes and black hair and wears crisp white shirts. He is a black-and-white photo, a postcard from Paris, a nineteenth-century novel. He looks best against the snow. He looks best against the snow and that's how I imagine him—have I admitted to imagining him? Gray eyes and black hair and music, music in his soul as I have in mine though he wouldn't know it.

(She tries to play again. A sputter. She sighs, preparing to try again.)

When you play the oboe, you must plan your breathing. You have to decide where to inhale, and where to let go.

(She takes a deep breath.)

The problem is, each time I take a breath I think—I am in love with Mr. Harnette!—and I nearly burst.

In the future I will discover three things, in the following order:

I was a better oboe player than I thought.

The oboe was rented for me not with school band funds, but by Mr. Harnette himself.

My love for Mr. Harnette was not unrequited.

Or maybe I already know that.

Maybe I'll write him a letter. I probably won't. The truth is I definitely won't but there he is—Mr. Harnette—his shades of gray against the snow, someone to return to in a circular breath that comes every so often as breath should
Full expansive not taking in more than it can give back
A breath that is just right, just enough to set loose
A note
Into the world as I went then
A song waiting to release itself
Steady Clear and
Free.

> *(Ainsley plays the oboe. The sound of a solo oboe, culminating in one long, sustaining note.)*

Ethan's Got Get
by Edwin Sanchez

Ethan, wet and drying his hair, sits by a lake. He takes a swig from a beer bottle. Next to him is a pail of golf balls. He calls out to his friend who is in the lake.

ETHAN: No, Willis, the other side.

    (He points.)

I already looked where you are. Now we're looking for a golf ball with a blue stripe around it. That's Mr. Allen's favorite. He'll pay me extra for that one. "Sentimental value."

    (Snorts.)

Old fool.

    (Drinks again and holds up the pail.)

Hey look, Willis, I got the town by the balls! Hell, I already paid off the scuba gear twice over just by selling their golf balls back to these guys. Guess when you're old your balls mean a lot to you. Hell, they're old enough. Youngest golfer here is forty if he's a day. They got so much free time, spend their days swinging a club at a little ball. Already made their money, they're set. Not me. But I'm gonna be a millionaire before I'm twenty-one, you watch. Okay, so this is small-fry stuff, chump change, but it's a start. This and the other three businesses I got going is gonna take me up and out. You find Mr. Allen's ball tonight and I'll think about taking you with me.

    (Waves to Willis and watches him disappear under water.)

No, I won't. Won't take anybody. Just be rich and alone. Finally.

    (Picks up one of the balls from the bucket.)

Now, how is something like this supposed to have sentimental value? A person, a person who leaves, now that has sentimental value. I mean, I can't go into a sporting goods store and buy a new father, right? Or buy back my mother's life so she's not tired all the time. Or get Ainsley one of her own so she ain't always trying to share mine. She's just like mama, a born loser.

    (To Willis.)

You find anything? Well, haul yourself outta there. I got VCRs to fix.

(To himself.)

Gotta be successful. Papa left 'cause he couldn't do it. I can. I will.

(Studies one of the balls.)

I got a couple of blue Magic Markers at home. Yep, looks like I found your ball, Mr. Allen.

Trying to Get There
by Eduardo Machado

AINSLEY: No. Ma, I won't pick up Ethan's dirty dishes and wash them for you. No, I'm sorry, Ma, I won't! *(She looks at her mother.)* No stay right there. I swear you won't pick them up either. I swear you won't! I demand you won't! No!

Why do I always have to fix everything for him, Ma? Dad left me, too, sure I was older but Dad left me too. Why do I always have to take care of everybody? I'm afraid that my entire life will be spent taking care of guys. You know it's the only thing that makes me feel worth something, that and playing music…. Do you worry about me about my future, huh? Ma, don't look away, Ma! Please don't look away. I don't hate him. From the minute he was born… I had to take care of myself. From the night he was born. And I have a missing toe to prove it. If it wasn't for Reuben, I wouldn't have anything, not even music. What am I inheriting, Ma?

Except for silence. Except for being a good girl and keeping my mouth shut. What will I inherit from you, Ma. Except for longing for a man that is never going to come back. My inheritance scares me, Ma. When I look at you I get scared. What will I become, Ma? Speak. Let me hear your opinions. I want to know what you think. Please talk to me. Don't turn on the TV. Please, Ma. Please. No I don't want to watch that show. 'Cause it's silly, Ma. I think TV is silly.

(She takes a dish. Smashes it against the floor.)

I guess nothing will ever make you scream, Ma. I'm going to read. Tell Ethan to sweep the floor.

Maid of Athens
by David Rambo

Ainsley, 19, screams offstage with a startled burst of pain.

AINSLEY: Shit! Oh…shit!
> *(She runs in wrapping a finger in a bloody swath of paper towel. It really hurts. She calls off.)*

I'm okay. I've got an ice cube on it. Aunt Lou, put the potatoes in a pot of cold water. Except the one I got blood on.
> *(To herself, raising her bloodied fist, and taking deep breaths.)*

Hold it above the heart. Come on, ice cube. Make it numb. Ice. Iceberg. Glacier. A big Alaskan glacier…on my finger. Kissing my finger, making the pain go away. Glaciers. Snow, in soft white drifts, like waves of icing on a wedding cake, like…

…Leonard Bernstein's hair. The summer I was eleven, and Reuben took me to Tanglewood. They remembered him, all the older musicians did, from when he played there. First clarinet. Reuben told them he was just teaching now and I was his star pupil. But they knew. It was a hot day, and when a drinker sweats, you can just smell it on them. We all could. And then, this…this wave of energy comes at us, and it's Leonard Bernstein. "Reuben! Reuben, God, where the hell have you been? Reuben, dear, darling, Reuben." And Leonard Bernstein's hugging Reuben and kissing him. Kissing! Then, Reuben says, "Lenny"—to Leonard Bernstein!—he says, "Lenny, this is Ainsley Belcher, my star pupil. She plays the clarinet." And then…
> *(She lowers the wounded hand, as if it's being held by Leonard Bernstein.)*

Leonard Bernstein kisses my hand! Can't look him in the eye, or I'll sink like the Titanic. So I'm looking at his hair, these waves of thick, soft, white hair. Like snow. Big, soft, Alaskan glaciers.
They call rehearsal, and "Lenny" looks up at me, and quotes Lord Byron, my favorite poet!
"Maid of Athens, ere we part,
Give, oh give me back my heart."

And he left. For three hours I sat on the grass watching rehearsal, and didn't move a muscle or even go to the bathroom, even when the orchestra took a break. I didn't move.

(She hums a passage from Beethoven's Ode *to* Joy, *"conducting" with the wounded hand.)*

After that, when I practiced up in the cake room, if my cheeks hurt, or the muscles in my jaw got tired, I couldn't feel it. Leonard Bernstein was there. Conducting. Kissing my...

(Her hand.)

It doesn't hurt anymore.

Moby Ethan at the Sculptor's Museum
by Constance Congdon

Scene begins in the dark. Suddenly, a flashlight is turned on, revealing the chin and face of Ethan. He's holding the flashlight under his chin so that the effect is eerie.

ETHAN: *(In a performance-like tone.)* Call me Ishmael.
    (In his normal voice, looking for the trustee with his flashlight.)
So, do you like that, Mrs. Chapin-Skinner? Because I could do something as good for the life of Mr. Daniel French if I thought about how I could illustrate the work of a sculptor. I could be holding a chisel or I could, like, cover myself with white flour and stand, like I was—check this out—like I was—could you turn on the light, Mrs. Chapin-Skinner?
    (Lights up on Ethan. He is standing in his jockey shorts.)
I think we need to, like, decide whether or not I'm going to be the sculptor or the sculpture. *Or.* I could just sit in a chair, in a suit, with a beard on—get where I'm going with this? And impersonate that sculpture of Abraham Lincoln over there. That might take less prep time. You see, at the Melville house I just recite a lot of *Moby-Dick*, or, if I hate the people I'm guiding, I recite *Pierre or The Ambiguities* and that usually gets them out of the house, so I can lock up and bike back to Stockbridge to catch the before-dinner tour of the Rockwell Museum. Because I need the money, of course.
    (Lights go out. Sound of a scuffle.)
Mrs. Chapin-Skinner! What are you doing? Good God!
    (Breaking away.)
Now this is just not right, so let go of me—let GO!
    (Sound of a crash. Ethan turns on his flashlight and investigates.)
Jesus! What have you done?? Mrs. Chapin-Skinner?? Look at this!! You have knocked over the Daniel French Museum Official Replica of the Abraham Lincoln Memorial Statue!! Ohmygod!! It's chipped!! Oh man! I am so fired!! Prudence!! Prudence!! You have been a very bad trustee tonight. If one cannot trust a trustee, then—YOU HAVE BELIED THE NAME OF TRUSTEE!!! YOU DO NOT DESERVE TO BE A TRUSTEE OF THE DANIEL FRENCH MUSEUM OR ANY

MUSEUM!! MRS. CHAPIN-SKINNER GET YOUR HANDS OFF OF MY PANTS!!! *JESUS!!*

(He flails at his assailant with his flashlight, until he drops it and he's in complete darkness again.)

Mrs. Chapin-Skinner? Are you all right? Prudence? Pru? I didn't mean to hit you that hard. Squeeze my hand if you can hear my voice. Just squeeze—

(But she squeezes his genitals.)

Oh my god. Ohmygod. Oh my god. Mrs. Chapin-Skinner, what are you doing now? Did you take out your teeth? Ahhh. Ahhhh. Ahhhhh. Call me Ishmael! Call me—ohhh, ohhh, ohhhhhhhh! Just call me, call me, call me! YESSSSSSSSS!

(He climaxes. Beat.)

Ooooo. Uh.

(Beat.)

Did you ever play the oboe, Mrs. Chapin-Skinner? Because you certainly have the lips for it. My sister says it takes really strong lips.

Turn Down
by Shirley Lauro

Ainsley at desk reading letter she's writing. Crumpled paper on floor.

AINSLEY: *(Warm, familial tone.)* Dr. Rudolph Silensky, Chairman, Admissions Committee, Boston Conservatory of Music.... Dear Dr. Silensky, *First,* let me express my happiness and great appreciation to the entire audition committee for selecting me at the Conservatory in the Woodwind Division for next fall. My deepest dream has come true...

(She stops at the end of the part she's written, thinks, then starts to write.)

Second, I—

(Stops, goes on.)

Is there any possibility of a late admission? Postponing until—

(Crosses this out, starts again.)

However, since my audition, I—

(Crosses this out.)

Unfortunately, however, now—until—

(Stops abruptly, tears sheet from pad, crumples it, throws to floor. Gathers strength, starts over, much more formal, distant tone.)

Dear Dr. Silensky... I want to inform the Committee that although...I am honored...to have been chosen for admission—-

(She stops again, then determined, pushes on.)

A deep family responsibility and commitment...make it...impossible for me to accept...at this time...

(Close to tears, she stops, stifles them, goes on.)

Thank you all for your consideration and—faith—in my talent—and... me...

(She breaks, sobbing, finishing.)

Sincerely...Ainsley Belcher—

(She puts letter in envelope. A beat. She goes to the phone, dials number she's written down on desk.)

Danville Correctional Facility? Yes—we spoke before? Ainsley Belcher? My brother Ethan. Right—hitchhiking and alcohol level—right. Well, *I'm* coming, so please tell the officers in charge there? I want a meeting.

Right off the turnpike you said, didn't you? So a couple of hours. *My* custody...the responsible adult...yes...well, with our mother...but she works every night...*I'm* home. Yes, and I'll straighten it out...he's an exceptional boy and this is just a fluke of some kind...so if you'll tell who's in charge about a meeting...thank you....

(Hangs up, starts out, remembers letter, gets it, looking at it a moment.)

Misadventure
by Donald Margulies

Ainsley bails Ethan out of jail after a misadventure.

The parking lot of the Danville, New Hampshire police station. She's fuming. He's sheepish. It's cold.

AINSLEY: *(To policeman offstage; laced with sarcasm.)* Thank you, officer. Thanks a lot. *(To Ethan.)* Get in the car.

ETHAN: *(Refusing.)* Un-uh.

AINSLEY: Get. In. The. Car.

ETHAN: No way.

AINSLEY: Ethan! Get in the car!

ETHAN: I refuse to get in the car when you're like this.

AINSLEY: Like what?

ETHAN: You're mad at me.

AINSLEY: I am not mad at you.

ETHAN: Yes you are; I can tell: Your nostrils are doing that thing.

AINSLEY: What thing?

ETHAN: *You* know, they kinda... *(He demonstrates by flaring his nostrils.)*

AINSLEY: GETINTHECAR!

ETHAN: What if you lose control and crash into a tree or something?

AINSLEY: I'm not gonna lose control.

ETHAN: How do *you* know? You might get this uncontrollable urge to smack me repeatedly and *then* what?

AINSLEY: I am not gonna smack you! Get in the car!

ETHAN: I've had enough trauma for one evening, thank you.

AINSLEY: *You've* had enough trauma!

ETHAN: Yes! The stigma of incarceration will haunt me for years.

AINSLEY: *(Softly.)* Get in the car. *(He shakes his head.)* Ethan, I am too tired and too pissed off—

ETHAN: Ah ha! *(She let her anger slip.)*

AINSLEY: *(Continuous.)* —to be having this argument with you in a police station parking lot in Nowhere, New Hampshire. I'm cold and I want to go home.

ETHAN: I like the cold; the cold feels good. It's sobering me up. I feel more awake than I've ever felt in my life.

AINSLEY: What were you *thinking*?! What in the world were you *thinking*!

ETHAN: I don't know.

AINSLEY: You don't *know*? Were you trying to kill yourself? Huh? Were you? *(He shrugs.)*

ETHAN: No. I don't know. Maybe.

AINSLEY: Maybe?! MAYBE?!

ETHAN: I don't know, I said.

AINSLEY: You selfish boy! You stupid selfish boy!

ETHAN: Good. Let it out. I'm glad we're talking now; it's much better than that nostril thing.

AINSLEY: How DARE you be reckless with your life! How DARE you!

ETHAN: Shhh! You're disturbing the peace. You want them to throw *both* of us in jail?

AINSLEY: What's *my* life worth if you trash yours? Huh? Have you thought about that?!! I'll have to live the next seventy-five years haunted every goddamn day by your pimply ghostly self. We're not just sibs, you stupid moron, we're soulmates. Don't you know that by now?!

ETHAN: *(Childlike, surprised by the depth of her rage, he nods; a beat, softly.)* I'm sorry.

AINSLEY: You drink yourself sick and go hitching on the Interstate?! Are you crazy?! Have I taught you nothing?!

ETHAN: Hey. A. I said I was sorry.

AINSLEY: Never mind being drunk and weaving on the shoulder with cars and trucks whizzing by at eighty miles an hour. Never mind that. What if a crazy person stopped to pick you up—a Jeffrey Dahmer type or something—

ETHAN: *(Amused.)* What?!

AINSLEY: —and took you away so you were never heard from again! Some boy scouts would come across your jawbone one day in the woods. It's a good thing the cops picked you up and threw you in jail. You could've been roadkill.

ETHAN: You're nuts, you know that? You've been watching too much television.

AINSLEY: Don't mock me. There ARE crazy people out there, you know, they're not just CREATED by the media. They exist! There are truly bad and sick people out there in the world who want nothing more than to destroy other people's happiness. *(He cracks up.)* Stop laughing! STOP IT!! It isn't funny! You scared me, Ethan! You scared me to death!!

(She throws punches at him; he protects his head with his hands, laughing until she really hurts him.)

ETHAN: Ow!

(She stops. Silence.)

That hurt.

AINSLEY: Good.

ETHAN: I can explain.

AINSLEY: Nothing you could possibly say…

ETHAN: Aren't you even gonna give me my due process? Aren't you?

AINSLEY: I don't see why I should.

ETHAN: I'm just a kid, you know.

AINSLEY: Oh, God. Is that your excuse? Is that your pissant excuse?!

ETHAN: Kids are *supposed* to act out and do reckless things. Right? If not while I'm young, when? When I'm old? When I'm forty?

AINSLEY: The key is surviving long enough to attain wisdom.

ETHAN: Okay, so let's chalk it up to the folly of youth. Okay? I've learned my lesson: I drank a whole lot of really shitty bourbon with some asshole I don't even like whose approval I inexplicably crave and blew Pizza Hut pizza all down my front and onto my brand new running shoes. Don't you think I'm humiliated enough? I just *bought* these shoes. Like a week ago.

AINSLEY: If you'd *killed* yourself…! If you'd gotten yourself killed for some stupid, peer-pressure, macho, adolescent, alcoholic misadventure…. If I'd *lost* you 'cause of it…. If I'd *lost* you…

(She finally lets herself weep; she turns away from him. He's impressed. Silence.)

Pizza Hut, huh. No wonder you smell like a dairy farmer.

ETHAN: I can't even smell it anymore.

AINSLEY: Trust me.

ETHAN: Oh, yeah, why should I trust *you*?

AINSLEY: Because you'd better. Because if you don't trust *me*, brother, you are a goner. You are toast. *(A beat.)* Now get in the car.

ETHAN: Still mad at me?

AINSLEY: *(Smiling.)* Get in the fucking car?

ETHAN: *(Smiles; a beat, as he gets into the car.)* Can we stop somewhere to get something to eat? I'm starving.

AINSLEY: We'll see. Phew. You stink.

(She starts the car.)

Something To Do With Bolivia
by Jon Klein

Ethan sits on the front steps of the post office at Harper's Ferry, writing a very large postcard. The discarded remains of previous attempts lie in a torn pile at his feet.

Oh, and he has a noticeably black eye.

Ethan pauses, squinting down at his writing, rereading something.

ETHAN: Shit. Careful, bro. This is from Mr. Spring Fling.
>   *(He tears it in half and throws it on the pile. He starts over with a new card.)*
Dear Ainsley—
>   *(Lights up on Ainsley, reading the postcard.)*
How's it goin'? Bet you thought I forgot you, but how could I ever forget you? You think I'd spend four weeks off trail with any girl who'd give me a lift to the grocery? Guess who I ran into down at Harper's Ferry. Your brother Ethan. Small world, huh. He was on some cheap rail pass, takin' on some history, and I just came off the Appalachian Trail. So we're shootin' the shit, and he tells me you been wonderin' what the hell happened to me. Man, was I glad to see your brother.
>   *(Ethan gingerly rubs his black eye.)*
Dickwad.
>   *(He resumes.)*
The thing is, I quit the postcards 'cause I ... lost my pen.
>   *(He stops, looking at his pen.)*
Damn.
>   *(He gets an idea.)*
Till now. Ta da! The thing is, Ethan said it reminded you of your dad's postcards, how they stopped without any warning. And you said what is it about men that they all need "time to think." But the truth is, guys *don't* need time to think. It's just that they can only think about one thing at a time. Take the old dude on this postcard—John Brown. Talk about a one-track mind. He fought off the entire US Army from a little

stone firehouse—just like the end of *Butch Cassidy*. Because all he could think about was slavery, just like all Butch could think about was Bolivia, and all Captain Ahab could think about was a big stupid whale. Add it all up, and what do you get? No justice, foreign territory, and a really long fishing trip. Hi, Dad.

(Ainsley frowns. He thinks about that, and scratches out the last two words. He resumes.)

Anyways, right now all I can think about is this trail, and getting to Georgia. I guess that's a little like Bolivia too. But I ... miss you, babe. You were the first. I promise.

(Ainsley beams, enraptured. He stops writing.)

Fat chance, you prick.

(He resumes.)

One last thing. Give your brother a break. I know you think he's a dumb-shit, but he hates to see you get hurt, which is why he came here to punch my fucking lights out...

(Ainsley stands up, furious.)

Shit.

(Lights out on Ainsley. He tears it in two and throws it on the pile. He pulls out another large postcard.)

Dear Ainsley...

Or Maybe Not
by Adele Edling Shank

Ainsley, sitting on the front porch after supper, talking to the frogs.

AINSLEY: I knew Mr. Harnette would be mad, but I didn't think he'd be, like, fireworks. Pouff. Pouff. Anger lighting up the sky. I knew he'd be awful sorry I'm not going, but there was no call for him to...he didn't have to say words like coward. Nobody ever called me a coward. I got the strength to go all right. I'm tough enough all right. He oughta ask that cop who put Ethan in jail if I'm tough. "I'm just trying to teach 'im a lesson." Well I let him know what I thought a lessons like that at about a hundred and thirty decibels and he goes, "Stop, stop! You gotta voice like an ax, my head is splittin'." So there Mr.-Harnette-think-you-know-so-much-about-me, you ask that cop if I got a spine or not. And you ask that basketball coaching English teacher who wrote "moron" on Ethan's essay about my spine. He got a hundred and sixty decibels and the diabolicalist headache ever was! Yeah, Mr. Harnette-think-you-got-me-pegged, you ask him if I'm a coward. And the dumbshit kid Jimmy, I almost made his brain explode when I found out he sold Ethan acid. Ask Jimmy if I've got a spine or not! And if I can take on a cop and a basketball coach and a drug dealer, I can stand up to a few musicians in Boston for sure!!

So, it's pretty clear to me we aren't talking about my spine here. It's not a question of how tough I am. It's a question.... It's more a question of.... Okay, I don't really know what it's a question of. I guess...I guess... Maybe I'm only tough enough for Ethan. Maybe I'm not tough enough for me.

Things don't feel right anymore. I can't remember when they stopped feeling right it's been so long. Suppose I didn't notice at the time. Or maybe I thought it was just a temporary dip. Now it feels like the Grand Canyon. And I can't figure out how to get things feeling right again. Maybe now I finally made the big decision, now I know I'm staying home with Ethan, maybe now I'll get some peace, and maybe things will feel right again. Or maybe not.

Dead Men Make No Dollars
by Val Smith

Lights up on Ethan, sitting in a puddle of water dressed in wet suit, mask and flippers sans tanks. He partially unzips the front of the suit. A cascade of golf balls pours out. He blows a golf ball out of his mouth.

ETHAN: Yes, Willis, I took a risk. Calculated, yes. Dangerous, yes. I AM grateful, alright? But underlying MY action was the loopy capitalistic all-American urge for monetary gain. I do not wish to die. I wish to make a *killing*. If anyone has a death wish around here, Willis, it's you. An *insincere* death wish to be sure, but a death wish however incompetently expressed is still a death wish.

(Long pause. Listens to Willis.)

Okay. Fine. *Let's* talk about it. Specifico numero uno. You open your mother's medicine cabinet. There is a bottle marked VALIUM. There is another bottle marked ASPIRIN. Which one do YOU, who can read, and who SINCERELY wishes to kill himself, choose?

Ejemplo number dos. Room full of people concentrating intensely on that fine, fine actress, Cameron Diaz in that superb film, *Something About Mary*. You walk through the room carrying a rope. It becomes obvious you are going to hang yourself. It becomes obvious you are going to use the so-called "chandelier" in your mother's dining room. Now, Willis, it wasn't that we cared more about Cameron Diaz than you. But anybody with half a fuckin' brain knows that wrought-iron dangle hanging from the cottage cheese in your mother's dining room probably cost the builder all of two dollars and fifty cents. With luck, it might support a balloon.

Ejemplo three. If you are going to use a rifle to shoot yourself, Willis, what do you do? Do you put it in your ear? Do you put it in your mouth? No. YOU decide that the most effective way to kill yourself is to take aim and I quote, "sever the artery that runs down the neck from the brain over to the shoulder." Unquote. Fuck me. So now, your mother has a plywood board over her bay window, a giant hole in her dining room ceiling and you have a chipped collar bone. And, Willis, Willis, —follow me here, *you are still alive.*

Yes, I too am still alive. Yes, thanks to you. Okay, okay. Bastando, aright? Truce. Okay. So. I will give up my shit IF you give up your shit. I will give up the most unbelievable underwater goldmine since, since, fucking… King Tut's tomb. *(Points to golf ball.)* Look, Willis. A Titleist. Near virgin condition.

> *(Throwing golf balls back in the pond. And another. And finally, he throws one at Willis and laughs.)*

Shit, Willis.

The Deal
by Jane Martin

Ainsley sits at a kitchen table with nine glass-bottled beers on it.

AINSLEY: I never drank nine beers before. I feel strangely free. Ethan, bring me
my toe out of the refrigerator, will you? I like to see my toe when I'm
drunk.

(He brings the toe. It's in a ziplock sandwich bag.)

Thanks. Two and a half years old, an' I cut this baby clean off with a
snow shovel the night Momma went to the hospital to have you. You
ingrate. One of a thousand sacrifices, baby brother. If ol' Reuben hadn't a
come along drunk as a lord, I might have bled to death, but, more impor-
tantly, I would never, never have played the oboe. Did you know Reuben
played with the Boston Symphony Orchestra for thirty years? That old
drunk, who would have thought it. He's got crystal pure tone. You play a
duet with Reuben, you downright feel fucked. He's eighty-one years old
come November.

(She opens the ziplock and dumps the toe into her hand.)

They sewed this baby on an' it lasted fourteen years till it snapped off that
time I fell when I was doing cross-country. I believe the moral to be that
you can't put something broken back together. Not in the long run. This
has proved true in all three of my romantic relationships. In each one, we
split an' then came back together an' then broke off forever. The toe
knows.

(She puts it back in the bag.)

I wonder how it came to be that I'm a supporting role even in my own
life. I mean I thought I'd star in my life, but it hasn't worked out that
way. You're the star of my life, brother mine. Whatever I am it's in rela-
tion to you. Second oboe. You know people hear about my toe before
they hear about me? I meet 'em an' they say, "Oh, sure, you're the one
keeps her toe in the refrigerator." Second fiddle to my own body parts. At
what point, Ethan, is it determined in your own life whether you are to
be a first chair or just a general all-purpose oboist? I believe it was when
you were born, Ethan, and I wasn't allowed to go to the hospital. I was
not...among the chosen, though I did, however, achieve self-mutilation

with the snow shovel. Well, "They also serve who only bleed and wait," right? I believe I'll put my claim to fame back in the freezer compartment and fix you some dinner. What, dearest Ethan, would you like for dinner? I was once offered admission to the Boston Conservatory of Music, and though our family mythology would have it that I gave it up on your behalf, my sad, wild brother, I actually declined on the basis that it was a hell of a lot of money just to come out playing second oboe. It seemed a...pretension to be expensively trained to be ordinary. Oh, it's best to know who you are...or so they tell you.

Blackfish
by Courtney Baron

Ethan stands with a bucket of ice (fish inside).

ETHAN: Women want to know how you got to be the way you are. Like screening for mental illness. A litmus test to make sure you're not going to get worse. You want to check out the closet before you put your nice clothes inside. I think I love my girlfriend. I know my illness, my crime, but I tell her, "My father left us for fish," took an extended ichthyological adventure. And that does fuck with me. But it's not my crime. This is a fish.

(He holds up the bucket.)

Seven years ago it's Christmas and Ainsley is wearing these tiny ornament earrings. I'm driving us home. She sings Christmas songs and I say, "Your mouth is a cathedral." This is an Alaskan Blackfish.

(He pulls a blackfish from the bucket.)

Ainsley wants to go home, but I have this magnet and it draws me to Lake Onota. She shows me the North Star and I tell her I know where Jesus is. You're wondering why I want to go to the lake in the middle of the fucking night. I'm drawn to where the fish are. But it's not my crime.

(He puts down the bucket and looks at the fish.)

Ainsley says I wouldn't know Jesus if he bit me in the ass. I don't know why, but this pisses me off and I shove her back in the truck. Now she's pissed too. She's holding on to the dash as we pass the cardboard nativity at the neighbors, I say, "See there's Jesus." And she cracks this smile, her smile, because kneeling in front of the plastic-baby-away-in-a-manger Jesus is Santa Claus. I'm laughing so hard, I barely feel the thud as I pull into our drive. I jump out to see what I've run over. The neighbor's old Doberman is lying at Ainsley's feet. I've run over it. Ainsley's sparkling, those ornament earrings. I say, "You look like a Christmas tree." She says there's a gift at her feet. Ainsley bends down and says that the dog is breathing. I think, "Your mouth is a cathedral. Bless me." And she's got tears and the dog whimpers and I don't know why but her disappointment kills me. I die. She watches me freeze. And I wait for her to forgive me. She pulls me down to the dog and she puts my hand in hers and runs it through the dog's fur. And I'm born again.

(He runs his hand over the fish.)

The Alaskan Blackfish freezes in the water every winter, freezes dead. And every summer it thaws out and lives again. Ainsley's disappointment freezes me. Then she grabs my hand and I'm revived. You can't tell this to your girlfriend. You can't say that you love your sister more than life, that Ainsley makes me an Alaskan Blackfish. I die and live over and over again for her. My father left us for fishing in Alaska. But the fish is here. I can't tell you why I know that if he had stayed I wouldn't breathe for Ainsley. But I do. I breathe for Ainsley. I'm a fish dying and reviving over again. It's the perfect crime. I'm a fish.

Star Skating
by John Olive

Ainsley enters, pulling on a robe. She opens the door and Ethan enters, shivering from the cold, stomping the floor, eyes burning from sleeplessness.

ETHAN: I went skating on the reservoir last night. It was amazing. The whole reservoir was smooth as ebony. Black. A mirror. It was like skating on stars.
(Laughs.)
I felt like a fish swimming upside down following Ethan Belcher as he soared and swooped under the stars. If I could just break through the ice I could fly…. Did Kimmy call?
(Ainsley shakes her head.)
She didn't? That's…. Well, that's okay. She's sleeping probably. We had an interesting night.
(Takes off his jacket, sits near Ainsley.)
Here's what it is. We keep our lives small. You know, in these tight patterns with very familiar players: you, Mom, Aunt Lou, Reuben, and Kimmy, and I used to think it was because I was afraid, of…not change so much as of breaking through the ice and discovering that, yes, the stars are much brighter out in the cold air which, oh shit, I now discover I can't breathe. Know what I mean?
(Laughs again.)
But that's not it. We keep our lives small so we can hear magic scratching at the door. If we're living too big, or we're distracted by the sound of money and our tantrumming little egos, we might miss it. All this time I was waiting for it and now I heard it so of course I had to go skating.
(Looks at Ainsley.)
Did I wake you up?
(Suddenly stands.)
I should take a shower. Is it too early to call Kimmy? Yeah, she should sleep. It's just that, well, you think I'm not clear now, you shoulda heard me last night.
(Laughs again.)
I slept, maybe, half an hour. I had such wild dreams, like nightmares but I always woke up laughing. Except one. I dreamed I was back on the

reservoir skating and as I looked down into the black sky there was a huge bird above me, matching me move for move, swoop for swoop, but when I stopped and looked up…. The sky was empty. That dream made me cry.

(Another beat.)

It's too early to call Kimmy. I can't wake her up. I'm too shivery to shower. Tummy's too tense for coffee. It's gonna snow today.

(Looks at Ainsley.)

What're we gonna do?

(A moment. Then Ainsley stands, goes to Ethan, takes his head in her hands and kisses him.)

AINSLEY: We'll clean out the cake room and put in a crib.

Barbra Live at Canyon Ranch
by Tanya Palmer

Ainsley enters with a clipboard and a towel over her shoulder. A woman, Barbra Streisand, is lying on her stomach on a massage table. Ainsley moves toward the table and begins to speak.

AINSLEY: Ms. Streisand? I've got you down here for a Lymphatic Balancing Massage, but Jeannie's locked up all the aromatherapy bottles in the cabinet and I can't find a key. So it looks like the Stress Buster for you! *(Putting down the clipboard.)* Just let me know if I'm doing it too hard. And no speaking, please, we find it creates tension in the sternocleidomastoid muscles. *(Pause.)* I have to tell you, we were all pretty excited when we heard you were coming to Canyon Ranch; Richie at the front desk is a HUGE fan. He performed "Woman in Love" at the talent show last summer and won first prize. He looks just like you, when he dresses up, down to the nails and everything. Okay, now this is the part where I really go for it, so don't be scared.

   (She starts whaling on Barbra's back, takes a deep breath, then goes back to moving slowly.)
Isn't that just the best feeling Babs? Do you mind if I call you Babs? That's what my Great Aunt Lou calls you so that's how I think of you. Aunt Lou was thrilled when I told her you were a guest here. She said that girl is a real talent and a class act! I told her that you were very polite except for the fact that you were always changing your massage appointment, which caused a few problems with scheduling and staff. But Lou said, listen Ainsley, that woman sings, she dances, she acts, she directs, she produces and she looks great doing it and I think that entitles her to change her massage appointment a few times. She argued so passionately that she almost convinced me. Okay, Babs, now I'm moving down to the lower back, where I'm going to stimulate and balance the body's immune system through gentle strokes with the fingertips. *(Pause.)* I'm musical myself, although I don't sing. Did you always know that you wanted to entertain? I think you have to really want to if you're going to make it to the top. For me, music is more private, a way of saying things that are really personal, things that are hard to put into words. Sometimes I have

conversations with music. Conversations with people who aren't there. I know that sounds weird, but I think you understand. Like that scene in *Yentl* when you're out in the woods just after you've hacked off your hair. You're on your way to the Yeshiva and you're looking up at the stars and singing to your dead father *(Sings.)* "Papa, can you hear me?" *(Pause.)* It's weird, isn't it, that we keep trying to bring them back, like they're this magic ingredient that will make our lives whole. I mean, at least in *Yentl* your dad was really nice and supportive. My dad didn't do much. He was okay, but he sure didn't instruct me in the Talmud or anything like that! Still, I wish I'd wake up and find he was home. *(Sings.)* "Papa, can you hear me? Papa, can you see me?" What'd ya think Barbra? Babs? Do you think he can?

Introducing Dad
by Susan Miller

*Ethan stands next to his unborn baby's newly assembled crib. He is nervous,
in awe, and trying to find words of introduction to a life on the way.*

ETHAN: Okay. Okay. Okay. I've been trying to think of something to tell you,
our first time alone like this. Well, my first time alone with the idea of
you. I mean, about…how to be.

　　(Beat.)

Hey, this used to be the cake room. You're in with the cakes now. There
were hundreds of them nobody ever showed up for. We moved them out
to make room for you. I used to hide in here when I was a kid, wondering
why they weren't picked up. Who'd of left them like that? You could get
crazy thinking about it. The wedding cakes, especially. Suddenly a girl
wakes up and knows its over. Leaves him, leaves the white frosting, a nice
life. There was this chocolate layer for some Jimmy guy's high school
graduation. Jimmy, we believe in you, it said. Jimmy, you did it, it said.
Did they just stop believing in him? Is that why they left his cake here?
Why would anyone want to leave something so sweet and perfect behind.
Except, I guess, if it reminded you of something you failed at or didn't
live up to.

　　(Beat.)

You don't even have a name yet. I mean, what do we call a thing like you?
It's just there's no words. There's no word for you. I want to give you a
name nobody else has. *Cake.* Or—or—*Batter.* Maybe, *Icing. Flash.* What
do you think? You're not talking but you're not quiet, either. You are a
noise. You're the biggest sound in the universe.

　　(Beat.)

I want to tell you things. I used to be full of what to say. But I can't make
you up. I have to get you right.

　　(Beat.)

You don't know me, but I know you. You are gonna be crazy beautiful.
You are brilliant. You're gonna be right here sleeping in this room. With
actual skin. And hands. This is a person coming. This is everything.

(Suddenly inspired.)

I want to name you *Story*.

(Beat.)

I don't know what a father's supposed to do, exactly. But I'm going to stay and find out.

(Beat.)

Tell me how to do it right.

Norman Rockwell's Thanksgiving in the Year 2000
by Joan Ackermann

ETHAN: *(Earnestly.)* Read it again.

AINSLEY: Did you just fart?

ETHAN: No.

AINSLEY: You did.

ETHAN: I didn't.

AINSLEY: You did.

ETHAN: Well. It's Thanksgiving.

AINSLEY: Oh right.

ETHAN: Read it again.

AINSLEY: "Dear Jim…"

ETHAN: Maybe we should say… "Dear Dad."

AINSLEY: We never do.

ETHAN: We don't?

AINSLEY: No.

ETHAN: Oh.

AINSLEY: "Dear Jim…"

ETHAN: We never write to him.

　　(She looks at him.)

ETHAN: So we never write "Dear Jim" or "Dear Dad."

AINSLEY: We've written to him.

ETHAN: When?

AINSLEY: Ethan…

ETHAN: I think we should say "Dear Dad." In honor of the occasion.

AINSLEY: Thanksgiving?

ETHAN: No. Me becoming. A dad.

　　(Ainsley stares at him.)

ETHAN: What. *What.*

AINSLEY: I'm just…assimilating. Your news. "Dear Dad…. Happy Thanksgiving."

ETHAN: Do we have his address?

AINSLEY: We have his address from…a few years ago. It should still work.

ETHAN: What if it doesn't?

AINSLEY: His loss. "We've had a terrific Thanksgiving."

ETHAN: What do you think they eat for Thanksgiving in Alaska?

AINSLEY: Turkey. "Lou came downstairs for the occasion. She pretty much stays in bed most of the time now. Reuben, you will remember, our tenant...." *(Pondering the phrasing.)* You will remember. You *will* remember, "made stuffing with roasted artichoke hearts." And now Ethan is farting them out his ears, just kidding. "You won't believe it but we finally cleared out the cake room. We need the space. Ethan's girlfriend Kimmy is going to have a baby and she's moving in. She's going to work for Mom in her video store." We should cross that out, right? A reference to Mom? *(Shrugs.)* Eh. Leave it in. "Thought you'd like to know. You're going to be a grandfather. Congratulations. Ethan and Ainsley."

    (She looks at him. His eyes are tearing up.)

    What's wrong? Ethan. What's wrong, sweetie?

ETHAN: I don't know. Nothing.

AINSLEY: Nothing? Your face is red, your eyes are watery.

ETHAN: I don't know. I'm happy... I'm.... *(He shakes his head, throws up his arms. Grins, doesn't know what he is.)* It was...nice of you.

AINSLEY: What.

ETHAN: To say Kimmy should move in. That was...I appreciate it.

AINSLEY: Stop. Your gas is going to your head. So, were you guys using birth control at all?

ETHAN: At all?

    (Ainsley just stares at him, knowing the answer.)

AINSLEY: What do you think they eat for Thanksgiving in Alaska?

ETHAN: Uh...I don't know if there are turkeys there. If they migrated over that...strait.

AINSLEY: That strait? The Bering Strait? You mean from Russia?

ETHAN: No.

    (Pause.)

AINSLEY: So. Are we sending this? This is okay?

ETHAN: Should we say some more?

AINSLEY: What more?

ETHAN: I don't know.

AINSLEY: You're a mess tonight.

ETHAN: Yeah.

AINSLEY: Let's eat some pie.

ETHAN: I finished it.

AINSLEY: You finished the pie?

ETHAN: Ainsley. You're my saving grace.

AINSLEY: Is that like *Saving Private Ryan*? You finished the pie?

ETHAN: Without you…I don't think I'd be alive.

AINSLEY: There was half a pie left.

ETHAN: I'm sorry.

   (She looks over her shoulder.)

AINSLEY: What's that noise?

ETHAN: There's a gutter loose. I'll fix it tomorrow.

   (Pause.)

AINSLEY: I'm gonna start a vegetable garden this spring, back where there's all that dead brush. I'm gonna clear it out and plant a whole bunch of vegetables.

ETHAN: You want me to go to Price Chopper and buy you a pie?

AINSLEY: No.

ETHAN: I will.

AINSLEY: Price Chopper is closed.

ETHAN: We could make one.

AINSLEY: I don't know why I'm hungry.

ETHAN: Do we have the ingredients?

AINSLEY: For another pumpkin pie? Actually, we do.

ETHAN: Let's make one.

AINSLEY: Okay.

ETHAN: Let's tell Jim…. We're making a pie. Write that. Post script. P.S.

AINSLEY: P.S. We're making a pie?

ETHAN: Yeah.

AINSLEY: All right. *(She writes.)* P.S. We're making a pie. At midnight. In your mother's oven. Come on over.

ETHAN: That's nice. That's good.

   (He wipes a tear from his eye. Ainsley reaches over and grabs his hand.)

AINSLEY: Ethan, you are *my* saving grace.

END OF PLAY

The Phone Plays

The Phone Plays

Among stage conventions, the "phone call" is a classic. How many times have you seen an actor on stage reach for the phone, dial a number, wait a moment, and launch into one side of a conversation? How many times have you heard a phone on stage ring, prompting an actor to pick it up, say "hello!" and *then* launch into one side of a conversation? Chances are, many times, for the telephone, the speaker phone, and the cell phone are as ingrained in the repertoire of 20th century theatre as they are in our lives.

In the standard theatrical phone call, one party stands on stage, while the other remains out of sight. In The Phone Plays at Actors' Theatre of Louisville, however, both parties remain hidden while the audience listens in. Actually, that's part of The Phone Play's appeal—listening without being seen or heard. It's a creepy, little pleasure, like eavesdropping or wire-tapping, but it can be so rewarding. And isn't it amazing what people will say on the phone!

Beyond the voyeuristic frisson, how much can really be accomplished in three-minute phone conversations? Can they epitomize the power dynamics of relationships at work? Anatomize personal beliefs? Evoke nightmares? Justify cruel acts of revenge? Or deconstruct the psychology of sales? We think Phone Plays can do all that and more—these five do.

The Reprimand
by Jane Anderson

BIOGRAPHY

Jane Anderson has premiered several plays at Actors Theatre of Louisville, including *Tough Choices for the New Century, The Last Time We Saw Her, Lynette at 3 A.M., Lynette Has Beautiful Skin* and *The Pink Studio*. Off-Broadway: *The Baby Dance, Defying Gravity*. Other Theatre: *Hotel Oubliette, Food and Shelter, Looking For Normal*. Film: *How to Make an American Quilt, It Could Happen to You*. Television: *The Baby Dance* (wrote and directed), 1961 segment of *If These Walls Could Talk II* (wrote and directed), *The Positively True Adventures of the Alleged Texas Cheerleader Murdering Mom*. Additional Credits: Peabody Award for *The Baby Dance*, Emmy Award, Best Teleplay for *The Positively True Adventures of the Alleged Texas Cheerleader Murdering Mom*.

HUMANA FESTIVAL PRODUCTION

The Reprimand was commissioned by Actors Theatre of Louisville and premiered at the Humana Festival of New American Plays in February 2000. It was directed by Jon Jory with the following cast:

Rhona . . . . Adale O'Brien
Mim . . . . Katie Blackerby

and the following production staff:

Designer . . . . Paul Owen
Sound Designer . . . . Jeremy Lee
Sound Engineer . . . . David Preston
Properties Designers . . . . Ben Hohman, Mark Walston

CHARACTERS

RHONA
MIM

The Reprimand

RHONA: …we need to talk about what you did in the meeting this morning.

MIM: My God, what?

RHONA: That reference you made about my weight.

MIM: What reference?

RHONA: When we came into the room and Jim was making the introductions, you said, "Oh Rhona, why don't you take the bigger chair."

MIM: But that was—I thought since this was your project that you should sit in the better chair.

RHONA: But you didn't say better, you said bigger.

MIM: I did? Honest to God, that isn't what I meant. I'm so sorry if it hurt your feelings.

RHONA: You didn't hurt my feelings. This has nothing to do with my feelings. What concerns me—and concerns Jim by the way—is how this could have undermined the project.

MIM: Jim said something about it?

RHONA: Yes.

MIM: What did he say?

RHONA: He thought your comment was inappropriate.

MIM: Really? How? I was talking about a chair.

RHONA: Mim, do you honestly think anyone in that room was really listening to what I had to say after you made that comment?

MIM: I thought they were very interested in what you had to say.

RHONA: Honey, there was a reason why Dick and Danny asked you all the follow-up questions.

MIM: But that's because I hadn't said anything up to that point. Look, I'm a little confused about Jim's reaction, because after the meeting he said he liked what I did with the follow-up.

RHONA: He should acknowledge what you do. And I know the reason why he's finally said something is because I've been telling him that you deserve more credit.

MIM: Oh, thank you. But I think Jim already respects what I do.

RHONA: He should respect you. But from what I've observed, I think—because you're an attractive woman—that he still uses you for window dressing. Especially when you're working with me. You know what I'm saying?

MIM: Well, if that's the case, Jim is a jerk.

RHONA: I know that. And I know you know that. But I think you still have a lot of anger about the situation and sometimes it really shows.

MIM: I don't mean it to show.

RHONA: I know that. Look, I consider you—regardless of what Jim thinks—I think you're really talented and I really love working with you.

MIM: And I enjoy working with you.

RHONA: Thank you. And that's why I want to keep things clear between us. Especially when we're working for men like Jim.

MIM: No, I agree, absolutely.

RHONA: *(To someone off-phone.)* Tell him I'll be right there. *(Back to Mim.)* Mim, sorry—I have Danny on the phone.

MIM: Oh—do you want to conference me in?

RHONA: I can handle it, but thank you. Mim, I'm so glad we had this talk.

MIM: Well, thank you for being so honest with me.

RHONA: And thank you for hearing me. I really appreciate it. Let's talk later?

MIM: Sure. *(Rhona hangs up. A beat.) (Mumbling.)* Fat pig. *(Hangs up.)*

END OF PLAY

Show Business
by Jeffrey Hatcher

BIOGRAPHY

Jeffrey Hatcher's plays, including *Three Viewings, Scotland Road, Smash, Sockdology, The Turn of the Screw, Compleat Female Stage Beauty, What Corbin Knew, Neddy, Miss Nelson is Missing!* and *One Foot on the Floor,* have been produced by Manhattan Theatre Club, Yale Repertory, South Coast Repertory, The Old Globe, Oregon Shakespeare, Alabama Shakespeare, Denver Center, Intiman, Milwaukee Repertory, Madison Repertory, Children's Theater Company, Primary Stages, Cincinnati Playhouse, St. Louis Repertory, The Empty Space and many more. He has won the Rosenthal New Play Prize and the Whitfield-Cook Prize, as well as grants and awards from the NEA, the Lila Wallace Fund and the Jerome and McKnight Foundations. He is an alumnus of the Playwrights' Center and New Dramatists. He has written for the TV series *Columbo.*

HUMANA FESTIVAL PRODUCTION

Show Business was commissioned by Actors Theatre of Louisville and premiered at the Humana Festival of New American Plays in February 2000. It was directed by Jon Jory with the following cast:

Voice..................................... Molly Binder
Barry .... William McNulty
Howard.................................... Brad Bellamy

and the following production staff:

Designer.................................. Paul Owen
Sound Designer .... Jeremy Lee
Sound Engineer............................ David Preston
Properties Designers.............. Ben Hohman, Mark Walston

CHARACTERS

VOICE
BARRY
HOWARD

Show Business

Sound of phone ringing. Click sound as phone picks up. A chipper female voice—recorded.

VOICE: Hello and thank you for calling TeleCharge. Please stay on the line and an operator will assist you! Thank you for calling TeleCharge!
(Click. Then a recording of Ethel Merman singing "There's No Business Like Show Business." Five or six seconds. Then another click. A dulled lobotomized male voice with a New York accent comes on the line.)

HOWARD: Hello this is TeleCharge what show please.

BARRY: Yes, I need to get four seats for this Wednesday's matinee of *Annie Get Your Gun.*

HOWARD: *(By rote.)* Four seats for the Wednesday, May 12th performance of *Annie Get Your Gun* at the Marriott Marquis starring the darling and delightful Bernadette Peters as the irrepressible Annie Oakley in this six-gun shoot-em-up revival of the durable and enduring Irving Berlin classic. What method of payment please. *(Beat.)*

BARRY: ...Howard? *(Pause.)*

HOWARD: ...er...

BARRY: Howard Morrison?

HOWARD: ...Uhhh—

BARRY: Howard, It's Barry Peyser.

HOWARD: Oh, uh, hi...Barry.

BARRY: ...What are you doing at TeleCharge?

HOWARD: ...Uhhh...I lost my job.

BARRY: Lost your job? How can you lose your job? The unemployment rate is, like, minus ten percent. What happened?

HOWARD: I was fired.

BARRY: That's not possible, you're a public school teacher. What did you do?

HOWARD: I questioned a student's answer on a test. He saw it one way, I saw it another.

BARRY: You're a math teacher.

HOWARD: Math is now a subjective study...like literary theory.

BARRY: So they fired you for that?

HOWARD: It was part of the settlement.

BARRY: Wow. And this is all you could get?

HOWARD: *(Offended.)* I always liked theater.

BARRY: Yeah, but—

HOWARD: I was the advisor of the Thespian Troupe.

BARRY: Still—

HOWARD: Look, I get half-price tickets for previews, it's not so bad.

BARRY: Half price?

HOWARD: Yeah.

BARRY: Can I get half-price preview tickets for *Annie Get Your Gun?*

HOWARD: …It's been running a year.

BARRY: Sorry, just thought I'd—

HOWARD: So what do you want, orchestra, mezzanine—?

BARRY: Orchestra.

HOWARD: Orchestra.

BARRY: Unless they're way off to the side.

HOWARD: Well, they're—

BARRY: 'Cause I'd really like to get as center as possible. And on the aisle.

HOWARD: "Every seat is good."

BARRY: Really?

HOWARD: That's what it says here. "Every seat is good."

BARRY: You haven't seen the show?

HOWARD: No.

BARRY: …Have you ever been in the Marriott Marquis?

HOWARD: One thing you learn quickly in the theater business is that nobody you know has ever been to the Marriott Marquis.

BARRY: How can you sell tickets for a show you haven't seen in an auditorium you've never been in?

HOWARD: Who are you, Herbert Marcuse? This isn't a moral issue.

BARRY: Well, it seems to me that if you're a salesman, you should be familiar with what you sell. Otherwise, it's deceptive.

HOWARD: You teach divinity. Have you ever been to Hell?

BARRY: *(Proudly.)* Sixth row on the aisle.

HOWARD: Look, I can get you side orchestra, no aisle, eight seats in.

BARRY: Might as well be in New Jersey. You really can't get me good seats in the orchestra?

HOWARD: I can get you good orchestra for *Perfect Crime* and anything at Classic Stage Company, I can't get good orchestra for *Annie Get Your Gun.*

BARRY: Have you seen *Chicago?*

HOWARD: No.

BARRY: *Kiss Me Kate?*

HOWARD: No.

BARRY: *Les Miz? Phantom?*

HOWARD: I don't like Broadway musicals, Barry! I like straight plays!

BARRY: Straight plays on Broadway, that'll be a cold day on 46th Street.

HOWARD: Look, will this be VISA or Mastercard?

BARRY: Are there any salespersons who do just musicals, maybe I should talk to them.

HOWARD: VISA. Or Mastercard.

BARRY: It's like saying, "Doc, you ever done brain surgery before?" "No, I prefer appendectomies."

HOWARD: I'm not playing Annie Oakley. I'm just facilitating the tickets!

BARRY: Facilitator, enabler, take your pick. You're on a slippery slope, Howard. One day you're selling a friend questionable seats for a show you know nothing about in a theater you've never visited, the next you're voting Republican.

HOWARD: Look, there are other customers waiting on the line.

BARRY: If they only knew the deception they're about to encounter.

HOWARD: Do you want the tickets or not!

BARRY: …Oh…okay.

HOWARD: Fine, four tickets, side orchestra for the Wednesday, May 12th performance of *Annie Get Your Gun* at the Marriott Marquis starring the darling and delightful Bernadette Peters as the irrepressible Annie Oakley in this six-gun shoot-em-up revival of the durable and enduring Irving Berlin classic.…Oh.

BARRY: What?

HOWARD: Bernadette Peters doesn't play that matinee. It's Susan Lucci.

BARRY: Have you ever seen Susan Lucci act? *(Click.)* …Hello? Hello?

(We hear Ethel Merman singing, "Let's Go On With The Show? Let's Go On With The Show!")

END OF PLAY

Trespassion
by Mark O'Donnell

BIOGRAPHY

Mark O'Donnell's plays *Marred Bliss* and *The Goblins Plot to Murder God* are featured in Actors Theatre of Louisville's collections of ten-minute plays. Off-Broadway: *That's It, Folks!*, *Fables for Friends*, *The Nice and the Nasty* (all produced at Playwrights Horizons); *Tots in Tinsletown*, *Strangers on Earth* and *Vertigo Park*. Mr. O'Donnell has also adapted *Scapin* and *A Flea in her Ear* for the Roundabout Theatre. Fiction: *Elementary Education, Vertigo Park and Other Tall Tales, Getting Over Homer* and *Let Nothing You Dismay*. His work has appeared in *The New Yorker, The New York Times, The Atlantic, Spy, The New Republic, 7 Days* and *McSweeney's*. Awards: Guggenheim Fellowship, the Lecomte du Nuoy Prize, Harvard's Academy of American Poets' Prize, Arena Stage's George S. Kaufman Fellowship.

HUMANA FESTIVAL PRODUCTION

Trespassion was commissioned by Actors Theatre of Louisville and premiered at the Humana Festival of New American Plays in February 2000. It was directed by Jon Jory with the following cast:

Gina . . . . Suzanna Hay
George . . . . Brad Bellamy

and the following production staff:

Designer . . . . Paul Owen
Sound Designer . . . . Jeremy Lee
Sound Engineer . . . . David Preston
Properties Designers . . . . Ben Hohman, Mark Walston

CHARACTERS

GINA
GEORGE

Trespassion

Phone rings three times. Receiver is clumsily fumbled from its cradle.

GINA: *(Groggy from sleep.)* …Wha'?… H'lo?…

GEORGE: *(Extraordinarily stupid—think Lenny in* Of Mice and Men *or even an imbecile Brooklyn accent—and he's drunk.)* Lenore. It's me.

GINA: Uhhh… There's no Lenore here. You have a wrong number.

GEORGE: *(Plaintively—pathetic rather than hostile.)* You called me a jerk tonight. Why?

GINA: You have the wrong number.

GEORGE: But why did you call me a jerk?

GINA: It's three o'clock in the morning. You have the wrong number.

GEORGE: But why did you call me a jerk?

GINA: *(Still patient, but strained.)* I don't know what to tell you. I don't know you.

GEORGE: Tell me you don't hate me like you said you did tonight.

GINA: You have the wrong number.

GEORGE: I love you, Lenore. Is it my problem lips? Is it because my ears are different sizes?

GINA: *(Strained.)* I'm not Lenore. There's no Lenore here.

GEORGE: I can hear your voice. I'm not that big a jerk! If you're talking it means you're there. Phones don't talk on their own!… Well, except for robot phones.
(Pause.)

GINA: *(Ominously calm.)* Fine. Tell you what, uh—What's your name, anyway?

GEORGE: It's George, Lenore. You know that, Lenore.

GINA: *(In a dull, fast, non-sexy voice.)* I suddenly see it all your way. I've been a fool. I can't wait to see you. Meet me at the junkyard at the edge of town right away.

GEORGE: Oh, Lenore! That's wunn'erful!!… But—It's raining real hard out, and there's lightning and all. And that dog at the junkyard is awful mean. It bit me up real bad that time I went looking for free videos. And—what if I got arrested for…what's it called?…trespassion?

GINA: I want to dress up extra special for you, George, so just wait there for me.

GEORGE: Oh, I will, Lenore! You're as beautiful as a…a…I was trying to think of something beautiful to say you're like, but I can't think of anything right now.

GINA: It doesn't matter. Hurry to my side!

(Thunder is heard in the background.)

GEORGE: I will! Oh Lenore! This is the first time you've ever been nice to me!

GINA: I can believe that!

(Click of phone hanging up.)

GEORGE: *(To himself.)* Wow. I still wonder why she called me a jerk.

END OF PLAY

Lovers of Long Red Hair
by José Rivera

BIOGRAPHY

José Rivera is the Obie Award-winning author of *Marisol* (1992 Humana Festival, Joseph Papp Public Theatre, Hartford Stage Company, La Jolla Playhouse), *Tape* (1994 Humana Festival), *Cloud Tectonics* (1995 Humana Festival, La Jolla Playhouse, Goodman Theatre, Playwrights Horizons), *References to Salvador Dali Make Me Hot* (South Coast Repertory), *Sonnets for an Old Century* (Greenway Arts Alliance), *The Street of the Sun* (Mark Taper Forum), *Giants Have Us in Their Books* (Magic Theatre), *Each Day Dies With Sleep* (Berkley Repertory, Circle Repertory), *The Promise* (Los Angeles Theatre Center, Ensemble Studio Theatre), *The House of Ramon Iglesia* (Ensemble Studio Theatre), *Brainpeople* (South Coast Repertory commission) and *Adoration of the Old Woman* (La Jolla Playhouse commission). His work has been translated to five languages and has been supported by the NEA, the Rockefeller Foundation, the Whiting Foundation, the Kennedy Center Fund for New American Plays, the Berilla Kerr Foundation and the Fulbright Commission.

HUMANA FESTIVAL PRODUCTION

Lovers of Long Red Hair was commissioned by Actors Theatre of Louisville and premiered at the Humana Festival of New American Plays in February 2000. It was directed by Jon Jory with the following cast:

Adriana . . . . .Roxanne Raja
Mario . . . . Bryan Taylor

and the following production staff:

Designer . . . . Paul Owen
Sound Designer . . . . Jeremy Lee
Sound Engineer . . . . David Preston
Properties Designers . . . . Ben Hohman, Mark Walston

CHARACTERS

ADRIANA
MARIO

Lovers of Long Red Hair

ADRIANA: I'm persecuted by lovers of long red hair. Always.

MARIO: Three in the morning, Adriana.

ADRIANA: Strangers on buses. Staring. Envious. It's always being *touched*—by thick fingers—with cigarette stains. Knuckles.

MARIO: You complain a lot.

ADRIANA: Every Halloween my mother kept me home. Afraid of a kidnapping. "Get the virgin with long red hair, make a soup out of her!"

MARIO: So unexpectedly ruining my night of cable and self-pity...I was thinking of long red hair when you called...

ADRIANA: Hear that?

MARIO: What?

ADRIANA: Breathing? Why do I hear breathing?

MARIO: This city is full of freaks. The criminal lonely. When they leave an apartment they leave their shadows behind. More alive and active than the cockroaches.

ADRIANA: Even in my sleep. There's breathing, Mario.

MARIO: Is that why you called me? You're spooked?

ADRIANA: I'm being watched.

MARIO: Are you alone?

ADRIANA: You don't hear that?

MARIO: I don't hear that.

ADRIANA: There's something—*waiting*. How do I know that? I just know it.

MARIO: I know about waiting.

ADRIANA: Except in the shower. It doesn't follow me into the shower. It's embarrassed. To see me in the shower. Soap down my long red hair. Steam in the eyes. This is only a theory. Why? Why does the waiting and watching and breathing stop at the bathroom door?

MARIO: So move. Or cut that red, red hair and stop...

ADRIANA: Every address I ever had. Uptown. Down. Across town. Dive. Doorman building. Every one. The same thing. The breathing, the watching, the waiting.

MARIO: That red hair, you know…burned my eyes on the very first day…left me demented.

ADRIANA: I almost expect it now. Since the old man died.

MARIO: Left me with a raving maniac's desire to TALK LOUD. To eat great meals. To improve my mind. And flex my physique. To negotiate a new treaty with the world. Make me respect it more. Bring me some of the finer things. That's what your red hair…

ADRIANA: Don't *even*…

MARIO: You pretend you don't have it. You don't have power. To slay men. To leave a trail of phantoms in your wake on city streets, on the job, in buildings across the street…

ADRIANA: Come *on*…

MARIO: But I'm one of the men on the bus. I'm one of the touchers. Thick fingers. Cigarette stains. Knuckles.

ADRIANA: …before I lose all respect for you. Let me at least pretend you have some originality.

MARIO: I'm in your apartment breathing and waiting and watching.

END OF PLAY

Beside Every Good Man
by Regina Taylor

BIOGRAPHY

Regina Taylor's writing credits include *Jenine's Diary*, *Watermelon Rinds* (1993 Humana Festival) and *Between the Lines* (1994 Humana Festival). *Watermelon Rinds*, *Inside the Belly of the Beast*, *Escape from Paradise* and *Millennium Mambo* (1994-2000, The Goodman Theater), *Oo-Bla-Dee* (1999, Goodman Theater and LaJolla Playhouse), *A Night in Tunisia* (2000, Alabama Shakespeare Festival). Ms. Taylor's television acting credits include Cora in *Cora Unashamed* for PBS Masterpiece Theater, Anita Hill in *Strange Justice* for Showtime, and Lilly Harper in *I'll Fly Away* for NBC. Film acting credits: *The Negotiator*, *Courage Under Fire*, *Clockers* and *Lean on Me*.

HUMANA FESTIVAL PRODUCTION

Beside Every Good Man was commissioned by Actors Theatre of Louisville and premiered at the Humana Festival of New American Plays in February 2000. It was directed by Jon Jory with the following cast:

Winnie Mandela . . . . Linda Sithole
Coretta Scott King . . . . Opal Alladin

and the following production staff:

Designer . . . . Paul Owen
Sound Designer . . . . Jeremy Lee
Sound Engineer . . . . David Preston
Properties Designers . . . . Ben Hohman, Mark Walston

CHARACTERS

WINNIE

CORETTA

Beside Every Good Man

WINNIE: If not him—then who.

CORETTA: No one.

WINNIE: You never even dreamed—?

CORETTA: I couldn't dream—couldn't even imagine—

WINNIE: Coretta, you are a liar—

CORETTA: Winnie!

WINNIE: Try.

CORETTA: No. I can't.

WINNIE: Because no man could compare—or are you afraid?

CORETTA: Afraid? No.

WINNIE: Perhaps you should be. Even as a widow. Perhaps you should be. To dream of another man and speak it out loud—such blasphemy—perhaps you should fear.

CORETTA: Our situations are very different. I'm sorry.

WINNIE: Sorry for what? Once you have been dragged down the mountaintop—There was nothing left. Nothing left of who I used to be. Now what I have belongs to me alone. I am no longer afraid to speak of love. I loved a ghost for many, many years. He was with me every day. Shared beds. Sat across me at the table at every meal. I could hear his voice in the wind. Feel his hands caressing me—Even though he was a ghost he was seen and felt. People would never see one without the other. We were inseparable— Siamese twins joined by vital organs, lifeblood mixed. So many nights I had wished for him to return—a man made of flesh and blood.

CORETTA: Stone monuments cannot keep you warm.

WINNIE: Yes. One day upon his return—I woke up as a ghost. His wife—cut off— Nothing left of us. I found my own bloody tongue. My own. Free.

CORETTA: I often wonder—what if? I remember the last day I saw him. What he wore, what he ate, what he said…. His smell is still sweet. His breath is still warm. His smile still so white and inviting. Always will remain so.

Fixed in time. Pieces neatly placed in a box in the mind's eye…. If he were to return—the box spills over on the floor like so many unjoined parts of this huge jigsaw puzzle.

WINNIE: Egyptian Kings—they buried the whole household with him…servants, wife—

CORETTA: He and I are forever joined—in life. Nothing will change that. Not time, death, divorce—other loves—There have been only a few earth-shaking men—Hannibal on the back of an elephant—taking the Alps. Shaka-Zulu matching spear against gun…madmen and martyrs. The best are either dead, near death, much too young or yet to be born. What's left?

WINNIE: One's self.

CORETTA: That I've always had. Yes, he and I will remain forever joined at the hip. Created each in the other's image. His greatness shines through me—

WINNIE: As your greatness shone through him.

CORETTA: Beside every great man—

WINNIE: Yes.

END OF PLAY